MEMORY SYSTEMS DESIGN
AND APPLICATIONS

MEMORY SYSTEMS DESIGN AND APPLICATIONS

Selected from

ELECTRONIC DESIGN

Edited by

DAVE BURSKY

Senior Editor, Semiconductors, *Electronic Design*

HAYDEN BOOK COMPANY, INC.
Rochelle Park, New Jersey

Library of Congress Cataloging in Publication Data

Main entry under title:

Memory systems design and applications.

    1. Computer storage devices—Addresses, essays,
lectures. I. Bursky, Dave. II. Electronic design.
TK7895.M4M463   621.3819'583   80–16274
ISBN 0–8104–0980–1

1	2	3	4	5	6	7	8	9	PRINTING
80	81	82	83	84	85	86	87	88	YEAR

Preface

In less than a dozen years, memory technology has increased RAM density by a factor of 64—from the original 1,024-bit MOS RAMs to the just being sampled 64-kbit (k = 1,024) devices. New memory concepts also have made their debut—the bubble memory, the charge-coupled device, the ultraviolet erasable programmable memory, the electrically reprogrammable memory, and more—just adding to the system designer's repertoire. And not only has the choice of memory types increased tenfold, but the performance also has increased by approximately the same factor. Today, there are MOS memories that can compete on a speed basis with the fast bipolar memories, save for the "superfast" ECL memory components. The day won't be far away, either, when even the speed of these memories will be attained by the MOS devices.

The eight sections in this book have been set up to provide a total overview of all the developments in the memory area, as well as provide the latest system design and evaluation information. Each of the major memory types is covered: dynamic RAMs, static RAMs, ROMs, PROMs, UV EPROMs, bubble memories, and CCDs. Each has its own applications niche in overall system design. The sharp system designer will use a mix of various memory types in different parts of the system to provide the optimum performance at the lowest possible cost.

Today, it's possible to fill a microprocessor memory space with just eight 64-kbit RAMs and replace a minidisk system with a few bubble-memory devices and their support circuits. Complete interpreter software such as BASIC can be purchased in ROM form, and "smart" displays can directly convert ASCII codes into alphanumerics. It won't be long before a complete computer with a high-level language, a megabyte of nonvolatile storage, and full alphanumeric display and keyboard will be able to fit in a pocket or on your wrist. And the memory devices that go into it will play a key role.

Memory components, though, are not just going into computers—as more and more consumer equipment receives digital "smarts," even your microwave oven and television set will take advantage of the new memory components. Nonvolatile memories, for example, have found their way into appliances and television sets to "remember" the last setting. And other types of memories have found their way into TVs to provide the picture-within-a-picture capability available on some deluxe models. So not only have the advances in memory technology aided the computer systems, but consumer equipment has benefited as well.

Dave Bursky

Contents

Section VI. Charge-Coupled Devices: Are They or Aren't They?

Section VII. System Application Examples Using RAMs

Section VIII. System Reliability and Testing Hints for RAMs

MEMORY SYSTEMS DESIGN
AND APPLICATIONS

SECTION I
Overviews of the Entire Memory Field

With new memory developments appearing almost every day, the system designer is hard-pressed to keep up with all the new products and improved performance limits that the new devices deliver. These first few articles provide an overall summary of the performance limits of today's technology and an overview of the available leading-edge products. These articles cover the spectrum of memory products—from the dynamic RAMs to the latest in bubble technology.

Memory-device specifications, which have remained relatively the same over the past few years (the same parameters, but much improved numbers) also must be examined by the designer to make sure the manufacturer's quoted specifications are accurate and are specified in a manner similar to that expected by the designer. Technology limitations also are examined, since today's memories are approaching the edge of manufacturing technology. Available processes are evaluated and projected into the next few years, based on processing and production equipment improvements.

Just what are some of the leading-edge products? Well, just emerging in the dynamic RAM area are the 64-kbit memories; in static devices, the ultra-high-speed, sub-50-ns 4-kbit devices; in UV EPROMs, 64-kbit units are just becoming available; and in bubble memories, 1-Mbit chips are starting to be sampled. These are just some of the developments that the articles in this section report on.

Storing the Most for the Least

DAVE BURSKY
Senior Editor, Semiconductors,
Electronic Design

Look inside a memory system today and you could find quite a collection of technologies being mixed and matched for the best possible performance for the lowest possible cost: tape, disk, bubble, dynamic RAM, and static RAM. Merely putting them together won't work because each memory technology offers a different performance limit in terms of access times, data storage density, and cost.

As for cost, it's being assailed on two fronts. As technological developments bring down the cost of memory by putting more bits on a chip or more bits per square inch on a magnetic material, user needs are forcing the cost per bit down almost to shelf-storage level by requiring that more data be stored on-line for faster access.

Match speed to system

Whether a system needs high-speed cache memories or slow archival systems, products are out there to meet most needs. From the semiconductor industry come the super-speedy bipolar RAMs for the fastest cache systems, and fast bipolar and NMOS products for the not-so-fast caches. Microprocessor systems have spawned a major demand for fast static RAMs, which are also finding their way into many computer main memories.

At the same time, μP systems, especially the latest generation of processors that can address megabytes of memory, are being visited from above by dynamic memories, popular with the mainframe manufacturers. However, most semiconductor memories share a limitation—they cannot transport data. Once power is turned off, RAMs lose their data content. To be transported, therefore, data must be stored on a nonvolatile medium that can be removed from one piece of equipment and plugged into another.

Over the past ten years, the traditional answer has been disk drives with removable media and magnetic tape drives with open reels, cartridges or cassettes. However, magnetic developments have thrown another contender into the ring—magnetic-bubble memories. Offering 10 to 100 times faster access time than disk drives, bubble memories are expected to be the next major addition to systems that require non-volatile storage of important data.

Some obstacles, too

At this point, however, bubble devices throw two major stumbling blocks—high per-bit costs and limited availability—at potential users. A bubble system with capacity equivalent to a floppy disk's, for example, could typically cost about three times more than the disk if the cost of the controller and interface are included. Even so, the advantages of bubble devices in harsh environments far outweigh the cost factors.

All this memory activity boils down to many different types of storage components, all with places to go:

- ECL bipolar memories: Very high-speed cache, writable-control stores, and processing sections of large computers.
- Fast static NMOS and bipolar memories: Writable control stores in medium-speed machines, fast μP main-memory systems, and main memories of some small-to-medium-size minicomputers.
- Dynamic RAMs: Main-memory systems of large computers, minicomputers, and even some large μP memory systems.
- CCDs: Large buffer memories for minicomputer systems, interfacing between the magnetic storage disks or tape drives and the RAM, or as plug-compatible disk replacements.
- Bubble memories: CCD-type applications, but also a wide range of applications where nonvolatility and ruggedness are absolute requirements and the cost differential is not a major concern.
- Disk drives (floppy, removable, nonremovable): Bulk storage for most minicomputer and mainframe systems, and μC systems needing several Mbytes of storage.
- Tape drives (cassette, cartridge and open-reel): Bootstrap back-up and small-system, noncritical-access-delay applications for the cassette and cartridge drives; large-computer, archival-memory applications for the open-reel drives.

The performance limits for the various types of

STORAGE TECHNOLOGY

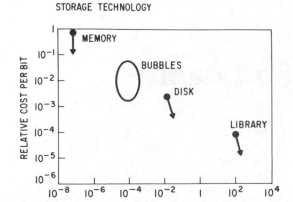

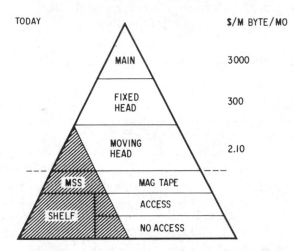

GROWTH OF ON-LINE DISK STORAGE

ENVIRONMENT... GROWTH ON-LINE CAPACITY... 1984
(IN 10^{12} BYTES)

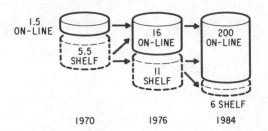

DATA COMPILED FROM VARIOUS PUBLIC SOURCES

DISK STORAGE TRENDS—
BIT DENSITY

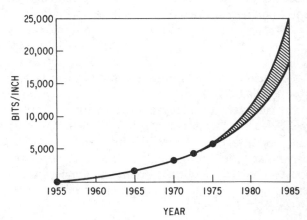

Filling the gap between main computer memory and disk and library storage, bubble memories will meet both cost and performance requirements (top left). The pyramid of memory storage types indicates that main computer memory accounts for the smallest percentage (bottom left), while on-line storage is predicted to grow (top, right) in quantity—and economically, thanks to the increase in bit density on the magnetic storage media (bottom right).

memory systems span a tremendous range—from tens of nanoseconds to several minutes for data access. Costs, too, run the gamut, from just a few hundred dollars for a small system to well over $10,000 for a large disk drive. Whether you're buying memory boards to plug into a computer system or memory boxes that connect to a system, there are many different aspects to examine before making the final choice. The same goes for disk drives and tape transports—one big decision here is whether to buy or lease the units. Because of the large capital outlay, many companies lease large disk and tape drives.

The 64-k response

With performance always the key to any system a storage device will find itself in, such components as the 64-k RAM have come to light. This particular advance is an example of the pressure put on semiconductor manufacturers for high-density products. With it, board capacities can be quadrupled with almost no power and performance penalties. What's more, with the cost per bit coming down, main memories probably won't get smaller, as predicted. In fact, they seem to be growing.

Many of the currently available minicomputers have addressing techniques that can handle megabytes of main RAM memory. And almost every new 16-bit μP can address at least 1 Mbyte, with one 16-bit going so far as to address 48 Mbytes. Recent developments, such as IBM's use of its own internally developed 64-k RAM, have brought the add-on memory prices for semiconductor RAM down to just $15,000 per Mbyte—about one-third the cost reported just one year ago.

Not all RAM developments are dynamic. Static RAMs are also speeding up and getting denser. And another year's time should see production devices with access times below 10 ns for bipolar chips and in the 35 to 45-ns ballpark for NMOS devices.

Leading the speed race are the ECL devices manufactured by companies such as Fairchild, Fujitsu and Motorola. Up to now, power-hungry (about 800 mW per device) RAMs have been the fastest commercial devices and they haven't had to look back. However, that picture is changing as technological improvements in both standard NMOS processing and vertical NMOS now permit n-channel devices to close in on bipolar speeds.

The race is worth the trouble, because NMOS

processing requires fewer mask operations, is thus simpler to use, and should result in lower device costs. In addition, the density potential associated with NMOS could mean a fourfold improvement over bipolar for the same die area. Another plus for NMOS processing is the special circuit tricks possible that permit static RAMs to be designed with low-standby-power modes. These reduce the power consumption of RAMs not being accessed to about one-tenth that of the active power.

The 2147, for example, when it was introduced by Intel in 1977, was not only the fastest NMOS product available (55-ns access), it also offered a low-power standby mode that reduced the active current by 85% —and its cost was competitive with bipolar devices that didn't have the low-power capability. Better still, the 2147 has not stood still—an even faster version, the 2147H, provides 35 to 45-ns access.

Static densities quadruple

Other technology tricks such as scaling and multiple layers of polysilicon interconnect permit major improvements in device density—are responsible for the nearly factor-of-four density increase for the same-size chip. One product of this will be the 2167, a 16-k × 1 fully static RAM, which is expected to be available from Intel toward year's end. With access times around 50 to 65 ns, the RAM will be the mainstay of many larger static main memory systems.

Putting statics in large memory systems does cost quite a bit more than putting in dynamic RAMs. However, if speed is critical, or the refresh overhead is hard to work with, or the system can't tolerate any wait states, static devices are the only choice. However, static devices are also growing in other areas —μP memories—and as EPROM replacements. The reason is simple: Byte-wide static RAMs are reducing the complexity of any system by cutting package counts by as much as eight to one.

Real bubble products do exist

The squeeze is on in bubble memories, too. Originally introduced to the commercial marketplace in 1977, the devices have grown from the 92-kbit unveiled by Texas Instruments up to the 1-Mbit devices that are on the way from TI, Rockwell, Intel and National Semiconductor. (Both Rockwell and TI expect to start shipping production-volume quantities of quarter-megabit devices by the end of the year.) In addition, performance has more than doubled in the past two years—access times have been cut from 10 to 20 ms down to 5 to 10.

Right now, there are few, if any, commercial memory products using bubble memories—a situation that should change during the latter half of this year. However, one commercial product using bubbles right now is a replacement for a formatted disk drive. Developed by the Bubbl-Tec Division of PC/M Corp. (San Ramon, CA), the system consists of two basic boards: a controller called the Bubbl-Board, and a memory card called the Bubble-Pac. The controller and memory cards plug directly into a Digital Equipment Corp. LSI-11 Q-bus backplane, requiring just one slot per board. One controller can handle up to 16 memory cards, which hold 40 kbytes each.

Meanwhile, both TI and Rockwell have developed evaluation boards for their quarter-megabit bubble chips. Each of the boards contains four chips for a 1-Mbit capacity, and one controller can handle several boards. One controller handles up to 16 Rockwell memory boards for a total system capacity of 2 Mbytes.

Still many times the cost of disk or RAM storage, prices for the bubble memory chips are expected to drop shortly as larger devices are introduced. Building systems with the bubble devices is a relatively straightforward task and many companies will eventually offer various forms of nonvolatile disk, tape and drum replacements and with the extra reliability

General comparisons of moving media

	0.5 in. reel	"Philips" cassette	3M-type cartridge	Floppy disk	Hard disk fixed media
Density	880 bpi	880 bpi	1600 bpi	3200 bpi	12,000 bpi
Tracks	9	2	4	77	550
Capacity (bytes)	18,500 k	550 k	2500 k	250 k	571,000 k
Transfer rate	180 kbp/s	9.6 kbp/s	48 kbp/s	250 kbp/s	14,000 kbp/s
Interrecord gap	0.6 in.	0.8 in.	1.3 in.	Not applicable	Not applicable
Mechanism cost	$3000	$500	$750	$750	35,000*
Media cost per byte in millicents	0.08	1.5	0.8	2.8	0.225

*Controller with two spindles (IBM 3870A)

factor of no electromechanical wear, the bubble memories are the ideal product to use in harsh environments, where mechanical devices would be subject to dust, gas, vibration, and other perils.

Disk drives have also seen a tremendous amount of technological improvement in the last few years. And if the disk-storage-subsystem technology IBM has openly discussed progresses at the rate the company has predicted (see ELECTRONIC DESIGN, April 26, 1979, p. 34), disk storage will eventually drop to about 35 cents per Mbyte. This expectation, though, is about two generations of equipment away, say IBM sources.

One current innovation is to take the fixed-block architecture for the file structure on a small disk and adapt it to many of the large disk systems, as exemplified by IBM's 3370 series of disk drives. These drives can store 571 Mbytes, and have an average access time of just 20 ms. The fixed-block architecture makes the space definition independent of tracks and cylinders.

The 3370 has an improved magnetic areal density, costs about a fifth as much as the older 3340 drive, yet stores the same amount of data. Using a 14-in. disk, the data density of the 3370 approaches 12,000 bits/in.

Smaller disks are also being used in many drives —8-in. disk drives are offering the user intermediate storage capacities with the same access times and at lower cost. The money savings comes from the reduced mechanical drive requirements and the materials saved in platters, power supplies and other related components.

Improvements in tape-transport technology have also helped the serial-access tape drives speed up and get more compact. Controller circuits have become more integrated, motors have been made more efficient and easier to control, better recording heads have been developed, and improved magnetic materials permit higher bit-packing densities.

All these memory-technology adjustments and advances are half the story, however. Computer system architectures are also changing—to accept the various types of memory components and subsystems and use them to the best advantage. Many computers are even being designed as microprogrammable systems with large writable-control-store memory areas, which permit computer operation to be altered just by changing the microcode.

Distributed performance booster

However, with the cost of the processor section dropping as LSI building blocks cut the component count, processing within the computer system will become distributed. Systems have already arrived containing several processors to increase over-all efficiency. Even the peripherals are getting smarter and can do more without the software control of the main CPU.

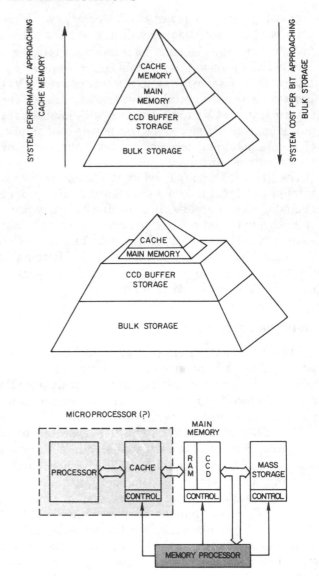

The hierarchy of memory within a computer system is changing from the organizations proposed in the mid-1970s (top) to the hierarchy suggested in the late 1970s (middle). Improvements in distributed control and device densities (bottom) are paving the way.

A typical example of the "smart" interface is the recently introduced 8089 I/O processor developed by Intel (Santa Clara, CA). A main CPU like an 8086 can be surrounded by 8089s and simply download commands to each device, which then goes off and executes the command. Then, when the 8089 is finished, it returns to the main processor and indicates it's ready for another command.

Hewlett-Packard (Santa Clara, CA) will shortly introduce an enhanced family of CMOS/SOS-based minicomputers using the distributed processing control concept. But not all the processing control will go to the I/O.

Smart memories will also brighten the future for many computer users by taking some of the memory-control burden off the CPU and permitting faster access to much of the stored data. For example, a smart memory system might look ahead and shift some data blocks from a slow disk file to high-speed RAM just so the processor won't have to wait for a disk access. If the program being run doesn't need the data pulled from the file, there's no time lost, but if the data are needed, several milliseconds of processing time can be saved.

In a nutshell, the large computer system of the future may well work through four levels of memory. The slowest—and lowest-cost memory will store the bulk of the data, often billions of bytes. Tape drives and hard-disk drives are the commonly used storage devices for the bulk memory with their access times of several seconds (tape) and tens of milliseconds (disks). From here, the data will be transferred to a faster medium, possibly magnetic-bubble or CCD bulk memory, where rapid accesses can be made without any mechanical wear. These memory devices offer access times in the 0.1 to 10-ms range.

Data from the bubble or CCD regions will then pass on to main semiconductor memory, which typically accesses in 150 to 600 ns and actively stores instructions and handles data.

The speediest processing and most critical instruction paths will be handled by the processing section itself, which will use high-speed cache RAM with access times at the board level of 30 to 100 ns.

Make the right connections

Once memory systems are purchased, finally, they're usually just plugged into the computer system and turned on, right? Not quite—even though memory systems are the simplest add-ons to a computer system that can be made, especially if the add-on memory is designed to plug right into the computer system card cage or interface.

Many companies offer plug-compatible memory cards that go right into the computer cabinet. Add-ins are available for just about every minicomputer and mainframe computer made. And beyond that,

there are memory systems designed to be "universal" memory boxes, which can be interfaced to any computer system with a single controller card.

Offered by Mostek, Intel, Intersil and several others, these universal memory systems provide users megabyte capacities without forcing them to go back to the computer manufacturer. However, among the various manufacturers that offer these add-on memory systems, there are no standards for the size or interface of the individual memory boards. Others, Monolithic System and MuPro to name two, offer plug-in cards for various minis and micros.

Trying to bring some order to the memory-system jumble, Intel has developed the Series 90 Memory System, which uses a bus that can support memory cards built from dynamic RAMs, static RAMs or bubble devices. The bus can handle up to 88-bit word widths (up to 80 bits with single-bit error correction and double-bit error detection).

With static devices operating in the normal RAM mode or dynamic devices operating in an interleaved mode, the System 90 can transfer data at up to 10 MHz. Able to hold up to 16 independently addressable memories, the System 90 modules can each directly address up to 16-Mwords. Thus, the total system capacity, is 256 Mwords.

The interface control structure system has been designed with a broad range of capabilities in mind. For starters, data transfers can be done in either synchronous or asynchronous modes, and interleaved operation of the various memory modules can be performed to speed up the over-all memory-system performance. Special direct data transfer and swap modes are also available.

In the direct-data-transfer mode, the contents of a word location are made available by a read operation and stored in a different word location by executing a write cycle. A swap operation first stores the contents of the data bus in the word location specified by the address, and the previous contents are automatically made available on the data bus.■■

Focus on Memories

DICK HACKMEISTER
Western Editor,
Electronic Design

A ravenous appetite for bit storage has propelled semiconductor memories so far along that each new product generation doubles and redoubles its bit density.

And this creates problems.

Manufacturers, eager to be the first on their block to announce yet another round of increased density, have developed a reputation for jumping the gun. To further complicate matters, it's not at all apparent which manufacturer's parts can be substituted for another's: A device that is second-sourced means only that there is another manufacturer who can supply a part with a similar function and pinout—but not necessarily the same performance.

The onus of true alternate sourcing is on you. You've got to nit-pick the specs to determine if you can safely swap one part for another. Not easy.

Try selecting a 4096 × 1-bit dynamic MOS RAM: One source specifies 39 ac parameters, repeated for each of four different grade parts, plus 13 common dc parameters, six timing diagrams and 22 footnotes. Selecting a MOS RAM means matching all those data to all the alternatives—and not just the "typical" numbers, either.

You've got to reckon with both the max and the min values because if you read the fine print, you'll find that "typical" is specified at room temperature—certainly not a valid condition in the real world, where memory devices sometimes operate hot as a pistol.

The parameter-priority paradox

With so many parameters to weigh, it is far too easy to take a pin-the-tail-on-the-donkey approach to device selection. But by listing the memories' parameters in order of importance, then comparing numbers, you can avoid feeling like a donkey's rear end.

Start with the power supply. Unless you're working on a full-blown mainframe EDP system, or something of that magnitude, you'll probably want to avoid designing-in a special power supply just for bit storage. Smaller μP-based control systems may not be able to justify the extra 12-V and −5-V supplies. So look for a memory that uses TTL power—just 5 V.

Basically it's a TTL world, and the memory manu-facturers know it; the trend is to provide parts that are compatible with your host system's power supply. For example, the available 2102-type static RAMs are second-generation 1101s. Unlike the older 1101s, which needed three supplies, the 2102s require only a single 5-V source.

Once you've narrowed the field down to single-supply parts, scrutinize the I/O levels and noise-margin specs. Those numbers, too, should conform to the host system. Adding level translators and the like can only complicate matters and leave more room for things to go wrong.

Don't use typical values—they represent the over-all average of a great many pieces and are not guaranteed by the manufacturer. Also, parts may be screened before shipment, so the average may actually be far away from the typical values stated.

"Min/max limits at worst-case voltages and worst-case temperature are the only responsible way to specify any semiconductor memory," a spokesman for Harris Semiconductor asserts. Some firms, like EM&M Semiconductor, are finally dropping the "typical" column from their data sheets.

After levels, check performance

With system power supplies and I/O levels out of the way, dive right into the performance specs. It takes power to move bits quickly, and the manufacturer who supplies rapid access time with low power consumption is offering high performance.

Here, too, you should specify in terms of the host system—a CMOS part may not be as fast as ECL, but it runs cool and might save you a lot of money on power supplies. On the other hand, bipolar devices are high performers that run hot. NMOS parts generally fall in between. Performance costs, so if you don't need the speed, save the money for a year-end bonus.

The Gaussian distribution ensures a spread of access times for any given production lot. After the manufacturing process is complete, semi houses almost always sort out the faster chips from the slower ones; the faster ones, of course, command a premium price.

Lowest performers are often identified with the basic part number, while faster ones get "dash numbers" (part-1, part-2). But there is no standard for such labeling, or binning. Remember that access doesn't start until all the address bits are presented to the chip—so be careful, and deskew the host system to get all the bits nicely lined up in time. Otherwise, you may think the part doesn't conform to the data sheet.

If you're buying many memories, give the vendor your production schedule. He may be able to integrate your requirements with those of another customers', and thereby save you money.

When analyzing input-threshold specs, which are sometimes given in terms of one of the supply voltages, be sure to use the worst-case situation. Output drive should be specified at the more rigorous V_{CC}min. Check the test conditions for load capacitance; for a given access time (t_{acc}), less capacitance means less performance.

For timing specs, look at the timing diagrams, and check the reference points. Worst-case evaluation should include 90% of the rising and falling edges on the waveform under consideration.

Some firms will offer you a precalculated power-dissipation parameter. Beware. There are several ways to calculate P_d, and you may not be getting the whole picture, especially if the memory is dynamic. It's best to calculate it yourself.

The graphs that often accompany semi-memory specs are to be used for trend projection only. These data, too, are only typical, and any individual part may not agree with the curve.

Some high-volume users write their own data sheets rather than trust published specs. "Rolling your own" avoids that ominous footnote: "Subject to change without notice." But don't try to incorporate all the best features of all the manufacturers into one phantasmagorial part. It can't be done. Like everything else in life, you get a semi memory only by compromising.

Which package?

Like most semiconductor products, a memory's package is important to both design and price. Ceramic packages are the top of the line. They perform well under the most adverse conditions and often cost as much as the chip inside, sometimes more. The chip fits into a cavity, which is sealed after bonding to protect the die and the bonding wires.

Plastic packages cost much less than the top-of-the-liners. But they're molded, and the plastic strains the die and bonding wires by flowing right over them. It doesn't take much to break a golden wire that is half the size of a blonde hair; consequently, the yields are lower. The ones that don't break are the ones that ship.

Manufacturers go to great lengths to match the plastic's coefficient of expansion to that of the silicon chip and bonding wires, but nothing is ever perfect.

Programmable read-only memories (PROMs) help you develop microprocessor-based computer programs. Data, usually microcode, are stored in the chip as charges on a floating-gate FET and can be erased and rewritten many times. Manufacturers claim data will remain intact for 10 years because the charges have no leakage paths. Exposing the die to intense ultraviolet light (through the quartz lid) for several minutes dissipates the charges, erasing the stored data pattern. Many PROMs have pinouts compatible with static RAMs and factory-programmed ROMs (electronic arrays).

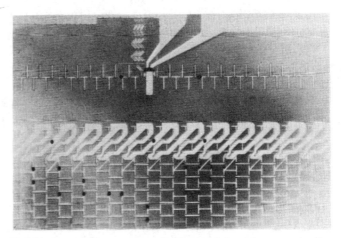

Bubble memories are no longer a laboratory curiosity. This 92,304-bit memory is available from Texas Instruments as the TBM-0103. The technology may provide even greater bit density—a million-bit device is expected within a year. The package contains a permanent magnet, the bubble-memory chip, and two coils that produce a rotating magnetic field. The chip is fabricated on a garnet substrate rather than silicon. Price: $200.

If the memory will experience many drastic temperature changes or will require a high degree of reliability, the chances are you can justify the extra cost of a ceramic package. A good compromise is "Cerdip," a modified-ceramic "sandwich" that offers the stability of conventional ceramic at lower cost.

Don't reinvent the wheel

After you've painstakingly picked through the specs for power-supply compatibility, I/O levels, noise margins, power-supply drain, access and cycle times, you will appreciate the opportunity to ignore something—the input leakage current. With MOS memories, leakage is usually not very significant. In practice, the device is either an open or a short.

Once you've narrowed the field to just a few candidates, contact the manufacturers for applications and reliability data—only then will you have covered all the bases. Semi firms put a lot of effort into their app notes, and one note might just have your complete design. Motorola, for example, offers an app note entitled *A Non-Volatile Microprocessor Memory Using 4-k NMOS RAM* (AN-732A).

Don't be afraid to specify a device that's been around for a long time. Older types, which presumably have their bugs ironed out and their designs optimized, get better yields. And since most manufacturers' specs have had a chance to converge, a pseudo-standardized part can emerge. Also, since they've been designed into a great many OEM products that still enjoy healthy sales volumes, they're not likely to be discontinued.

On the other end of the stick—new memories—watch out for the data sheet that's stamped "PRELIMINARY." That usually means the manufacturer hopes to ship a lot of devices, but right now the part is "being sampled"—a euphemistic way of saying that the producing semi house is sticking its big toe in to see if the market is hot or cold.

Having pored over the specifications, you are ready to select a RAM. Different RAMs have different attributes—and some have special needs.

Move slowly with dynamic RAMs

For example, dynamic RAMs require refreshing, and that can lead to trouble. When you specify a dynamic RAM, be especially careful to consider all the timing details. Watch out for specs that don't, without good reason, include 90% of the transition edges.

Vendors balance density, power and speed, so you can specify a part that optimizes the characteristics most important to you and trade off those you don't need. Another compromise to consider is density vs dollars. The new 16-pin, 16-k parts will soon be cheap enough to compete with the assortment of 4-k devices now available.

If it's a 4-k you're considering, maybe you can replace it with a 16-k part, pin for pin, level for level and nanosecond for nanosecond. For instance, the chip-select pin—pin 13 in the standard Mostek pinout—becomes A_6 in many of the 16-k devices. With a DIP switch or a jumper, you can design a field-upgradable memory board—just pop out the 4-k, do a little hardware change and pop in the 16-k. Presto! You've increased the board's capacity by four—that is, with 4-k RAMs that allow you to do so.

Desirable features to look for in 16-k RAMs include: page-mode addressing, row-address-strobe refreshing

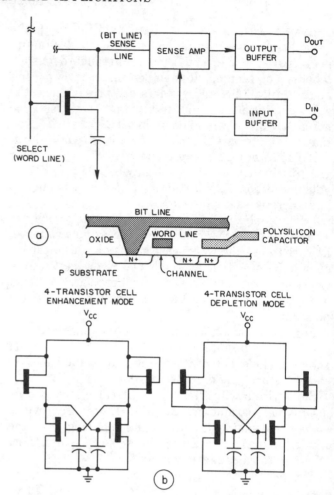

(a)

(b)

Dynamic RAMs store data in small capacitors. The presence or absence of a charge represents a ONE or a ZERO. Since the capacitor will leak away most of its charge in a few milliseconds, it must be continually refreshed (a). **A static RAM is basically an array of flip-flops.** One side or the other of each memory cell is "ON" at any time, and this defines whether the cell is storing a ONE or a ZERO. At least four transistors are needed to make a single memory cell. Consequently, static RAMs consume more power and need more chip area (b).

and (long overdue) ±10% power-supply variations. Choose between latched or unlatched outputs and 64 or 128-cycle refresh.

You should understand the difference between Read-Modify-Write cycles and plain old Read cycles and Write cycles. R-M-W is a timing mode that slices nanoseconds off the cycle time. If you expect the software to be doing a lot of file updating (as opposed to number crunching), use R-M-W to access a word, modify all or part of the word, then restore it immediately. You'll design a more efficient machine.

If *anything* on your data sheet is unclear, don't hesitate to contact the manufacturer. Almost everything on a timing diagram is interrelated, and if you don't completely understand what's going on inside the part, you can't make a valid selection. Besides, once you know one device thoroughly, you'll be able to comprehend all the others.

The standard pinout for the 16-k generation will probably be Mostek's 16-pin arrangement: a power supply in each corner, input and output across from each other, and address bits increasing in significance in a counterclockwise manner. Most likely, the next generation of 16-k memories will see no change in the refresh rate—it will remain one or two ms.

The 16-k generation

Dynamic RAMs—almost always implemented in NMOS—are available in 16, 18, and 22-pin DIPs. Be sure to check out all the manufacturer's types—some may be more readily available than others.

The MK4116 family of 16-k memories from Mostek offers access times down to 150 ns. The company's 4-k × 1 families include the MK4022, 4027, 4096, and 4200, with 200-ns devices over the full commercial temp range of 0 to 70 C.

A 250-ns, 16-k × 1 device from Intel, the 2116, comes in three different t_{acc} bins. This industry leader's 2108 is an 8-k × 1 chip with 200-ns access. Intel's 4-k parts include a number of bin selections in the 2104 and 2107 families.

A 16-k × 1 memory from Texas Instruments, the TMS4070, comes in three bins, according to access and cycle times. TI's 4-k line includes the TMS 4030, 4050 and 4060. Another 4 k, the 4051, takes TTL-compatible clocks.

A 16,384-bit dynamic RAM, the MCM-6616, is produced by Motorola in four bins. And for something in a 4096, look into the company's 6604 and 6605. Access times are as low as 150 ns for the 6605.

A 16-k chip offered by Fairchild has the most meaningful designation: F16k. You can get it in three timing bins. Fairchild also makes the only bipolar 4-k dynamic RAM—the 93481C, and it's fast—100 ns from 0 to 70 C.

The quickest 8-k chip anywhere is the 7008-10 with a 150-ns t_{acc}. It's from newly merged Intersil/AMS, which also produces a 16 k, the 7116, as well as a good selection of 4-k devices: the 7005, 7027, 7270, 7271, 7280, 7505, and 7507. Another 16 k: NEC's μPD-416. The 411, 414 and 418 are NEC's 4096-bit parts.

Fujitsu rounds out the 16-k choices with its MB8116, and its 4-k contributions include the 8107, 8215 and 8224.

National Semiconductor has six 4096-bit dynamic RAMs—the MM4270, 4280, 5270, 5271, 5280 and 5281. Access times range from 150 to 270 ns, a pretty tight span.

Signetics offers the 2660, 2675, and 2780—all 4-k × 1. The 2260 is one of the better specified devices.

Other manufacturers of 4096 × 1 dynamic NMOS RAMs include Advanced Micro Devices, Electronic Arrays, RCA, Panasonic, Rockwell, Synertek, Toshiba, Western Digital, Monolithic Memories, Hitachi and Siemens.

Static RAMs: smaller but steadier

Static RAMs usually lag behind dynamic ones in density, but come in a wide assortment of sizes and technologies. For example, static emitter-coupled-logic (ECL) RAMs are the fastest of all commercially available memories. They get down to 10-ns t_{acc}, and illustrate nicely the balance of density, speed and power. ECL RAMs span the density spectrum from 64 to 1024 bits, and they run hot. (Beware of the smaller ones—t_{acc} may not be specified at high temperatures.)

Introducing $\overline{CAS}$ and $\overline{RAS}$

The column-address strobe ($\overline{CAS}$) and the row-address strobe ($\overline{RAS}$) appeared around 1974, when linear addressing began to limit the number of addresses in cost-effective 16 and 18-pin packages.

The old 1103, with 1024 × 1 addressable words in an 18-pin package, used 10 precious pins just for address definition. Going to 2-k and then to 4-k addresses would have required 11, and then 12 pins —clearly unacceptable for a part meant to be inexpensive.

$\overline{CAS}$ and $\overline{RAS}$ solve the dilemma by splitting the address bits into most and least-significant halves and delivering the bits to the memory in two "waves." Thus, the number of pins required to define any given address can be cut in half.

With $\overline{CAS}$ and $\overline{RAS}$, up to 65,536 discrete addresses can be described with a mere eight pins. These eight pins describe one of 256 rows—as well as one of 256 columns. (Both row address and column address are internally latched and decoded.)

Consequently, only 10 pins—$\overline{CAS}$, $\overline{RAS}$ plus eight more—are necessary, and that is why 4096 × 1 dynamic MOS RAMs (type 2104) need only a 16-pin DIP, whereas the older, smaller 1103 needed 18 pins.

Multiplexed addressing is one reason that chip density will continue to quadruple, rather than merely double: One more pin devoted to addressing doubles the number of columns, but also doubles the number of rows. So the size of the internal cell matrix can grow by a factor of four.

The 65-k limit of eight address pins will probably be breached by one of two schemes. Adding a ninth address pin will allow for up to 262,144 addressable locations. But adding a third multiplex pin will provide "three-dimensional" addressing, with a whopping 16,777,216 locations in a single package.

Need more information?

The products cited in this report don't necessarily represent the manufacturers' complete lines. For complete details, circle the appropriate reader service card number. More vendors and information may be found in ELECTRONIC DESIGN's GOLD BOOK.

Advanced Micro Devices, 901 Thompson Pl., Sunnyvale, CA 94086. (408) 732-2400. (Ben Anixter)

American Microsystems, Inc., 3800 Homestead Rd., Santa Clara, CA 95051. (408) 246-0330. (Russ Knapp)

Electronic Arrays, Inc., 550 E. Middlefield Rd., Mountain View, CA 94043. (415) 964-4321. (John Lipnisky)

EM&M Semiconductors, Inc., 3883 N. 28th Ave., Phoenix, AZ 85017. (602) 263-0203. (F. L. Krch)

Fairchild Semiconductor Div., 464 Ellis St., Mountain View, CA 94042. (415) 962-5011. (Frank Rittiman)

Fujitsu America, Inc., 2945 Kifer Rd., Santa Clara, CA 95051. (408) 985-2300. (Ron Gorshe)

General Instrument Corp., 600 W. John St., Hicksville, NY 11802. (516) 733-3099. (Brian Cayton)

Harris Semiconductors, Inc., P.O. Box 883, Melbourne, FL 32901. (305) 724-7257. (Steve Harris)

Hitachi America, Inc., 2700 River Rd., Des Plaines, IL 60018. (312) 298-0840. (Yukio Suzuki)

Hughes Aircraft Co., 500 Superior Ave., Newport Beach, CA 92663. (714) 548-0671. (Gary Desrochers)

Intel Corp., 3065 Bowers Ave., Santa Clara, CA 95051. (415) 246-7501. (Bill Regitz)

Intersil , 10900 N. Tantau Ave., Cupertino, CA 95014.　　(408) 996-5000.

Monolithic Memories, Inc., 1165 E. Arques Ave., Sunnyvale, CA 94086. (408) 739-3535. (Ray Gouldsberry)

MOS Technology, Inc., 950 Rittenhouse Rd., Norristown, PA 19401. (215) 666-7950. (Jules Hertsch)

Mostek Corp., 1215 W. Crosby Rd., Carrollton, TX 75006. (214) 245-6921. (Derrell Coker)

Motorola Semiconductors, Inc., 5005 E. McDowell Rd., Phoenix, AZ 85008. (602) 962-2821. (Jerry Prioste)

National Semiconductor, 2900 Semiconductor Dr., Santa Clara, CA 95051. (408) 737-5891. (Ron Livingston)

NEC Microcomputers, 5 Militia Dr., Lexington, MA 02173. (617) 862-6410. (Dick Koerner)

Nitron. 10420 Bubb Rd., Cupertino, CA 95014. (408) 255-7550. (Dave Fletcher)

Nortec Electronics Corp., 3697 Tahoe Way, Santa Clara, CA 95051. (408) 732-2204. (Leon Mittman)

Panasonic Industrial Div., 1 Panasonic Way, Secaucus, NJ 07094. (201) 348-7275. (Terry Kobayashi)

Raytheon Semiconductor, 350 Ellis St., Mountain View, CA 94042. (415) 968-9211. (Dave Uimari)

RCA, Rt. 202, Somerville, NJ 08876. (201) 685-6810. (Don Carley)

SGS-ATES, 79 Massasoit St., Waltham, MA 02154. (617) 891-3710. (Ruben Sonnino)

Siemens Corp., 186 Wood Ave. S., Iselin, NJ 08830. (201) 494-1000. (Claus Bahr)

Signetics, 811 E. Arques Ave., Sunnyvale, CA 94086. (408) 739-7700. (Ralph Kaplan)

Solid State Scientific, Industrial Center, Montgomeryville, PA 18936. (215) 855-8400. (Al Genchi)

Synertek, Inc., 3050 Coronado Dr., Santa Clara CA 95051. (408) 984-8900. (Bob Cushman)

Texas Instruments, Inc., PO Box 1443, Houston TX 77001. (713) 494-5115. (John Hewkin)

Toshiba America, 5235 N. Elston Ave., Chicago, IL 60630. (312) 545-5123. (Ken Motoe)

Zilog, Inc., 10460 Bubb Rd., Cupertino, CA 95014. (408) 446-4666. (Dave West)

Representative 1-k ECL RAMs include Motorola's MCM10146 and 10415, Fairchild's 10415 and Fujitsu's 10415.

TTL RAMs can't go quite as fast as ECLs—they bottom out at about 50 ns. But then, TTLs consume fewer milliwatts than ECLs while covering the same density range.

With one notable exception (Fairchild), the densest bipolar TTL RAMs are made by Signetics (82S110), Fairchild (93415), TI (54 S 314), National (93425), Raytheon (5500), AMD (93415), Intersil (55 S 08), NEC (2205) and Hitachi (2501). These are all 1024 × 1 bits. Fairchild's 4 k, the 93471, is a TTL-compatible static RAM with an eye-popping 55 ns access time. It uses an integrated-injection-logic technique.

At 15 μW/bit, complementary MOS (CMOS) RAMs take the low end of the power scale. CMOS memories are available in 16 to 1024-bit arrays, and in access times from 80 all the way to 1500 ns.

The highest-density CMOS RAMs are made by Harris (6508), RCA (5501), Intersil (6508), Solid State Scientific (5502), AMI (6508), National (74 C 929) and Toshiba (5007). Hughes has recently entered this arena with a 32 × 8 CMOS RAM and two shift registers.

The line between p-channel and n-channel MOS is quite distinct. While the highest-density PMOS RAM is a mere 256 bits, static NMOS RAMs are available from 1024 to 4096 bits. Almost all new designs are being implemented in NMOS.

An NMOS process that promises to provide even denser memories than standard NMOS is the vertical MOS technique developed by American Microsystems. Fabricating the transistors vertically in a V-shaped groove—instead of in a horizontal plane—reduces RAM cell size by almost 50%, yielding a smaller, faster part. The first VMOS product is the AMI S4015-3, a 45-ns static RAM, with a chip size of only 4400 square mils—about half that of the Fairchild 93415, a bipolar equivalent of the 1-k × 1 VMOS RAM.

The one on the cover

Today's largest capacity static NMOS RAMs are all organized as either 4 k × 1 or 1 k × 4. (For clarity, those devices with *1-k × 4* organization will be indicated in italics: 4 k × 1 will be in normal type.)

EM&M Semi's 4402 ties NEC's μPD 410 for the quickest t_{acc}. The former yields its data in 100 ns maximum over 0 to 70 C—very good performance for a MOS device. The latter is available in three bins. Other 4-k parts from EM&M are the *4104*, 4200, 4801 and *4804*, each with a number of bin selections.

Intel's recently introduced family of 4-k static RAMs boils down to two basic type numbers with a total of six bin selections. The *2114* comes in an 18-pin DIP; the *2142* features two additional control pins.

Mostek's *MK4404* needs only a single 5-V supply. Mostek's other static RAM, the *4104*, carries a 200-ns t_{acc}, as does the *MK4404*. Signetics offers one of each—the *2614* and the 2316.

National's two static RAMs, the *5255* and the *5256* are "nibble" (half-byte) organized. Also, its 5257 4 k is a "× 1." Intersil's 7114 is available in four bins and the *7141* also has 4 grades of t_{acc}.

Nitron has two "× 1" parts—the 4402 and 4200. The 4200 uses only two power supplies, −5 and 12 V. The

4104 is Nitron's 1-k × 4. Another Fairchild memory, the *3445*, is nibble-organized.

The fastest (55 ns) 4096-bit static RAMs in the business are in Fairchild's 93470/71 series. Implemented in TTL, the /70 is usable over the full military temperature range of −55 to 125 C.

General Instrument makes two kinds of NMOS static RAMs—the RA3-4402 and RA3-4200.

Advanced Micro Devices offers the *9130* and the 9140 series. The 9145, an unconventional 4-k × 1 NMOS RAM, uses a relatively new technique—clocking—that cuts down on the power consumed. You can consider it a hybrid, falling somewhere between dynamic and static, whose popularity will increase as static devices grow in density. The 9145, in wafer form, is shown on the cover. ■■

A special thanks to the following individuals for their help in organizing the material in this article: Bill Blood, Motorola; Brian Cayton, GI; Richard Florence, CompuCorp; Joe Heesbeen, Macrodata; John Hewkin, TI; Ralph Kaplan, Signetics; Fran Krch, EM&M; John Latham, Rockwell; Harry Masuda, Signetics; Jerry Prioste, Motorola; Bill Regitz, Intel.

Standards for Dynamic MOS RAMs

R.C. FOSS
President, Mosaid, Inc.,
Ottawa, Canada

R. HARLAND
Vice President,
Mosaid, Inc., Ottawa, Canada

Increasing demands for lower cost, higher bit density, and better performance have caused a proliferation of new semiconductor memories—particularly dynamic MOS RAM chips. But, instead of developing a line of standard parts, manufacturers have devoted most of their efforts to maximizing performance and density—which usually means devices with unique "new" problems that result from not eliminating problems in available families.

Today, available 4-k, n-channel dynamic RAMs include at least five pin-out versions of three different packages, with numerous electrical-specification variations. Yet perhaps 90% of the market needs might have been satisfied with but one standard chip design.

This variety stems largely from the lack of a single part with good enough performance and low-enough cost to command undisputed leadership. Some of the types produced are fast, but draw excessive power and are noise sensitive. Other types offer good PC-board density, but have doubtful manufacturing economies and few alternate sources.

However, as the 16-k RAMs are beginning to appear, standards for dynamic RAMs are also beginning to emerge. In dynamic RAMs, Mostek parts have established a clear technical lead. Their specs have been sufficiently tight to delay alternate sourcing of their parts and even to discourage some companies enough to drop out of the game altogether. In static RAMs, standards are coalescing more painfully. The Mostek MK 4104 will likely set one standard. But the competition of the scaled-up 2102A and the fast Intel parts will prevent a single device standard from emerging.

Who sets the standards?

In the early days, the Intel 1103 was pretty much the standard. Tricky to build and even trickier to use, it was still second-sourced by enough companies to lead the field. With the coming of the 4-k RAM, the Motorola 6605 and the Intel 2107 introduced the 22-

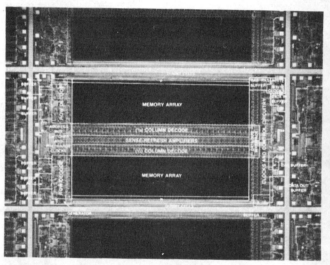

1. A combination of high speed and low power in this 16-k Mostek MK 4116 dynamic RAM results from new approaches in the design of on-chip peripheral circuits and sense amplifiers.

pin package (with different pinouts). But Texas Instruments' 22-pin version became the standard, and the Intel 2107A and 2107B followed.

Meanwhile, Mostek pioneered the 16-pin, multiplexed-address part, the MK 4096. With the emergence of the Mostek 4-k MK 4027 in 1976 and the general acceptance of the 16-pin, multiplexed-address concept, 22-pin parts and their 18-pin derivatives became obsolete. One important factor influencing this move was that the 4027, unlike its predecessors—the 4096—used standard silicon-gate processing.

A powerful argument for the 16-pin format is that it can be readily converted to a high-board-density 16-k RAM, by replacing the $\overline{CS}$ input with an input carrying the two extra address bits. So far, only Mostek (MK 4116) and Intel (2116) have shipped significant quantities. But despite the common pinning there are substantial differences between these seemingly similar memories.

Mostek sets the pace

The Mostek 4116 is setting the standards because of its circuit design (Fig. 1). A combination of high speed and low power requires new approaches to the on-chip peripheral circuits and to the sense amplifiers. Nearly all earlier designs, including the 2216, use sense amplifiers in which load current drawn from V_{DD} is traded off for cycle time set by the period needed to pull up a bit-line.

To escape this compromise requires balanced, all-dynamic sense amplifiers. Such circuits are more complex and difficult to lay out. More serious still, are the design problems created by the need for the Y-access circuits to connect both sides of the divided bit line to the read/write circuits when a bit line is selected. If this is not done, an all-dynamic sense amplifier will not allow read-modify-write cycles (see box).

Prior to MK 4027 and MK 4116, only the National 18 and 22-pin parts used balanced all-dynamic sensing. Failure to do so accounts for other companies' first attempts at 16-pin designs winding up with specifications incompatible with either the older 4096 (which uses all-dynamic, but unbalanced, sensing) or the 4027. It now seems certain that all future dynamic-RAM designs must feature all-dynamic sensing to be performance-competitive.

A second key area in dynamic-RAM design in which Mostek sets the pace is the address buffer.[1] Although detecting TTL levels should be a slight problem compared with the correct sensing of less than 10^6 electrons of stored charge in a memory cell, poor address-buffer design has caused many designs to founder. Unfortunately, a poor buffer shows up by its effects on the decoders, and the obscure errors created are very pattern-dependent.

2. Folded bit lines and a dynamic load-steering circuit minimize power drain in the Intel 2104A 4-k dynamic RAM. The device, which is a second source to the Mostek 4027, has a 16-pin package.

Finally, Mostek is leading the way in shrinking the chip dimensions. A reduction in line widths by x tends to give a speed advantage of x^2 since transistor gains increase by x and gate-capacitance loads diminish by x. A reduction in all linear dimensions achieves similar results, since transistor gains now stay constant and capacitance loads decrease as the square. When the MK 4027 first appeared, it used layout dimensions close to accepted industry standards. But later versions shrank 15%. The MK 4116 has come out in this smaller version from the start, and further size reductions are forecast.

Second sourcing—but how?

A key element in the success of any part is the degree to which it is "second-sourced." But in memories especially, care must be taken when defining a second source. On the one hand, users can sometimes accept quite different parts, maintaining system compatibility only at the board level. On the other hand, identical parts might be used interchangeably to simplify procurement, testing, spares logistics and maintenance.

Until very recently, this latter option was hardly available. Parts to the same nominal specification usually differed so much in second-order "unwritten spec" parameters that they were not fully interchangeable. The MK 4027 was the first n-channel dynamic RAM to be copied exactly by second-sourcers.

There is a hidden paradox in second-sourcing: While having identical multisourced parts seems ideal, if a design problem emerges in production, all identical second sources will be affected. Some 1103 pioneers were hurt in this way when the now-famous "column disturb" problem was discovered.

So despite the inconvenience, using different designs aimed at the same specifications has its advantages. For example, the new Intel 2104A approach to balanced all-dynamic sensing is totally different from that in the 4027, which it second-sources (Fig. 2). However the differences are minor and can be accommodated by users. But, as always with differing designs, it would be risky to consider the parts entirely interchangeable or intermixable.

Meanwhile, the pin-out for 64-k RAMs has been defined by JEDEC as identical to 16-k parts but with the V_{CC} pin converted over to the eighth-pair of address bits. What is not yet generally agreed is whether V_{DD} stays at 12 V, or is established at 5 V or some other intermediate nonstandard voltage. If V_{DD} is not 5 V, then V_{CC} must be derived internally for the output buffer which can be done readily.

The problem in fixing the V_{DD} level comes from having to reduce line widths and clearances to keep chip size compatible with standard 16-pin package-well dimensions. A 12-V supply bootstrapped internally to 16 V or even 20 V is likely to be incompatible with smaller dimensions. On the other hand, a nominal 5-V V_{DD} will give intolerably small internal voltage margins.

One possible way to increase operating margins is to use two cells per bit, as in the 2104A. This ensures that a stored ONE is always compared with a stored ZERO and vice versa, rather than being compared with an intermediate-reference level. Near-perfect balance can be achieved, too, but only by increasing the silicon area of the chip. However, the increase isn't so great, since the array itself does not double in size, and is in any case only 30% to 45% of the total chip area. Indeed, the total chip area might actually be reduced if the fabricating technique allows fine line widths and a 5-V V_{DD}.

Eliminating the $-V_{BB}$ supply is another way to reduce chip area. An on-chip generator might replace the external supply, as in several present static RAM designs. But the problem with using an on-chip generator for dynamic parts is that large peaks of substrate current occur because of capacitance coupling from the bit lines and other parts of the circuit. To minimize such current spikes calls for either an external decoupling capacitor or still more constraints on the circuit design.

As an intermediate step on the road to the 64 k, 16-k parts may emerge with 5-V-only power requirements. The problems will not be easy to solve, but unless some way is found to exploit advanced fine-

Why all-dynamic sensing?

The balanced flip-flop sense amplifier, used in all first-generation, balanced, one-transistor-cell RAM designs, gives the classic speed-power trade-off. Current taken by the sense-amplifier loads can be reduced only by increasing the time taken to pull up the 1 pF or so of bit-line capacitance. However, sense time or access time needn't be affected, because bit lines can be precharged high. It is the read-modify-write cycle, in particular, which is extended.

The extension occurs because the Y decoder gives access to only one half of the divided bit-line; and a ZERO read-out from the side remote from this access can be written back in only as a ONE at a rate set by the charging current available from the sense-amplifier load. If a dynamic circuit is used to cut off the wasted load current fed to the low side, then a ONE level cannot be written back in.

Thus, the key problem is arranging the Y decoder to give balanced access to both sides of the divided bit line. One method, used in the MK 4116, is to run the decoder up the center of the array along with the sense amplifiers. Another is to fold the bit-line halves parallel to each other, giving access to both halves at either end. This method is used in the NEC µPD 414D and Intel 2104A, and lends itself to a two-cells-per-bit format.

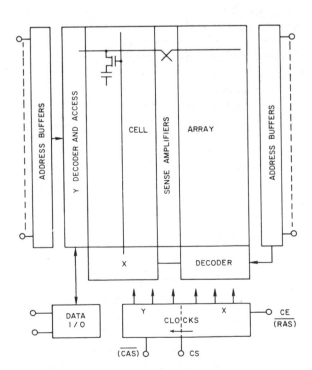

A first-generation dynamic RAM, which used a balanced flip-flop sense amplifier, has Y-access to only one half of a divided bit line.

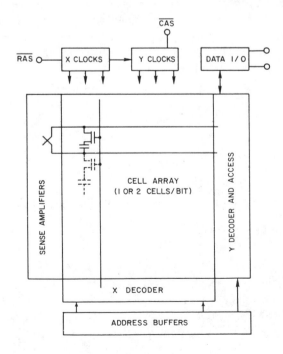

An Intel 2104A-style RAM with folded bit lines. These lines allow easy Y-access to both halves of a divided bit line.

line-width processes in dynamic designs then static RAMs, which use them now, will become more attractive than dynamic RAMs in performance and cost.

The future of dynamic RAMs

While 64-k dynamic RAM chips are now being promised, 4-k parts are still being actively developed to serve the real market. In early 1976, 16-k RAMs before year's end were promised by every supplier. Most have yet to emerge and it still seems reasonable to expect volume availability of multisourced equivalent parts in 1978.

Beyond the 16-k, the crystal ball gets cloudy. The 16-k dynamic RAM is a happy combination of reasonably well-proven processing and well-developed circuit techniques that fit a chip nicely into a standard package, while offering a good balance of performance features. This act will be hard to follow.

Advanced MOS processes at or beyond the limits of optical photolithography will be needed to improve real densities. (A 64-k chip in a larger package will be only a marginal benefit.) Smaller geometries will likely require that the 12-V supply and the still higher bootstrap levels currently used be eliminated. This would match the trend to 5-V-only parts but would create a new set of design problems.

While such difficulties probably will be overcome during this decade, it is also likely that different companies will solve the problems in different ways, and what happened in the early days of 4-k parts will happen again. As a result, acceptance of any one approach would be delayed, and the 16-k would have an unusually long-life—several years at least.

Outlook for static RAMs

Right now, a MOS static RAM has more than twice the area of a dynamic RAM, but this ratio may not stay constant if short-channel advanced MOS technologies now emerging in static RAMs can't be applied to dynamic RAMs. Unfortunately, the 4-k static is being standardized in an ad hoc way resembling the early history of the 4-k dynamic RAM. The situation is also complicated by three distinct though overlapping areas of static-RAM use—and a design that is best for one won't necessarily serve another as well.

One area is the replacement of bipolar RAMs in applications requiring access times faster than 50 ns. Such parts use all-static design to match bipolar functions. But they are more difficult to fabricate, and then they require more power than the slower static RAMs. But even with these two drawbacks, these fast static RAMs are likely to be an improvement over bipolar standards.

A second area—microprocessors—has been traditionally served by simple all-static parts like the 2102 and its 4-k successor, the 2114. But this area is now diverging. Since μP systems are nearly always

Progress in dynamic RAMs, 1973 to the present

Mfg.	Part no.	Bits	Pins	Remarks
T.I.	TMS 4030	4 k	22	1st commercial 1-T cell
M.I.L.	MF 2107C	4 k	22	1st clocked-source sensing
Intel	i 2107B	4 k	22	
T.I.	TMS 4050	4 k	18	1st 18-pin part
T.I.	TMS 4051	4 k	18	TTL-level CE clock
T.I.	TMS 4060	4 k	22	Re-specified TMS 4030
National	MM 5280	4 k	22	1st All-dynamic sensing
National	MM 5270	4 k	18	Nonstandard 18-pin
Intel	i 2104	4 k	16	
Motorola	MCM 6604	4 k	16	
AMD	Am 9060	4 k	22	Similar to TMS 4060
AMD	Am 9050	4 k	18	Similar to TMS 4050
Mostek	MK 4027	4 k	16	Leading 4-k part
Intel	i 2104A	4 k	16	Mosaid Inc. patents cover these two
NEC	μPD 414D	4 k	16	
Intel	i 2116	16 k	16	1st 16-k RAM
Mostek	MK 4116	16 k	16	Leading 16-k part

synchronous, it is better to design a static RAM cell with clocked peripheral circuits as in the MK 4104. This largely avoids the speed-power trade-off inherent in the static inversions of the address buffers and decoders in all-static parts.

Clocked-periphery circuits result in much lower power consumption, which particularly benefits systems with battery back-up and may even allow n-channel MOS to replace CMOS in some applications.

Compounding the variation in circuit techniques is a divergence in package styles and pinnings. An early 4-k static part, the AMD 9130/9140, used a 22-pin package. But later 4-k memory designs are all aimed at 18-pin packages for reduced cost and better board-packing density.

Process standards

In the 4-k RAM, several variations of n-channel technology were used. Most were silicon gate processes, but the industry was about evenly divided between "coplanar" processing and "standard" processing, whereby a uniformly grown field oxide is etched to define active device locations. In the former, field oxide is selectively grown and device areas are screened by silicon nitride to inhibit the field-oxide's growth. Coplanarity reduces step heights and can save an ion-implant masking step used in controlling field-threshold voltage. On the other hand, coplanar processes have been associated with gate-oxide-quality problems giving "stuck ONEs" and/or refresh failures.

Other variations existed: Some parts used a "buried-contact" masking step to provide direct connection between polysilicon and n-diffused regions. Even "philosophical" differences existed. Some companies used relatively large chips, claiming that relatively generous layout rules increased yields. Others used tight rules to achieve small chip sizes.

At the 16-k level, however, there is more standardization—for now. Silicon-gate coplanar processing is standard. The two layers of polysilicon reduce cell area that doesn't contribute to cell capacitance. A diffused bit line and a metal word line are used in the process. The extra pitch between bit lines allows sense amplifiers to be laid out without a buried-contact masking step.

In addition, relatively tight layout rules are forced on 16-k chip design by the need to ensure that the chip will fit in the well area of a 16-pin package. As a result, the maximum allowable chip width of the 16-k memory is about 145 mil.

Prices keep tumbling

This year, 4-k RAMs have become readily available at less than 0.1¢ per bit, which has reduced the cost of memory systems dramatically. By year's end, according to predictions, 16-k RAMs will be at this level. And the 16-k devices are already saving in overhead circuitry and board area, among other things.

However, the same techniques that can lower the 16-k prices might produce still cheaper 4-k parts. A chip area of less than 15,000 mil^2 on a basic four-mask process with scratch protection should give yields of 150 good chips per wafer or more—provided that the part design and/or spec do not cause significant parametric yield loss. With low-cost assembly, a price in the region of $2 seems attainable.

With most interest centered on 16-k parts, such prices may not materialize. But if they do, then 16-k parts will find it difficult to beat the 4-k price per bit until 1979. As always, price may not follow costs too closely in such a competitive market. At any rate, the pace of RAM development shows no sign of slackening in the near future. ∎∎

References

1. Foss, R. C. and Harland, R., "Should MOS RAMs be TTL-compatible?" *Electronic Design*, June 7, 1976, p. 107.

Memories Have Hit a Density Ceiling

SAM YOUNG
Strategic Marketing/Applications Manager,
Mostek, Carrollton, Texas

In ten years, MOS memories have gone from medium-performance (p-channel) devices to high-performance (n-channel) ones. RAM-cell structures have shrunk from three devices per cell to one, densities have increased by a factor of 16, and access times have dropped by factors of two or more. Process refinements and circuit innovations brought the MOS RAM to where it is—and where it would stay without process innovations.

The problem is that with today's best technology —line widths of 5 μ and one-element-per-cell structures—ROMs have hit a density ceiling of 64 kbits, dynamic RAMs of 16 kbits and static RAMs of 8 kbits. The next generation—64-k RAMs, 128-k ROMs, etc. —won't come without new ways to increase densities. But fortunately, new ways are being developed.

A dynamic beginning

It all started with the 1024-bit MOS dynamic RAMs —the 1103 from Intel (Santa Clara, CA) and the 4006 from Mostek—the first semiconductor memories to gain wide acceptance. Built from p-channel MOS technology, these devices made large, solid-state memory arrays possible by incorporating all decoding circuits on the same chip as the RAM array. Both were dynamic memories and used a capacitive storage technique to hold each bit value, a technology that required periodic refreshing to retain data (the charge held in the MOS capacitors leaked away). A major difference between the two was that the 1103 required MOS-level clocks and some complex timing, while the 4006 was TTL-compatible and had minimal timing requirements.

There were other similarities. For one thing, both the 1103 and 4006 used a three-transistor cell for each bit stored (Fig. 1); the big difference was that the 1103 used separate read and write buses. In both cases, though, the 1024 bits were housed in about 20,000 sq. mils of silicon—a density that promised to displace core memories and make large systems simple to implement. However, it wasn't until even higher-density products were introduced that the takeover became noticeable.

The first of the higher-density devices, the 4096-bit dynamic RAM, provided quadruple the density—and a lot of confusion by coming out in at least five major designs: two different 22-pin models, two different 18-pin models and a "maverick" 16-pin multiplexed device. As today's products clearly show, the maverick 16-pin design not only took hold as the industry standard for the 4096, but also for the 16,384 and 65,536-bit RAMs.

However, to make those higher-density and higher-speed RAMs possible, p-channel technology was aban-

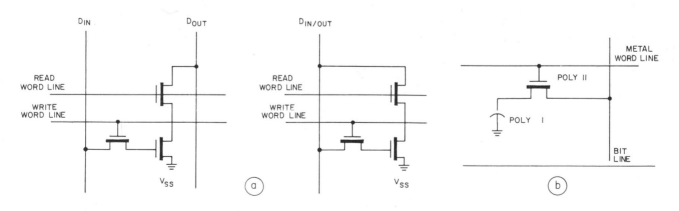

1. The first high-volume 1024-bit MOS RAMs, the 1103 from Intel (left) and the MK4006 from Mostek (middle), used a three-transistor cell for each bit (a). Newer designs, like the 16-k MK4116 use a single transistor cell (b).

NMOS: It began with a "spin"

Ever since it was developed, Mostek's NMOS process has been evolving

SPIN (self-aligned polysilicon interconnect n-channel) is a metal-gate process that uses aluminum for the MOS gate electrode as well as for signal and power-supply conductors. Usually requiring larger geometries, it was not suited for high-density products.

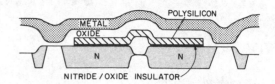

Poly I is a single-level, polysilicon, n-channel, silicon-gate process in which doped polysilicon is deposited and used for the gate electrode of the MOS transistor as well as for a single interconnection vehicle. When used as a conductor, doped poly introduces circuit delays, so it's normally used just for short distances.

The mainstay of many MOS RAMs, Poly I offers good speed/density characteristics. The MK4027 manufactured with this process is the smallest and fastest 4-k dynamic RAM available today, with a die size of 11,900 mil² and an access time of 120 ns.

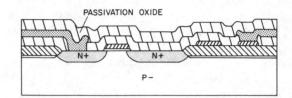

Poly II is a double-level, polysilicon, n-channel, silicon-gate process for high-density dynamic-RAM products. An enhanced Poly I, it uses a second level of polysilicon as the storage cell capacitor plate. This process permitted a reduction of cell area from 1.008 mil² (MK4027) to 0.55 mil² (MK4116). Like Poly I's polysilicon level, Poly II's other polysilicon level is used to form device-gate electrodes as well as some signal interconnects.

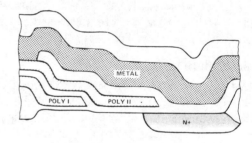

Poly R is a single-level, polysilicon n-channel silicon-gate process that also includes intrinsic polysilicon for use in static cell-load devices. This process eliminates the depletion-transistor-type load normally found in static RAMs, and virtually doubles the packing density of static cells. When introduced, the Poly R process used in the MK4104 kept the storage cell to 2.75 mil² about half that of earlier static RAM cells (5.5 mil²). And with the intrinsic loads drawing less than 1 nA each, Poly R is a low-power as well as high-density process.

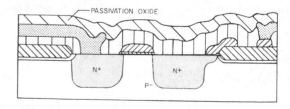

Scaled Poly 5 is the scaled-5-V circuit process for the next generation of products. It can be used with Poly II or the Poly R processes. This process, therefore, not only takes advantage of the technological evolution that is driving the growth of NMOS for semiconductor memories. It also makes much larger contributions by increasing speed, density and reliability, and lowering cost.

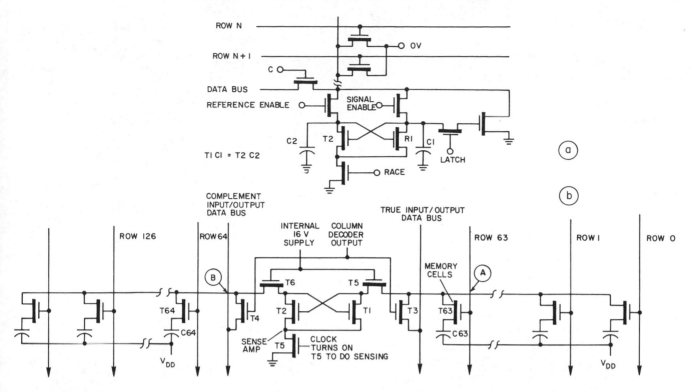

2. **Two basic types of sense amplifiers** are used to detect the tiny charge stored on the RAM capacitors: the single-ended (a) and the differential balanced (b). Almost every RAM made today uses the balanced version.

doned and n-channel processing brought on-line. N-channel allowed the low threshold voltages needed for TTL compatibility, its speed was inherently greater —and, most importantly, it permitted device densities to really grow. Along with n-channel processing there came a new storage-cell design that permitted a bit to be stored using a single transistor and a capacitor instead of three transistors and a capacitor: another big density increaser.

But with two amplifying transistors eliminated, new sense-amplifier designs had to be developed to boost the very small signal levels that had to be detected. The levels out of the memory matrix dropped from volts to millivolts. The two most popular techniques included a single-ended sense-amp design (Fig. 2a) and a balanced differential sense amp (Fig. 2b). The balanced amplifier which was much better, has become the dominant method.

Another technique (developed by Mostek) that permitted an active load to be used instead of a passive load for writing through the sense amplifier reduced the RAM's power dissipation by half.

Sense amplifier design is crucial

But without the sense amplifiers, there wouldn't have been any single-transistor cells. So difficult was it to sense the signals from the cells that the one-transistor cell wasn't introduced until three years after the three-transistor cell was unveiled.

As its name implies, the one-transistor cell is a minimal structure—a capacitor stores digital data as a high or low level and a transistor selectively connects the capacitor to a digit/sense line (Fig. 3). Conduction through the transistor is controlled by its gate, which is electrically connected to the other gates in a row. When a row is enabled by the row decoder, all transistors in that row become conductive, and transfer the charge from their respective capacitors to the corresponding digit/sense lines, destructively reading data. Each column has its own sense amplifier, which detects the charge and amplifies the signal created by the charge. The amplified signal is a full logic level—either at ground or close to V_{DD}.

During a destructive read, the transistors stay conductive, and part of the amplified signal is fed back to the cell input to refresh the cell. To maximize the signal fed to the sense amplifier means that cell capacitance should be large and digit/sense-line capacitance small. These two capacitances form a divider that attenuates the signal from the cell.

However, integrating a large number of bits on chip means that the cells have to be small and that many bits have to share the same digit/sense line. As a result, this line is long and has a high stray capacitance. To keep the attenuation acceptable, then, cell capacitance must be maximized and digit-line capacitance minimized.

A double-layer polysilicon process helps maximize cell capacitance; simply cutting a digit line in half reduces its capacitance. The sense amplifier is then located in the center of a digit line, and senses a

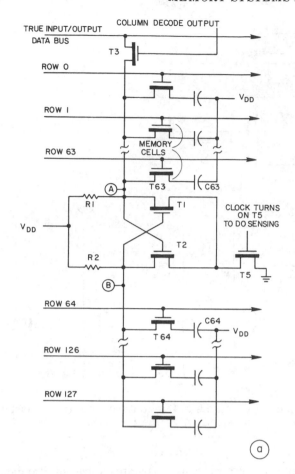

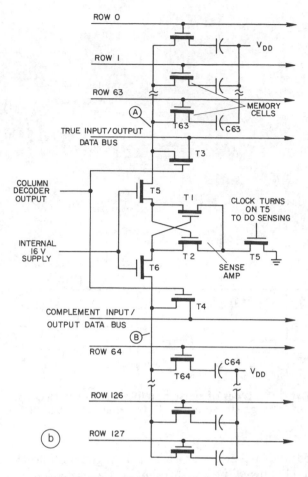

3. **Two versions of the balanced amplifier** are used in different RAM designs. The static amplifier (a) draws about double the power of the dynamic amplifier (b), but it's easier to design and lay out on the chip. Both types of differential amplifiers have similar sensitivities for detecting and amplifying small signals.

differential voltage between the two halves of the line.

In 16-k designs, the cell capacitance is typically about 0.04 pF and the stray capacitance of half a digit line about 1 pF. Thus, the signal from the cell is attenuated by a factor of 25 before being sensed by the amplifier.

Basically, a sense amplifier consists of a balanced flip-flop. Since the addressed cell, working with a dummy cell (a special cell used to adjust the voltage on the half-digit line not containing the addressed cell), guarantees an initial voltage imbalance to the flip-flop, the flip-flop's positive feedback causes it to latch up. The half-digit line with the lower initial voltage goes to ground while the other half-digit line goes to V_{DD}, or in the case of a dynamic sense amplifier, remains close by.

Two basic types of balanced differential sense amplifiers have found their way into commercial memory chips: the static amplifier (Fig. 3a) and the dynamic amplifier (Fig. 3b). Neither does a better job of detecting and amplifying small signals. However, the load resistors in the static amplifier (R_1 and R_2) consume quite a bit of power, typically more than half that of the entire chip. Dynamic amplifier designs don't have these resistors and dissipate much less power. However, there are critical design and layout

problems to solve for dynamic amplifiers—some so severe that many chip designs choose to pay the power-consumption penalty for using static-amplifier designs.

Meanwhile, process techniques were being developed to improve yield, density and performance. For a brief history of process development, see the box on p. 20.

Once the amplifier design was established, the 4096-bit RAM became an "industry standard." The first one was the MK4096 in 1973. Its successor, the MK4027, dramatically reduced chip size from the original 19,000 mil² to the current 12,000, and cell size from about 1.5 mil² to 1.008 mil².

After the MK4027 came a 16-k RAM, the MK4116, whose cell size came all the way down to just 0.55 mil². The process that yielded this cell-size reduction was called Poly II.

Packing things in

Until now, device density has been increased by reducing the number of elements per cell, as well as by a two-dimensional reduction in geometry. The two-dimensional reduction results in a "squeezing" of signal lines and spaces. The slope of the graph in Fig.

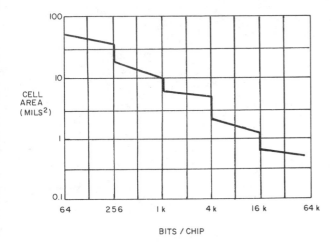

CELL AREA (MILS²) vs BITS / CHIP

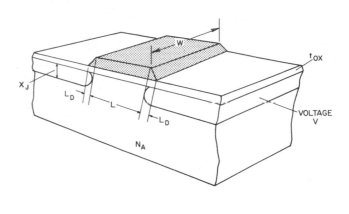

4. Memory-cell area continues to drop as more and more bits are crammed into each chip. There are limits, however: production capabilities and scaling requirements.

6. True transistor scaling means that all dimensions are reduced. Even the voltage must be lowered to compensate for the reduced channel lengths (L).

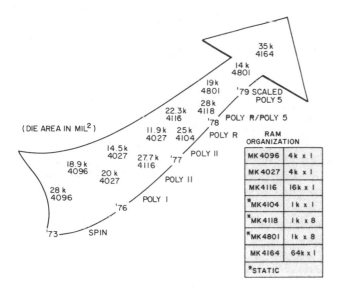

RAM ORGANIZATION	
MK 4096	4k x 1
MK 4027	4k x 1
MK 4116	16k x 1
*MK 4104	1k x 1
*MK 4118	1k x 8
*MK 4801	1k x 8
MK 4164	64k x 1
*STATIC	

5. A dynamic evolution: Over the past six years, the dynamic RAM has progressed from a 4096-bit, 20,000-mil² chip to a 65,536-bit, 35,000-mil² chip, in 1979, by combining circuit and process innovations.

4 illustrates the squeezing mechanism while the vertical steps show cell-element reduction. There is, however, an anomaly in the graph around the 4-k region. A significant area reduction was obtained by a process change—silicon-gate instead of metal-gate. In general up to now, this two-dimensional squeezing has produced up to 40% reductions (see chart in Fig. 5).

At the same time, chip size has doubled with each new RAM generation while the number of bits per chip has quadrupled. A process called Poly II has already reduced the area occupied by a transistor and capacitor effectively to the area of just one of those components. Therefore the memory cell element count

has reached its minimum, which means that the next generation of memory products hinges on process innovations for added density.

So the stage is set for three and four-dimensional scaling, or scaled Poly 5.

Scaling actually refers to circuits in which *all* physical dimensions—length, width and depth—have been reduced by a scaling factor, K, along with the operating voltage. Fig. 6 shows all the dimensions of a typical device that are affected by scaling. To operate at 5 V when previous versions operated at 12 V, a device must have a K of 5/12. Table 1 compares the scaled Poly 5 factors with a brute-force 5/12 reduction process and currently used NMOS technology.

Modifications to the brute force approach were made for scaled Poly 5 to make the process usable for production devices. For example, substrate resistivity was changed from the calculated 6 Ω-cm to 30 Ω-cm to minimize what would have been undesirably high junction capacitance and body effects.

Reaping the benefits

The most significant advantage of scaling is that chip area goes down by a factor of K^2. At the same time, performance goes up: smaller devices packed closer together will have shorter propagation delays, with less power dissipation per device. Table 2 illustrates the performance difference scaling can make by comparing two 64 kbit ROMs, one built with a standard high-density NMOS process (the MK36000), and the other (the MK9009) with scaled Poly 5.

Reliability factors change to some extent. Power dissipation drops by a factor of K^2, voltage stress decreases by a factor of K, and current density increases by a factor of 1/K. The increase in current density, however, will not affect reliability, because

Table 1. Standard NMOS vs scaled Poly 5

Device parameter	Current N-MOS	Scaled by	Scaled poly	"Brute force"
Channel length L (μ)$_0$	5	5/12	2.5	2.1
Oxide thickness t_{OX} (Å)	850	5/12	500	354
Doping concentration N_A	10^{15}	12/5	5×10^{14}	2.4×10^{15}
(substrate resistivity)	(10 Ωcm)		(30 Ωcm)	(6 Ωcm)
Power supply voltage (V)	12	5/12	5	5
Junction depth Xj (μ)	1.2	5/12	0.4	0.45
Lateral diffusion L_D (μ)	1.0	5/12	0.3	0.41

Table 2. Two 64-k ROMs—head-to-head

	MK 36000	MK 9009
Die dimensions	183 x 190 mils	105 x 109 mils
Die area	34,770 sq. mils	11,445 sq. mils
No. of die/wafer (3 in.)	170	575
Min. poly width	5.0 microns	2.5 microns
Min. line width	2.5 microns	1.0 - 1.5 microns
Junction depth	1.3 microns	0.4 microns
Access time	80 ns (typ.)	40 ns (typ.)

Table 3. Genealogy of geometry requirements

	1960 Discrete	1965 Digital	1970 P-MOS	1975 N-MOS	1980 Poly 5 (NMOS)
Leading Technology	Discrete	Digital	P-MOS	N-MOS	Poly 5 (NMOS)
Line width (Microns)	>10	7 - 9	5 - 8	3.5 - 5	2
Interconnect Technology	Metal	Metal	Metal	Metal/ poly	Metal/ double level poly

Table 4. Memory applications: a wide spectrum

Cost ←					→ Performance
	Electronic games	Microprocessor applications	Mini computers	Mainframe	Cache memory
Performance	1μs - 450 ns	450-200 ns	250-150 ns	200-100 ns	100-30 ns
Product	RAM ROM EPROM	SRAM ROM EPROM	DRAM —	DRAM CCD —	D/S RAM —

of the conservative guidelines used in the past. Field strength and power per unit area remain the same.

With device sizes shrinking, production methods are getting close to their maximum tolerances. New photolithographic processes will have to be developed to match the reduced line widths required by the next-generation circuits. Table 3 compares technologies and line widths that have emerged since the first commercial ICs appeared in 1960. Manufacturing goals for 1980 are set on devices with 2-μ dimensions. However, there are still some problems to overcome. For one thing, today's measuring equipment has an accuracy to within ±0.18 μ (10% of what is to be measured). Moreover, standards are only accurate to within ±0.1 μ, and contact printers have a runout of ±0.75 μ on 4-in.-diameter wafers.

Obviously, to meet future production needs, accuracy had better be improved. Methods such as electron-beam mask making, projection printing and X-ray lithography are making headway.

As devices have improved and cost has come down thanks to circuit innovations and process improvements, the applications for semiconductor memories have grown. As Table 4 shows, applications for various types of memories span a spectrum ranging from electronic games to cache memories. At the game end, technology improvements resulting in low cost are most significant, while at the cache end, performance is the main beneficiary. So much so that cache as well as microprogram memory markets, hitherto dominated by speedy bipolar memories, have become fair game for high-performance MOS devices.

Future MOS generations will see improvements in density and performance. Current dynamic RAM products, for example, now feature TTL-compatible I/O characteristics, but still require multiple power supplies for operation. Next-generation memories will provide complete TTL compatibility and operate from a single 5-V power supply.

ROMs and UV EPROMs will improve in density immensely: 64-k ROMs are already on the shelves, and 32-k EPROMs are starting to appear. What's more, some companies expect to have 64-k EPROMs shortly.

ROM pinouts have been virtually standardized for the past several years. The 24-pin package has managed to hold ROMs with 8 through 64 kbits. This upward compatibility is accomplished merely by changing the chip-select functions to address lines as the density increases—all other pins remain the same (Fig. 7a). The same pin configuration has also been applied to EPROMs, and more recently, to byte-wide static RAMs (Fig. 7b).

But now that density has reached 64-k, the 24-pin package has become a problem. Since more pins are needed to accommodate the output enable function, a program pin, or more address lines, there's been a split in the ROM/EPROM/RAM pin-configuration standards.

To increase pin availability, a 28-pin package family has been developed (Fig. 7c) and configured so that there's no compatibility with the older 24-pin products beyond the 16-kbit level.

The pinout is set up so that pin 24 of the 28-pin package pinout is for an active-high chip-select function and pin 2 is for a 64-k address—on the 24-pin package, pin 24 is for the V_{CC}, and pin 2 is unused. ROMs below 64 kbits will be offered in a revised 24-pin package that will permit upgrading or downgrading without any major board changes.

Static RAMs have also been major growth products, aided mostly by the microprocessor market. Special power-saving techniques such as Edge-Activated, Address-Activated and Chip-Enable switching of internal high-dissipation elements have given the

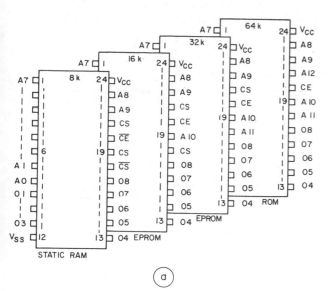

STATIC RAM

(a)

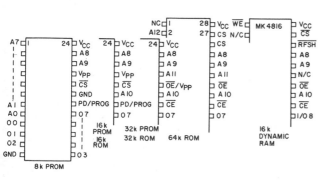

STATIC RAM

(b)

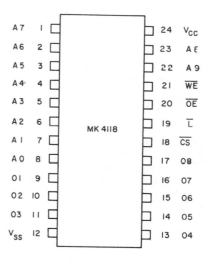

(c)

4096-bit statics another stronghold—in large OEM applications. In addition, pinouts of byte-wide static RAMs are set up to be pin-compatible with the 1 and 2-k EPROMs to aid system development.

How the next generation of static RAMs will perform is previewed in the MK4801 and MK4118, 1-k × 8, static RAMs. The 4801 offers access times ranging from 55 to 90 ns, comes in a 24-pin DIP, has a chip area of 19,000 mil² and will be built with scaled Poly 5. A slower but pin-compatible version, the 4118, is built with the single-level Poly R process (see box p. 20) and will come in versions with access times from 120 to 300 ns (Fig. 8).

With a compact-cell design to achieve its high density, the 4801 is totally designed for speed. It has an Address-Activated interface that permits asynchronous operation for the user while main-

A0 — A9	ADDRESS INPUTS	$\overline{WE}$	WRITE ENABLE
$\overline{CS}$	CHIP SELECT	$\overline{OE}$	OUTPUT ENABLE
D_{IN}	DATA INPUT	$\overline{L}$	LATCH
D_{OUT}	DATA OUTPUT	O1–O8	DATA IN / DATA OUT PORT
V_{SS}	GROUND		
V_{CC}	POWER (5 V)		

8. **Low-cost byte-wide static RAMs** like the MK4118 offer high density for small systems. A higher performance version, the MK4801, is pin compatible.

7. **Standardized ROM pinouts** have been available for memory sizes from 8 through 64 kbits (a). EPROMs and RAMs have also been built to fit in the 24-pin ROM pinout (b). However, more than 64 kbits means extra address lines, so the 24-pin package must be abandoned for a 28-pin (c).

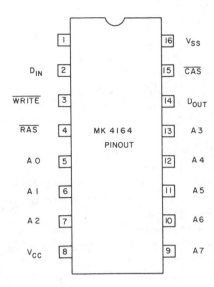

9. **The 64-kbit dynamic RAM** will fit into the same 16-pin configuration as earlier 16-k's. However, it'll require just one 5-V supply instead of the three supplies needed by the 16-k's. In the case of the MK4164, a special function will be included on the otherwise unused pin 1.

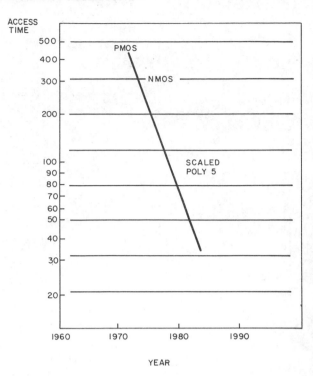

10. **With access time projected to shrink below 20 ns** by 1990, dynamic RAMs will have to take advantage of both improved processing and circuit innovations. Otherwise it will be impossible to meet the goals.

taining the advantages of clocked circuit technology inside. And a fast chip-select path permits external decoder delays without impacting access time.

The 4118 adds an output enable and a latch function. This permits the RAMs to be used with 16-bit microprocessors that have common address and data I/O —like the Z8000 from Zilog (Cupertino, CA) and the 8086 from Intel. Both RAMs come in the 24-pin DIP configuration (Fig. 7b). The 4118 can be used in the asynchronous mode like the 4801, or it can operate in a synchronous mode, like the 4104 4-k RAMs. To operate in the synchronous mode, the latch function will latch the status of the address and chip-select pins so any changes on the lines won't affect the operation.

The ever-changing dynamic RAM

Dynamic RAMs are also being reorganized. For example, a 2-k × 8 organization will highlight the 4816, currently under development at Mostek. It will operate from a single 5-V supply, come in a 28-pin DIP, and have access times in the 100 to 150-ns range. Designed for cost-sensitive applications, the 4816 is well suited to microprocessor systems.

More accurately a pseudostatic RAM, the 4816 includes refresh circuitry on its chip. The refresh has two modes of operation: When the refresh pin is pulsed from high to low and then back again, an internal counter will replace the external addresses and a RAM cycle occurs, refreshing one row of cells. This operation must be repeated 128 times every 2 ms. For standby-mode, the refresh pin may remain active—in fact, the RAM will execute a refresh cycle approximately every 16 μs, which will satisfy data-hold requirements without outside help. This feature great-

ly simplifies control circuitry needed and eliminates all address multiplexer components.

The next generation of OEM dynamic memories will be the 64-k × 1 RAM (with alternative organizations to come: 16-k × 4, 8-k × 8). Like its predecessor, the 16-k, the 64-k × 1 device will use the 16-pin, multiplexed address package. Unlike its predecessor, though, the 64-k RAM will operate from a single 5-V supply and offer a sub-100-ns access time.

In 1979, Mostek will sample a 5-V-only, sub-100-ns 64-k-RAM built with the scaled Poly 5. Expected to have a chip size of 35,000 mil², use 2-μ geometries and come in the familiar 16-pin package (Fig. 9), the RAM will also add something new. With only one supply, there's a spare pin on the package (pin 1)— it'll be used to provide a new system feature or control function.

The goal is a 128-cycle refresh every 2 ms to make the RAM pin-compatible with available 16-k units. The 128 cycles would then require the same seven address pins of the 16-k's instead of eight that some other manufacturers will require. To maintain the compatibility for all refresh circuitry, pin 9 (A_7) won't be used as a refresh address. The RAM's dissipation will be a low 300-mW—even though it operates at twice the frequency of the earlier 16-k's.

Performance should evolve as depicted in the graph of Fig. 10. The techniques needed to achieve a usable 64-k RAM require several breakthroughs that are currently being proven on predecessor devices. ∎∎

Dynamic Memories Offer Advantages

JERRY WINFIELD
Applications Engineer,
Mostek, Carrollton, Texas

Faced with a need to expand memory, you can choose from two basic types: static and dynamic RAM. Because most microprocessors, like the 8080 or 6800, do not provide any control signals or operating modes that would simplify the interface of dynamic RAM to a microprocessor, designers usually prefer static RAM because it's "easier to interface." But before you follow suit, see what dynamic memory has to offer.

Tables 1 and 2 compare the requirements of the two RAM types when used with a Z80 μP. For a 4-k $\times$ 8 RAM, there is little difference in power consumption and cost, but the static approach needs 39 chips, while the dynamic alternative requires only 15. The ratio $15/39 = 0.38$ is indicated in the "relative size" column.

For the larger memories of Table 2, differences are more pronounced: compared with a 16-k $\times$ 8 static RAM, equivalent dynamic memories are vastly superior in power consumption (40% and 21% of static RAM) and size (31% and 10% of static RAM). Even the cost can be much lower (70% with 4-k chips).

Dynamic RAM does have disadvantages—above all the need for a refresh cycle. But if you use a suitable μP, the problems are minor.

The Z80, for instance, is designed to ease interfacing to dynamic RAMs by providing four memory control signals, and a refresh time slot.[1] The signals are memory request, read, write, and refresh.

During the op code fetch cycle, the Z80 also provides a time slot that allows the memory to be refreshed without sacrificing system speed. The refresh cycle is executed during the last two T states of the op code fetch cycle, while the CPU is decoding the op code. During this time period the memory is idle, so that the refresh cycle is "transparent" to the operation of the CPU.

Furthermore, the Z80 provides the refresh row address on address bits A_0 to A_6 during the fetch cycle. The refresh address is automatically incremented each time a refresh cycle is executed.

Timing is the key

Of the Z80's three memory cycles (Fig. 1), the most critical for access time is the op code fetch cycle. Excluding TTL delays, the worst-case access time for the op code fetch is 450 ns (Fig. 1a), while the worst-case access time for the memory-read cycle is 640 ns (Fig. 1b). These access times assume a clock frequency of 2.5 MHz, and are referenced to memory request ($\overline{MREQ}$).

The Z80 microcomputer system puts the extra T-state to good use by placing the refresh cycle in that time slot. No "wait states" or clock "stretching" are required.

To keep track of the row in the memory matrix that is to be refreshed, the Z80 has a dedicated register, R. For the refresh cycle, the Z80 puts the contents of the R register on address lines A_0 to A_6 and

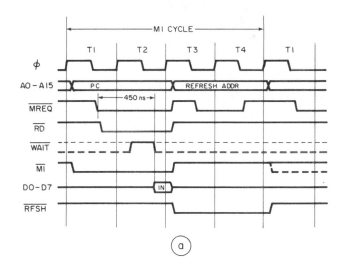

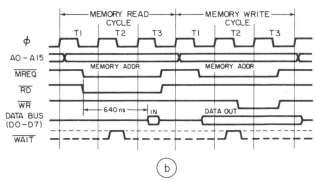

1. **The instruction fetch cycle of the Z80** (a) is longer than the memory read or write cycle (b). The extra time is used to refresh dynamic memories.

automatically increments the R register when an op code fetch is executed. The Z80 memory control signals perform the following functions:

- Memory request ($\overline{\text{MREQ}}$) indicates that the address bus holds a valid memory address for a memory-read, or memory-write.
- Read ($\overline{\text{RD}}$) indicates that the CPU wants to read data from memory or an I/O device. The addressed I/O device or memory uses this signal to gate data onto the CPU data bus.
- Write ($\overline{\text{WR}}$) indicates that the CPU data bus holds valid data to be stored in the addressed memory or I/O device.
- Refresh ($\overline{\text{RFSH}}$) indicates that the lower seven bits of the address bus contain a refresh address for dynamic memories. The current $\overline{\text{MREQ}}$ signal is used to refresh all dynamic RAMs in the system.

Mostek's MK4027 (4 k × 1) and MK4116 (16 k × 1) 16-pin dynamic memories use a special address multiplexing technique that loads the address bits into memory and allows each memory to be packaged in a 16-pin DIP. The MK4027 needs 12 address bits to select one out of 4096 locations, and the MK4116 requires 14 bits to select one out of 16,384.

Refresh your 16-pin RAM

The internal memory can be thought of as a matrix: The MK4027 matrix is 64 × 64, while the MK4116 matrix is 128 × 128. To select a particular location,

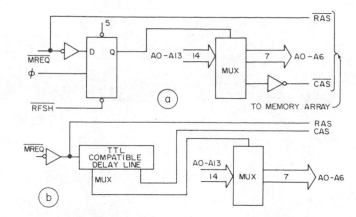

2. Memory timing signals can be generated differently for small (a) or large (b) memory arrays.

a row and column address is supplied to the memory. For the MK4027, address bits A_0 to A_5 form the row address and bits A_6 to A_{11} the column address. For the MK4116, address bits A_0 to A_6 form the row address and bits A_7 to A_{13} the column address.

Both the row and column addresses are strobed into the memory by negative-going signals, one called row-address strobe ($\overline{\text{RAS}}$), the other a column-address strobe ($\overline{\text{CAS}}$). They latch the address bits into the memory for access to the desired memory location.

To retain valid data, the MK4027 needs 64 refresh cycles every 2 ms, while the MK4116 needs 128 refresh cycles every 2 ms, due to its larger memory matrix. In other words, an MK4027 has to be refreshed every

Table 1. Comparison of 4-k × 8 static and dynamic RAMs

Device used	Number of RAMs	Support ICs	Voltages, currents	Over-all power[1]	Relative power	Relative cost[2]	Relative size
21L02 1 k × 1 static	32	7	+5 V @ 1.26 A	6.3 W	1	1	1
MK4027-4 4 k × 1 dynamic	8	7	+5 V @ 0.42 A +12 V @ 0.25 A −5 @ 0.03 A	5.25 W	0.83	0.90	0.38

Table 2. Comparison of 16-k × 8 static and dynamic RAMs

Device used	Number of RAMs	Support ICs	Voltages, currents	Over-all power[1]	Relative power	Relative cost[2]	Relative size
21L02 1 k × 1 static	128	28	+5 V @ 5.04 A	25.2 W	1	1	1
MK4027-4 4 k × 1 dynamic	32	16	+5 V @ 0.55 A +12 V @ 0.60 A −5 V @ 0.03 A	10.1 W	0.40	0.7	0.31
MK4116-4 16 k × 1 dynamic	8	8	+5 V @ 0.42 A +12 V @ 0.25 A −5 V @ 0.03 A	5.25 W	0.21	1.08	0.10

Notes (1) Power requirement of dynamic RAMs is based on Z80 operating at 2.5-MHz clock frequency.
(2) Relative cost includes RAMs, support ICs, power supply, and PC board.

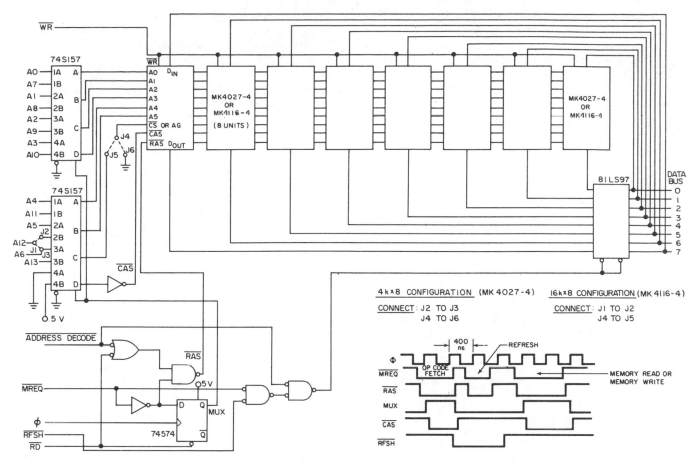

3. **The schematic for a 4-k × 8 memory** makes provisions for expansion to 16-k × 8 bits.

32 µs, while the MK4116 needs refreshing every 16 µs. The memory is refreshed each time a read or write cycle is performed, or by a $\overline{RAS}$-only refresh cycle. (For detailed information on the MK4027 and the MK4116, write for the manufacturer's literature.[2])

The Z80 needs some help

When interfacing a Z80 to a 16-pin dynamic RAM, two timing signals not generated by the Z80 are necessary: the switch multiplexer (MUX) and the column address strobe ($\overline{CAS}$). You can provide them in several ways: Fig. 2a shows a circuit that's best suited for a small on-board memory, while Fig. 2b shows one that suits a separate memory board.

The complete schematic for a small "on-board" memory (Fig. 3) can accommodate either the MK4027-4 or the MK4116-4. Control signal $\overline{MREQ}$ is gated with $\overline{AD}$ (address decode) or $\overline{RFSH}$ to generate $\overline{RAS}$, while $\overline{MREQ}$ and Φ generate MUX. The column address strobe $\overline{CAS}$ is then generated by an output of one of the 74S157 multiplexers.

This design can easily be expanded from a 4-k × 8 memory to a 16-k × 8, by changing two jumpers and installing eight MK4116s. You can wire these jumpers directly into the board, or route them to a DIP socket, into which you insert a DIP header that's appropriately wired for the desired memory.

A circuit for large memory boards (Fig. 4) provides

a memory capacity of 16 k × 8 or 64 k × 8, depending on which memory chip you use. Again, you can easily upgrade a 4-k × 1 memory using MK4027 by substituting MK4116s and changing a DIP header that has pre-wired jumpers.

This circuit generates the switch multiplexer (MUX) and column-address strobe ($\overline{CAS}$) differently from the circuit in Fig. 3. A two-tap TTL-compatible delay line controls the timing for MUX and $\overline{CAS}$ and is controlled, in turn, by $\overline{MREQ}$. This timing method references all memory timing from $\overline{MREQ}$—which simplifies the timing for a DMA system—while the circuit of Fig. 3 requires both $\overline{MREQ}$ and the Φ clock.

The control, address, and data lines for the circuit in Fig. 4 are buffered with Schmitt-trigger devices to provide high immunity to possible noise on the backplane.

You should terminate memory lines that have a heavy capacitive load (A_0 to A_5, $\overline{CS}$, $\overline{CAS}$, and $\overline{WRITE}$) with series resistors which help suppress undershoot. Neither the MK4027 nor the MK4116 can tolerate voltages more negative than −1 V.

When you use the MK4027, the two 74LS138 3-to-8 decoders together permit addressing to start on any 4-k boundary. With the MK4116, only one decoder is necessary to give 16-k-boundary addressing. If you use two DIP sockets as shown in Fig. 4a, you will find it easy to select the starting address for either chip.

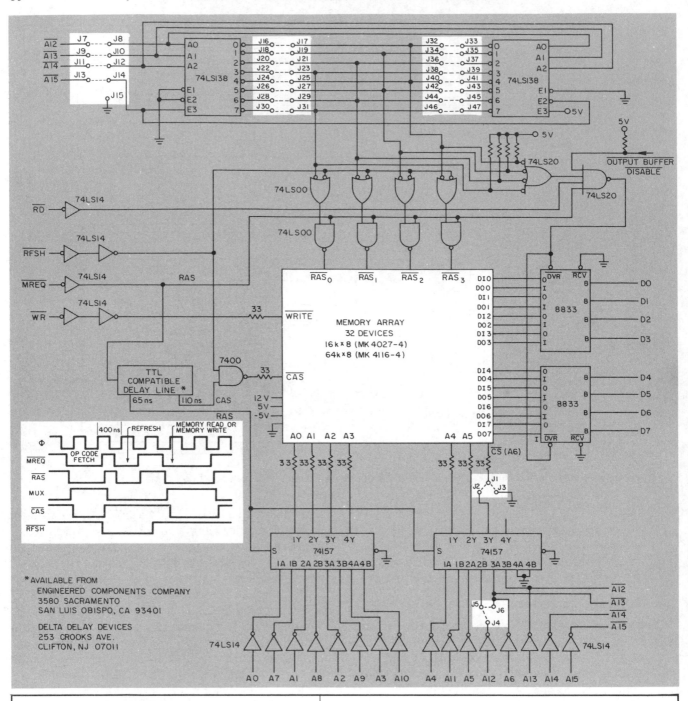

16-k × 8 CONFIGURATION (MK 4027)

CONNECT:
J1 to J3
J5 to J6
J7 to J8
J9 to J10
J11 to J12
J13 to J14

64-k × 8 CONFIGURATION (MK 4116)

CONNECT: J1 to J2   ADDRESS: 0-FFFF
J4 to J5   CONNECT: J32 to J33
J8 to J11   J34 to J35
J10 to J13   J36 to J37
J12 to J15   J38 to J39
J14 to J15

ADDRESS:	0-3FFF	ADDRESS:	4000-7FFF	ADDRESS:	8000-BFFF	ADDRESS:	C000-FFFF
CONNECT:	J24 to J25	CONNECT:	J16 to J17	CONNECT:	J40 to J41	CONNECT:	J32 to J33
	J26 to J27		J18 to J19		J42 to J43		J34 to J35
	J28 to J29		J20 to J21		J44 to J45		J36 to J37
	J30 to J31		J22 to J23		J46 to J47		J38 to J39

4. **A large dynamic RAM-board** can also be expanded with a special jumper-DIP (white).

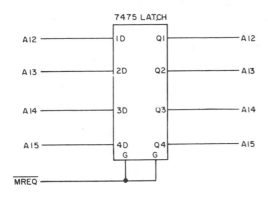

5. To suppress a glitch that could destroy rows of data, use this simple quad latch.

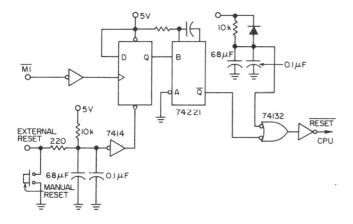

6. This auxiliary circuit limits the length of reset signals to prevent memory loss.

Don't jeopardize your memories

To support the memory circuits shown in Figs. 3 and 4, you need a 7475 quad latch (Fig. 5), because the Z80 cannot guarantee that the address bus will be valid at the end of an op code fetch cycle. This quirk doesn't affect the dynamic memory directly because the address is latched internally.

However, the $\overline{RAS}$ decoding circuit will be affected by a change on the address bus, which may cause a "glitch" on the $\overline{RAS}$ line that can destroy one row of data (64 or 128 locations) in the dynamic memory.

The following conditions may destroy dynamic memory content if they persist for more than 1 ms: manual reset, wait-state operations, and bus acknowledge. So you use a circuit that generates a short reset pulse, three clock cycles long (Fig. 5), to prevent the accidental destruction of memory content.

Remember, to refresh dynamic RAM properly, the Z80 must be able to execute op codes. A halt instruction meets this requirement, because it continually executes an op code fetch. (Incidentally, the execution of the halt cycle is the worst-case condition for the Z80 in terms of power dissipation.)

When you design a dynamic memory, proper power distribution and PC-board layout are very important. Power-supply voltage V_{DD} and ground should be laid out in a grid to help minimize the power-distribution impedance, while V_{BB} and V_{CC} needn't be gridded since they have lower supply currents. To help reduce system noise, a 0.1 μF, high-quality ceramic capacitor is recommended on both V_{CC} and V_{BB} for each device, and one 0.1 μF on V_{CC} for each row of eight RAMs.

Lines such as A_0 to A_5, $\overline{CS}$, $\overline{CAS}$, and $\overline{WRITE}$ are best bused together as rows. Then all the rows can be bused together at one end of the array. Avoid interconnecting these rows. Lines carrying $\overline{RAS}$ are bused together as a row and then connected to the appropriate $\overline{RAS}$ driver. The layout for a 32-device array can be put in a 5 × 5 in. space on a two-sided PC board.■■

References

1. *Z80 CPU Technical Manual,* Mostek Corp., 1215 W. Crosby Rd., Carrolton, TX 76005.
2. *Mostek Memory Products Catalogue,* Mostek Corp.

SECTION II

Dynamic RAMs: Designing with the Latest Devices

The new "breed" of dynamic RAMs, the 5-V-only devices, are just starting to emerge and capture the designer's eyes. RAMs with capacities of 16 and 64 kbits will be available from many companies starting in 1980 and will eventually replace the triple-supply 16-kbit RAMs designed into many computer system applications. Designing with these new devices requires a complex decision based on the economics of the particular system and the benefits resulting from the use of the improved devices.

The 64-kbit RAM, of course, will offer not only a quadrupling of the density on the board but also an improvement in system access time and a reduction in system complexity due to the elimination of the multiple power supplies. The last two benefits also are possible with the use of the single supply 16-kbit RAM. However, with the prices of the multiple-supply 16-kbit RAM holding at between five and ten dollars in large quantities, the more expensive single-supply 16-kbit units must clearly show a performance advantage to be used. And the prices for the 64-kbit RAMs also must drop at a very stiff rate to be economical—current sample prices of well over $100 per chip are expected to drop as the initial learning costs drop.

The articles in this section go over some of the design guidelines for using these advanced memory circuits. The differences in the various manufacturer's versions are noted and compared to show how they will perform in various system applications. This will be critical in the next few years, since there are at least three possible pin variations for the devices just being introduced. System designers will have to evaluate them all and select the best one for their system.

Single-Supply, 16-k Dynamic RAM

EDWARD METZLER
Product Manager, Intel Corp.,
Santa Clara, California

JAMES OLIPHANT
Marketing Manager, Intel Corp.,
Santa Clara, California

While 16-k dynamic RAMs are firmly established in memory system designs, RAM technology continues to be improved in response to user demands for a wider range of choices among devices. It's not simply a matter of making RAMs faster and easier to use. Users also want RAMs that are compatible with both current devices *and* the coming, denser units. The first dynamic RAM to satisfy all these requirements is the Intel 2118.

Organized as 16 kwords × 1 bit, the 16-pin 2118 is designed to operate in systems requiring 100-ns access. It is also the first 16-k × 1 RAM to operate with a single +5-V supply and to offer very low maximum levels of operating (190 mW) and standby power (16 mW).

Except for its supply, the Intel 2118 is functionally compatible with existing 16-k devices, such as the Intel 2117. Not only that, the 2118 will also be voltage and pinout-compatible with future 64-kbit RAMs. What that means is that high-performance, 5-V-only memory systems can be designed now and have their density increased simply by plugging in future 64-k dynamic RAMs.

The compatibility with both 16-k and 64-k RAMs can be seen in the pinout and package designs for the 2118 (see Fig. 1). Indeed, the only functional difference between the 2117 and the 2118 is that the 2118 requires just the one 5-V supply. For the devices in Fig. 1, 128 refresh cycles are required every 2 ms. With such compatibility, performance can be upgraded with minimal wiring changes on the control and memory cards.

One supply in demand

Most NMOS dynamic RAMs, including the current 16-k's, use −5-V substrate bias and +12 V of drain voltage. The smaller size of the MOS transistors lead to density, power, and performance improvements, but require a lower positive supply to avoid source-drain punch-through.

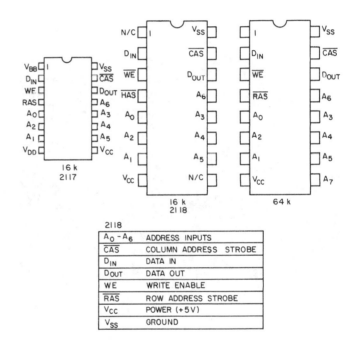

2118	
$A_0 - A_6$	ADDRESS INPUTS
CAS	COLUMN ADDRESS STROBE
D_{IN}	DATA IN
D_{OUT}	DATA OUT
WE	WRITE ENABLE
RAS	ROW ADDRESS STROBE
V_{CC}	POWER (+5 V)
V_{SS}	GROUND

1. **Pinout compatibility** allows 2118 RAMs to replace present-generation 2117 16-k dynamic RAMs and also lets forthcoming 64-k RAMs replace both without significant changes.

The 2118's positive supply has been lowered to +5 V, and the negative-voltage substrate bias is internally generated—its operation is both automatic and transparent. And without an externally supplied substrate bias, the 2118 can fit into newer high-performance microprocessor systems without additional power supplies. In mainframe memory systems also, the single supply simplifies the lay out of storage boards, while cutting power-supply costs.

The 2118's sub-100-ns access, is much faster than current 16-k RAMs (see Fig. 2). But the 2118 doesn't dissipate nearly as much power as current 16-k dynamic RAMs, most of which dissipate as much as 460 mW. The 2118 dissipates no more than 190 mW, and just 16 mW during standby, which reduces power-distribution costs and cooling requirements. More-

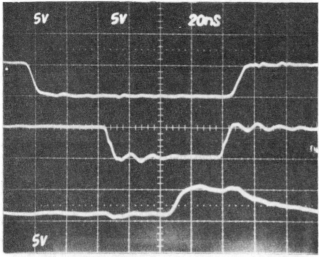

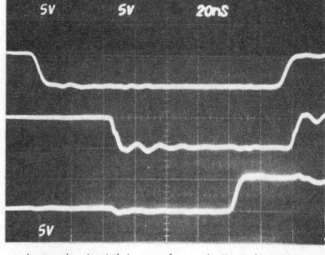

2. **Access time comparison** for 2118, left, and 2117 right, shows row address strobes, top, column-address strobes, center, and output data waveforms, bottom. Note that the 2118 has an access time less than 100 ns.

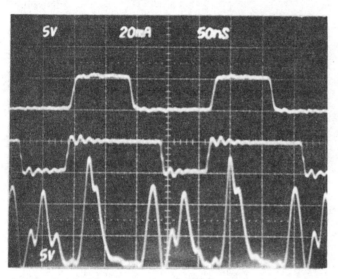

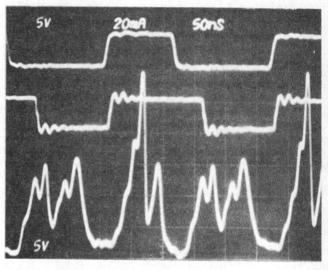

3. **Current waveform** comparisons (bottom) show I_{CC} for 2118, left, and I_{DD} for 2117, right. Top waveform is row address strobe and middle waveform is column address strobe. Note the 2118's lower transients.

over, the 2118 draws very small transient currents through its +5-V input (see Fig. 3).

Design with the 2118

To see how the 2118 fits into the design of a high performance memory system, take a 64-kword memory with 16 bits per word and 125-ns access time. Bear in mind, first of all, that the timing conditions for multiplexing the 2118 must be satisfied while using relatively slow TTL interface circuits.

In any high-speed multiplexed dynamic RAM memory, the timing problems primarily stem from the delays from a memory start signal to the appropriate device clocks. In a 64-kword memory system four time periods in all (Fig. 4) must be minimized:

■ t_1, the delay from memory start to the latest occurrence of control clock $\overline{RAS}$ at the 2118 input.

■ t_2, the address-hold time between the latest occurrence of $\overline{RAS}$ and the earliest occurrence of address changes in column addresses.

■ t_3, the time between row-address and column-address multiplexing (skew).

■ t_4, the time between the latest occurrence of row addresses multiplexed to column address and the earliest occurrence of control clock $\overline{CAS}$.

So to take full advantage of the 2118, you must configure the interfaces to minimize not only absolute delay through peripheral circuits but also skew through the logic circuits/drivers (for more on skew, see box). To accomplish this:

■ Select all logic gate types for minimum delay and skew for the function desired. (In some cases, this means that it may be more desirable to use a simpler TTL logic gate than a more complex TTL gate that has more skew.)

What is skew?

Skew is the difference between the minimum and maximum delays of two or more logic paths. In dynamic-RAM memory systems, skew is important when considering the timing between the control clock's logic path and the address path. Since in dynamic RAM systems, addresses must arrive at or before a specified time relative to the input clocks, the *minimum* clock timing must not exceed the *maximum* address path timing:

ADDRESS TIME

CLOCK TIME

The logic gates used in the address-timing path presumably have their maximum delays. The logic gates in the clock timing path presumably have their minimum delays. Since addresses must arrive at the memory device at or before the clocks, the clock may have to be delayed to allow for the addresses to become valid. This "artificial" delay directly reduces access time and must be minimized.

There are two ways to minimize skew:

1. Select devices whose minimum and maximum delays are as close together as possible.

2. Use gates in the same IC package for both paths. For example, if logic gates labeled A in the figure were in the same IC package, one can have a maximum delay, and the others will also be very close to maximum.

■ Minimize the output loading on these gates.

■ Minimize skew by placing parallel gates that lie in the critical timing path in the same IC package. For high-performance control logic that includes all these factors, see Fig. 5.

The control logic is designed to drive the memory board. Note that in this configuration, the control clocks RAS and CAS for a given side and row on the board are driven from the same IC package to minimize skew (see Fig. 5). Likewise, the seven addresses required for all eight 16-k RAM devices in a particular row of the card come from drivers in the same IC package (see Fig. 6).

For the address-multiplexing portion of the control logic, the latches, multiplexers and drivers have also been chosen for their minimum delay and skew characteristics.

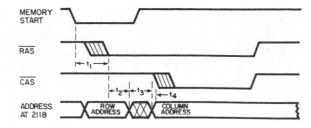

4. **Memory timing design** requires attention to four time periods which all must be minimized. Skew must also be minimized.

As you can see in Fig. 6, system addresses MA_0 to MA_{15} for the 64-kword card are brought onto the card and latched by 74S257 gates. The two 74S158s do address multiplexing between the low-order row addresses and the high-column addresses.

Refresh addresses (generated by counters) are OR-tied to the latch outputs of the low-order system addresses as shown. Using a two-input multiplexer instead of a four-input will minimize skew (save about 4 ns) when switching from row to column addresses.

Finally, the addresses are buffered by 74S240s driving the memory array. Capacitive loading is minimized on these addresses by having each driver drive a moderate amount of memory devices—in this case, just 16.

Control timing generation

To generate timing for the row and column address strobe clocks and for row and column address multiplexing, use precision delay lines as shown in Fig. 5. The taps on these delay lines are at 5 ±1-ns increments, so you can achieve maximum flexibility in timing by choosing taps. Timing stability is excellent, since the delays remain within ±1 ns of nominal, with respect to the delay line input.

During a read or write cycle, the appropriate RAS signal is activated on the selected row of devices on the storage card. This row is selected by the decoder (Fig. 6) from system addresses MA_7 and MA_{15}. Moreover, you'll be able to bring addresses MA_{16} and MA_{17} onto the card to allow for upgrading to higher-density (64-k) memory devices; a jumper is provided to help this upgrade.

Again, the RAS and CAS clock drivers for a given row of memory devices are contained in the same IC package, which saves about 10 ns of skew in these paths.

In this control logic, refresh is synchronized with a system clock. This type refresh eliminates delays associated with refresh arbitration (between a read/write cycle and a refresh cycle) that could be as high as 40 to 60 ns.

Timing calculations

With the control logic designed, we calculate worst case system delays. There are two ways to perform such calculations:

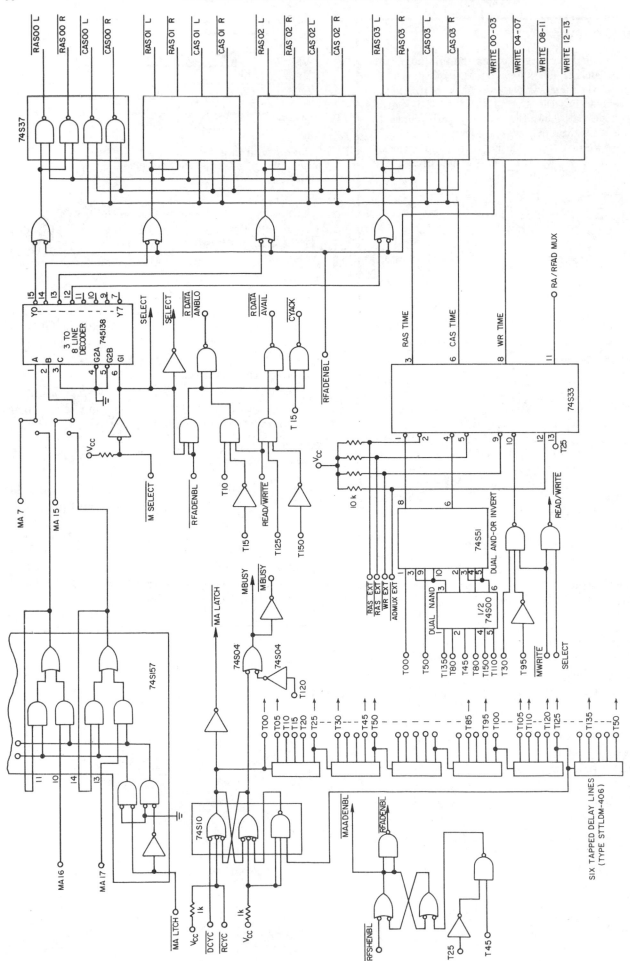

5. **Timing generator/clock driver** for memory board using 2118 16-k dynamic RAMs is built using standard TTL logic, but skew and delays are minimized. Six tapped delay lines help generate timing.

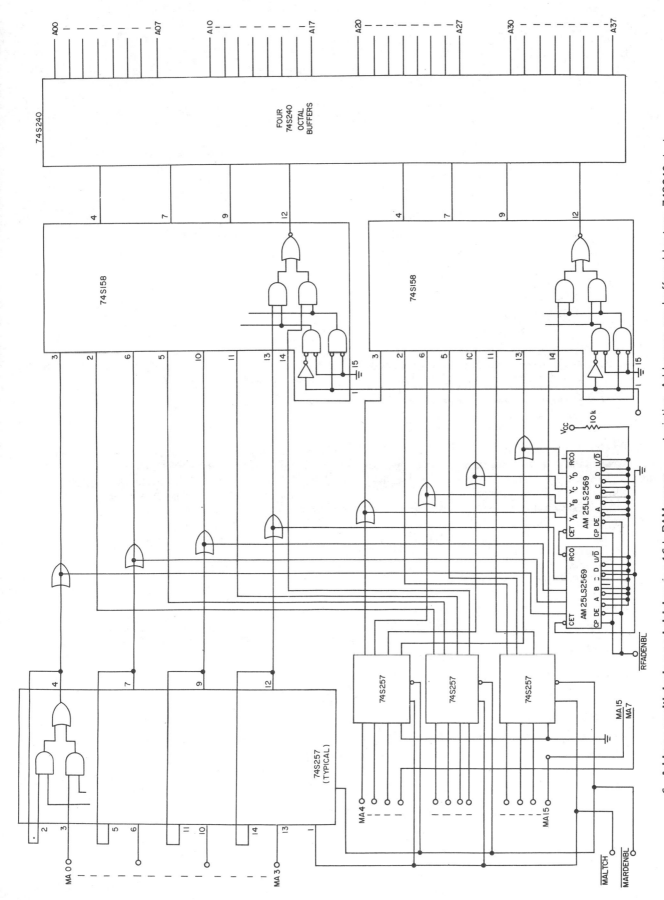

6. **Address multiplexing and driving** for 16-k RAMs uses TTL circuits chosen for minimum delay and skew characteristics. Addresses are buffered by type 74S240 devices and each driver serves 16 RAMs.

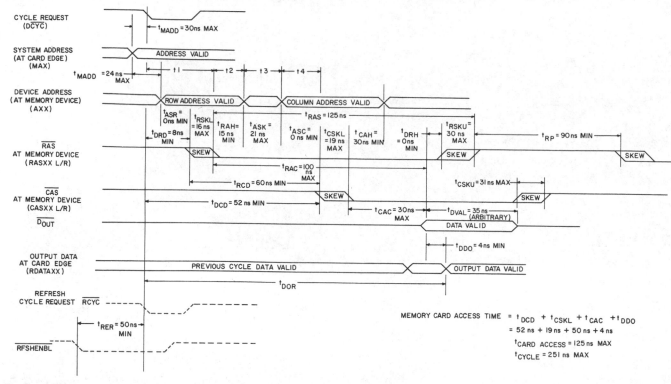

7. Complete memory-system timing chart shows how worst-case card access time of 125 ns can be achieved using 2118 16-k dynamic RAMs. Timing analysis is based on TTL data-book entries.

Guidelines for timing analysis

To make a timing analysis in a logic design for worst-case conditions, assume that the TTL devices have certain characteristics. To get the fast times shown in Fig. 8, use the following guidelines:

1. All propagation delays are taken from industry TTL data books:

    Max = Data book entry
    Typ = Data book entry
    Min = 1/2 of data book typical value, which is generally considered good practice.

2. Device-to-device skew (same package) = 0.5 ns max for Schottky TTL; 2 ns max for 74S240 buffer driver.

3. The STTLDM-406 is a special 25-ns delay line with active outputs (available from Engineered Components Co., San Luis Obispo, CA) whose propagation delay is 5 ns ±1 ns per tap. (Within a line, the tolerance is not cumulative; for example, the delay from the input to the third tap is 15 ns ±1 ns.)

4. Capacitive loads add 0.05 ns/pF to the propagation delays specified in the data books. Schottky-TTL input capacitance is 3 pF. Printed-circuit board traces are 2 pF/in.

5. PC-board etch adds no skew to array address/control timing signals. The etch adds 4 ns to over-all access time.

6. Timing components are immediately adjacent to each other. The etch delays in the delay-line timing chain are negligible.

---

1. A true worst-case analysis, using specified maximum and minimum delays for peripheral circuits plus all delays due to capacitive loading from driven device input capacitance and PC-board etched conductor patterns.

2. A statistical worst-case analysis, which assumes that all devices can't be in their worst-case condition at the same time. Since the statistical approach can be justified only in large systems with hundreds or even thousands of components, the timing calculations used here are based on true worst-case analysis.

The simplified timing diagram for the control logic shown in Fig. 7 is similar to that shown in Fig. 4, but presents the specific timing conditions of the control logic in greater detail.

The timing conditions shown in Fig. 7 assume a loading effect on the TTL drivers of 0.05 ns/pF. The maximum capacitive load specified in TTL data books for high-current MSI devices is 50 pF. The RAS/CAS drivers each drive 68 pF, which represents the effects of clock input capacitance of the 2118 and 2 pF/in. of printed circuit etch lines on the board.

Fig. 7 shows that using a 100-ns 2118, you can get a true worst-case card access of 125 ns, with the multiplexing and driving overhead minimized. In fact, you can cut the access times to 115 ns if you adjust the taps on the delay lines to "personalize" the card for a particular combination of peripheral devices. In very high-performance systems, that's the only way to get minimum access time. ■■

64-k Dynamic RAMs Are Here

DAVE BURSKY
Senior Editor, Semiconductors,
Electronic Design

The 64-kbit dynamic RAM will soon be available from almost a dozen manufacturers.

With these RAMs, designers will be able to quadruple memory system densities without losing any power dissipation or speed.

In fact, the new RAMs will actually operate at lower power levels than available 16-k RAMs. What's more, many of the devices won't be multiple-supply units that have been discussed at previous meetings of the International Solid-State Circuits Conference —they'll require just a single +5-V supply. Access times will be about the same as 16-k's, with typical times in the 100 to 200-ns range. But over-all system reliability should increase—for the same size configuration there will be one quarter the number of memory chips and interconnects.

Get your samples here

Samples of 64-k devices have been quietly available since mid-year from Fujitsu America (Sunnyvale, CA). While these parts have been evaluated by large users, they suffer from requiring two nonstandard supplies (+7 V and −2.5 V)—a condition that could inhibit their acceptance in the memory system design community. Specified the MB8164, the Fujitsu RAM comes in three versions—an N suffix with a 200-ns access and 330-ns cycle, an E version with a 150-ns access, and an H model with a 120-ns access and a 320-ns cycle.

The MB8164 uses a 128-cycle, 2-ms refresh and dissipates a fairly high 385 mW. It won't start cheap—single samples cost $285 (for the MB8164E), and 100-quantity prices are $178 each.

Fujitsu also has available partial memory versions, the MB8132, of the 64-k RAMs. With only half the array functional, it will be available as an

Storing 65,536 bits and offering a worst-case access time of 150 ns, the TMS4164 from Texas Instruments is the first U.S. manufactured 64-k dynamic RAM.

upper or lower-half version (H or L suffix) in all three speed versions. Prices for the E version of the partials are $110 and $72.50, respectively, for unit and 100-quantity lots.

Fujitsu, though, won't have the sample market to itself for long. In a major move, Texas Instruments has just announced its 64-kbit dynamic RAM—the TMS4164 (see ED No. 19, Sept. 13, 1978, p. 37). The first U.S.-based manufacturer to announce sample availability—this coming October—Texas Instruments will unveil many technological innovations in its memory.

Innovation yields low power

For starters, the TMS4164 will operate from a single 5-V supply, thus offering complete TTL compatibility and simple system design—something the +7/−2-V products don't offer. (Most of the dual-supply units have open-drain outputs and must be pulled up via external resistors to the proper levels.) Moreover, the TMS4164 won't dissipate much power—200 mW maximum, or about 60% that of currently available 16-k RAMs.

The low power dissipation stems from eliminating the bias generator

normally needed and giving the RAM a 256-cycle, 4-ms refresh, which eliminates half the 512 power-hungry amplifiers usually needed. And a 256-cycle refresh won't overburden existing system timing operations. Indeed, nothing happens to the timing generator—only an eighth bit is added to the refresh counter and the address multiplexer.

The TMS4164's access time will be just 150 ns, maximum, and cycle times will be as short as 250 ns. The key to this performance is a TI secret. But what's known is that the company has managed to eliminate the need for any substrate bias generator, yet maintain the address and data-line capability to handle undershoots of up to −1 V, and reduce the line-to-line spacing for the aluminum metalization from the typical 6 μm to just 4 μm. And some new sense amplifiers have been designed to handle lower signal levels.

Moreover, the internal structure of the RAM has been redesigned so that over 30 major internal clocking signals are generated by the RAS and CAS signals, and the clocks are set up so they provide a nonskewing timing sequence to help speed up operations.

Even a redesigned cell layout has decreased internal area, the storage capacitance of the cell has increased: cell area is now about 200 square μm, yet the capacitance has been upped to about 50 femtofarads—almost a 20% increase.

The chip itself has an area of just 33,000 square mils and contains about 140,000 devices. Masks for the chip are generated using electron-beam lithography, and the wafers are made using the masks and standard projection printing techniques. Line widths are a tight, but producible, 2.5 to 3 μm.

Meanwhile, many other 64-k RAMs are being developed from U.S. manufacturers such as Intel, Mostek, Motor-

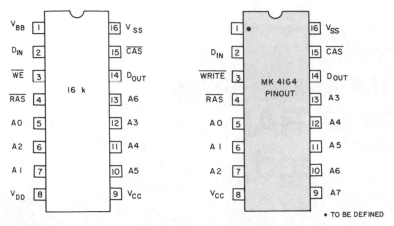

Upgrading a 16-k RAM system to a 64-k RAM system will be relatively simple as this comparison of the two JEDEC standard pinouts shows. Only the definition of pin 1 and the number of refresh cycles still have to be nailed down.

ola, and National Semiconductor, and Japanese manufacturers such as Hitachi, NEC, OKI and Toshiba. But none will be available until the first quarter of 1979 (see Table).

The RAMs are coming

But while there will eventually be many 64-k RAMs, there won't be many standardized ones. For instance, only TI and National Semiconductor are developing 256-cycle, 4-ms refresh RAMs. All other devices slated for introduction will be 128-cycle, 2-ms units.

The single power supply is also open to question. Not all manufacturers think they can make a single-supply 64-k RAM, and some are using pin 1 of the 16-pin package as a negative supply terminal. But that could mean either the −2-V supply used by Japanese manufacturers or the −5-V supply proposed by some U.S. vendors.

As a matter of fact, pin 1 isn't completely reserved by any means. Companies bringing out a single +5-V part are divided into two factions: Texas Instruments and several others want to keep the pin disconnected, while Mostek and other companies are considering a special function control for pin 1.

So, by this time next year, there could be three different versions of the 64-k RAM: a dual-supply model, a single-supply model with nothing on pin 1, and a single-supply version with a special function on pin 1.

Just what that special function will be is also open to speculation. It could be some sort of a test function or a system-control function. Possible applications include a refresh control, a chip select, a capacitor decoupling point for the substrate, a timing control point, a data-ready signal, and an output enable. Test functions might include an output-buffer disable, or some sort of array-enable capability.

What's more, don't forget that there will be units with a 128-cycle, 2-ms refresh rate and those with a 256-cycle, 4-ms refresh. With a 128-cycle refresh, 64-k devices can be completely compatible with currently used 16-k RAMs. No signal lines have to be transposed, and the refresh controller doesn't have to be modified.

Two choices for refresh

The 256-cycle models, on the other hand, can't really use existing 16-k RAM systems since they require an eighth address line and an eighth bit on the refresh counter and multiplexer. In most cases, however, that eighth bit is already in the system and can be used, since most multiplexers and

How the 64-k RAMs will perform

Manufacturer	Model	Access time	Refresh	Supplies	Active P_D	Pinout	Availability
Intel	N/A	150 to 200 ns	128 cy, 2 ms	+5 V	330 mW	Standard 16-pin	Samples 2q. '79
Mostek	MK4164	80 ns typ	128 cy, 2 ms	+5 V	300 mW	Standard 16-pin	Samples 1q '79
Motorola	MCM6664	150 to 200 ns	128 cy, 2 ms	+5 V	Under 400 mW	Standard 16-pin	N/A
National Semi-conductor	MM5295	Less than 150 ns	256 cy, 4 ms	+5 V	Under 250 mW	Standard 16-pin	Samples 2q. '79
Texas Instruments	TMS4164	100 to 150 ns	256 cy, 4 ms	+5 V	250 mW	Standard 16-pin	Samples 4q '78
Fujitsu	MB8164	120 to 200 ns	128 cy, 2 ms	+7 V/ −2 V	385 mW	Modified 16-pin	Delivering
Hitachi	HM4864	120 ns max	N/A	+5 V	350 mW	Standard 16-pin	Samples 1q '79
NEC	N/A	150 ns typ	128 cy, 2 ms	N/A	400 mW	Standard 16-pin	Samples 1q, '79
OKI	N/A	N/A	128 cy, 2 ms	+7 V/ −2 V	Under 400 mW	Modified 16-pin	Delivering in Japan
Toshiba	N/A	N/A	128 cy, 2 ms	+5 V	Under 400 mW	Standard 16-pin	Samples latter '79

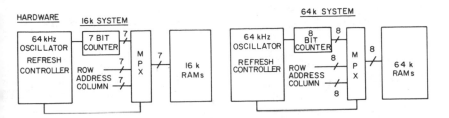

Changing over from a 16-k system to a 64-k requires no timing changes if 64-k RAMs with 256-cycle refresh are used. Just an eighth bit must be added to the multiplexer and the refresh counter circuits, and an extra address line.

counters come in 4-bit sections.

Systems designed to use the 256-cycle 64-k RAMs can easily be modified to use the 128-cycle 64-k RAMs, but not the reverse—the timing and multiplexing have to be altered.

The refresh overhead time always subtracts from the time a dynamic RAM can be used by the processor, but if it can be done fast enough or while the CPU does another job, the refresh can be made transparent to the CPU. If transparent refresh is not possible, then the system must stop the CPU for one cycle every 15.6 μs (4 ms divided by 256 cycles). Some systems may even use a burst mode and do all the refresh-

ing at the beginning of the refresh period, but that causes large system current surges.

The lower the overhead time of the RAM, the better the system performance. To compare the earlier 16-k RAMs with the 256-cycle, 64-k RAMs, Texas Instruments used the TMS4116 16-k and the TMS4164 as the models. For a 375-ns cycle time 16-k RAM, system overhead is estimated as 128 $\times$ 375/2, or 2.4%. Similarly, for a 64-k system the overhead comes to 256 $\times$ 250/4, or 1.6%—almost a 33% reduction. However, it's the array size not the refresh cycle speed, that causes the improvement—a 128-cycle, 2-ms, 64-k

RAM provides the same overhead advantage.

The two clocks on the TMS4164 RAS (row address select) and CAS (column address select) control the gating of the 8-bit addresses into the RAM. The row-address set-up time for the TMS4164 is 0 ns, and the hold time is 15 ns. Column address set-up time is −5 ns, and the RAS/CAS spacing is 15 to 50 ns. As a result, a system designer has 35 ns to change addresses and bring CAS low without extending the access time beyond 150 ns.

Savings abound for systems

But no matter which 64-k RAM is used, it will offer tremendous savings in board real-estate, and improve overall system performance since power consumption, access times and cycle times can also be reduced. And, depending on which manufacturer's claims you believe, chip costs will start to tumble fast, especially with the 256-cycle refresh designs.

Chip size affects the final cost of the memory considerably—the smaller the chip, the lower the device cost. But,

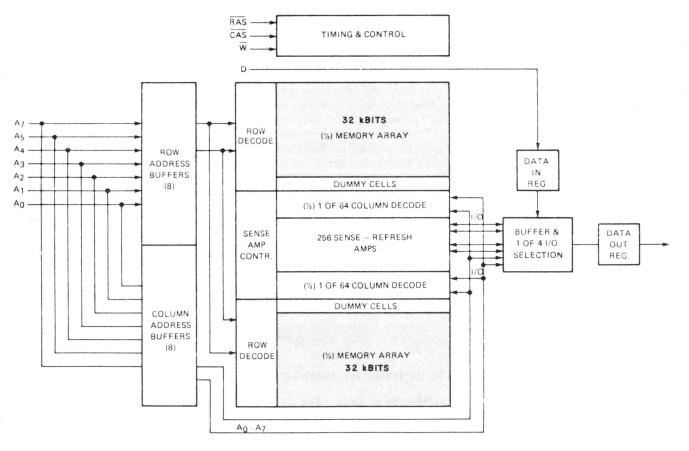

Inside the TMS4164 are two 32-kbit arrays of memory cells and only 256 sense amplifiers. Why? The RAM uses a 256-cycle, 4-ms refresh rate. This reduced number of amplifiers (other 64-k RAMs use 512) also means that the power dissipation will also be lower—just 200 mW for the complete chip.

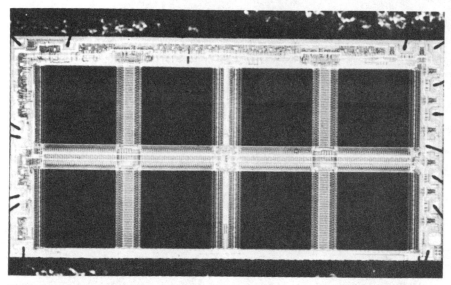

First of the Japanese 64-k dynamic RAMs to enter the U.S. market, the Fujitsu MB8164 offers three versions—a 200-ns, a 150 and a 120-ns access time model.

that stems from a host of behind-the-scene factors—yield, producibility, testability and more. And, the smaller the chip, the faster the memory since there's less parasitic capacitance to slow down signal transfer, and shorter signal paths.

The price trend of dynamic RAMs has already been established by the 4 and 16-k devices, each of which has cut the cost per bit by factors of two or three depending on the maturity of the production cycle. By 1981, when 64-k RAMs are expected to mature, costs will be in the 10 millicent/bit range—about one-third the cost of today's 16-k RAMs.

Testing the large RAMs, though, is one of the largest contributors to the device cost. Some tests can't even be run on a commercial basis since each device would take days. So, new methods of picking the best tests and evaluating the results will also have to be found to make the 64-k RAMs economical.

A stand-out in the crowd

Incidentally, not all the dynamic 64-k RAMs being developed will be organized as 64-k × 1 bits. For instance, NEC is developing not only a 64-k × 1 chip, but also two other configurations—a 16-k × 4 organization and an 8-k × 8 version. No other information is available yet as to the expected circuit performance. Other companies are also examining the feasibility of these organizations.

The one drawback that seems to be surfacing is the lack of alternate sourcing that will be needed for OEM ap-plications. However, all companies listed in the table are doing their own development work and have developed proprietary products that might, just might, be pin compatible in most cases. This is especially true for the non-U.S. based manufacturers.

One of the reasons that joint development of alternate source agreements has lagged is that the many processes going into the various RAMs are incompatible. For example, Texas Instruments uses a process called SMOS (scaled MOS) with a double-level polysilicon-gate structure. Mostek, on the other hand, uses its own version—Scaled Poly 5. Fujitsu uses a double-poly embedded-field-oxidation process.

What's more, the companies consider many of the details of their processes proprietary, so it isn't easy to exchange information. However, Fujitsu is currently negotiating with a U.S.-based manufacturer for an alternate-source pact on its MB8164 dynamic RAMs.

Before the 64-k, 5-V dynamic RAMs finally appear, some companies will preview with families of 5-V, 16-k dynamic memories. Indeed, Intel has just introduced the 2118, a 16-k × 1-bit dynamic memory that requires just a single 5-V power supply.

Static RAMs are catching up

Meanwhile, large static memories are being developed for small system applications. Texas Instruments offers the TMS4016, for example, a 2048 × 8 bit static RAM that operates from a 5-V supply and resides in a 24-pin DIP. Its maximum access/cycle time of 150 ns makes it suitable for many small systems. It is also pin-compatible with the currently available 16-k, 5-V only UV EPROMs made by several manufacturers. Mostek and EMM Semiconductor (Phoenix, AZ) also have similar parts—the 4118, and 8108, respectively, which are 1024 × 8-bit static RAMs.

Other companies are also planning mixes of static and dynamic technologies. Zilog (Cupertino, CA) is currently developing a 4-k × 8 pseudostatic memory circuit—actually a dynamic RAM with all the refresh circuitry included on the same chip. This way, the interface to the CPU will require just one line to control the refresh.

In other memory areas, such as CCDs and bubble memory technologies, much development work is taking place. Meanwhile, major developments have recently been unveiled in another big technology area: magnetic bubbles. In fact, a major step forward has been taken by Texas Instruments and Rockwell (Anaheim, CA), which have both announced 256-kbit memory chips. And in the CCD area, 64-kbit devices are finally starting in high-volume production, and larger devices are still on the drawing boards.■■

64-k RAM: In Line to Succeed 16-k

SAM YOUNG
Strategic Marketing/Applications Manager,
Mostek, Carrollton, Texas

Just as the 16-k × 1 dynamic RAM proved to be the most important component in the semiconductor memory industry for the 70s, the 64-k × 1 RAM is a sure bet to be the premier memory for the early 80s. As usual, there will be a proliferation of manufacturers and products, but it will use a standard package—the address-multiplexed 16-pin DIP that won out over the nonmultiplexed 22-pin design for the first 4-k device.

Developed in 1973, Mostek's maverick 16-pin package has been adopted by JEDEC as the standard for the 64-k RAMs (see illustration). Since pin 9 is free due to the 64-k's single-supply requirements, it is available to hold the additional address bit that brings density up to 64-k. This seems to settle the 64-k standard question, but there are still important secondary considerations:

- What is V_{DD} (+5, +7, +8, +12, etc.)?
- What is a proper refresh interval—128 or 256 cycles?
- What is on pin 1?

Form, fit and function

The 64-k performance table (see p. 35), based on a study by a leading industry analyst, illustrates the controversy surrounding the choice of power supply levels for the 64-k. Multiple-voltage parts, while easier for manufacturers to design, suffer the same drawbacks in 64-k devices that they did in 16-k parts: power turn-on must be sequenced to avoid coupling effects that could drive the substrate bias positive, which destroys the RAM; added power sources are required to supply the additional voltage requirements; and higher costs that result from these and other drawbacks.

Two approaches to refresh

The question of refresh cycle comes down to a choice between two approaches: 256 cycles every 4 ms or 128 cycles every 2 ms. In either case, the processor interference figure of merit is identical—64 cycles/ms.

Internal circuit-design tradeoffs govern which approach is best for specific devices. Basically, 128-cycle, 2-ms refresh requires twice the number of internal sense amplifiers, which increases die size. However, since each sense amp has half the loading, the available signal is dramatically increased. And, of course, storage for only a 2-ms interval is required in the refresh operations.

As far as the user is concerned, as long as a part meets specification, availability and cost objectives, either approach will do. The only significant difference is that one additional bit is required on the refresh counter for the 4-ms part. If taken into account during system design, this should not create compatibility problems.

Another area of controversy in 64-k design centers on pin 1. Texas Instruments has chosen to leave the pin open. Motorola put a refresh function on pin 1 that simplifies the refresh operation. Mostek intends to use pin 1 as refresh—full details of the design will be available later in the second quarter of 1979.

The on-chip refresh incorporates an internal counter for refresh addressing. As a result, an additional refresh address field does not have to be generated and multiplexed into the memory. In addition, the problem of row address simultaneously activating all $\overline{RAS}$ lines for refresh has been eliminated without logic being required in the critical access path.

During power-fail modes, all drivers to the RAM except $\overline{RAS}$ and $\overline{REF}$ may be turned off to conserve precious battery reserves. This is not possible with $\overline{RAS}$-only mode refresh. Since, on the Mostek part, pin 1 may be left open, this feature will not prevent downward compatibility with parts from those semiconductor vendors who have chosen to simplify the refresh operation for users.

User in the middle

The user, whose major concern is compatibility, sits in the middle of

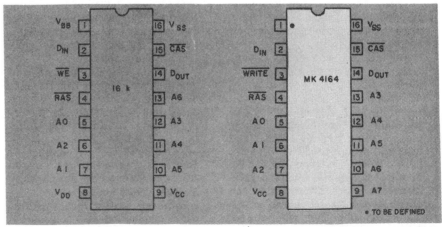

Standard 64-k RAM package, adopted by JEDEC and based on Mostek's package scheme, leaves the function of pin 1 to be defined later. Various suppliers have various uses: Some intend to leave it open, others to use it for refresh.

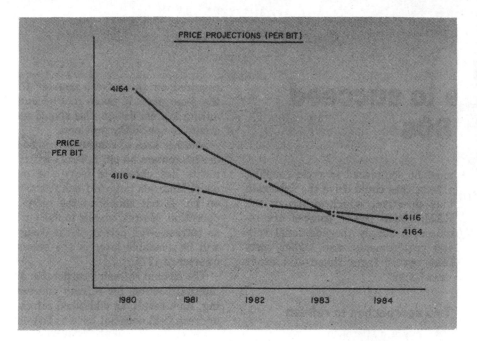

PRICE PROJECTIONS (PER BIT)

PRICE PER BIT

4164

4116

4116

4164

1980   1981   1982   1983   1984

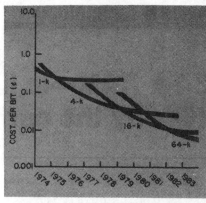

Learning-curve price reductions for RAMs show rapid decreases. Texas Instruments' projections (above) show 16-k and 64-k RAMs crossing in 1981. Mostek (left) predicts crossover during 1983, but also a second-generation 16-k that will prolong the 16-k.

Answers to the 64-k questions

The 64-k RAM is provoking a rhubarb among 64-k RAM designers by giving rise to several debatable questions, including: How many refresh cycles to use? What to do with pin 1? Can you live without substrate bias? And how many supply voltages will be needed to run the RAM?

Responding to the question of how many power-supply levels will drive the RAM, Sam Young sees the market place driving the design. "It's a 5-V TTL world," Young notes, "and the user is not going to use a part requiring multiple supplies if he can get one that uses a TTL-compatible 5-V only supply."

But will the user wait for it if he can get a 64-k part now, albeit one requiring multiple power supplies?

Young's answer: "The user can't get the 64-k device at the right price he wants in quantities he needs now."

For the user who simply cannot wait for the single-supply 64-k, Mostek will offer a soon-to-be-announced 5-V-only, 32-k device, to be called the 4532. Mostek already has the 4332, a three-supply 32-kbit module using two MK4116s. "The user can design products with the hybrid 32-k device (two 16-k RAMs in one package) and get the performance he needs with most of the packing density he wants now," Young explains. Then, when the 64-k parts come into sufficient volume

production or cross the 16-k/64-k price crossover point the 64-k can replace the smaller capacity parts with no redesign.

"With the 32-k RAM package, you do not need to conquer the learning curve—this has already been conquered with the 16-k devices," Young adds. "Hybrid packages are not a dead-end technology. We can continue to have dual or even better density with this enhanced-packaging approach."

Closely related to the question of multiple supplies is the issue of whether or not to bias the substrate on the chip. The multiple-supply designers "cop-out" and generate it off-chip while the 5-V-only purists argue over whether to ground the substrate or generate the bias on-chip.

According to Young, generating the bias off-chip creates problems for the OEM in his system design, while having no bias creates a potential yield problem.

"If you generate bias off-chip you get noise induced in the bias depending on the layout of the board that will contain the memory, hence a significant consideration for the board designer. Moreover, it increases the number of power-supply corners to be tested from two to four, thus dramatically increasing test time."

Generating the bias on-chip, while eliminating the noise problem completely and reducing test

time, does produce its own chip-design problems. Young feels, however, that if the designer comprehends what the chip is going to do under various switching conditions, he can design these problems out. The part then can be tested exactly as if it were in the final system, as far as substrate effects are concerned.

"Another gain from on-chip bias," Young adds, "is that we can set the bias where we want it to optimize the RAM's performance. In some of our other memories, for example, we use a feedback path to vary the substrate voltage to adjust the threshold exactly where we want it."

Beyond the substrate bias and power supply questions, there is the ongoing discussion of how many refresh cycles to use—128-cycles every 2 ms or 256 every 4 ms—and how to handle pin 1.

From the manufacturer's point of view, the 128-cycle approach is better since the part only has to retain data for 2 ms rather than 4 ms—this improves yields.

In addition, while a 128-cycle refresh requires 512 sense amps compared with the 256 required by the 256-cycle refresh and thus more silicon area, it also provides much more signal because each amplifier drives half the cells as the 256-cycle design.

From the user's point of view, the refresh-counter logic used for these controversies. And there's more—besides power supply and refresh cycle incompatibility, the devices also vary in their performance in power consumption and access times.

The competition among suppliers goes beyond the initial design battle. The race is on to see who builds volume and gets down the cost-learning curve the fastest. By-1 organized dynamic RAM products follow a familiar cost-learning curve: the larger the volume, the lower the average selling price—a commonly used model predicts that each time the industry's cumulative volume doubles, selling price decreases by 10 to 25%, depending on product type.

Initially, each successive generation costs more on a per-bit basis than its

64–k RAM performance

Company	Model	Chip area (mils²)	Access time (ns)	Number of pins	Power supply voltages
Fujitsu	MB8164	48,000	120 to 200	16	7, −2
Hitachi	HM4864	48,000	120 max	18	8.5, −3
Intel		43,000	150 to 200	16	5 only
IBM		65,000		40	8.5, −2
ITT		54,000		16	7, −2
Mostek	MK4164	40,000	90 to 150	16	5 only
Motorola	MCM6664	39,000	150 to 200	16	5 only
National	MM5295		less than 150	16	5 only
NEC		52,000	150 typ	16	5 only
Siemens		35,000		16	8, −2
TI	TMS4164	33,000	100 to 150	16	5 only
Toshiba		40,000		16	8, −2

predecessor. But eventually "crossover" occurs, as cost per bit drops. As it turns out, the system crossover point occurs significantly before the device crossover point. This is due to the higher-density device's reduced parts count, which, in turn, reduces board area and power-supply requirements.

Down the learning curve

The early learning-curve model for the 16-k showed system crossover at four times the 4-k × 1 RAM price plus three dollars in large quantity prices. The 16-k, first introduced in 1975, did not cross over on a per-bit basis until late '78, or three years after its introduction. Among several predictions for 16-k/64-k price crossovers is one from Texas Instruments (see curves on p. 34), which aggressively shows the crossover occurring sometime in the first half of 1981.

A more conservative prediction by Mostek, based on historical facts with device production difficulty factors comprehended, predicts the 16-k/64-k crossover in 1983. Inherent in the Mostek curves is a second generation 16-k extending the 16-k's product life cycle. The second-generation device will also use a 5-V-only power supply.

The question of availability

One question remains: When will multiple suppliers of 64-k devices with compatible parts be in volume production? Fujitsu, Motorola and Texas Instruments have already announced samples. TI and Fujitsu have been "sampling" since the summer of 1978, not quite volume production, but a start.

The history of 16-k dynamic RAM availability offers valuable insight

into the possible 64-k availability. The 16-k was first introduced in the fourth quarter of 1975 by Intel, with TI running a close second. Mostek's came out in the first half of 1976. Quantities of 16-k RAMs shipped by the semiconductor industry grew tremendously each year since 1975.

- 1975—less than 1000 devices.
- 1976—less than 100,000 devices.
- 1977—About 1.8 million devices.
- 1978—About 20 million devices.
- 1979—More than 60 million devices are forecast.

In retrospect, supply was not even close to adequate until 1978 and even then huge shortages existed. It is also useful to note that the first two devices that were introduced are now extinct, and TI's device never became a production part.

The 16-k device required a relatively minor process change—from a Poly I to a Poly II process. Device sizes, geometries and design techniques remained relatively constant. The 64-k, on the other hand, requires a circuit design technology change to achieve exclusive 5-V operation, and a major process change in going to scaled geometries.

Two new buzz words

Two of these process buzz words are H-MOS and Scaled Poly 5. In addition, National Semiconductor has announced a Triple Poly process, which adds one additional dimension to the task. The scaled geometries also require new advanced state-of-the-art equipment in order to be manufactured.

The 64-k is a certainty, and it will become the RAM of the 80's. When it will be available in volume quantities at a cost-effective price is the $64-k question. ■■

64-k RAM with Single Supply

SAM YOUNG
Strategic Marketing/Applications Manager,
Mostek, Carrollton, Texas

The 64-k dynamic RAM represents the start of a new cycle in product design. Getting a jump in that cycle means getting acquainted with all aspects of the new memory as well as gauging how it may affect future designs. This boils down to examining not only the key element in a 64-k dynamic design—the chip—but also the main beneficiary of such a design—the system.

The chip

The experience gained from designing with 16-k dynamic RAMs like the MK4116 has set the ground rules for developing a 64-k:

■ The chip must be well below 50,000 square mils to produce a reasonable yield (cost-effective on a per-bit basis when compared to 16-k RAMs).

■ The die must be reliable (all 65,536 bits must be functional and "hard" failures should be minimal).

■ The RAM should operate from a single 5-V supply (and not draw more power than the earlier 16-k units).

■ The RAM should not be any harder to use than the 16-k devices, and preferably easier (for a comparison of pinouts and major specifications of the 16 and 64 k's, see the table).

The squeeze is on

But to get the necessary density—65,536 bits—on a less than 50,000-square-mil chip, the dynamic RAM cell must be physically reduced to about half the size of the 16-k dynamic cell. And with a smaller cell size, capacitance—which is directly proportional to capacitor size—must be smaller. Furthermore, since only a 5-V supply will be available, the stored voltage in the cell will also have to come down (the 16-k RAMs use a 12-V supply to store the charge). Thus, only a small amount of charge can be stored in the cell for a ONE while the lack of charge represents a ZERO.

However, the small difference in charge between a ONE and a ZERO means that a relatively small signal will be imposed on the bit line when the cell is read. To make the signal more detectable, several things can be done in the RAM design:

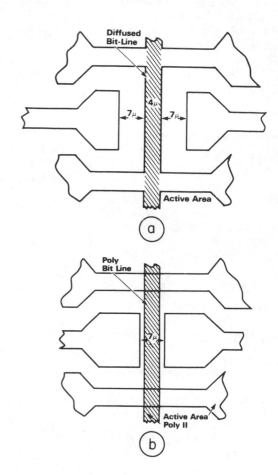

1. Built with a diffused-bit line, the 4116 memory cell (a) does not maximize capacitance for available area. By using a polysilicon-bit line instead, the 4164 crams the most capacitance possible into the die area (b).

■ Maximize the capacitance of the cell, keeping in mind the area limitations.

■ Maximize the voltage stored on the cell, keeping in mind that the supply is now limited to 5 V.

■ Minimize the capacitance on the bit line. The cell can be maximized by using a polysilicon-bit line instead of the diffused or ion-implanted line used in the 4116 (Fig. 1). This eliminates the wasted space between the active plate of the capacitor and the bit line, and thus increases the capacitor's area so that it extends up to the edge of the bit line. With no space left between the capacitor and the bit line, the capaci-

Compare 4116 and 4164 specs and pinout

Pinout comparison					Features	MK4116	MK4164
MK4116	MK4164	Pins	MK4164	MK4116	Organization	16 k × 1	64 k × 1
V_{BB}	$\overline{RFSH}$	1	16	*	V_{SS}	Access time (ns)	150/250	90/200
DI	*	2	15	*	$\overline{CAS}$	Cycle time (ns)	320/410	180/400
$\overline{WE}$	*	3	14	*	DO	Refresh period	2 ms	2 ms
$\overline{RAS}$	*	4	13	*	A_6	Number of ref. cycles	128	128
A_0	*	5	12	*	A_3	Power, max (mW)	462	300
A_2	*	6	11	*	A_4	Power/bit, max (μW)	1.22	0.31
A_1	*	7	10	*	A_5	Page mode operation	Yes	Yes
V_{DD}	V_{CC}	8	9	A_7	V_{CC}	Input levels (V_{IH}/V_{IL})	2.4/0.8	2.4/0.8
						Input levels (max)	6/−1 V	6/−1 V
						Output hold time	10 μs	Infinite

*same as 4116

tor can be about 50% larger in area than a capacitor using the same layout rules but a diffused bit line.

Maximizing the stored charge requires several design techniques. In contrast to the 4116, which has the 12-V supply voltage minus the threshold drop of a gate access transistor written into the cell, the 5-V 4164 cell is designed to eliminate the threshold loss and receive the full 5 V. But to write the full supply voltage in, first the gate of the cell-access transistor must be driven to a voltage more positive than the supply voltage by an amount equal to the threshold voltage of the transistor (this activity is sometimes referred to as bootstrapping the word line). Then the bit line, if high after sensing, must be driven all the way to the supply voltage. To do this, an active pullup circuit, built into each bit line, selectively pulls its bit line up to the supply voltage if the sense amplifier has left it in the ONE state, without affecting any bit lines brought to ground.

Unlike a load resistor, an active pullup wastes no power trying to bring a low bit line high. With the bit line restored to the full supply level or ground level at the end of the active pullup cycle, and with the word line driven to a voltage above the supply, the cell can be charged to the full supply voltage or set to ground —which eliminates the threshold loss of previous-generation RAMs.

Before the cell contents can be sensed, however, the word line must be driven high to a voltage at least one threshold above the starting voltage of the bit lines. When this is done in the 4164, the full charge stored in the cell is transferred from the cell to the bit line. This increase in differential charge between a stored high and a stored low results in a stronger signal on the bit line before sensing.

Capacitor connections change, too

Another design approach separating the 16-k RAM from the 64-k is to tie the top plate of the cell capacitor to ground—this minimizes the loss of signal going into

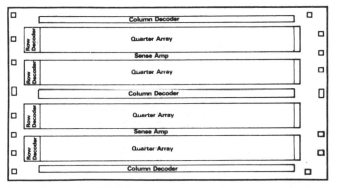

2. **Dividing the 64-kbit memory array into four subarrays** maximizes the signal available to the sense amplifiers.

the sense amplifier. In the 4116, the top plate is connected to V_{DD} (to simplify manufacturing). If, when a ZERO is written into the cell, V_{DD} happens to be at a relatively low value—say 10.8 V—and then increases, say, to 13.2 V before the low value is sensed, the sense amplifier signal margin drops. Since the top plate has a △ of 2.4 V, the capacitor storage node is also moved positively by the same △. Now the sense amplifier must sense a ZERO even though the ZERO level stored on the cell is 2.4 V instead of 0 V, which should be there for a stored low.

Once the cell capacitance and cell's differential voltage are maximized, the next step in the design cycle is to maximize the voltage developed on the bit line. The solution is to minimize the bit-line capacitance. And the way to do that is to keep the line as short as possible.

In the 4164, this is done by dividing the memory array into four blocks (the 4116 has only two memory blocks). As a result, individual bit-line segments can be less than one-quarter the vertical dimension of the chip rather than just under half the vertical dimension, as in the 4116. What's more, the bit lines are set up not to run through the column decoder, as they do on the 4116. In the 4164, the column decoders are located on the outer sides of the memory blocks, further reducing the length of the bit lines (Fig. 2).

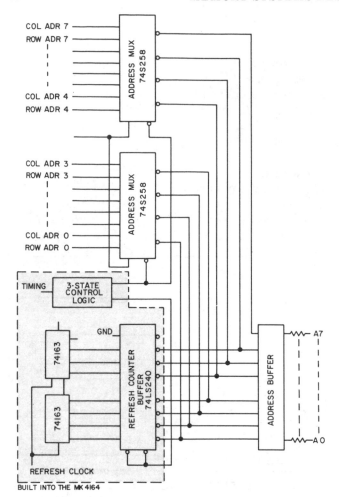

3. Multiplexing address and refresh signals usually requires several multiplexers, two counters and a control unit. With 4164s, however, the circuitry in the dotted area can be eliminated, since those functions come built-in.

When the signal reaches the bit line, the sense amplifiers take over and amplify the signal. In the various 64-k RAMs announced by several vendors, there will be either 256 or 512 sense amplifiers. To keep its bit line short, the 4164 uses 512, a design that puts 64 cells on either side of the sense amplifier instead of the 128 cells that would have been required with 256 amplifiers.

In the 4164, the sense amplifiers perform as close to the ideal as possible (zero offset). The number of components whose exact matching critically determines offset voltage has been minimized. Furthermore, all pairs of components—especially the critical pair—are matched as closely as possible since any offset voltage subtracts directly from signal margin. The sense amplifiers in the 4164 will be no less sensitive than the sense amplifiers introduced by the 4027 4-k RAM and used in virtually all 16-ks.

However, no matter how good it is, the sense amplifier will not suffice if the charge in the cell gets wiped out by an invasion of alpha particles. These invaders have only recently been exposed as the cause of soft errors in the 16-k RAM, and for the next few

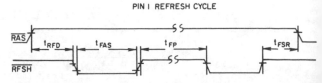

PIN I REFRESH CYCLE

NOTE: DATA OUT WILL REMAIN VALID THROUGH A PIN I REFRESH CYCLE AS LONG AS $\overline{CAS}$ IS HELD ACTIVE (LOW)

4. **The simple pin-1 refresh control of the 4164** require that the $\overline{RAS}$ control line be kept high while the $\overline{RFSH}$ line goes through its cycle.

years they will have to be tolerated in the 64-k RAM

For a large memory system, this means having som form of error-detection-and-correction logic. Soft er rors per RAM could be as bad as one error per 100(hours or as good as one error per 10^6 hours. In system containing about 1000 RAMs (8 Mbytes, for instance) error rates could range from about one per hour t(about one per 1000 hours.

Keep the data refreshed

To maintain charge in the storage cells, then, the 4164 requires 128 refresh cycles within a 2-ms period. The alternate approach of 256 amplifiers, each servicing 256 cells, requires 256 refresh cycles.

Although the 128-cycle, 2-ms and 256-cycle, 4-ms approach produce the same total overhead time, the former refresh eliminates the burden of supporting a 4-ms interval. In any present dynamic RAM system, external logic provides refresh functions (Fig. 3) that can be grouped into three functional areas:

1. A way to cycle through the 128 row addresses required to refresh the cells.

2. Logic to permit the row-address strobe (RAS) command to go simultaneously to all RAMs during a refresh cycle, and not just to the selected bank of chips as during a normal cycle.

3. An interval timer to determine when a refresh cycle is needed, and circuitry to generate the refresh signals when needed.

Since the 4164 has just one power supply instead of three, pin 1 is initially uncommitted, and thus available for a special function like refresh control. Such an assignment does require some circuitry, built onto the RAM chip.

This approach has been taken on the 4164, and as a result, uncommitted pin 1 has a refresh function —an approach echoed by Motorola.

Put refresh logic on the chip

Circuits built into the 4164 execute the first two refresh functions previously listed. A counter on the chip can cycle through the various row addresses, so that when a separate refresh command is given to the chip, it will refresh the row addressed by the internal counter. This eliminates the need for an external counter and the logic that applies the address to the

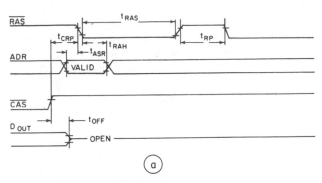

RAS – ONLY REFRESH (WITH CAS HIGH)

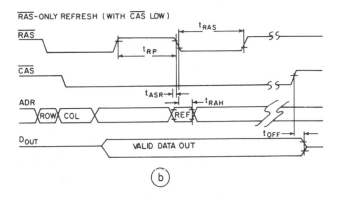

RAS-ONLY REFRESH (WITH CAS LOW)

5. **In the RAS-only refresh of the 4116** (a), the data output is not valid during the entire refresh period. In the 4164, a modified RAS-only refresh keeps the valid output data (b) available much longer.

RAM during the refresh time. And, since this function is enabled when pin 1 is pulled low (independently of the RAS command), the external RAS logic isn't needed either.

When initiated, the refresh cycle ignores the external address inputs as well as the states of the column-address-strobe (CAS) and write-enable (WE) signals. The RAS line, however, must be left high for the internal refresh function (Fig. 4). So, a system can be set up simply by tying all the pin 1's to a common node and pulling that node low each time a refresh operation is desired. Normal RAM accesses make use of the RAS, CAS and WE control lines.

However, the 4164 RAM chip does not include a refresh timer, for two reasons. Not only would it be a difficult function to test, but it would be difficult to build so that it has a low power requirement and a very stable frequency (independent of power supply, temperature, and process variations). If a timer with wide frequency variations had been integrated into the chip, its slowest frequency would have had to be high enough to meet the minimal refresh requirements. But with poor frequency control, the fastest frequency would have performed refresh more often than necessary, which would have increased standby-power dissipation significantly.

At any rate, the 4164 does provide two refresh modes, the self-refresh controlled by pin 1, and the "standard" system refresh mode of the 4116 16-k RAM.

Pin 1 may be left unconnected without impairing device performance when using the standard RAS-only refresh.

The 4116 refresh operation begins with a valid refresh address on the address lines before RAS goes low. If the CAS line returns high (inactive) within the t_{CRP}-ns specification, the output will go open circuit. If CAS remains low, the data read from the previous cycle remain on the data output. However, if CAS had gone high within the t_{CRP} spec and come back low following a RAS signal, the data on the output will change to the data at the address locked-in by CAS and RAS. By definition, this is a simple read cycle and thus it is merely a subset of a refresh cycle.

The hidden refresh of the 4164 is an enhancement of the 4116 refresh, and is designed so that the output circuitry will be hidden to refresh operations—either RAS or pin 1 modes. In Fig. 5b, a read cycle followed by a RAS-initiated refresh shows the differences if you compare the data-out waveform to the 4116's data-out sequence in Fig. 5a. The 4164 data from the read cycle stay valid through the refresh cycle, while for the 4116 the data output must remain open or change to the data in the cell being refreshed. Thus, the 4164 requires simpler external circuitry in the data-output path, and in many cases eliminates the need for off-chip latches.

Data can now remain valid while a refresh operation takes place. Output data, caused to appear by a negative edge of the CAS input, remain valid as long as CAS remains low. And CAS can be kept low indefinitely, as long as the normal refresh requirements of the RAM are met.

The 4164 handles all types of page-mode cycles including read, write, or read-modify-write cycles. In fact, the number of page cycles handled is limited only by the RAM-refresh requirements, which is a significant enhancement over the capability of the 16-k

The system

Designing systems built with 64-k RAMs can be much simpler than designing with 16-k's, particularly when the 64-k offers the advantages of the MK4164: density, greater performance, improved timing, enhanced page mode, pin-1 refresh capability and 5-V-only operation.

In addition, all RAS lines don't have to be simultaneously active during refresh as in 16-k systems, where multiple rows of chips must be activated and one-of-n decoders are commonly used to select which of the n banks of chips will be accessed. The problem is, these decoders cannot select all outputs simultaneously for a refresh operation.

During 16-k RAS-only refresh, the RAS line must be active to more than one row simultaneously in order to reduce refresh-interference time. One common technique that brings RAS to all RAMs simultaneously is shown in Fig. 6a. The signal that indicates a refresh

Testing 'counts'

One problem associated with building any function into a memory chip is testing that function. The refresh counter is a case in point. Simply writing data into the memory, waiting for 2 to 10 ms and then testing the memory and finding the contents unchanged in no way guarantees that the counter is performing properly. Many memory cells can actually retain data for 100 ms, so a missing refresh cycle will not be detected during a short-running test.

The 4164, however, provides a 100% functional counter test in an indirect but foolproof way. After writing background into the RAM (say all ZEROS) during normal write cycles to establish a reference, special provisions in the 4164 take over. They permit a write during a modified pin-1 refresh cycle while inhibiting the write operation during a normal refresh cycle. This is done by bringing $\overline{RAS}$ low after pin 1 is pulled low.

When $\overline{RAS}$ is low, the column circuitry and the write circuitry are enabled to allow a write function to be executed. After both pin 1 and $\overline{RAS}$ have been pulled low, both the $\overline{CAS}$ and $\overline{WE}$ lines are pulled low. As a result, the data present on the data-in line (a ONE) is written into the cell whose row and column addresses have been defined by the internal address counter.

Following this cycle, 127 identical cycles write a single bit into each of the other 127 rows. If the internal counter functions properly, when the data are read out, 128 bits—ONEs in a background of ZEROS—should be there, one for each output state of the counter. If the counter has malfunctioned, one or more bits will be missing, which indicates a skipped state.

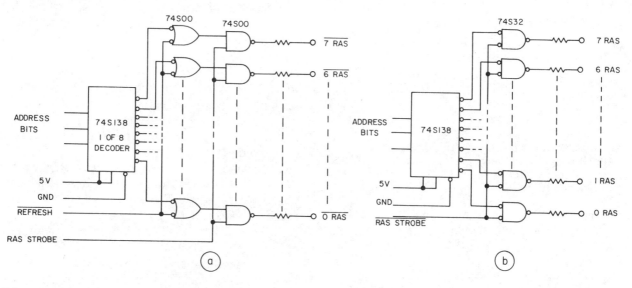

6. In most memory systems using 16-k RAMs, the $\overline{RAS}$ signals not selected by a decoder are gated-on when a refresh is required (a). If 4164s are used with $\overline{RAS}$-only refresh, one level of gating can be eliminated (b).

Uncovering the alpha particle

An alpha particle isn't much—just a helium atom nucleus emitted as radiation from such radioactive materials as thorium and uranium. But when trace amounts of these elements appear in semiconductor packages, their alpha particles get close to the memory chip itself—should they hit the RAM at a certain angle with enough energy, they could make the data in the RAM cell change.

Fortunately, the RAM suffers no permanent damage—just a soft error—and the next time the cell gets written it will behave normally. However, an alpha-particle hit does generate many electron-hole pairs on the chip. While, in a p-type substrate, the holes are majority carriers and cause no problem, the electrons are minority carriers and diffuse until they either recombine with the holes or are collected by an n-type diffusion or implant in the chip. That is a problem.

The storage cells of the RAM are such n-type regions, so they can collect the stray electrons. The collected electrons discharge the cell by some fixed amount of charge depending upon the number of electron-hole pairs generated by the alpha-particle hit. Thus, the amount of charge stored in a cell is extremely critical.

For example, if a cell is charged to 5 V to represent a high, or to 0 V to represent a low, the sense amplifier will typically use 2.5 V as the threshold to distinguish between a ONE or ZERO. If an alpha-particle hit causes the high cell to lose more than 2.5 V worth of charge, the sense amplifier will erroneously read the cell as a ZERO instead of a ONE.

Besides the cell, bit lines can be affected by the alpha-particle hits. Charge could be removed from the bit line, or from the complementary bit line on the other side of the sense amplifier. As a result, the sense amplifier may sense improperly, causing a soft error.

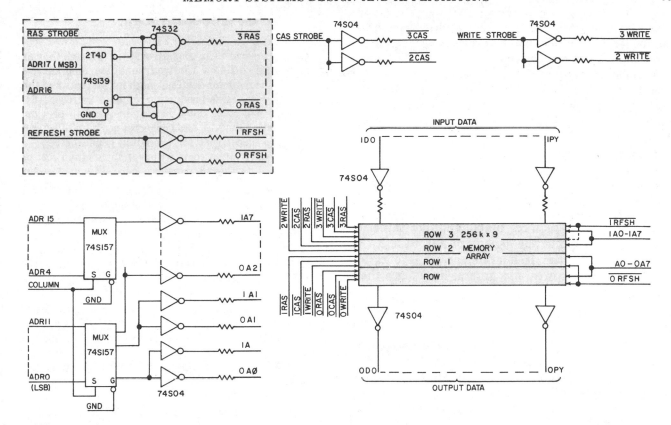

7. All the circuitry for a typical 256-k × 9 array using the 4164 dynamic RAMs is shown here minus the timing generator for refresh timeouts. By taking advantage of the pin-1 refresh, the circuitry required can be minimized.

request is ORed into the decoder path to override the deselected signal on the n−1 output lines of the decoder. However, with the gating lying in the critical path that determines the RAM access time, system performance could be hampered.

Such is not the case with the 4164, whose external logic for the pin-1 option is shown in Fig. 6b. This circuitry, simple to begin with, can be further simplified in a small system by eliminating the buffers and placing the decoder near the RAMs. A typical 256-k × 9-bit array with the drive logic for the 4164 RAMs requires that only the logic within the dotted lines remain active in battery-backup applications (Fig. 7). All address drivers, data in/out drivers, and timing control other than $\overline{RAS}$ can be shut off during battery-standby operation. The power dissipation will be considerably lower than if a $\overline{RAS}$-only refresh is used for standby.

The use of pin-1 function also eliminates performance delays that would be introduced if address generation or synchronization is required during refresh cycles. In systems whose refresh and CPU-cycle requests are asynchronous, the memory controller requires a settling time, which it uses to determine the type of cycle to execute when a refresh and a CPU cycle are requested simultaneously. If the controller finds that a refresh cycle will be executed, additional settling time will be needed to stabilize the refresh address. With the 4164, however, no time will be wasted, since the refresh address is generated on-chip.

Conventional refresh is a rather drawn-out affair. First, the refresh logic flags the memory controller to indicate that the next cycle to be executed will be a refresh. The refresh-request signal then gets generated by a counter set to a frequency determined by the system's cycle steal, the system's cycle time, and the number of refresh cycles required by the memory devices during a specified time.

Steal the cycles to do the refresh

When the refresh-request signal is generated, the memory controller switches to the refresh mode, and a refresh cycle begins after the current memory cycle ends. First, the memory controller must bypass the $\overline{RAS}$ decoder so that all memory chips simultaneously receive the $\overline{RAS}$ signal. Next, the controller must disable the $\overline{CAS}$ clock and generate a signal that tells the refresh logic to send a refresh address to the memory array. Then, a refresh control signal disables the CPU address to the memory and enables the refresh address.

With all these conditions set up, the controller performs the refresh with an operation time the same as that for a read or write cycle. At the end of the cycle, the controller switches back to CPU operation. If 4164s are used in such a system, however, the refresh timing becomes greatly simplified. After the controller determines that a refresh cycle is required, it disables the normal timing sequence, generates the pin-1 RFSH signal (which resembles a $\overline{RAS}$ pulse), and enables the normal timing sequence at the end of the refresh cycle. With the 4164 taking care of all the addressing problems for refresh, the cycle-steal refresh can be done very efficiently.

However, even greater system-design simplification stems from the elimination of two power-supply connections. For one thing, shorts among the V_{BB}, V_{DD} or V_{CC} supplies are no longer a concern since there is no V_{BB} supply to worry about. And even the number of decoupling capacitors can be significantly reduced: Only one supply requires decoupling, not three.

In general, while the pinout of the 64-k RAMs follows that of the 16-k units, board layouts are simpler for the power and ground lines since there are fewer lines to bus. Any interconnect should provide a low inductive pass between the RAM and its capacitors, a low ground impedance to reduce induced noise, a minimal ground offset between TTL memory drivers and the memory chips, a constant impedance reference for signals traversing the board (thus reducing reflections), and a reduced inner-signal crosstalk due to a reduced signal-to-ground spacing.

Fighting noise

The MK4164, in particular, though designed to use standard TTL interface devices without any level enhancement, still requires good signal routing to minimize any possible noise problems, notably crosstalk. This can be limited by the spacing between signal lines, the lengths of the parallel lines and the proximity of the lines to grounds. The number of signals simultaneously switched will also affect the amount of crosstalk generated. Signals sensitive to noise spikes should not be placed near groups of signals simultaneously switching at inopportune times.

Other ways to minimize noise include decoding $\overline{RAS}$ so that it occurs on only one memory word simultaneously. Address lines, $\overline{WE}$ and $\overline{CAS}$, can reach all chips in an array simultaneously.

In addition, resistors in series with the various signal lines help eliminate any signal ringing caused by signal mismatches between the driver and the line. Without the resistors, signal characteristics violate the RAM specifications. However, if a slow driver is used (such as a low-power Schottky device) and the interconnect lines are short, resistors can be omitted.

There are other techniques to minimize ringing—another resistive load at the end of the line, or Schottky-diode clamps. Both of these techniques, though, have drawbacks not associated with the resistors-in-series technique. However, they are useful when the highest possible speed is required and the delays incurred from the series resistors cannot be tolerated.

Is the 64-k economical?

The answer is an unequivocal yes. Though they are expected to follow the traditional learning curve of all semiconductor devices—high initial costs and then rapid declines as production volumes increase—64-k RAMs will come down in cost faster than previous-generation devices, and their cost per bit will actually end up below that for preceding generations.

Indeed, system costs will drop faster than cost per bit, despite the bit density's fourfold enhancement. Not only can the number of boards in a large system be reduced by a factor of four, but fewer interface and buffer circuits are needed, the number of capacitors can be cut by 2/3 and power requirements by 50%, and two supplies out of three can be eliminated. And most likely, over-all system reliability will increase.

For it's part, the cost-per-bit crossover should occur in 1983—this estimate uses the 16-k RAM as a model and adds-in a delaying factor due to the introduction of a 5-V-only high-performance 16-k device, the MK4516 from Mostek and other companies (see graph).

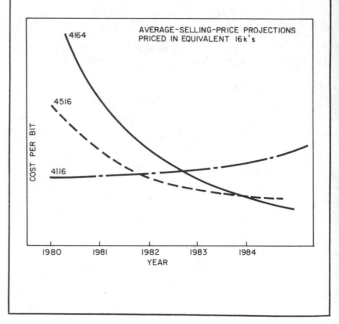

While the future appears to be bright for the 64-k × 1 dynamic RAM, there are other organizations coming—soon to be introduced will be an 8-k × 8 configuration that mates directly with microcomputer systems. Not only will this byte-wide pseudostatic RAM contain the self-refresh features of the MK4164, plus an additional automode refresh for battery-backup applications, but it will have circuitry for reducing synchronization problems. Known as the MK4864, the 8-k × 8 will be available in 1980 and will be pin-compatible with the other members of Mostek's pseudostatic RAM family. Only one TTL logic chip is needed by the RAM to interface to various microprocessors. ∎∎

SECTION III

Static RAMs: Byte-Wide is the Word

Although the dynamic memory has its place in large computer memory systems, many of the small microprocessor applications do not need all the benefits offered by the dynamic devices, nor are users willing to pay the refresh penalty. Static RAMs offer the user an alternative to the dynamic memories. However, there are now two types of static devices from which to choose—the fully static (including edge-triggered types) and the pseudostatic devices that are actually a dynamic memory with the refresh circuitry included on the chip.

Until recently, however, static memories were only available in organizations that provided only 1, 2, or 4 output bits. The microprocessor, though, has changed all that. Since many of the CPU buses are 8 bits wide, a new class of 8-bit-wide static RAMs has been developed to directly mate with the microprocessor buses. And these byte-wide RAMs are available in either static or pseudostatic types. Fully static devices are great for systems in which minimal control is needed and access must be fast. The pseudostatics, however, typically offer double the density, although their access times are slower, and they also require some external operation control to trigger the internal refresh before the chip's internal time-out circuit causes an auto-refresh operation.

The articles in this section contain most of the latest information on the newest static and pesudostatic RAMs available today. Many of the system design guidelines and component tradeoffs are examined so the system designer can make the best choice.

Get Top Memory System Performance with MOS RAMs

KIRK F. MacKENZIE
Static RAM Marketing/Applications Manager,
Intel Corp., Aloha, Oregon

Until recently, costly bipolar memories were the only devices that could keep up with computers' increasing speed requirements. The 2147 HMOS RAM, introduced by Intel and now available from several vendors, spearheaded a new approach to delivering bipolar performance with static operation while providing MOS densities, power levels and economy.

With a 4-k × 1 array that accesses in 55 ns (Fig. 1), the fully-static MOS RAM includes a unique power-down capability. When not required, active power is cut by 85%, placing the device in a stand-by mode. And being fully static, the 2147's operation and timing requirements are straightforward.

Large numbers of these RAMs are going into cache and control store memory sections of large hierarchical computer systems. With the high-speed RAMs, the processor can operate at its fastest cycle time and process data much faster. And applications don't end there. Since it's a comparatively low-cost NMOS product, even main computer memories are starting to use these RAMs.

Approaching the ideal

Judging from the multitude of alternate sources, the 2147 approaches an ideal memory—it is fast, fully static, operates from a single +5-V ±10% power supply and has an automatic low standby power mode. Actually, there are four versions available—the 2147, a 70-ns access time model; the 2147L, a 70-ns low-power option version, the 2147-3, a full 55-ns device; and a full MIL temp version, the M2147, which has an 85-ns access time. Housed in the industry-standard 18-pin DIP pinout, the RAM design uses a conventional six-transistor cell.

The 2147's high performance comes by way of the HMOS technology developed by Intel. A scaled version of previous NMOS technologies, HMOS uses 3.5-micron channels, 700-A oxides and 1-micron junction depths. Performance is further enhanced by the reduction of junction capacitances through the use of an on-chip back-bias generator that typically provides a −3-V back-bias voltage.

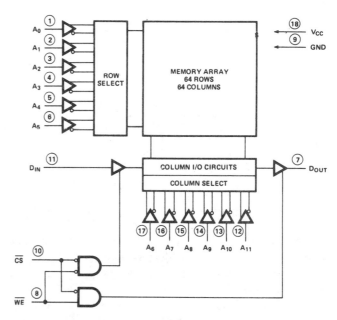

1. **Offering a blazing access time of 55 ns,** Intel's 2147 static, 4-k HMOS RAM cuts power consumption with its automatic power-down operating mode.

Because the 2147 is fully static, basic device operation is particularly simple. Data are simply accessed from either the Chip Select or Address Valid signals, whichever comes last—as the Read Cycle waveforms show in Fig. 2. Clocks, address setup, address hold, and address multiplexing are not required. Therefore, performance degradations due to system skews are minimal.

Since the $\overline{CS}$ input is not a clock and does not have to be cycled, multiple read or write operations can be performed during a single select period. No time is lost between operations for a pre-charge requirement, which allows the 2147 to be cycled at its access time for improved performance over clocked, or "edge-activated," static RAMs.

Historically, fully static RAMs have meant constant power dissipation at high active levels. The first fully static RAM to break with this tradition, the 2147 combines an innovative design approach with the benefits of HMOS to achieve low power—without the need for a clock.

READ CYCLE NO. 1

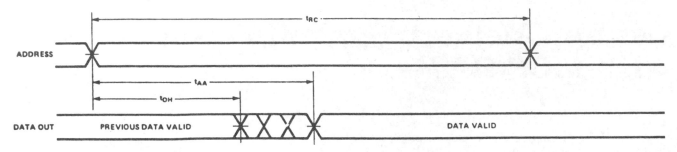

READ CYCLE NO. 2

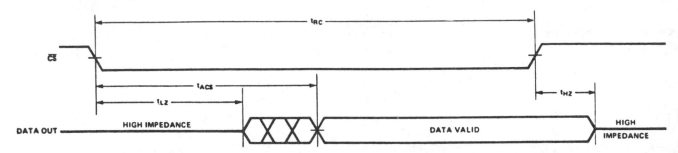

2. **Data are accessed** from either the Chip-select or Address-Valid signals, depending upon which comes last.

Whenever the 2147 is deselected, power dissipation automatically drops to a fraction of the active power, and remains at the low standby power level (I_{SB}) as long as the device stays deselected. Internal power requirements drop because unnecessary portions of the internal peripheral circuitry are turned off (see scope trace in Fig. 3). I_{SB} remains stable over voltage and temperature variations.

The 2147's automatic power-down feature saves in two ways. It reduces power requirements as the duty cycle decreases (Fig. 4a) because the memory spends more time in the deselected, low-standby-power state. As the duty cycle approaches zero, average power dissipation approaches the standby level. Also it saves power in larger memories where only a fraction of the total memory is active at any time—typically 4 kwords. Additional memory beyond the active block is added at standby power levels (see Fig. 4b).

Power savings in a system

To get a good idea of the power savings possible, examine a typical system that uses the 70-ns 2147L, which has a 100-mA typical active current and a 7-mA typical standby current. For a 64-k × 16 memory (256 RAMs), the first 4 k of memory requires 0.86 A, typical, assuming a 50% duty cycle. This is calculated by multiplying 16 devices by (50% × 100 mA + 50% × 7 mA). The remaining 60-k × 16 memory requires only another 1.68 A, typical (240 devices × 7 mA). The total system requirement is 2.8 A at 5 V, or 12.4 W. Without the auto power-down feature of the 2147,

the system power requirements jump to 128 W.

Two important characteristics of the 2147 should be considered. First, it requires more decoupling than a constant-current device. The I_{CC} makes a transition from standby current levels to active current levels during selection, then back again during deselection. To keep the supply within tolerances during these transitions, localized high frequency decoupling is required. Adding one 0.1-μF ceramic capacitor to the board for every other RAM, and one 22-μF bulk electrolytic decoupler for every 16 RAMs is the recommended amount of decoupling.

Second, the relationship of Chip Select Access time (t_{ACS}) to Deselect Pulse Width (t_{DPW}) must be observed (see Fig. 5). For continuous back-to-back cycles with no intervening deselection, t_{ACS} equals the Address Access time (t_{AA}). For deselect pulse widths less than a cycle time, t_{ACS} typically increases 5 ns because of the time lost in repowering the array. Even deselect pulse widths as narrow as a few nanoseconds are affected by this.

As t_{DPW} lengthens, t_{ACS} eventually speeds up. Certain nodes in the RAM are equalized during power-down to provide compensation for the time lost in powering up. This shaves time off t_{ACS}, and just how much depends on the Chip-Select pulse width. For a 40-ns pulse width, t_{ACS} equals t_{AA} in a typical device. For a longer pulse width, t_{ACS} speeds up to about 5 ns faster than t_{AA}. Short deselect times cause absolutely no problem for the device, but the slight increase in Chip-Select Access time must be allowed for. The device specifications account for this characteristic by speci-

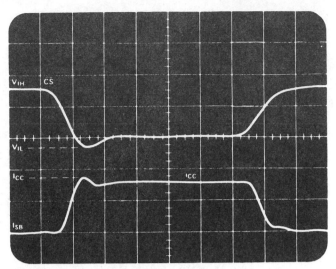

3. When the auto power-down goes into effect, the 2147's current requirement drops as sections of the internal array are turned off.

Manufacturers of 4-k static RAMs

INTEL	Santa Clara, CA
AMD	Sunnyvale, CA
AMI	Cupertino, CA
EMM/SEMI	Phoenix, AZ
FUJITSU	Santa Clara, CA
INTERSIL	Cupertino, CA
MOSTEK	Carrollton, TX
MOTOROLA	Austin, TX
NATIONAL	Santa Clara, CA
NEC	Wellesley, MA
SIGNETICS	Sunnyvale, CA
SYNERTEK	Santa Clara, CA
T.I.	Houston, TX
TOSHIBA	Chicago, IL
ZILOG	Cupertino, CA

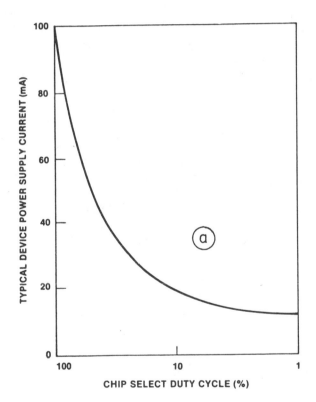

4. As their duty cycle decreases, the RAMs' power requirements drop; they spend more time in the deselected state

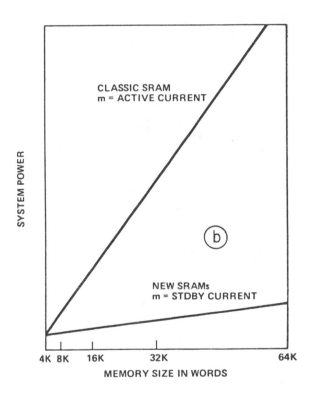

(a). Then only one bank of 2147s remains on at one time, allowing large systems substantial power savings (b).

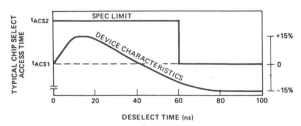

5. One major timing consideration—the relationship of Chip-Select access time to Deselect pulse width—must be dealt with. For deselect pulse widths of less than a cycle time, the access time typically increases by 5 ns.

fying two Chip-Select Access times, t_{ACS1} and t_{ACS2}.

The 2147's pinout, which follows the industry standard, was chosen for optimal performance and layout. All manufacturers but one have selected this pinout (or a clocked variation) for their medium and high performance 4-k × 1 static RAMs (see Table).

The device's simple and efficient layout places the V_{CC} and ground at the corners, which simplifies routing and decoupling of the supplies (Fig. 6a). The address pins are placed to allow the address lines to be routed together, as are the data and control lines.

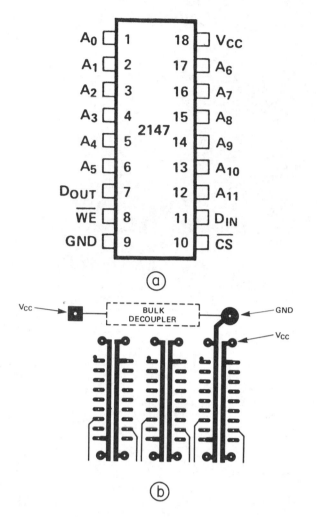

6. **The 2147's pinout** keeps V_{CC} and ground on the corners (a). The PC layout keeps the supply voltage fairly constant across a two-layer board (b).

The pinout minimizes cross-coupling effects by using the data pins to separate the control and address lines. This separation reduces Miller-capacitance effects between the address and control lines, whose signals frequently make near-simultaneous transitions. The interconnection cross-coupling from the data lines to either the address or control lines is minimal because of the usual perpendicular routing of the data traces to other traces.

The gridding used in the layout of Fig. 6b runs supplies both horizontally and vertically at every device location. This highly recommended gridding—in conjunction with the decoupling previously mentioned—keeps the supply voltage acceptably constant across a two-layer PC board.

Since RAMs like the 2147 operate in the high-speed world that was previously reserved for bipolar devices, line terminations are sometimes required to eliminate excessive overshoots, and the problem of ringing inputs must be faced. MOS inputs, which differ from bipolar inputs, do not provide input diode clamps. The 2147 incorporates an input protection circuit (Fig. 7)

in which an n+ diffused resistor is used to limit current transients from static discharge. The protection device provides an enhanced junction breakdown voltage. The diffused resistor forms a diode to the substrate.

Positive overshoots during a V_{IH} transition are no problem for the 2147. These overshoots seldom exceed the maximum input specification, and the levels that result from the ringing generally remain above the 2147's input threshold voltage of, typically, 1.5 V.

Negative overshoots during a V_{IL} transition also present no problem. To have an effect, the overshoot must be sufficiently negative to forward bias the device's input diode. This requires the overshoot to be 0.6 V more negative than the substrate ($V_{BB} = -3$ V typically), and it must last more than 20 ns—the input diodes approximate turn-on time. In the majority of designs, these conditions are not met. The diode is therefore not forward biased, and the overshoot has no effect.

In cases where the diode is forward biased, the small charge in the overshoot is injected into the floating substrate, slightly increasing the back-bias. As a result, device threshold voltages are raised and junction capacitances are decreased. Since these two changes have opposite effects on access time, the net change is limited to at least one or two nanoseconds (usually faster). The injected charge does not affect device reliability.

Negative overshoot can cause a problem if the subsequent ringing exceeds the input threshold voltage. If this occurs, the input buffer's reaction slows down as it tries to follow the changing input. This can lengthen a Read Access time by the time it takes the input lines to quiet down. For a Write cycle, addresses should be stabilized prior to an active Write pulse to eliminate the possibility of multiple selection and problems with stored data.

Terminations cut ringing

To avoid excessive ringing, use any of the terminations shown in Fig. 8. The series resistor is easiest, but it costs a few nanoseconds of performance. A typical resistor value is 10 to 33 Ω for high-speed Schottky gates. The parallel resistor network does not cost performance when matched to the line impedance, but does draw considerable power and imposes loading factors on the bus drivers that feed the RAMs. A Thevenin equivalent resistance of 100 to 200 Ω is typical for two-layer boards; it's less for multi-layer boards.

The R-C network saves power over the parallel resistor network, depending on frequency. Choose the resistor to match the impedance of the line (100 to 200 Ω). The capacitor should have about one-tenth the impedance of the resistor (i.e. C = $10/2\pi fR$, about 30 to 150 pF). A simple Schottky diode clamp may also be considered.

During a negative overshoot, the protection device is too slow to have much of a clamping effect. However, when the input is held at a dc negative level exceeding about −1 V, the protection device turns on and supplies current from ground to the input. Depending on the input voltage, the current can go as high as several milliamps.

System power-on does not immediately activate the 2147 back-bias generator. It begins functioning only when the V_{CC} supply has reached approximately 2.5 V. During this interval, device current can exceed standby specifications because internal threshold voltages are lower without back-bias, and device currents are consequently higher. The amount of current depends on whether the device is deselected ($\overline{CS}$ high) or selected ($\overline{CS}$ low).

If the device is selected, the power-on current rises quickly toward full active power (140 to 180 mA), as shown in Fig. 9a. Although no problem for the device, which has been designed to handle this current level, this current can cause a problem for the power supply. The supply was designed to handle current at or near device standby current levels, such as in a large memory application.

Deselect RAMs to keep power down

An obvious way to eliminate this problem is to keep the devices deselected during power-on. Simply use 1-k pull-up resistors to V_{CC} on the $\overline{CS}$ inputs, which raises $\overline{CS}$ as the power comes on. This holds the power-on current to about twice the standby current level (I_{SB}), which is considerably less than full active current (see Fig. 9b). However, this is still not quite as low as I_{SB}, and the power supply must be designed accordingly. A maximum power-on current spec (I_{PO}) is included in the 2147 data sheet for this purpose. Device current values range from 30 to 70 mA, depending on the version selected.

The time constant of the internal back-bias generator is about 10 to 100 μs—several times faster than most power supplies, whose constant is typically several milliseconds. Therefore, the dc curve of Fig. 9b represents what can be expected of a 2147 during ac power-up. The time spent within a specific voltage range will be determined by the time constant of the power supply—not the RAM.

Putting the RAMs into a system using the suggested guidelines is relatively simple. Fig. 10a shows the basic block diagram for a 16-kword memory card using 64 of the 2147 (55 ns) RAMs. The card is designed to interface to a system that has an 18-bit address bus, a 16-bit data bus and a multi-line control bus.

The data bus can be organized as either a common I/O bus of 16 lines or a separate input and output bus totalling 32 lines. Within the card, data input and output lines are separate. Data written into the memory are latched and buffered by latches. The same goes for data read out of the memory.

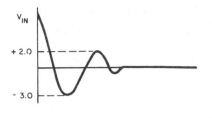
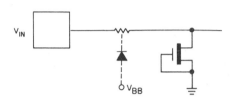

7. **Input ringing,** which consists of overshoots and undershoots (a), requires an understanding of the input circuitry for termination considerations (b).

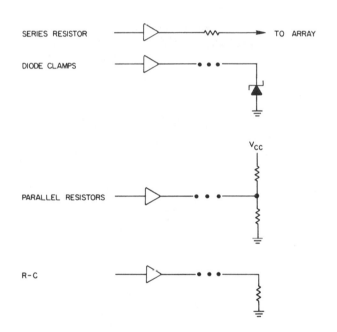

8. **To prevent excessive ringing,** simple termination schemes such as these can be used. However, depending upon the specific system limitations, no single technique is always the ideal solution.

Since the memory is static, the control bus consists of only two lines—a $\overline{REQ}$ line that initiates each memory cycle, and a $\overline{WR}$ line that defines whether a read or write cycle will take place. Simplified timing waveforms for the system are shown in Fig. 10b. Addresses are established 30 ns prior to a cycle and latched by the time $\overline{REQ}$ initiates the cycle at t = 0 ns.

The status of $\overline{WR}$ at the beginning of the cycle determines whether a Read ($\overline{WR}$ high) or Write ($\overline{WR}$ low) is executed. If a Read is executed, data are available at the card edge at t = 75 ns. If a Write

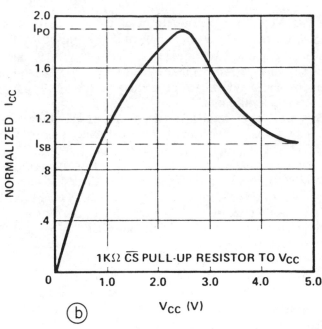

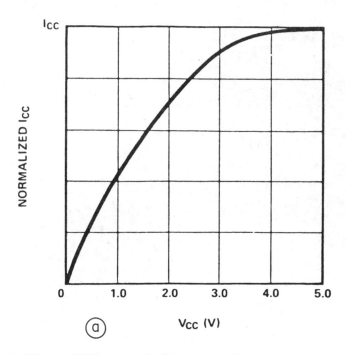

9. When a RAM sytem is first powered up, the supply current can approach a fully active power level (a). During power on, though, all RAMs can be kept deselected to minimize the start-up current from the power supply (b).

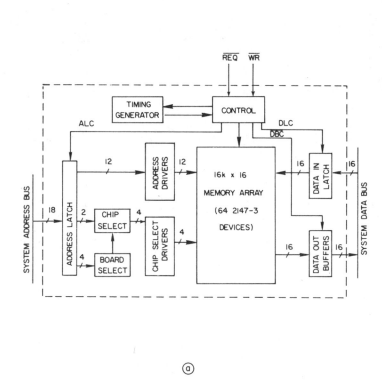

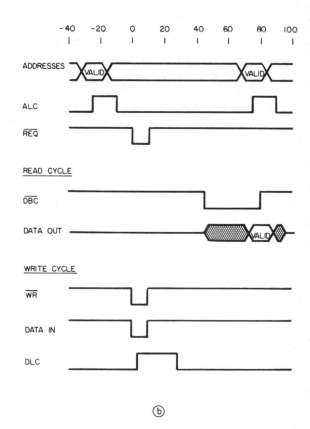

10. A typical, 16-kword (16-bit words) static RAM system is based on the 2147-3 (a). This memory system provides an over-all cycle or access time of 100 ns, as shown by the timing waveforms (b).

is executed, the input data are latched at the beginning of the cycle and the write is completed during the cycle.

The maximum time required to complete either a Read or Write operation is 100 ns.∎∎

Fast 4-k and Byte-Wide Static RAMs

DAVE BARNES
Western Editor,
Electronic Design

New 4-k and 8-k static MOS RAMs are competing for socket territory with older static designs, especially in high-speed cache and microcomputer system designs. The battle is being joined on several fronts:

■ Speed: Superfast, 4096-bit MOS RAMs are challenging bipolars in the 50-ns cache race. Meanwhile, 100 to 500-ns, 8-k and 16-k devices, organized in 1-k and 2-k × 8-bit configurations, offer micro designers convenient cost-saving configurations while maintaining fast access time.

Improved 1 k and 4-k bipolar statics with 30 to 50-ns speeds nevertheless still are the choice for the fastest TTL and ECL cache and buffer systems.

■ Power: Automatic, on-chip, power-down switching in new MOS statics can cut power drastically whenever a chip is unselected.

■ Unclocked vs clocked RAMs: You can now get truly static storage coupled with either static or clocked (dynamic) access circuits on the periphery of a chip. Main differences are in addressing flexibility and average power consumed.

■ Organization: Right now, 4-k × 1 and 1-k × 4 RAMs dominate but byte-wide "by-8s" may yet take over, as they ease power drain and simplify chip-selection logic. With clocked or power-down RAMs, the wider words tend to save power, since fewer chips are on at a time.

■ Pinouts: A wide choice is already on the market, and JEDEC standards are still not approved. This means designers must make prudent choices on their own.

■ Capacity: The number of bits per chip is growing, but 1-k statics still dominate shipments. The consensus is 4-k statics will grow to be a volume commodity by the first half of next year—but by then, several firms will be sampling or shipping 8-k and 16-k

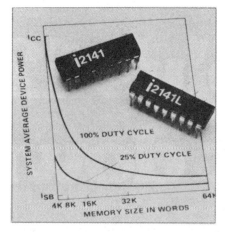

These 4-k × 1 static RAMs from Intel go on low-power standby automatically. The 2141L low-power versions require only 40-mA supply current (I_{cc}) in active operation and 5 mA on standby, which saves over 90% of the power consumed by conventional, fully static RAMs.

statics. And one firm will sample a 32-k quasistatic before the end of this year.

Speed: which nanoseconds?

Most of the new statics are in the 200 to 500-ns access-time range, which makes them suitable for MOS μPs. Meanwhile, many manufacturers are on the brink of producing 150 and 120-ns NMOS 4-k RAMs. But remember clocked parts have cycle times slower than their access times. And it's the cycle time that determines how often you can read or write in a chip. The chart on p. 66 gives specifications on some of the leading static RAMs.

On the other hand, the HMOS 2147 from Intel (Santa Clara, CA) and the VMOS 4017 from AMI (Santa Clara, CA), both with 55 ns access times, are leading an attack on bipolar RAMs, those ultrafast units that serve bipolar

bit-slice μPs and other fast processors as cache memories, writable control stores and scratchpads. Clocking doesn't apply here (yet), so cycle time is the same as access time. But there are two specs on access time to watch out for.

Address access time (t_{AA}) is familiar —the number of nanoseconds you wait to get data, after address bits stabilize on the RAM inputs. But there's also *chip-select* access time (t_{ACS})—the number of ns after chip-select occurs and before you get data. Chips are known by their address access times, because T_{ACS} is usually no problem. But when power-down and fast access time are combined in the same RAM, an important tradeoff exists.

Actually, the latter of the two events (chip select and address settling after the respective access times are added) governs how fast your RAM can read. And to figure out write speed, you have to add two access times again: address-write (t_{AW}) and chip-write (t_{CW}).

But chip-select pulses often arrive a few nanoseconds after addresses settle, because they're often decoded from the address lines themselves. So most RAMs have a t_{ACS} shorter than t_{AA} to allow time for the decode gates to derive the chip-select term.

The 4017 has a t_{AA} of 55 ns and a t_{ACS} of 30 ns, while the Fairchild bipolar 93471 RAM has a t_{AA} of 30 ns and a t_{ACS} of 25 ns. As long as the address decoding takes less than 25 or 5 ns, respectively, the RAMs will perform just as fast in a memory system as a glance at their t_{AA} specs implies.

But Intel's 2147 may not. Its t_{AA} is 55 ns, but its t_{ACS} is 55 ns if the chip has been deselected for more than 55 ns, and 65 ns if deselected for less. This is because deselection starts the chip's powering down process, and some time is lost in powering back up.

Avoid short turnoffs, then, and the

2147 will recycle at 55 ns—provided you can get the chip select decoded that soon. The AMI 4017 and the 93471 don't have this problem, because they don't have the valuable power-down feature. But Motorola's MCM 2147 claims to have the power-down feature without short turnoff time problems.

One other caveat on speed: The 2147 and the 4017 are specified with min/max ns values, but the Fairchild 93471 data sheet has only typicals. And the best production testing has about ±2 ns accuracy.

A hot issue

As the trends of more memory per system and more memory per chip continue, the problem of too much heat per board becomes inevitable. RAM manufacturers are reducing chip power, not only to cut heat, but to cut power-supply and cooling costs for the OEM.

Though the single +5-V supply has become the rule for virtually all static RAMs, the approaches to cutting power consumption vary.

As the chart indicates, one major way to cut average power per chip is to clock dynamic MOS peripheral circuits. Another is automatic on-chip power-down, which is controlled by the chip-enable (chip-select) pin. Indeed, one static RAM, the 8-k 8108 from EMM Semi (Phoenix, AZ) features both clocking and power-down, for impressive savings in the standby mode (see chart).

With either power-down or clocking, power buses on the PC board should have lower inductance than buses used for full-power statics. And there should be more decoupling capacitors because current transients in the 5-V lines are large and rapid.

Second-sources for the Intel 2114 static RAM abound. The SY 2114 from Synertek (Santa Clara, CA), the 7114 from Intersil (Santa Clara, CA) and the 9114 from AMD (Sunnyvale, CA) have minimum output drives of 3.2 mA, compared with Intel's 2.1 mA. AMD's 9124, available in sample quantities now, is also 2114-compatible, but adds the power-down feature. AMI's 2114H under development will draw about 800 mW to achieve a breakthrough speed of 70 ns.

While most RAMs are still spec'd for 5 V ±5%, Texas Instruments (Dallas, TX), National Semiconductor (Santa, Clara, CA) and Motorola (Austin, TX) among others, have begun designing commercial statics to stand ±10%, as the military has long required.

"If a manufacturer cannot meet ±10% on a consistent basis, he doesn't have enough margin in his design as it relates to his process," argues Ron Livingston, National Semiconductor's memory marketing manager for MOS statics.

The lowest-power 4-ks come in CMOS—standby power is at the microwatt level. But CMOS RAMs still feature premium costs. However, as more CMOS equivalents of NMOS static RAMs appear, the price gap is narrowing. Acknowledging that today's CMOS:NMOS price ratios range around 3:1 or 4:1, Intersil's memory marketing manager Ron Hammer sees the ratio "heading for only about 1.6:1, but with a nine-to-18 month lag behind NMOS."

Since RAMs are volatile, battery backup is often used in systems where data must not be lost when power goes down. Most static RAM types reliably retain stored data when their +5-V power is lowered to +2.5, so batteries need not supply full operating power. Various manufacturers spec 2.0 V for data retention, and AMD's 9130/9140 are okay down to 1.5 V.

Another battery approach is pin separation. Some RAMs have a 5-V pin for the array and another to power the peripheral circuits that complete the chip. Only the array needs power when the system is inactive.

Meanwhile, unclocked RAMs are getting the business from clocked statics. Since the fully static (unclocked) RAMs have static peripheral circuits as well as static flip-flop circuits in their storage arrays (see box), they draw relatively constant current, whether or not they are reading or writing data. Being direct-coupled, fully static RAMs pay relatively constant attention to their address inputs, too.

Not so with cooler-operating clocked statics, also known as edge-triggered, synchronous or edge-activated. The leading edge of the chip-enable (CE) pulse sets off the dynamic peripheral circuits in a clocked static, and triggers the various internal clocks that get the read/write jobs done. Then the peripheral circuits revert to ultralow power drain. The static array is the only significant load until the chip is accessed again.

The state of the address inputs is ignored by a clocked RAM, except at the CE-fall instant and for a few nanoseconds after. The advocates of fully static RAMs argue that their

Static RAMs are easier to use

Static RAMs are usually easier to use than dynamic RAMs because they require no refresh logic. They use a complete flip-flop to store each bit, instead of a capacitor. Since capacitor charges tend to leak away, dynamics must be refreshed, usually about every 2 ms, either by data accesses to all rows, or more typically by external refresh circuitry. Refresh usually uses about 3% of the chip's time, but often can be done when the CPU doesn't need memory access.

Dynamic cells do have fewer parts than static cells, so dynamic die sizes are smaller for the same capacity, and prices are lower. But statics are making inroads—especially in small systems, where the elimination of refresh logic saves a significant amount of power, space and/or cost.

Some new statics use only four transistors per cell instead of six, by replacing the two depletion-load transistors connected to V_{DD} with two smaller polysilicon resistors. Proponents of the four-transistor design report better margins, lower power, and smaller cell size.

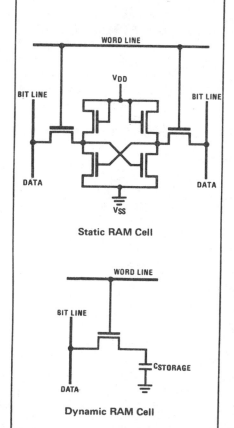

Static RAM Cell

Dynamic RAM Cell

4k and 8k static RAM types

	Device type	Process	Organization, words × bits	Power (mW) on/standby (max)	Access/cycle times (ns)	No. of pins	Original developer
Fully static RAMS without power-down	2114	HMOS	1k × 4	525/525 to 370/370	200/200 to 450/450	18	INTEL
	4044/4046	NMOS	4k × 1	649/649 to 370/370	150/150 to 450/450	18/20	TI
	4045/4047	NMOS	1k × 4	550/550 to 400/400	150/150 to 450/450	18/20	TI
	AM 9114	NMOS	1k × 4	525/525 to 370/370	200/200 to 450/450	18	AMD
Fully static RAMS with chip select power down	2147	HMOS	4k × 1	945/160 to 735/53	55/55 to 70/70	18	INTEL
	4244 4245	NMOS	4k × 1 } 1k × 4 }	~300/50	150/150 to 450/450	18	TI
	2141	HMOS	4k × 1	385/110 to 200/28	120/120 to 250/250	10	INTEL
Clocked static RAMS	8108	NMOS	1k × 8	270/60	300/450	22	EM & M SEMI
	4801	NMOS	1k × 8	250/50	90/150 to 250/350		MOSTEK
	26104	NMOS	4k × 1	320/242 to 165/127	150/240 to 350/510	18	ZILOG
	4104	NMOS	4k × 1	116/28	200/310 to 300/460	18	MOSTEK
CMOS static RAMS	IM 6507	CMOS	512 × 8	33/.005 (@25°C)	400/670 (@25°C)	24	INTERSIL
	HM 6504	CMOS	4k × 1 }	35/.005	170/240 300/420	18	HARRIS
	HM 6514	CMOS	1k × 4 }	35/.005	170/240 300/420	18	HARRIS
	MWS 5114	CMOS/ SOS	1k × 4	250μW	450	18	RCA
	CDP 1825	CMOS/ SOS	1k × 4	5.0 mW	300	18	RCA

(Left margin, vertical: LOWER POWER)

RAMs are easier to understand and use as well as accessible all the time, while the clocked RAMs have cycle times about twice as long as their access times. But the clocked-static proponents point to the considerable power saved and relaxed timing requirements for address validity.

"Of course, clocked approaches are borrowed from dynamic RAMs, and tend to be more complex and less reliable, and dynamic circuits take more space," notes Intel's Rick Pashley, who led the design of the 50-ns 1-k 2125 and the 55-ns 4-k 2147. "Some clocked designs have to give over 60% of the chip to the peripheral circuits," he says.

But Roger Badertscher, responsible for component development at Zilog, says, "Clocked approaches are certainly reliable. We use clocked logic on everything we make. In our 6104 clocked RAM, the peripheral portion is large percentagewise because our dynamic peripheral circuits can tolerate a much smaller, high-impedance array. In a fully static design, the cell has to drive the sense amp in both polarities; in ours, only one."

The Zilog (Cupertino, CA) 6104 RAM and the Mostek 4104 are similar clocked static RAMs. Neither has power-down. But Mostek specifies much lower power, while Zilog offers higher speed. Both are compatible with the pinouts of the Intel 2147 and 2141, but socket compatibility, of course, requires that the chip-select line be strobed for each access.

Going straight to 16k

The future for static RAMs is at best a mixed bag. While AMI, Intersil, RCA and Synertek may introduce 16-k statics next, in the belief that the industry won't really stop off at 8 k, Intel is working on a clocked 1-k × 8 for microprocessors. National expects to have an 8-k next year, and TI is planning to introduce two fully static RAMs late this year, a 1-k × 8 and a 2-k × 8 that will have the 2716 EPROM pinout. And Fairchild is considering both MOS and I³L statics in 4-k × 4 and 2-k × 8.

Intersil's 16-k, scheduled for introduction in the first quarter of 1979, will be a 24-pin RAM with better than 200-ns access time. And EMM Semi, while sampling the 8108 1-k × 8, is working on a 16-k static.

RCA says it intends to skip the 8-k static RAM derby and plunge directly into 16-k's. The company feels that the price-per-bit of its 16-k will simply be much more attractive than any 8-k's. RCA's 16-k will be CMOS/SOS, of course, and first cut samples should be available late this year, with production quantities by the middle of 1979.

A sub-100-ns MK4801 1k × 8 static from Mostek, the MK4801—scheduled for sampling in August and volume shipments in the fourth quarter of 1978 —will feature both clocking and power-down as options. This byte-wide 300-mW RAM has 24 pins, with a pinout similar to the EMM 8108 and the Intel 2716 EPROM.

So far, getting 16-k on a static chip is challenging enough. But Zilog reports that samples of a clocked 32-k quasistatic RAM will be available late this year (see ED No. 11, May 24, 1978, p. 54). Access time is estimated at 200 to 250 ns, cycle time 300 to 450 ns. The clocked 32-k will have a dynamic storage array, but with a totally hidden on-chip refresh circuit, it will look just like a static in any μP environment.■■

Wide-Word RAMs Are Smart Enough

SHEFF EATON
Memory Development Engineer,
Mostek, Carrollton, Texas

DAVE HUFFMAN
Memory Applications Engineer,
Mostek, Carrollton, Texas

WARD PARKINSON
Memory Development Engineer,
Mostek, Carrollton, Texas

Until recently most leading-edge memory chips have been designed primarily for large mainframe storage. To use them in microprocessor systems required not only considerable adaptation but also additional ICs to interface the memory chips. But now comes a new breed of smart memory chips—a 2-k × 8 dynamic RAM and two fully static 1-k × 8s—specifically designed for μP applications, and cache memory uses as well.

While conventional memory chips can accept only read, write, and select commands, the smart memory devices do that and more: Besides accepting additional commands, they present parallel data on byte-wide outputs, and provide many other features for users, including the following:

- 5-V-only operation.
- Automatic power-down.
- Automatic refresh for dynamics.

- ROM/PROM/EPROM compatibility.
- Output enable (OE) command.
- Chip select (CS) command.
- Latch command—for synchronous operation.

To see the design tradeoffs possible with this family, see Table 1.

The 16-k dynamic MK4816 (with single-pin refresh) and the 8-k static MK4118 can both be used readily with any of the present-generation and new generation MOS microprocessors such as the Z-80, Z-8000, 8085, and 8086. For high-performance applications, another 8-k static (MK4801) provides a choice of 55, 75, and 90-ns access times.

The new parts are configured as 1024 words × 8 bits in fully static designs or as 2048 words × 8 bits in an internally refreshed format. The refresh timing cycles are supplied by the chip itself and are largely transparent to the user. Whatever the configuration, the Mostek RAMs typically dissipate a low 200 to 300 mW of power, and offer fast data access down to 55 ns.

The memory-use spectrum

The impact of this family cannot be appreciated fully without noting that semiconductor memory applications cover a broad spectrum, from low-speed uses in games to very high-speed applications in cache memory. For μP applications, medium-performance RAMs generally suffice, and cost is a major selection factor. But as Fig. 1 shows, cache memory users pay a higher price for high speed.

In the center of the spectrum is main-store memory, which has relatively balanced density, performance, and cost requirements. A typical main-store memory is 32 bits wide and 1/2 to 1-million words deep. Memories this large (in fact, most memories larger than 64-k to 128-k bytes) warrant some sort of error-detection/error-correction scheme, which favors a "by 1" or serial-output memory device.

So far, the NMOS dynamic RAM using address

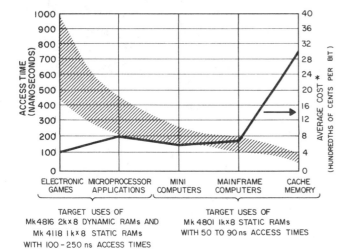

(BASED ON ACTUAL INDUSTRY SURVEYS; SOME ANOMALIES ARE DUE TO COST VARIANCES IN CERAMIC vs PLASTIC PACKAGES, AND QUANTITY BUYS)

1. **Today's memory-use spectrum** is dominated by the tradeoff between device cost and speed. The new byte-wide RAM designs will compete in all areas.

multiplexing and a "by 1" bit-serial organization has been the most efficient and cost-effective for main memory. So long as the needed memory depth is greater than the depth of the available by-1 memory chips, the by-1 minimizes the number of lines, the input and output capacitances, the pin count, the board area and the cost. However, while by-1 RAMs are excellent for conventional main storage applications, they are less than attractive for many others.

The most dynamic growth over the past four years has come from electronic games and μP-based products. Increased use of memory in such systems has been the key item in penetrating low-cost/high-volume markets. As a result, both general-purpose minis and dedicated microcomputers have come down in price while staying functionally equivalent. Indeed, CPU cost is so low in this area that μP system costs tend to be in proportion to memory requirements.

Until the 2114 (1-k × 4) static RAM, it took eight 2102-type RAMs to implement 1-k × 8 of memory. Before the 2114, few RAMs were designed to interface directly with a microprocessor, because chip designers concentrated on the processors themselves. Even the better RAMs would not work with all processors.

ROM and PROM grabbed a lot of attention because of their nonvolatility, which was needed for fixed instruction set storage, usually a bigger requirement than RAM. ROMs and PROMs have always been "by 4" or "by 8" because of the convenience of putting instructions in the least amount of packages.

Why byte-wide RAMs?

Recently however, three trends have stepped up the demand for wide-word RAMs—declining cost of μPs, further improvements in memory density and cost, and the emergence of high-volume dedicated-computer markets such as the automotive market. Such applications as μP memory, CRT refresh memory, CRT buffer memory—being very shallow—all lend themselves to a "by 8" memory organization and its minimum number of packages.

Cache memory, high speed buffer memory, writable control store, scratchpad memory and terminal/communications buffer memory stress speed much more heavily than cost. Fast bipolar memories have usually been used here, at the expense of package count, cost, and high power. However, recent technological innovations such as scaling and the four-transistor (six-element) static cell concept enable MOS memories to compete with bipolar for cache.

Though cache applications have a large number of bits, there are usually a small number of words; that is, they are wide but shallow memory matrices. For instance, a typical cache memory in a minicomputer is 32 bits wide but only 2-k to 4-k words deep. Clearly, a wide-word memory chip is most efficient here.

MK4816—fast but low-cost

The MK4816 16-k dynamic RAM is the first 5-V-only dynamic MOS memory. It's also the first wide-word dynamic RAM, and the first RAM designed specifically for present and future microprocessor systems. Using small dynamic-memory cells offsets the cost of the slightly greater overhead circuitry required for proper operation of dynamic memories.

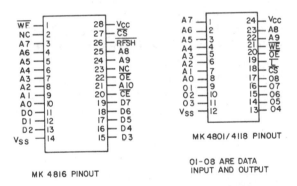

2. **The 16-k dynamic RAM (MK4816) pinout (left) features** single-pin refresh. The 4801/4118 statics have 2708/2758 compatible pinout. All these designs use common I/O pins for data.

Table 1. Characteristics of new byte-wide RAMs

Type number	Memory organization	Process/ pinout	Access time	Unique features	Other leading features

MK4816	2 k × 8 dynamic	N-channel Si gate
		
		28 pin
			100 typ.	First byte-wide dynamic
				First 5-V only dynamic
				
				First one-pin refresh
					Edge-activated™
					  150 mW active,
					  25 mW standby
					Competes with 2102 and 2114 statics,
					  cutting cost and space

MK4801	1 k × 8 static	Scaled Poly 5 24 pin	55 75 90	First 2 mil² static RAM cell Fast as the 4 k × 1 2147	Fully static 250 mW typical Double capacity at double speed, compared to 4 k statics now dominant

MK4118	1 k × 8 static	N-channel Si gate
		
		24 pin
			120
			150
			200
			250
				Faster than the
				  X8s now available
					Fully static
					Lower cost than 4801
					Competes with 2102 and
					  2114 static, cutting cost and space

The MK4816 is designed to minimize the off-chip support circuits, while maintaining the internal efficiency of a dynamic RAM. Its cell size is three times smaller than in typical static cells, while its die size —29,000 mil²—approaches that of 4-k static RAMs. Built with standard N-channel silicon gate technology, the device requires only a single +5-V power supply.

High speed, low-power operation stems from edge-activated dynamic logic, which produces a typical access time of 100 ns at a power-dissipation of only 25 mW standby and 150 mW active.

System-oriented features include single-pin refresh, automatic refresh in battery back-up mode, and common data I/O. Full TTL compatibility is also provided on all inputs and outputs. See Fig. 2 for the pinout.

The MK4816 can handle a variety of read, write, and refresh cycles. Read and write cycles are initiated by the falling edge of chip enable ($\overline{CE}$) which also latches the state of 11 address inputs and the chip select input. In a read cycle, data become valid after one access time assuming that both $\overline{CE}$ and $\overline{OE}$ (output enable) are low. After the data are read or written, the memory returns to a precharged condition.

After it's fully precharged, the internal logic will initiate a refresh cycle, provided the $\overline{RFSH}$ pin is brought low during the previous cycle. Waveforms for this type of latched-refresh cycle, together with those for typical read and write cycles, are shown in Fig. 3. Since the single-refresh step renews the charge in only one row of the RAM matrix, 128 such steps must take place every 2 ms.

Although latched-refresh operation is particularly convenient for achieving refresh in minimum time, the chip may also be refreshed simply by clocking the $\overline{RFSH}$ pin 128 times every 2 ms, while $\overline{CE}$ remains high. In this as in all types of refresh cycles, addresses are generated internally and automatically incremented and stored at the end of each refresh cycle. Since the on-chip refresh function in the 4816 uses an extremely small part of chip area, it's clear that, at least for wide-word RAMs, refresh is more efficiently performed on-chip.

Ultimately, the single-pin refresh concept could be extended to fully static operation, by means of an internal oscillator to generate refresh-request pulses at fixed intervals. But this function has not been implemented on the MK4816 because of the long access and cycle times involved and because arbitration logic always has some finite probability of indecision. In such "hidden refresh" designs, if an external cycle is requested at precisely the same time as an internal refresh request, arbitration logic allows either cycle to go ahead, with the other immediately following. From a user's viewpoint, such a "hidden-refresh" device appears totally static with an access time equal to one refresh cycle time plus a normal access time.

Instead, the 4816 has a battery back-up or self-refresh mode, which is initiated after $\overline{RFSH}$ has been low for about 15 μs. During the self-refresh mode, the states of all inputs except $\overline{RFSH}$ are ignored and refresh is performed automatically through refresh-request pulses derived from an internal oscillator. A rising edge on $\overline{RFSH}$ terminates the self-refresh mode and active read or write cycles can follow after one cycle time.

The self-refresh mode, with its fully automatic on-chip timing, is also particularly useful for single-step operation, since it is not necessary to provide external refresh pulses between instructions. The memory will always refresh itself independently of the time interval between clock pulses. Data can be read during the self-refresh mode since output data will remain valid throughout the self-refresh interval if $\overline{CE}$ and $\overline{OE}$ are held low.

The MK4816's memory matrix is structured around a single row of 128 sense amplifiers each fed by a

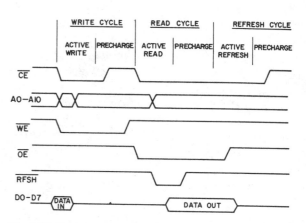

3. **The MK4816 2-k × 8 RAM** combines edge activation with latched refresh. Refresh request is stored for execution after the read cycle.

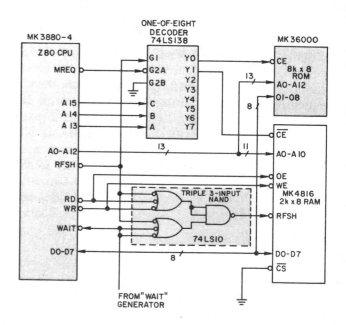

4. **The MK4816 dynamic RAM's built-in control logic** simplifies interfacing to a Z-80 μP. This design uses only one logic gate, but supports single-step operation.

Wide-word memory devices—a response to changing needs

As the spectrum of microprocessor applications continues to expand and as high-speed, general-purpose computers continue to grow, the semiconductor industry is preparing for a surge in memory demand. Designing products that will ease the system designer's work, the industry is providing the most cost-effective, highest-density and highest-performance memories ever.

Bit density for semiconductor memory has increased steadily and quickly since the integration of an R-S flip-flop into the integrated circuit. In just 15 years, single-bit memories have given way to 64-kbit memories. There was one goal behind this evolution: Replace core-implemented main memory with something cheaper and smaller.

But core replacement is no longer a problem. Now the concern is differing consumer/industrial memory requirements. Where typical μP systems have a more fixed need for memory per CPU at lower cost per bit, cache and scratchpad memories require very high performance, with less emphasis on cost. The result? High-speed, but low-cost MOS RAMs—both dynamic and static.

The new dynamic and static chips are configured in a "by 8" or "byte-wide" organization. They will be effective for those applications outside main store memory where a "by 1" bit organization is either not attractive technically (because of system constraints such as power) or not efficient for implementing wide-word shallow memories.

balanced bit line loaded with 64 memory cells. Data from both ends of eight selected bit lines are amplified, latched and buffered into eight data I/O pins. Input addresses are derived from either the external address pins or the internal refresh counter. Refresh-request pulses controlling the refresh counter are derived either from the $\overline{\text{RFSH}}$ pin itself or the internal oscillator, which also doubles as the charge pump for generating the negative substrate bias.

Architecturally, the MK4816 is easy to use with all microprocessors. As shown in Fig. 4, it can be connected directly to the Z80 with only one logic gate added for single-step capability. The 8085 also interfaces easily by taking advantage of the 8085's status bits (S_0 and S_1) to refresh the MK4816 following each instruction fetch.

Latched refresh is particularly easy to implement in microprocessor systems since $\overline{\text{RFSH}}$ can be delayed slightly from $\overline{\text{CE}}$ to accomplish asynchronous refresh in minimum time. The MK4816 may also be used in multiplexed data and address systems, with the $\overline{\text{OE}}$ pin for control, and in CRT systems where the normal sequential addressing automatically refreshes the memory by addressing all positions within 2 ms.

While recognizing that clocked, dynamic RAMs with automatic refresh will clearly be the most cost-effective byte-wide RAM for use with microprocessors, MOSTEK has also developed two fully static 1-k × 8 RAMs. Functionally alike, and identical in pinout, the 4801 and 4118 differ only in production process and in speed.

Bit density way up

With a die the same size as the 4816's and using the standard N-channel production process and tolerances, the 4801 typically runs a 50 to 90 access/cycle with typical power of 250 mW. This means an 8-to-1 increase in bit density per chip over the 93415 bipolar 1-k × 1, and 15-to-1 decrease in system power per bit.

Low power and high speed are achieved using a 2-mil² cell that eliminates connections to V_{cc}. Power is fed to the cell from the column lines, through 1-nA intrinsic poly load resistors (see Fig. 5).

This economical design limits the matrix current to just 8 μA. Column and row decoders are modified tree decoders (Fig. 5) that dissipate only leakage current in both active and standby modes.

The key to the 4801's high speed is an ECL-style linear differential amplifier for sensing the column signal (Fig. 5). The differential amplifier's output is amplified and translated to full TTL levels with a strobed differential latch. The strobe signal, derived by sensing an address change or address activation, allows fully static ripple-through operation.

Since a completed cycle results in automatic chip power-down until the next address change, the user doesn't have to deselect the chip, but can use the simple, fast $\overline{\text{CS}}$. The result is a chip that is as easily used for retrofit as for newer clocked systems.

Some very useful features on both the 4801 and 4118 increase their flexibility. As shown in Fig. 10 several control functions have been added. In addition to the normal R/W, and $\overline{\text{CS}}$ (chip select) there is also $\overline{\text{OE}}$ (output enable) and $\overline{\text{L}}$ (latch). Both $\overline{\text{L}}$ and $\overline{\text{OE}}$ inputs may be used to simulate a clocked RAM for easy interface to any μP (see Table 2).

The 4801 and 4118 may be tied to any μP or mini bus without SSI interface devices. The pinout, like a 2708's or 2758's, may be used interchangeably with EPROMs or bipolar PROMs to assist in μC product development (see pinout in Fig. 2).

Besides being able to interface easily in a "clocked" mode, both the devices may also be used as fully static ripple-through RAMs. The latch input may be tied high, $\overline{\text{OE}}$ low, and the part can be used to replace directly eight 93415/425s, eight 2102s or two 2114s. This means existing designs can be upgraded for improved density, power and cost.

Some conflicts occur when these common-I/O three-

Table 2. Truth table for 4801/4118 1 1 k × 8 RAMs

$\overline{OE}$	$\overline{WE}$	$\overline{CS}$	Latch	Mode	Output	Power
L	H	L	H	Read selected	D_{out}	Address activated
L	H	H	H	Read selected	Open	Address activated
H	X	X	H	Chip deselected	Open	Address activated
L	L	X	H	Write address & $\overline{CS}$ latched until cycle terminated by $\overline{WE}$ ⬧ H	Open (D_{IN})	Active
—	—	—	L	Latches addresses and $\overline{CS}$ at state present when latch switched low.	See above	Standby

Available at speeds as low as 55 ns max, the 4801 is the first high-speed, byte-oriented memory chip. Two important applications for this high-density 1-k × 8 RAM are cache and read/write microprogram memory for efficient emulation of different instruction sets with a bit-slice μP. Both applications require fast read cycles, while caches need a fast write cycle as well. Typically, the depth of these memories is shallow, less than 16-k, with words that can be 72 to 100 bits wide. For these applications, the by-8 organization makes the 4801 ideal.

Consider $\overline{CS}$. There has lately been much interest in using this pin to power-down the chip on by-1 memory parts. This is done in Intel's 2147 4-k × 1 but only by making $\overline{CS}$ delay similar to t_{AA}.

On the 4801, $\overline{CS}$ gates the outputs only and inhibits write when disabled. Since $\overline{CS}$ delay is just 30% of t_{AA}, memory depth can be expanded incrementally from 1-k up without the additional delay of a decoder to allow memory expansion. Further $\overline{OE}$ is provided to assure that three-state can be used rather than open collector and to resolve the problem of two chips being on simultaneously.

In the write mode, addresses and $\overline{CS}$ are automatically latched on the selected chip when R/$\overline{W}$ goes high, which avoids the early write of a previously selected cell when entering a write cycle. On a typical static part, every address bit must settle and write before any bit change. But autolatch on the 4801 chip can substantially improve skew sensitivity of write timing relative to address. Further, the addresses are internally held after R/$\overline{W}$ goes high for as long as the chip needs to complete the write cycle.

Meanwhile, the addresses on the bus may be changed in preparation for the next read or write cycle. This also relieves the address-to-write skew on the trailing edge of write.

Loading on the address lines is significantly im-

state RAMs are used to replace separate I/O, open drain/collector products. But these are painlessly resolved by correctly using $\overline{OE}$, the latch input, or both. But even without $\overline{OE}$, and even when RAMs with access times of 50 and 90 ns are used in parallel, bus conflicts are resolved on-chip. During read accesses, the outputs of the 4801 are first opened at 30% of T_{AA} and closed later in the cycle. Similarly, the t_{ON} time transition of $\overline{CS}$ is slower than t_{OFF} ($\overline{CS}$). Holding the R/W pin low for a write cycle unconditionally opens outputs in 20 ns.

The 4801 can be used with popular minicomputers that time-multiplex the address and data by having the latch input trap addresses and $\overline{CS}$. Data inputs are trapped on the rise of R/$\overline{W}$ during a write cycle.

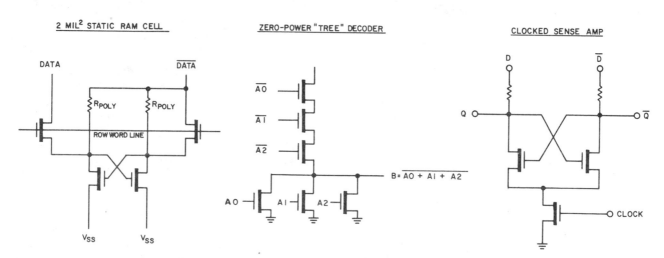

5. **The MK4801 static RAM's 55-ns access time** is the result of streamlined circuits. The basic RAM cell (left) uses four transistors and two polysilicon resistors instead of the conventional six-transistor circuit. Three decoders (center) use only leakage current, regardless of chip activity. The linear differential sense amplifier (right), based on high-speed ECL practice, gets strobed whenever the addresses change.

proved by replacing eight 93415s with one 4801 or 4118. This also improves board density 4-to-1 (since the 4801 is in a 24-pin package) and pin count by 5-to-1.

The 4118 is slower than the 4801, but it's also more economical. It has the same pinout and operates in the same modes. The differences stem from the process technologies that are used to manufacture the two devices.

Since the 4801 is intended for high-speed, high-performance applications, it is offered in 50, 75, and 90-ns speed selections and is manufactured using Mostek's new "Scaled Poly 5"™ technology, which will eventually reduce chip size to approximately 14,000 mil^2. The 4118, on the other hand, will be run

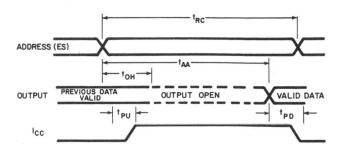

6. The 4801/4118 byte-wide static RAM's three-state outputs have a definite "output open" period during a read cycle—which eliminates bus contention when two chips are accessed successively. Current drops as cycle ends.

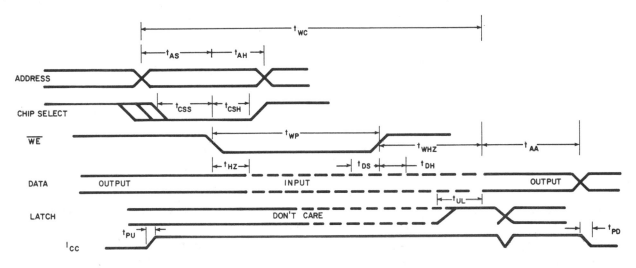

7. The write-cycle timing of the 4801/4118 8-k static uses the fall of $\overline{WE}$ to clock the addresses and the $\overline{CS}$ status into on-chip storage latches. For the rest of the write pulse, external addresses may change without affecting the write operation—a valuable feature when the RAM is used with multiplexed buses.

on Mostek's standard N-channel silicon gate production line and is intended for μP applications calling for 10% power-supply tolerance, TTL compatibility, density, low cost, and easy interface. Its access/cycle times are 120, 150, 200, and 250 ns.

Future trends

Obviously, if history means anything, the trend toward higher density will continue—2-k × 8 statics are under way and 16-k × 1 are planned. These new static RAMs will eventually have to go to a 28-pin package, at least.

Dynamic byte-wide RAMs should also start proliferating. Since this market is geared to reducing space and cost, the dynamic, byte-wide trend may move into any of several directions. On one hand, semiconductor vendors are heavily involved in designing 64-k × 1 dynamic RAMs. On the other hand, it is reasonable to expect that a family of devices will also emerge, organized as 4-k × 8 and 8-k × 8.

However, with rock-bottom cost and space weighing in more heavily than specific implementations, several vendors are considering clocked static RAMs with multiplexed data and address, which will reduce pin count considerably for specialized applications. With a multiplexing scheme, 1-k × 8 of RAM could be in a 300-mil wide, 18-pin package.

Clocked multiplexed RAMs can be implemented two ways. One is to multiplex the eight outputs onto eight of the 10 address pins using two clock cycles—one for address and the second for data. But unless the data are unmultiplexed and remultiplexed off-chip to achieve 16 bits of address and data, data width will be limited to 8 bits.

A better alternative is to multiplex eight bits of address, followed by eight more bits of address, and then multiplex eight data bits onto the same 8-bit bus, using hard-wire select to choose a given package. This method requires three clock cycles for eight data bits or four cycles for 16 data bits.

This latter concept, used successfully at the 4-bit level on the Intel 4004 μP, can result in a very low-cost minimum-pin-count byte-wide memory with the best packing density. The most severe limitation (because of the number of clock cycles) would be lowered data bandwidth, but the success of multiplexed 16-pin dynamic RAMs and the demands for lower costs will outweigh this drawback.■■

Pseudostatic RAM Offers Dynamic Density

FRED JONES
Product Line Manager, MPD,
Mostek, Carrollton, Texas

Tired of the trouble it takes to refresh dynamic RAM but still want dynamic density? Pseudostatic RAMs offer a way out. They fill the gap between static and dynamic RAM by combining dynamic cells with on-chip logic, refresh and interface circuits.

Above all, they are easy to work with. To appreciate how easy, examine the read, write, and refresh cycles of a typical pseudostatic RAM like the MK 4816 and how easily it interfaces with the Z80, 8085 and 6800 microprocessors. Then see how byte-wide architecture simplifies designing with the pseudostatic.

Although static and dynamic memories both have read and write cycles, dynamic RAM requires a periodic cell-refresh cycle to replenish decaying electrical charge and thus ensure data retention. In dynamic-RAM systems, this means that periodically the MPU provides the memory with both an address and a refresh signal, or special circuitry must be added to accomplish the refresh function. With some dynamics, refresh has to occur 256 times every 4 ms, in others 128 times every 2 ms. Either way, the system is burdened with extra processing overhead. What's more, systems with battery backup or extended DMA operation need to generate refresh while the computer is idle. Not so with pseudostatics working in memory systems. Not only do pseudostatics simplify refreshing, they simplify power-down and battery backup operations.

Refreshing addition

For example, the 4816 uses one-transistor storage cells and requires 128 refresh cycles every 2 ms. However, a special on-chip refresh circuit, controlled by pin 1 ($\overline{\text{RFSH}}$), executes the required refresh cycles internally, which eliminates off-chip generation of refresh addresses.

This system-oriented design feature also minimizes the number of required off-chip support circuits. In many applications, the one-chip refresh makes the part appear totally static to the user—hence, the term "pseudostatic RAM."

There are three ways to use the on-chip refresh (Fig. 1a). One way is to strobe $\overline{\text{RFSH}}$ active low for a minimum of T_{RD1} during device standby, which causes an internal refresh cycle to execute immediately. This way the MPU need only ensure that 128 cycles of refresh occur every 2 ms.

Another way is to pull $\overline{\text{RFSH}}$ low a short time (t_{CSR}) after the falling edge of the chip-enable signal ($_{CE}$), which initiates an active cycle (Fig. 1b). This cues the on-chip refresh circuitry for a latched refresh cycle, which occurs automatically after the current active cycle is completed.

A third alternative conveniently maintains data during power-down or μP single-step operation when memory isn't being accessed. Holding $\overline{\text{RFSH}}$ active low for more than 20 μs (Fig. 1c) initiates this mode, called auto-refresh. Thereafter, the RAM automatically initiates a single refresh cycle nominally every 15 μs. The mode is terminated automatically when $\overline{\text{RFSH}}$ goes high. During the auto-refresh period, all of the inputs of the random-access memory, except for the refresh, are inhibited.

A read cycle is initiated by the high-to-low transition of $\overline{\text{CE}}$. At the activating transition of $\overline{\text{CE}}$, the addresses and the status of chip select (CS) are latched on a chip. (Fig. 1c shows read-cycle timing relationships.) The short setup and hold times of the on-chip latches permit easy interfacing to μP systems. Write Enable ($\overline{\text{WE}}$) isn't latched on-chip and must stay high (in active) while $\overline{\text{CE}}$ is low (active during the read cycle).

The 8-bit word specified by the address field will be available at the data I/O buffers at the $\overline{\text{CE}}$ access time. The output-data buffers are enabled or disabled by Output Enable ($\overline{\text{OE}}$), a signal that eliminates problems of devices with common data I/O in three-state environments. (Note that $\overline{\text{CE}}$ going inactive also disables the output data buffers.)

Two endings

An active read cycle is completed when fetched data are read from the I/O buffer or when $\overline{\text{CE}}$ goes inactive. The end of a read cycle initiates an automatic precharge, which shortens chip-enable precharge time, T_p, to approximately one-fifth that of the $\overline{\text{CE}}$ access time.

A write cycle is also initiated by $\overline{\text{CE}}$'s falling edge,

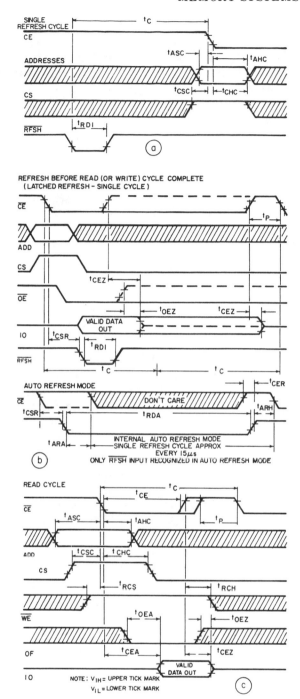

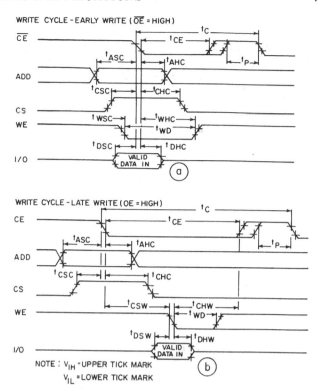

2. When a write enable (WE) occurs in relation to a chip enable (CE) determines if an early (a) or late (b) write occurs in a pseudostatic RAM.

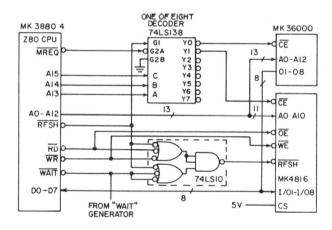

3. Interfacing dynamic RAM to a Z80 is simple since the MPU generates its own refresh level—and even simpler with pseudostatics because the RAM needs no address from the MPU.

1. An MPU can refresh pseudostatic RAM one of three ways: by periodically generating RFSH (a); by using the RAM's automatic refresh circuit-on-chip when RFSH is latched on-chip; and by automatically refreshing when RFSH is held low (b). For read operations, all qualifying levels and addresses are latched on-chip (c).

with the falling edge of WE relative to that of CE determining whether an early or a late write cycle is executed (Figs. 2a and b). During the entire write cycle, the output-enable signal stays high (false) to prevent bus contention on the common I/O port.

Like the read cycle, the write cycle must end before the automatic precharge occurs. Pulling the WE control line low or pulling CE high completes a write cycle.

During such a cycle, WE control going low latches input data and address on-chip, which eliminates the need for additional off-chip registers. With the late-write cycle, including on-chip address, data, and CS latches permits direct interfacing to processor systems with common address/data-I/O buses.

Bringing these pseudostatic cycles into the real world is very simple. For example, all it takes to interface the 4816 to a Z80 are a decoder and a 74LS10 three-input NAND gate, since the Z80 provides the necessary timing and address signals required for refresh (Fig. 3).

With dynamic RAMs, transparent refresh occurs during the second half of the Z80 op-code fetch cycle, T_3 and T_4. In this period, the MPU issues a 7-bit refresh address on the address bus's least significant bits and a refresh strobe indicating that a refresh cycle can occur. If the refresh address is to be used during refreshing, the MPU's memory-request signal ($\overline{MREQ}$) must activate the refresh cycle. Only during this signal are refresh addresses guaranteed to be stable.

The 4816 also uses the Z80-generated refresh timing signal. But since it has its own on-chip refresh counter, it does not need the μP-generated refresh address. Thus, a memory-refresh cycle is activated by $\overline{RFSH}$ alone, without the conditional gating, with memory request ($\overline{MREQ}$) needed with conventional dynamic RAMs.

Birth of a byte-wide family

The MK 4816 is the first of the Micro Memories, a coming family of byte-wide memory components from Mostek. With byte-wide organization for easy interfacing with microprocessors, the family uses the industry-standard 28-pin package for ROM, EPROM and now RAM products. This compatibility permits mixing different memory types in a common memory array using the same socket locations and peripherals. It also allows the designer to verify system firmware with low-cost RAM before committing to the less flexible EPROM or unalterable masked ROM.

The 4816's 28-pin package permits expansion to high densities, where pins 2 and 23 can address 8 k × 8 of memory. In addition, the family's pinout permits the designer to use one socket location for memory increments of 1 k through 8 k.

Coming after the 4816 will be two 1-k × 8 versions, the MK 4808 and MK 4809. Larger versions—4-k × 8 and 8-k × 8 will be forthcoming.

The table below shows the number of chips and board real estate required for an 8 k by 8 memory array. Compared to fully-static RAM, these parts result in considerable board space savings.

RAM board areas

Pins	Type	Chips required	Board area required*
28	4816 (2-k × 8)	4	5.4 sq in.
18	2114 (1-k × 4)	16	9.12 sq in.
24	8308/4118 (1-k × 8)	8	9.92 sq in.

*Includes minimum space for decoupling.

To exploit the 4816's on-chip refresh capability, the 74LS10 gates maintain data by entering the auto-refresh mode when the MPU halts or enters a wait state. Holding $\overline{RFSH}$ low keeps the auto-refresh mode active on the RAM. This interface allows the RAM to be used during the MPU's single-step mode by initiating an auto-refresh mode between the instruction executions.

Auto-refresh also permits operation in a power-down battery-backup mode. When a power failure is detected, the MPU's wait line can be pulled low, causing the RAM to enter auto-refresh. All inputs of the 4816 except refresh are inhibited; therefore, the MPU and associated logic power can be powered down as long as $\overline{RFSH}$ stays low and the 4816's supply remains within the allowable limits. If single-step capability or power-down backup is not required, the 74510 logic can be removed and the refresh output signal from the Z80 can be connected directly to the refresh input of the MK 4816.

The Z80/4816 combination allows easy, transparent DMA by stealing refresh cycles, since memory-data retention does not depend on MPU-generated refresh addresses. During an M_1 cycle, an arbitrator can decide if a refresh cycle or DMA should occur during the MPU's T states, which are reserved for transparent refresh. In addition, the arbitrator must guarantee a minimum 128-cycle memory refresh every 2 ms. All CPU-generated refresh cycles not needed for memory refresh are available for DMA.

Interfacing to an 8085 μP is no more difficult for the 4816, but extremely difficult for a conventional dynamic RAM. The problem is, the 8085 provides neither refresh addresses nor a timing signal to initiate a refresh cycle.

However, it does provide status bits that can be used to determine when to refresh. Status bits S_0 and S_1, when high, indicate an op-code fetch. With this status information and the 8085-generated $\overline{RD}$ signal, transparent refreshing can occur in the second half of the op-code fetch cycle.

Fig. 4 shows the logic to accomplish transparent refresh using the 4816 after each op-code fetch. The 74LS00 NAND gate decodes the status bits and generates the refresh signal. Although the refresh scheme appears functionally identical to the method used with the Z80, significant differences exist. With the Z80, the refresh signal is issued to the 4816 after the chip-enable signal goes high (false). With the 8085, the refresh signal is issued during an active fetch cycle, which causes the 4816 to execute a latched refresh cycle.

Although the 8085 has a multiplexed address and data I/O bus, the 4816 can be connected to most such multiplexed buses without additional latches or registers. In this configuration, the falling edge of $\overline{CE}$ causes the RAM to latch addresses and $\overline{CS}$ status. With the 4816's late-write feature, the falling edge of the $\overline{WE}$ strobe causes the RAM to latch the data. To use

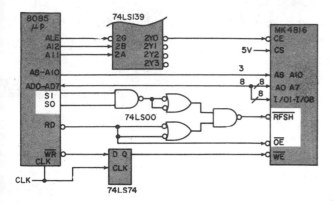

4. **Simplify pseudostatic refreshing** by using status from the 8085's pins S_1 and S_0 to determine when the MPU is not accessing memory.

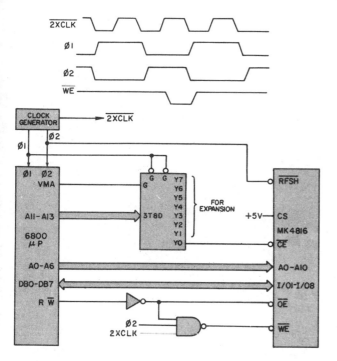

5. **The most common dynamic RAM refresh** with the 6800 microprocessor uses a hidden refresh during phase 1 of the MPU clock cycle.

the late-write cycle, data must be valid during $\overline{WE}$'s high-to-low transition.

Data set-up and hold times of memory during late write are referenced to the falling edge of $\overline{WE}$, a characteristic of low-power edge-activated devices like the 4816. Since the 8085 specifies the input data set-up and hold times relative to the rising edge of $\overline{WR}$, a single D flip-flop generates $\overline{WE}$ for the 4816 from the 8085 $\overline{WR}$ strobe and provides proper timing.

Unlike the Z80 or 8085, the 6800 does not provide refresh-timing strobes, status information, or refresh addresses. But it can refresh a dynamic RAM. The most common way is to use a hidden refresh during phase 1 of the CPU clock cycle, leaving phase 2 for CPU read or write cycles. However, with conventional

dynamic RAMs, this method could require clock stretching to increase the effective clock cycle.

Several 4816 features minimize problems associated with squeezing a refresh cycle into the phase-1 time slot. For one thing, the RAM requires no added circuits to multiplex the refresh addresses onto the memory-address bus. This is because the RAM has an on-chip refresh counter and ignores external addresses during a $\overline{RFSH}$-stimulated refresh. For another, the memory's separate refresh strobe, which has noncritical timing requirements, eliminates the need to $\overline{OR}$ a refresh clock with the chip-enable signal. What's more, the 4816's automatic precharge mode requires less critical clock precharge timing. Finally, using nonmultiplexed addresses, in an application where low-power and low-speed address drivers are common, gives faster apparent access times.

Fig. 5 shows how the 4816 interfaces to the 6800 microprocessor. The circuit causes a refresh cycle every phase 1. A counter can be used to divide the phase-2 clock, so that the refresh signal occurs less frequently. Input data from the 6800 are valid late during phase 2. The three-input NAND gate generates a write enable from the MPU read/write control line.

Byte-wide advantages

Besides interfacing easily with a variety of different —even 16-bit—μPs, the 4816 offers several design advantages which permits most of the interconnects to be bused horizontally across the array. That's because in a typical system layout, the chip-enable decoding is the only signal that does not run horizontally through the array. The signal pinout produces a clustering of common signals, which is ideal for interfacing to bus-oriented microprocessors. In addition, the critical control signals will invariably be located at the top of the array, the addresses down the middle, and the data I/O at the bottom. bottom.

In addition, the 4816 readily lends itself to designing with two-sided printed-circuit boards, with a power-distribution scheme that offers several advantages:

■ A heavy ground (V_{ss}) path under the IC provides a low inductive path between the RAM and its decoupling capacitors.

■ A low ground impedance reduces induced noise.

■ A heavy horizontal ground path minimizes ground offset between memory drivers and memory chips.

■ A heavy ground under the signal lines results in a constant impedance transmission line for signals transversing the array. This makes terminating techniques effective.

■ Proper signal-to-ground spacing reduces intersignal crosstalk.

Careful attention to power buses can reduce noise within the array and maximize signal-noise margins. However, otherwise satisfactory bus schemes do not eliminate the need for decoupling capacitors within the memory array—edge-activated RAMs still require a high current for very short intervals. Still, with most typical layouts, a 0.1-μF high-frequency ceramic capacitor for every two 4816s is sufficient. However, decoupling every device is recommended when practical. ■■

SECTION IV

ROMs, PROMs, and UV EPROMs: The Permanent Memories

In just the last 5 years, the number of PROMs has increased from about 60 available types from about a dozen manufacturers to well over 250 devices made by almost two dozen vendors. Along with the growth of the PROM selection, new devices, such as the UV EPROM and the EEPROM have been added to the list of available devices from which to choose.

With the addition of so many new devices in a short time, there are many differences in device pinouts and performance. The reports in this section cover the latest developments in the ROM and PROM area and also delve into some of the evaluation problems faced when trying to establish a new device's reliability.

Just where is the state of the art? Well, for bipolar PROMs, densities are at the 16-kbit level for commercial units with access times in the 70 to 90 ns range. UV PROMs are just reaching the 64-kbit level, and samples became available in late 1979. The EEPROMs are just starting to make some waves, with some 16-kbit devices unveiled in late 1979.

Each of these device types services a particular market area, since the general device performance is drastically different from family to family. For instance, bipolar PROMs tend to go into the high-speed applications, since they have access times well below 100 ns. The UV EPROMs and EEPROMs have access times in the 250 to 500 ns range and are well suited for microprocessor-based systems. For applications in which the PROM will have to be reprogrammed but can be removed from the board first, the UV EPROM is quite suitable. However, if the data must be updated, say on an hourly or daily basis, the EEPROM would be well suited for the application.

ROMs and PROMs Are Moving, Part 1

DAVE BARNES
Western Editor,
Electronic Design

Eventually, ROMs will be pin-compatible with EPROMs, and both will be functionally compatible with all the leading microprocessors. But right now, a number of key parameters—density, speed, pinout compatibility, single-vs-multipulse programming, microprocessor compatibility and power—are still being handled differently enough to produce dissimilar ROMs and EPROMs.

Density, for one, is a real mixed bag. While some 32-k and 64-k ROMs have been announced, 8-k and 16-k ROMs remain the workhorses. Meanwhile, both Texas Instruments and Intel have announced 32-k EPROMs, which are being second-sourced. And several companies are even planning ROMs to 128-k and EPROMs to 64-k, at least. But the 8-k 2708 is still the industry mainstay, with two different versions of the 16-k 2716—one 2708-compatible, the other not—vying for sockets.

As for speed, MOS memory for MOS microprocessors should have access times and cycle times near 500 ns. But Intel's 32-k and 64-k MOS entries will have 300-ns access time and 400-ns cycle times, while Signetics is offering a 32-k ROM with 450-ns access time. VMOS versions from Mostek Corp. will be aimed at 200-ns access and below.

Pinout compatibility is going two ways. Most designs progress from a breadboard stage using EPROMs to a final masked-ROM version. But sometimes memory needs grow. So, two kinds of pin compatibility are being worked into today's changing ROM/EPROM families. The first allows ROM to replace EPROM in the same socket. The second allows one or more doublings (in the range of from 8-k to 64-k) of either kind of storage in the same socket. The user makes virtually no PC-board changes and merely plugs in a higher-density memory DIP.

EPROM/ROM COMPATIBLE FAMILY

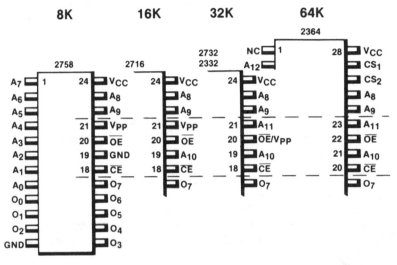

In the pinout scheme adopted by Intel, minimal jumpering allows interchange of ROMs and EPROMs of four different sizes, in the same 28-pin socket. Chips from 8-k to 64-k have the same pinouts except for pins 19, 20 and 21.

Single-pulse programming is starting to replace older approaches. Programming for Intel's 2708 8-k EPROM and earlier chips involves many trips through all addresses, with the whole chip being programmed at once. But now the 8-k 2758 and 16-k 2716 and larger EPROMs can be left erased, and can be programmed a word at a time in the field, even in the system. And repetitive high-voltage pulsing has given way to a single TTL-level pulse.

Microprocessor compatibility must take into account the fact that since many new microprocessors multiplex both addresses and data onto the same bus, memories must spend fewer nanoseconds outputting data onto the bus. The time can be cut by using a separate output-enable command to connect the ROM or EPROM output briefly to the bus when the output data are stable.

Intel has this feature in its 8-k device, and plans to have it in devices up to 64-k. But some ROMs, because their makers didn't see the multiplexed bus coming, have no such provision, so they'll have to be modified.

With multiplexed buses, especially, addresses need to be clocked into the on-chip latches at the correct nanosecond, so dynamic I/O circuits that propagate the clocking are a natural step.

The 2708, 2716 and smaller EPROMs are fully static, but newer chips, like the Intel 2732 and 2764 are dynamic, or edge-activated.

Power seems to be heading toward the day when all memory will work from a single 5-V supply, and accept 10% variations in that voltage. But that day will be a while in coming. Intel's 16-k 2716 fits these criteria, and the company's 2758 makes a single-supply version of the 8-k 2708 available. But TI has introduced a three-supply 16-k

Refresh your memory

ROMs and EPROMs are non-volatile memories: They retain data perfectly without dc power being applied to the chip.

Unlike RAMs, they never need clocking or refreshing to keep their data alive though some use clocked peripheral circuits to save power. Many field-programmable or reprogrammable ROM types have been developed though they can never be programmed as easily as RAMs.

■ ROMs. With their data contents determined by metal masks applied during chip fabrication, masked ROMs are programmed once and for all, and simply can't be reprogrammed. Generally the least ex-pensive type (once the data or program contents have been finalized and quantity lots of ROMs can be fabricated), they come in both MOS and bipolar types. The bipolar ROMs offer more speed, but recent MOS ROMs have the edge in density (bits per chip) and cost.

■ PROMs. Also available in MOS and bipolar, PROMs depend on fusible links being blown to store data. The basic fuse material in the early PROMs was nichrome, but new materials reportedly feature easier programming and/or better guarantees against fuses growing back together during use.

To program the data contents of either a PROM or an EPROM yourself, you may have to spend $1500 to $4500 for a PROM programmer.

■ EPROMs. These devices store data bits in charges rather than in metal pathways. But like PROMs, EPROMs can usually be erased with a 20-minute dose of ultraviolet light, then reprogrammed with high voltages, like PROMs.

■ EAROMs. Unlike EPROMs, they don't have to be removed and erased, and they can be selectively erased.

Nitride EAROMs allow you to change any word and erase and reprogram only those portions of memory that require updating.

---

version of the 2708, the TMS 2716, while adding a single-supply 16-k similar to Intel's 2716—the 2516.

Power-down

Another innovation, called power-down, means that less power is consumed when the chip isn't enabled. But the TI 2516 has no power-down and a new 32-k EPROM from TI has power-down but no output enable.

While there are enough differences to keep compatibility at bay, there are also important common points. For example, byte-wide organization and 24-pin packages are popular, at least from 2-k to 32-k. Three-state outputs are also a big choice, because many memory chips can be wire-ORed.

There is even an unofficial industry standard, the widely second-sourced Intel 2708 × 8-k EPROM. Its pinout and functionality are duplicated and extended not only in other EPROMs, but in masked ROMs and bipolar PROMs as well.

The 2708 features multipulse whole-

Current and projected capabilities of semiconductor ROMs

		Read-only-memory device types				Other semiconductor memories (for comparison)	
	Characteristics	ROMs: MOS types	ROMs: bipolar types	PROMs: bipolar types	EPROMs: MOS with UV erase	RAMs: dynamic MOS	RAMs: static MOS
General characteristics	Non-volatile Field-programmable Reprogrammable Special requirements	Yes No No None	Yes No No None	Yes Yes No Programmer	Yes Yes Yes Programmer, erase lamp	No Yes Yes Refresh logic	No Yes Yes None
Today's typical specifications	Chip capacity	32 kbit	8 kbit (TTL) 1 kbit (ECL)	8 kbit	16 kbit	16 kbit	4 kbit
	Read time Write time No. of pins Power supplies	300-450 ns N/A 24 +5V	20-50 ns N/A 24 +5V	30-60 ns 50 ms/bit 24 +5V	450 ns 50 ms/bit 24 +5V	150-400 ns 150-400 ns 16 +12, +5, -5V	150-400 ns 150-400 ns 18/20 +5V
Recent advances	Chip capacity	65 kbit (sample qty.)	1 kbit (ECL at 10 ns)	16 kbit (sample qty.)	32 kbit (sample qty.)	64 kbit (to be announced)	8 kbit (available)
Probable specifications by 1980	Chip capacity	128 kbit	16 kbit	32 kbit	64 kbit	64 kbit (in production)	16 kbit (in production)

chip programming, and three supply voltages: +5, +12 and −5 V.

But interestingly, Texas Instruments—not Intel—has introduced a 16-k EPROM whose features are compatible with the 2708. Intel's 16-k, the 2716, offers a single 5-V power supply, single-pulse single-word programming, and a power-down feature to conserve power.

While the Intel 2716 is more advanced, TI's TMS 2716 needs to have just three of its 24 pins changed to replace a 2708 in the same socket, and allow memory capacity to be doubled. All timing and programming parameters stay the same. Replacing a 2708 with the Intel 2716 isn't nearly as easy or fast.

The TMS 2716 uses just 540 mW for 16 kbits, while the TMS 2708 uses 800 mW for 8 kbits. But the TMS 2716 still requires 5% tolerances on its power supplies.

Meanwhile, TI has come out with a 16-k whose functions and pins are identical to the Intel 2716—a new device called the TMS 2516.

One major distinction between Intel's 2716 and the 2708 is how they're programmed for ultraviolet erasure, to set all the bits back to ONE. Several minutes of ultraviolet lamp exposure is the only way. But while the 2708 design is completely programmed in one continuous operation, the Intel 2716 may be programmed piecemeal. That is, although erasure affects all 16,384 bits, any location may be programmed at any time either individually, sequentially, or randomly.

Programming for a single bit takes

Cutting out bus disputes

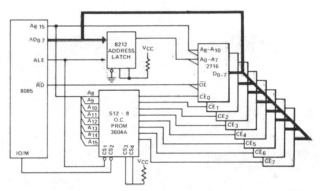

TRADITIONAL 16K EPROM SYSTEM

"CORRECT" EPROM SYSTEM

To eliminate timing overlaps and bus contention in all Intel ROMs and PROMs above 16 k, Intel has reversed the roles of the $\overline{CS}$ pin, usually used to select one of the several EPROM chips (above left) and the PD/PGM pin, usually commoned for all EPROM chips. Not only that, but those two pins have been renamed to reflect their new uses.

Pin 18, or PD/PGM (power-down/program), is now called $\overline{CE}$ (chip-enable), since putting the chip in power-down mode really disables it. Pin 20, or $\overline{CS}$ (chip select), is now called $\overline{OE}$ (output enable), and is the common strobe for all EPROMs.

The key to wiping out bus contention is to feed OE with a narrow strobe at the correct phase of the memory cycle. In the example (above right) the RD (read) signal from the 8085 does the strobe job correctly.

The timing diagrams below correspond to the two hardware versions above. The traditional decode scheme may put information on the shared bus too early, or leave it on too long, which will cause contention when two drivers pull in opposite directions on the same bus line. The two drivers almost become a short from 5 V to ground, and can send a glitch to other parts of the system. But the proper narrow OE strobe makes this impossible.

Most μPs, even those that do not multiplex data and address, make a suitable strobe signal available, asserts Intel, which advocates this new approach for all μP systems.

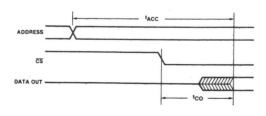

TIMING IN TRADITIONAL SYSTEM

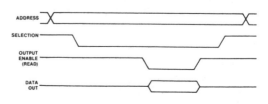

TIMING WITH "CORRECT" CONTROL

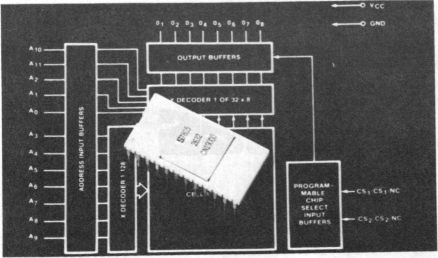

Like most new memory chips this 32-k MOS ROM from Signetics is completely TTL compatible and operates from a single 5-V supply. Access time is 450 ns.

Storing calibration offsets

The General Instrument ER1400 nitride erasable ROM stores important correction data for an unusual calibration scheme in the Series-6000 amplitude measurement system, a microprocessor-controlled digital multimeter with many computing features. It's from Racal-Dana (Irvine, CA).

All analog circuitry is located in a removable, interchangeable module (see photo). Since the rest of the instrument's circuitry is digital, and needs no calibration, the instrument may be repaired or replaced without affecting calibration.

For calibration, a standard full-scale input signal is converted to digital and combined with full-scale readings stored in RAM. The difference between the two digital values, equivalent to a shift in calibration, is then stored in the GI EAROM, which, being nonvolatile, keeps the information available. For actual readings, then, the stored data can be used as a correction factor.

The EAROM also holds zero-correction calibration information for 27 nodes within the analog section of the meter, which means changes in offset, gain, or attenuation can be corrected. In addition, limits on drift errors can be inserted by the user. The meter takes normal error into account to provide correct readings, but when the error exceeds the preset limit, it warns the operator with an error alert on a LED.

only 50 ms; for all memory bits, approximately 100 s.

The 2758, Intel's updated 8-k EPROM, takes 50 s to erase all memory bits. It has all the 2716 features: single-power supply, power-down mode, and single-word programming.

Having matched the Intel 5-V 2716 with its own TMS 2516, Texas Instruments has lost no time announcing the TMS 2532 32-k EPROM—static rather than clocked, but with a power-down feature that reduces current drain when the chip is deselected. Moreover, the TMS 4732 32-k ROM plugs directly into a TMS 2532 socket, with no board changes, so long as the second chip-select input (CS) is coded active high.

The next step for TI seems to be to expand this series in two directions—downward to match the Intel 2758 8-k part, and upward to provide a 64-k EPROM. Although no announcements have been made, many believe that 64-k parts from TI and others will appear in the next year.

Looking down the road

While digital system designers now have available a variety of high-speed 32-k and 64-k ROMs and 32-k EPROMs, they can look forward to even greater bit densities and faster access times for these device types.

Indeed, Mostek, using a high-performance 2 and 3-micron MOS process called Poly-5 has already built sample quantities of 64-k ROM chips sporting speeds in the 90-ns range, and during the next year is expected to increase this density to 128 kbits with no loss of speed. This means that designers can use these denser MOS parts in many microprogrammed system applications were fast-turnaround program management has required the faster but more expensive bipolar ROMs.

While most MOS ROM suppliers are using scaled versions of the standard n-channel silicon-gate process to reach higher densities and performances, a few manufacturers are turning to other MOS processes for next-generation devices. Most developed of these new processes is AMI's VMOS technique, which the Santa Clara-based manufacturer hopes will lead to high volume production of 64-k and 128-k parts. TI is also working on this approach. ■■

ROMs and PROMs Are Moving, Part 2

DAVE BARNES
Western Editor,
Electronic Design

Even as PROM users turn more and more to new, large MOS EPROMs for all but the fastest applications, bipolar PROMs are showing significant improvements in speed, density and function that may help them recapture many of the sockets previously lost to the MOS devices and sign the death warrant of bipolar ROMs.

For example, 4-k and 8-k bipolar PROMs from such manufacturers as Monolithic Memories (Sunnyvale, CA) are appearing with 45 to 50-ns access times. (Typical bipolars operate two to four times as fast but cost twice as much per bit as the more popular 2708 and 2716 MOS EPROMs.)

Density is also improving: 16-k PROMs are coming to market, while new functions, such as on-chip latches, registers and power-down features are appearing on new PROM chips from several manufacturers.

One major stumbling block remains to using bipolar PROMs: the lack of standardization in the fuse-blowing procedure for devices from different manufacturers. Now, at least, the procedure is being made the same throughout most device families. The JEDEC committee 42.1, formed early this year, probably won't consider industry-wide standards in programming until it has dealt with bipolar pinouts and functionality. In addition to the nichrome fuse material, there are now polysilicon, titanium-tungsten, and platinum silicide.

Meanwhile, PROMs are affecting the survival of masked bipolar ROMs. As PROM prices drop with increased production and competition among suppliers, fewer and fewer ROMs are being sold for today's equipment.

"The bipolar ROM business below 4 k is dying, and the bipolar ROM business above 8 k will never happen," says one industry expert. Another agrees:

"Today, we can actually sell PROMs cheaper. Also, you can usually find several PROM sources, while ROMs have only one source or two."

PROMs are favored over ROMs today by makers and users alike. Semiconductor maufacturers are eliminating custom-made ROMs—hence shortruns—to streamline production. For the OEM user, PROMs are a way to stock four or five types instead of 40 or 50; a way to take delivery while final programming changes are still looming; and a way to get quantity pricing by sharing part types among several different end products.

The trend away from ROMs toward PROMs is not so new, but the tradeoff point keeps moving. Two years ago, for instance, if you needed more than 2 kbits per chip and more than 2000 chips, you'd save money by using a ROM. Now it's a tossup at 8-k whatever the quantity, though at 16-k, ROM still appears more attractive for more than

2000 parts. PROMs are also increasing their popularity by including more on the chip. Both MMI and AMD (Sunnyvale, CA), with registered PROMs, and Harris (Melbourne, FL) and Signetics, with their latched PROMs, now include on the PROM chip the circuit functions that would normally follow in the next chip. If you're pipelining data for a microprocessor, you need latches or a full register on the PROM output. With the combination chips, you save half to three-quarters of the space on the PC board, and get a slight boost in speed as well.

The speed race

EPROMs are still slower than PROMs, but cost roughly 1.5 to 2.5 times less per bit. Moreover, they come in big sizes and talk well to microprocessor interfaces.

But bipolar PROMs aren't going to stand still. And surprisingly, MOS may

Bipolar PROMS

	Total Bits	No. of words	Best speeds (ns)		Signetics	MMI	Harris	Fairchild	Intel	Intersil	AMD	National	Raytheon	TI	Motorola	Fujitsu	NEC
			Schottky	Low-power (Schottky)													
8 bits wide	16k	2k	70	120	•	•	•										
	8k	1k	50	-		•	•	•	•				•	•		•	•
	4k	512	45	-		•	•	•	•	•	•	•	•	•			•
	2k	256	45	-		•	•	•					•	•			
	512	64	40	-		•	•							•			
	256	32	25	35	•	•	•				•	•	•		•		
4 bits wide	16k	4k	70	-	•	•							•				
	8k	2k	60	75	•	•	•	•							•		
	4k	1k	50	65	•	•	•	•		•	•	•	•		•	•	•
	2k	512	45	55	•	•	•	•	•	•	•	•		•	•	•	•
	1k	256	45	55	•	•	•	•			•	•	•	•	•		•

Double metal shrinks bipolar PROM cells

Combining its usual polysilicon fuse with two layers of metal instead of one has enabled Intel to make a 4096-bit PROM with a cell size of just 1.3 square mils, a total die size of 15,000 square mils, and an access time of 50 ns. The PROM is the 3605A, scheduled to reach distributor's shelves in September.

These numbers put the 3650A ahead of two current Intel PROMs: the company's original 4-k PROM, the 512 × 8 3604—2.3 sq mil bit size, 24,300-sq-mil die size, 70-ns access —and the 1-k × 4 3605—1.7 sq-mil bit size, 20,500-sq mil die sizes and 60-ns access times.

Each cell in the 3605A has its own unshared bit line and word line, both metal. The second layer of metal replaces a diffusion layer and, according to Intel, produces better control of parasitic resistances that limit the programming current.

While the availability of programming current is being eased by the metal, the uniformity of the fuse resistances is being improved by a new polysilicon doping method. As a result, says Intel, programmability and reliability are better despite the smaller cell size.

---

actually help bipolar technology stay faster. Virtually everything that's being learned in the HMOS and other MOS density-improvement efforts will transfer directly into bipolar processes. "Advances in MOS are primarily gains in photolithography, all of which apply equally well to bipolar," says Signetics' Steve Jasper, the bipolar marketing specialist who heads the JEDEC 42.1 subcommittee. "We'll be announcing a very high-density bipolar part about WESCON time that uses the same new techniques as MOS."

For even higher PROM speed, bipolar TTL may give way to ECL. Ed Bohn, bipolar memory marketing manager at National Semiconductor, Santa Clara, CA, notes that developing 512 × 8 and 1-k × 4 ECL PROMs in the 20-ns range is being seriously considered. It's not clear yet whether these chips would contain TTL translators to make them TTL-compatible, like the National 2901A-1 bit slice.

However, speed isn't everyone's concern. Signetics will be sampling a low-power Schottky version of its best-selling 1-k × 8 PROM, in the next two months. The 55% power cut from 170 mA to 80 mA, will increase access time from 70 to 175 ns in the 82LS180/181.

Low-power Schottky also figures prominently in the Monolithic Memories generic family of titanium-tungsten PROMs announced in June ("PROM Family Is Fastest and Densest," ED No. 12, June 7, 1978, p. 155).

Most sizes in the MMI will be available in a choice of high-speed Schottky (S); low-speed Schottky (LS); power-switched Schottky (PS); and registered Schottky PROMs with either asynchronous (RA) or synchronous (RS) enables for their three-state outputs.

The power-switched versions, like those from Harris and Raytheon (Mountain View, CA), cut power consumption back by 70% to 80% until the chip gets enabled.

Programming is critical

In general, manufacturers stress that when you program a PROM, you are completing the manufacturing of a semiconductor part. Be absolutely sure that the programming voltages, currents, pulse forms, and times comply with the manufacturers' recommendations. The manufacturers are eager to help with this, and will even test samples of your finished results to validate your method.

Most modern commercial PROM programmers do comply with PROM specs, and increasingly intelligent PC modules are emerging that permit older PROM programmers to deal correctly with the new programming methods. They also help handle the newer parts, like PALs (programmable array logic), FPLAs (field-programmable logic arrays), and FPGAs (field-programmable gate arrays).

Various new nonnichrome fuses have come into use in the past few years, and claims have been made that each new one is better. However, several industry experts point out that all are adequate, provided that exact compliance with the maker's programming specs is rigidly enforced.

"Fuse problems were just about licked three years ago, if you programmed the PROM right;" that's the consensus of many users. Makers of PROM programmers agree, adding that one useful trick is to have two verify voltages, like 4.8 and 5.8, to test adequately for a clean blow.

The fuse-link method of programming developed for the PROM is used also in such related logic devices as FPLAs, FPGAs and PALs. Still another "cousin" of the PROM is due from Signetics in the fourth quarter of 1978. Called a logic sequencer, it's a modulo-64 state machine right out of the textbooks. With 16 inputs to AND/OR gating, 8 outputs to a register plus 6 outputs fed back internally, it runs on an 11-MHz clock.

One important class of PROMs duplicates the pinouts of MOS EPROMs. Evidently, it's difficult to produce a PROM that's directly pin-compatible with the Intel 2716 MOS EPROM; so far, only Harris has one.

However, the 2708 pinout is available in bipolar PROM from Harris, MMI, Signetics, Fujitsu, NEC, Motorola, TI and Raytheon.

For that matter, the 2708/2716 pinout may not be the most useful package for applications that surround PROMs with TTL chips. Many will prefer the "skinny dip" pioneered by MMI, a 24-pin package with only 300-mil width.

Examine a PC board filled mostly with 16-pin packages, all of which are 300 mils wide: Note how much disruption a wider package introduces, say the skinny-DIP proponents. You'll see that the ability to put PROMs in the same-width packages really can save layout work and lots of "real estate."

Why is the skinny-DIP possible now, while the world has always made 24-pin packages 600 mils wide? Because today's chips are smaller.

To fit into a skinny-DIP package, a die can't be greater than 140 mils—but it can be 280 mils long. The more experienced process engineers don't fight the skinny-DIP trend. They're more confident tackling these shapes than they were a few years ago.

As suppliers get on top of the packaging problem, still another application area is opening up where bipolar and MOS may clash.

There is a speculation that the faster new 16-bit MOS microprocessors, such as the Intel 8086 and Zilog Z8000, will need ROM fast enough to give bipolar PROMs a new market. But rumors persist that leading MOS houses are working on an "E²PROM," to fill that same need. ∎∎

Power Switch ROMs and PROMs

JERRY GRAY
Design Manager, Monolithic Memories, Inc.,
Sunnyvale, California

Most TTL-based ROMs and PROMs can be operated by applying power only when you actually want to access the information they hold. But you must take some precautions if you want to operate successfully in this mode.

Examine the power switch in Fig. 1. If the input is taken to ground either through a switch or through the output of a TTL gate, base current flows through R_1 to turn on the pnp transistor. If the input is allowed to float or be pulled high by a TTL output, resistor R_2 turns the transistor off.

When the pnp transistor turns on, the V_{CC} terminal of the ROM rises rapidly to a voltage just below that of the V_{CC} supply. The difference is determined by the V_{CE} (SAT) of the pnp transistor. When the transistor is turned off, the V_{CC} for the ROM decays to a low value (Fig. 2). Turn-on time is how long it takes for the input signal to propagate through the switch and raise V_{CC} to the 4-V level, at which most ROMs and PROMs are fully functional—even though not all the device specs may be met.

Now it's time to propagate

Once the device's V_{CC} has reached 4 V, time is required for all inputs to propagate through the device and establish the correct output state. This is true regardless of whether the inputs are stable before V_{CC} is switched on, or whether V_{CC} and the inputs are switched at the same time.

The required propagation time is approximately t_{AA}, the address-access time given in the data sheets. Typically, ROMs and PROMs reach the correct state within 20 ns of the specified t_{AA}. So the "worst-case enable time" of a power-switched device is given as follows:

$$t_{enable} = t_{on(pnp)} + t_{AA} + 20 \text{ ns.} \qquad (1)$$

Notice that the turn-off time for the power switch in Fig. 2 is specified at 1.5 V, where most TTL PROMs are "off," and their outputs floating. If V_{CC} is dropped instantly to 1.5 V, the outputs will be "off" and floating within 10 ns. The worst-case disable time is thus given by the following equation:

$$t_{disable} = t_{off(pnp)} + 10 \text{ ns.} \qquad (2)$$

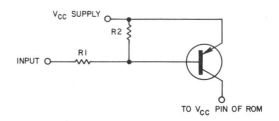

1. **ROMs and PROMs are power-switched** with a simple pnp transistor circuit in the V_{CC} line.

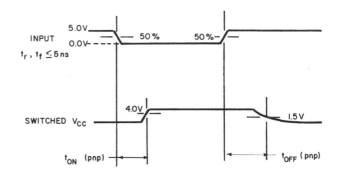

2. **The output waveform of a pnp switch** lags the input wave by t_{on} at the start, and by t_{off} at the end of the switching period.

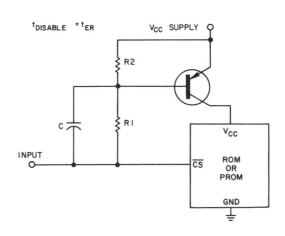

3. **Switching performance is improved** with a speed-up capacitor, and in addition by feeding the switching input to the ROM's $\overline{CS}$ pin.

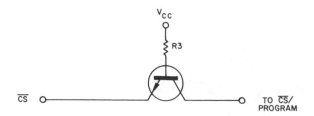

4. **PROMs require an npn transistor** at the $\overline{CS}$/Program input to avoid excessive loading of the input wave.

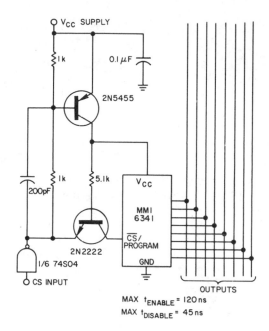

MAX t_{ENABLE} = 120 ns
MAX $t_{DISABLE}$ = 45 ns

5. **The complete schematic for a PROM switch** is developed for the 6341 PROM from Monolithic Memories.

Table 1. Suitable pnp switching transistors

No. of ROMs/PROMs	Some suitable pnp transistors
1	2N5455, 2N3467, 2N4402
2	2N3467, 2N3244
4	2N3467, 2N5023
8	2N3467

The actual disable time can be quite long because $t_{off(pnp)}$ consists of two components: the turn-off time of the pnp transistor, and the decay time for V_{CC}. Because pnp transistors with good current-handling ability often have lousy turn-off times, you must be very careful to chose the right transistor for a pnp power switch. Several recommended transistors are listed in Table 1.

The decay time for V_{CC} depends on the current, I_{CC}, of the ROM or PROM. As V_{CC} approaches 1.5 V,

I_{CC} drops very rapidly, and all or part of the current may turn on the output of the ROM. Accordingly, the $t_{off(pnp)}$ specified for the power switch may be quite high.

You can improve the performance of a pnp power switch in several ways. But two of the most effective are the following:

1. Use a speed-up capacitor in parallel with R_1 of the basic power switch in Fig. 1. This capacitor provides overdrive for turning the transistor on and off. The value should be such that the time constant, R_1C, is approximately equal to the fastest cycle time at which the power switch will be used. This technique, however, does not improve the decay time of V_{CC}.

2. Tie the input of the power switch to a $\overline{CS}$ (chip enable) input of the ROM or PROM being switched. You thereby force the outputs into the OFF state as soon as the input to the power switch goes high. This means that while V_{CC} is decaying to 1.5 V, the outputs are held off, because the $\overline{CS}$ input is high. The internal $\overline{CS}$ buffer becomes ineffective when the outputs are turned off by V_{CC}.

With this second technique, the disable time is no longer represented by Eq. 2, but rather given by the t_{ER} time specified on the ROM or PROM data sheet:

$$t_{disable} = t_{ER}. \qquad (3)$$

PROMs have special needs

What sets PROMs apart from ROMs is the fact that a $\overline{CS}$ input is also used as a programming input. The $\overline{CS}$/Program input is designed in such a way that voltages higher than V_{CC} provide the internal currents necessary to program the device. Even at 5 V, this current can be very high. Consequently, when V_{CC} is reduced by the power switch, the normal input-current spec does not apply. Instead, the $\overline{CS}$/Program input and all signals tied in parallel with it are loaded down; while you expect a logic "1," it may be a "0."

This peculiarity can cause you headaches if you choose the $\overline{CS}$/Program input in the improved switching scheme of Fig. 3. The loading of the $\overline{CS}$/Program input is normally high enough to keep the input at a low level, and the pnp transistor remains on. Sometimes the whole system oscillates.

Fortunately, the following solution is simple, and works regardless of whether the $\overline{CS}$/Program input is tied to a signal lead, or to the input of the power switch (Fig. 4): An npn transistor is used as a one-way switch to ensure that no current flows from the driver to the $\overline{CS}$/Program pin. The small delay through the npn transistor can be ignored.

Here comes the new generation

The solution shown in Fig. 4 effectively changes the $\overline{CS}$/Program input into a $\overline{CS}$-only input. But you don't necessarily have to apply this solution in the case of second or third-generation PROMs, which often have

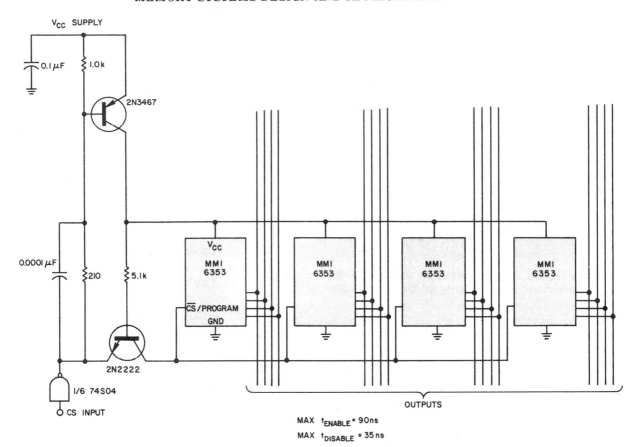

6. **This example for power-switching a PROM array** uses four MMI 6353 PROMs, for which the values of resistors and capacitors are optimized. You should get a cycle time of approximately 1 μs.

no $\overline{CS}$/Program input. If the chip-enable pin does not have to go to a high level for programming, you can be sure that the npn transistor (Fig. 4) is not needed. A small memory like the MMI 5330/31 can do without the Program input. The MMI 5380/81, a l-k $\times$ 8 bit configuration does not require the PROM solution either, because it was designed with power switching in mind: Zeners prevent the input circuit from being loaded down. If you want to power-switch PROMs, you really must know their design.

Even if your PROM turns out to be of an earlier variety, the outlined remedies work well. In Fig. 5, only one PROM is being switched with the concept described, while in Fig. 6, four PROMs are being switched. In both cases, the components give good operation in a system with a cycle time of 1 μs.

The worst-case enable time in both cases is the t_{AA} from the data sheet, plus 30 ns. The worst-case disable time is t_{ER} from the data sheet. While the 2N2222 is used in Figs. 5 and 6, other transistors with fast turn-off time—like the 2N3444, 2N4275, and 2N5134—work just as well. ■■

Stop Dropped Bits in EPROMs

JOHN E. GRIFFIN
Vice President, Turner Designs,
Mountain View, California

To get a better handle on how your EPROMs are behaving, obtain erase data with quantitative tests instead of the usual pass-fail tests. The profile you get will enable you to

- Monitor the intensity of your EPROM eraser.
- Determine or confirm thresholds of EPROM erasure from various manufacturers and lots.
- Identify EPROMs with underprogrammed or hard-to-erase bits.
- Gather quantitative data that can pinpoint failure modes.

A Go-No-Go erase verification works fine for most production EPROM programming, but only if you make an erase profile of a representative sample of each production lot to establish proper erase times and to prove satisfactory programmer performance.

Suppose you erase a 2708 EPROM for 30 minutes, put it in your PROM programmer and punch the Erase-verify button. The PROM programmer will reply with either an "erased" or an "unerased," answer. If the answer is "Unerased", you put the EPROM back into the eraser for another 10 minutes. Then you return it to the programmer and hit the Erase-verify button again, which now indicates "erased".

What have you learned? Only that one or more of the 8192 cells in the 2708 didn't erase during a 30-minute period, but did erase in 40 minutes. You *don't* know if those cells are typical. And you *don't* know if some cells erased quickly because they're underprogrammed or leaky.

Plot an erase profile

However, it's relatively easy for you to test all the memory cells completely in a representative sample of EPROMS. The test takes an EPROM—with all its bits thoroughly programmed according to the manufacturer's directions—erases it for a few minutes, then counts the number of unerased bits. The process is repeated until there are zero unerased bits.

Once you've plotted the data on a graph to get the EPROM's erase profile (Fig. 1), you can view the behavior of all 8192 bits—and make more informed decisions on the EPROM's behavior.

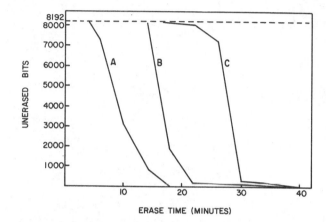

EPROM erase profiles can pinpoint behavior problems and confirm a vendor's specified thresholds. Curves for three different EPROMs show ideal erasure characteristics (A), and progressively worsening dropouts (B and C).

How do you count unerased bits? The simplest way is to let your microcomputer development system do it for you, with a program like the one in Fig. 2. This program assembles and runs on an Intel Intellec MDS-800 system. Changing just a few words will allow it to run on an Intel iSBC 80/10 or iSBC 80/20 System. There is only one external call (console out), and address-sensitive parameters are consolidated with equate statements at the start of the program.

Assuming you have an MDS-800, and Intel UPP (universal PROM programmer), and a CRT or teletypewriter, assemble the program and burn it into a 2708 EPROM. To execute the program, load it into location 0800H-0BFFH, in one of several ways. If your MDS-800 has a PROM card, you can keep the EPROM on that card and use the monitor's Move command to transfer it to 0800H. Or you can simply plug the 2708, with the program, into the UPP and use the PROM transfer command (such as TTX0800, 0BFF). The program will have to be loaded only once per session, and won't be altered by execution.

After loading the program into its execution location, see that the contents of the EPROM get transferred to 0C00H-0FFH, where the program expects to see it. All you have to do is plug the EPROM into the UPP and type in a TTX0C00, 0FFF. To execute the program, type in G800.

Less than a second later, the answer appears on your console as "NNNN Unerased Bits." You should assign and record an identification number for each EPROM, and record the number of unerased bits and the total erase dose applied to the EPROM before the readout. You should also maintain a consistent set of operating conditions when the EPROM is read into memory.

Use recommended supply voltages. And remember that the sense amplifiers of some EPROMs are light-sensitive. So for consistent data, make sure the EPROM lid is covered during readout. Don't use an adhesive tape that leaves a residue on the lid, since the residue may be opaque to UV light. Black electrical tape works fine.

EPROM erase times vary considerably, so choose an erase interval that will let you observe bits dropping out over at least four intervals. For starters, use erase intervals of five minutes for 2708s, 15 seconds for 1702s and two minutes for 2716s.

In Fig. 1, ten 2708 EPROMs from various lots and various manufacturers were erased for 2-1/2 hours, programmed to all zeros on the Intel UPP, and erased in a Turner Designs Model 30 for the intervals shown. A straight-line lamp and a parts tray that slides on a rail ensure a constant dose from one erase interval to the next.

Note the different shapes of the three curves, chosen to represent the sample of 10. Curve A describes an EPROM that behaves the way you'd like. Once the first bits erase, the bulk of the remaining bits follow quickly.

Curve B gets off to a great start, but then—a sharp dive. It takes just seven minutes to erase all but eight bits. But it takes another 12 minutes to erase the last eight bits. That could lead to trouble.

Curve C shows an EPROM that drops about 64 bits after 20 minutes. The majority of bits erase only after seven additional minutes of erase. If you're having data-retention problems, watch those bits dropping out earlier than the norm. Looking at the end of curve C, you see that about 200 bits did not begin to erase until after 29 minutes. After 41 minutes, all bits are erased.

Using the data

One quick benefit of the erase-profile curve is that you can use it to monitor the intensity of your erase light—not only the reduction in light as the lamp ages, but also the light's uniformity over the entire active area. If you're thinking of using a UV light meter to monitor your erase light, bear in mind that off-the-shelf meters are hard to apply to such measurements. Meters under $1000 usually use filters over the sensors, and the filters can become opaque when exposed. Consequently, readings can drop 50% or more after a half hour's exposure.

More expensive meters come with more stable interference filters to limit sensitivity to 2537-Å

mercury resonance, which erases the EPROMs. Unfortunately, the wavelength of light passed by interference filters varies sharply with the angle of light. Light at 30° to the normal will erase your EPROMs just fine, but will just barely get through an interference filter. The solution: Take a few prime EPROMs, number them, and plot curves of erased bits vs erase time. You can repeat the tests later.

The materials currently found in EPROM lids are far more stable when exposed to ultraviolet light. The lowest-grade materials show less than a 10% drop in transmission after extended exposure, not even close to the 50% or more for meter filters. What's more, both distance-to-lamp and light-acceptance angle are identical for the test EPROM and your production parts.

The erase time required for a properly programmed EPROM depends entirely on the total dosage of UV light. Thus, the erase profile of your test EPROM becomes the most accurate check on the efficiency of your eraser.

What's the right dose?

Published specifications exist for proper erase doses; erasers are rated in $\mu W/cm^2$ of available energy. However, when a quality-control problem crops up, the first concern that comes to mind is whether you're erasing long enough. Everyone has seen product changes occur after data sheets are printed, and everyone has encountered subtle effects that can adversely affect erase time—lamp aging and dirt on the lid, for two. Rather than guess at the correct dose for a specific lot of parts, measure it independently of the characteristics of the EPROM and the eraser.

For a given lot of EPROMs and a given eraser, all you'll need are the erase profile and a glance at your watch.

From profile curves, the threshold of erase is the time required to erase the last (worst-case) bit. But before you believe that number, look at the shape of the curves—for all the EPROMs. Are the curves smooth and consistent from part to part? If so, you can trust the numbers. The correct dose includes a safety factor in the erase threshold.

If you're going to plug the EPROMs into your development system for just a few days and reprogram them, a safety factor of two is adequate. Install the EPROM in a life-support instrument, and a factor of five is appropriate.

If the plotted curves aren't uniform, you'll have a hard time determining the correct dose. If one EPROM out of 10 needs a threshold significantly longer than the others, see if that EPROM comes from a different manufacturer—not all EPROMs of the same type are manufactured by the same process.

If all your EPROMs come from one manufacturer and one lot, check how long it takes to erase the last few bits. In critical applications, you may wish to run a profile on *all* parts.

```
;START THE CODE
;(MDS-800 VERSION)

EXIT    EQU     0FF0FH  ;YOUR MONITOR RE-ENTRY POINT
                        ;USE 0008H FOR SBC 80/10 OR SBC 80/20
START   EQU     0800H   ;WHERE THIS PROGRAM RESIDES
DATAH   EQU     0CH     ;WHERE PROM UNDER TEST RESIDES
CO      EQU     0F809H  ;CONSOLE OUT: ASCII CHAR IS PASSED IN C REG
                        ;01E6H FOR SBC80/10; 000FH FOR SBC 80/20
RAM     EQU     03D00H  ;5 BYTE SCRATCH PAD. LOCATE ANYWHERE
LAST    EQU     04H     ;01H FOR 1702, 08H FOR 2716
        ORG     START

BEGIN:  MVI     H,DATAH ;LOWEST PROM ADDRESS
        MVI     L,0H
        LXI     D,0H    ;D,E ACCUMULATE UNERASED BITS (BINARY)

NEXT:   MVI     B,08H   ;INITIALIZE BIT COUNTER
        MOV     A,M     ;FETCH BYTE FROM PROM
        PUSH    PSW     ;SAVE IT

AGAIN:  MOV     A,B     ;GET BIT COUNT
        CPI     00H     ;ZERO WHEN 8 BITS ARE SHIFTED
        JZ      NXTADD  ;GET NEXT PROM WORD
        POP     PSW     ;OTHERWISE GET A BACK
        RRC             ;ROTATE IT INTO THE CARRY
        PUSH    PSW     ;SAVE IT
        JNC     AGAIN1  ;BIT WAS A ZERO. USE JC FOR 1702 TYPES (ERASED BIT=0)
        INX     D       ;BIT WAS A ONE. ADD ONE TO D,E

AGAIN1: DCR     B       ;DECREMENT THE BIT COUNTER
        JMP     AGAIN   ;TRY FOR THE NEXT BIT

NXTADD: POP     PSW     ;STACK ADJUST ONLY
        INX     H       ;ADDR OF NEXT PROM WORD
        MOV     A,L     ;INTO A FOR TEST
        CPI     00H     ;IF L WAS ZERO, CHECK H
        JNZ     NEXT    ;IF NOT, CONTINUE
        MOV     A,H     ;GET H INTO A
        CPI     DATAH+LAST;HL=DATAH+03FFH+1 WHEN DONE (2708)
        JNZ     NEXT    ;MORE BITS TO COUNT
        LXI     H,RAM   ;FINISHED! H,L POINTS TO SCRATCH PAD
        CALL    BNBCD   ;BINARY TO BCD CONVERSION

        JMP     FINISH  ;PRINT THE RESULTS


BNBCD:  PUSH    PSW     ;SAVE VARIABLES
        PUSH    B
        PUSH    D
        PUSH    H
        XCHG            ;GET NUMBER IN HL, ADDR IN DE
        LXI     B,-10000
        CALL    DECNO   ;GET MSD
        LXI     B,-1000
        CALL    DECNO
        LXI     B,-100
        CALL    DECNO
        LXI     B,-10
        CALL    DECNO
        MOV     A,L     ;GET LSD
        ORI     030H    ;MASK FOR ASCII
        STAX    D       ;STORE IT
        POP     H
        POP     D
        POP     B
        POP     PSW
        RET

DECNO:  MVI     A,30H   ;30H TO A
        PUSH    D       ;SAVE ADDR
        MOV     E,L     ;SAVE BINARY
        MOV     D,H
        INR     A       ;INCREMENT DIGIT
        DAD     B       ;SUBTRACT
        JC      DECNO+3 ;RESULT NEGATIVE?
        DCR     A       ;YES, RESTORE DIGIT COUNT
        MOV     L,E     ;BINARY NUMBER
        MOV     H,D
        POP     D       ;AND ADDRESS
        STAX    D       ;STORE DIGIT
        INX     D       ;INCREMENT POINTER
        RET

FINISH: LXI     H,RAM   ;POINT TO DECIMAL RESULT MSD
        MVI     A,05H   ;NUMBER OF BYTES IN RESULT
        CALL    PRMSG   ;PRINT MESSAGE ROUTINE
        LXI     H,TEXT  ;POINT TO TEXT
        MVI     A,40    ;NUMBER OF BYTES IN TEXT
        CALL    PRMSG   ;PRINT IT
        JMP     EXIT    ;RETURN TO YOUR SYSTEM MONITOR

PRMSG:  ORA     A       ;TEST A=0
        RZ              ;A=0 WHEN DONE
        DCR     A       ;DECREMENT NUMBER OF BYTES REMAINING
        PUSH    PSW     ;SAVE A
        MOV     C,M     ;CHAR INTO C
        CALL    CO      ;YOUR CO ROUTINE DOES THE WORK
        POP     PSW     ;GET A BACK
        INX     H       ;POINT TO NEXT CHARACTER
        JMP     PRMSG   ;TRY FOR MORE

TEXT:   DB      ' UNERASED BITS
        END
```

A program to run an unerased-bits profile on EPROMs can be assembled and run on a µC development system, like the Intel MDS-800. Written in 8080 assembly language, the program calculates and prints out the number of unerased bits left after various erase intervals.

If the last few bits seem stubborn, you may have learned something. Naturally, not all 8192 cells in a 2708 EPROM have the same characteristics. Both erase and programming times may differ. However, if the part is good, and the programming performs to spec, a normal statistical pattern will describe the differences.

The pattern shapes the EPROM erase-profile curve. A few bits erase early, a few late, with a smooth curve in-between. Problems occurring within the EPROM or the programmer often change the shape of the curve sharply. It's easy to observe those underprogrammed bits erasing much earlier than the norm. Sometimes, just a few bits refuse to erase, even after receiving three times the dose needed for most of the bits. The shape of the erase-profile curve will tell if this is so.

There are several reasons for hard-to-erase bits. Although EPROMs are visually inspected before shipment, occasionally a small fleck of foreign material shakes loose and lands on the die. If the material is opaque to UV light, it extends the erase time for those memory cells within its shadow.

Flecks may also shake loose later or even become bonded to the die by the heat or programming. Lid contamination can also cast a shadow on the die. Cleaning the lid clears the problem.

Hard-to-erase bits often cause a failure to verify after programming. If you suspect this reason, note which specific addresses and bits fail to verify. Plot an erase-profile curve. But if as you approach the end of the test, you find 10 or 20 unerased bits, use your development-system monitor to display the entire contents of the EPROM before the bits erase. You can now see if there is a correlation between the hard-to-erase and the failure-to-verify bits.

If the erase time for the last bit is still within the data-sheet limit, simply erasing the EPROM longer may suffice. In an application where you'd prefer to use only the best of the in-spec parts, you can screen out those parts along with hard-to-erase bits and evaluate the best parts separately.

Occasionally, an EPROM will appear to have failed a QC test. But did the programmer really do it? Or maybe the eraser? You can test known-good EPROMs and compare the new profile data with the data gathered earlier on those same EPROMs. And you can compare erase times for the failed parts with those for other EPROMs in the same lot, as well as with your reference EPROMs. That way, you can tell if the failed parts are under-erased because of a drop in light intensity, or if the erase times or stuck bits don't represent the lot.■■

Evaluate Ultraviolet EPROM Data Retention

ROBERT WOODS
Manager, Quality and Reliability Assurance,
Electronic Arrays, Mountain View, California

With over a dozen manufacturers of ultraviolet-erasable PROMs, a good way to determine a unit's quality is to measure its ability to retain data under varying external conditions, such as temperature. Of course, when you use any memory ICs, you would like to know that the data they hold will be retained no matter what the power supply or temperature does. But this is especially critical for UV EPROMs since stored data can readily be eliminated if the stored charge dissipates.

Data loss occurs most rapidly at elevated temperatures—so much so that memory degradation increases at an exponential rate as temperatures go up. However, you can turn this fact to an advantage, by performing accelerated testing to determine how well a UV EPROM will retain its data under normal conditions.

To guarantee that the data-retention capability is influenced by as few outside factors as possible it is essential that each unit to be tested be completely erased and then thoroughly programmed according to the manufacturer's directions even before you begin to test the memory chips.

To determine retention, use MTBF

When an EPROM produces an incorrect output, you can say it failed. The mean time between failures (MTBF) then becomes a good measure of the retention capability, or reliability, of an EPROM. MTBF, in this case, refers to the amount of time that may be expected to elapse from the beginning of life until the first failure. From here on, a failure is defined as a loss or alteration of one or more bits of stored data.

The MTBF of a device is a function of the number of units being operated or tested, the elapsed time of the test and the number of failures that occur. For example, if 100 units are tested for 1000 hours and two failures occur, the observed MTBF is 100,000 hours divided by the two failures, or 50,000 hours.

Actually, failures tend to be distributed randomly over time. The confidence level that 50,000 hours is the true MTBF and that one or more additional failures will not occur in the next few hours is low. For this reason some statistical treatment is usually performed to provide a more realistic MTBF at a specified confidence level.

One of the most common ways to figure MTBF statistically is the Chi-square distribution, tables for which are available in any standard handbook of statistics. The associated MTBF formula is simple:
$$MTBF = 2T/\chi^2,$$
where T is the number of device hours (number of units $\times$ test time), and χ^2 is a value selected from the excerpted portion of the Chi-squared table shown.

To use the Chi-squared table, first determine the number of degrees of freedom, n, which is solely a

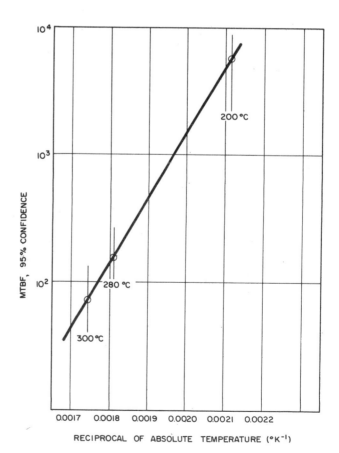

1. **By plotting the log of the MTBF** against the reciprocal of the absolute temperature, you get a linear graph. The slope is the failure-acceleration factor.

function of the number of failures, f, and equal to 2f + 2.

In the example that had two failures, n=6. Look up the value of χ^2 for six degrees of freedom. The column in the table is determined by the confidence level you want. Normally used values in the semiconductor industry are 60 and 90%; however, to keep things conservative, pick a 95% confidence level. Thus, the value of χ^2 is 12.592.

You can now calculate, with 95% confidence, an MTBF of *no less than* 2 × 100,000/12.592, or 15,883 hours—less than one-third the observed MTBF of 50,000 hours.

Another term frequently used in reliability predictions is the failure rate—which is nothing more than the reciprocal of the MTBF. Thus, the failure rate of the devices tested in the example is 1/15,883 or 6.3 × 10^{-5}. Or you can multiply the value by 10^5 and express it as 6.3% per 1000 hours.

Armed with the MTBF and failure rate, you can quantify the effect of external conditions such as temperature on your data reliability. If tests are conducted at two or more temperatures, for instance, the MTBFs at specified confidence levels can be calculated and the results plotted (MTBF vs temperature). Remember: The thermal effect on reliability is exponential. Your best plot will be the log of MTBF vs reciprocal of absolute temperature.

Run some tests

Now that you have the basic formulas, take a typical test situation to see what UV EPROM reliability looks like. The graph shown in Fig. 1 was generated from tests run on three test lots of EA2708 8-kbit EPROMs at 200, 280 and 300 C:

Lot 1: 14 units programmed and stored at 200 C for 1198 hours; no devices lost data. MTBF at a 95% confidence level is 5599 hours.

Lot 2: 30 units programmed and stored at 280 C for 24 hours; one device lost data. MTBF at a 95% confidence level is 151.8 hours.

Lot 3: 24 units programmed and stored at 300 C for 19.25 hours; two devices lost data. MTBF at a 95% confidence level is 73.4 hours.

The plot of the MTBFs follows the well-known Arrhennius relationship, which states that temperature accelerates failure rate by a factor, F, such that:

$$F = \exp([E/K][(1/T_1) - (1/T_2)]), \qquad (1)$$

where F is the acceleration factor, expressed as the ratio of MTBFs at two temperatures, E is the thermal-activation energy expressed in electron volts, K is Boltzman's constant (8.63 × 10^{-5} eV/°K), T_1 is the lower of the two temperatures expressed in °K, and T_2 is the higher temperature, also expressed in °K.

As a result, E is the value that determines the

failure rate (MTBF) acceleration factor between any two temperatures. It also describes the slope of the curve in Fig. 1. Since the MTBFs have been empirically determined in each of the three lots, F can be found. And E can be determined by reversing the equation. Reshuffling the equation, to solve for E, you get:

$$E = (K/[(1/T_1) - (1/T_2)]) \ln(MTBF_1/MTBF_2). \quad (2)$$

Plugging in the values for the MTBFs at 300 and 200 C, you get E = 1.014 eV. To verify this answer, use the calculated value of E and compute the MTBF at the 280-C point. Substitute these values in Eq. 1, and F becomes 36.379. Now $MTBF_2$ can be determined from the following relationship:

$$MTBF_2 = MTBF_1/F, \text{ or}$$
$$MTBF_2 = 5599/36.379$$
$$= 153.9 \text{ hours.}$$

The result is very close to the empirically calulated value for Lot 2.

Don't jump to conclusions, however: The activation energy determined in this example describes the effect of temperature on *one* type of EPROM's data retention. This value is associated with a specific combination of failure mechanisms that relate directly to the processing steps involved. Don't assume that the value applies to another device type, another manufactur-

Sample Chi-squared table

f	0.75	0.90	0.95	0.975	0.99	0.995
1	1.323	2.706	3.841	5.024	6.635	7.879
2	2.773	4.605	5.991	7.378	9.210	10.597
3	4.108	6.251	7.815	9.348	11.345	12.838
4	5.385	7.779	9.488	11.143	13.277	14.860
5	6.626	9.236	11.071	12.833	15.086	16.750
6	7.841	10.645	12.592	14.449	16.812	18.548
7	9.037	12.017	14.067	16.013	18.475	20.278
8	10.219	13.362	15.507	17.535	20.090	21.955
9	11.389	14.684	16.919	19.023	21.666	23.589
10	12.549	15.987	18.307	20.483	23.209	25.188
11	13.701	17.275	19.675	21.920	24.725	26.757
12	14.845	18.549	21.026	23.337	26.217	28.299
13	15.984	19.812	22.362	24.736	27.688	29.819
14	17.117	21.064	23.685	26.119	29.141	31.319
15	18.245	22.307	24.996	27.488	30.578	32.801
16	19.369	23.542	26.296	28.845	32.000	34.267
17	20.489	24.769	27.587	30.191	33.409	35.718
18	21.605	25.989	28.869	31.526	34.805	37.156
19	22.718	27.204	30.144	32.852	36.191	38.582
20	23.828	28.412	31.410	34.170	37.566	39.997
21	24.935	29.615	32.671	35.479	38.932	41.401
22	26.039	30.813	33.924	36.781	40.289	42.796
23	27.141	32.007	35.172	38.076	41.638	44.181
24	28.241	33.196	36.415	39.364	42.980	45.559
25	29.339	34.382	37.652	40.646	44.314	46.928
26	30.435	35.563	38.885	41.923	45.642	48.290
27	31.528	36.741	40.113	43.194	46.963	49.645
28	32.620	37.916	41.337	44.461	48.278	50.993
29	33.711	39.087	42.557	45.722	49.588	52.336
30	34.800	40.256	43.773	46.979	50.892	53.672
31	35.887	41.422	44.985	48.232	52.191	55.003
32	36.973	42.585	46.194	49.480	53.486	56.328
33	38.058	43.745	47.400	50.725	54.776	57.648
34	39.141	44.903	48.602	51.966	56.061	58.964
35	40.223	46.059	49.802	53.203	57.342	60.275
36	41.304	47.212	50.998	54.437	58.619	61.581
37	42.383	48.363	52.192	55.668	59.892	62.883
38	43.462	49.513	53.384	56.896	61.162	64.181
39	44.539	50.660	54.572	58.120	62.428	65.476
40	45.616	51.805	55.758	59.342	63.691	66.766
41	46.692	52.949	56.942	60.561	64.950	68.053
42	47.766	54.090	58.124	61.777	66.206	69.336
43	48.840	55.230	59.304	62.990	67.459	70.616
44	49.913	56.369	60.481	64.201	68.710	71.893
45	50.985	57.505	61.656	65.410	69.957	73.166

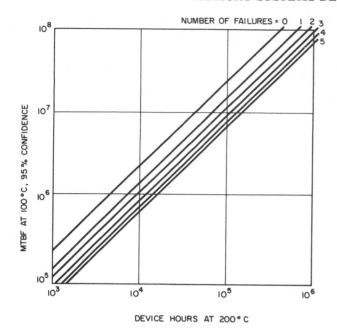

2. **This nomograph of MTBF at 100 C vs hours at 200 C** can be derived from the MTBF at 200 C multiplied by the acceleration factor.

er's EPROM or any other device attributes. However, the techniques used are universally applicable.

Use the data to good advantage

You are now in a position to use the data generated to predict memory lifetimes at normal operating temperatures. Using the same EPROM as a model, you can find the acceleration factor from 200 C to 100 C (70-C ambient with a 30-C rise in junction temperature) with a thermal activation energy of 1 eV:

$$F = [\exp (1/8.63 - 10^{-5})]([1/(273+100)]$$
$$- [1/(273+200)]) = 711.8.$$

The MTBF at 100 C and a 95% confidence level is, thus, 5599 × 711.8, or 3.99 × 10⁶ hours (455 years) —a failure rate of 0.025% per 1000 hours. By plotting MTBF against device hours, as in Fig. 2, you can determine the EPROM reliability. For example, if 10 units are tested for 100 hours at 200 C and one failure occurs, the abscissa of the graph is entered at 10 × 100 (1000) hours, and the ordinate value corresponding to one failure can be read out—about 1.5 × 10⁵ hours (the MTBF at 100 C with a 95% confidence level).

Using the same graphic procedure you can easily construct a graph that relates any two temperatures. Just bear in mind the following relationships:

$$MTBF = 2T/\chi^2$$
$$MTBF_1 = (F) (MTBF_2) = (2T_2/\chi^2)(F).$$

With the acceleration factor calculated by the Arhennius relationship, the appropriate values of device hours and the Chi-squared value can be entered to provide the points for the graph. ∎∎

SECTION V

Bubble-Memory Components and Systems

The bubble-memory devices, the most unusual of the memory technologies, uses no semiconductor material but provides the highest storage capacity of any memory component. They offer almost all the ideal characteristics—ruggedness, nonvolatility, reliability, and density—with only a few drawbacks—relatively expensive (high cost/bit), unproven, and just moderate speed (access times are typically between 5 and 10 ms). Although devices have been fabricated in the laboratory in the last 10 years, the last 2 years or so have seen the first commercial offerings become available to the designer.

And the growth of the device density has been astounding—from the introduction of the 92-kbit device to the now being sampled 1-Mbit devices. Because the devices are not silicon-based, specially designed support circuits have to be used if system component count is to be minimized. Almost all the bubble-memory manufacturers are working on these system support components, and several manufacturers have already introduced such components to support their bubble-memory devices.

Now, with almost a dozen bubble-memory devices available, selecting the one that best meets your present and future system design needs can be a difficult job at best. The articles in this section provide most of the detailed technical information about the bubble devices and support components that the vendors have available. Details of device operation as well as system organizations are included as well as some projections of where the bubble devices are heading and the technology that will be used to get them there. All the major commercial bubble-device manufacturers are represented and their latest products included.

Bubble World Swelling with Density

DAVE BURSKY
Senior Editor, Semiconductors,
Electronic Design

Bubble memories certainly aren't lacking for design improvements and innovations—in fact, they're coming from all sides. Increased density, of course, remains a paramount goal, but so do more efficient design, greater reliability and commercial production. As a result, the bubble-memory world is being populated with new concepts in magnetic structures, device organizations and subfunction design (detectors, generators, stretchers, gates, etc.), as well as material and measurement techniques.

Among these developments are

■ A dual-conductor magnetic circuit technique that will eliminate the bulky external magnetic coils now needed for bubble-memory operation.

■ New device organizations—folded-loop, ladder and multiple-bit—that will increase density.

■ A contiguous-disk design that threatens to outshine chevron propagation structures.

■ Much more effective bubble-detection techniques.

■ Improved material processing to make bubble yield more commercially feasible.

■ Planar-deposition approaches to manufacturing bubble devices.

All these items and more came to light at the third International Conference on Magnetic Bubbles held in Indian Wells, CA.

Major technological innovations to increase density are on the way. A notable one, a dual-conductor magnetic-circuit technique from Bell Laboratories (Murray Hill, NJ), will do away with the bulky external magnetic coils currently burdening bubble-memory operation. Not only will this technique cut the package volume by 33%, it will help increase memory density by a factor of four, according to Andrew Bobeck of Bell.

Two layers on one

Basically, this approach puts two layers of metalization on top of the magnetic epitaxial layer. Oval holes cut into each layer overlap so that the final pattern looks like figure-eights.

Separated by a 1500-Å layer of silicon dioxide for insulation, these metal layers replace the rotating magnetic field coils, and the hole pattern outlines the path the bubbles will follow in the material underneath. Before the metal layers are deposited, however, the material receives an ion-implant dosage of 3×10^{13} neon ions at an energy level of 100 keV. This better defines the bubble path and eliminates the formation of undesirable hard bubbles.

However, because the external field coils and the permalloy layer on the chip have been eliminated, the inductance has been reduced—thus, the drive current requirements have also dropped. As a result, the fields can be changed faster, thus permitting an increase in operating frequency, possibly to as high as 1 MHz.

IBM in San Jose, CA, is also promising a factor-of-four density increase—but without changing lithography techniques, says Ta-lin Hsu. Also from IBM is a crosshatch metalization layer, which, as Dr. Voegeli describes it, could end of allowing 1-Mbit memory chips with 2-μm features.

Densities of a megabit and even larger look promising thanks to other new device organizations, including ladder-type structures from Bell, mul-

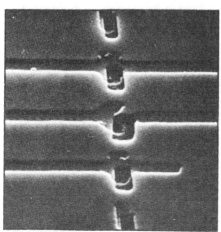 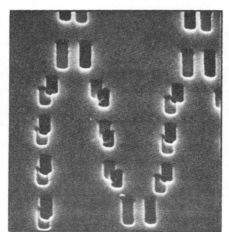 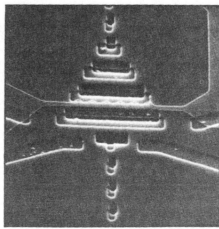

Various SEM photographs of a contiguous-disk structure developed by Bell Laboratories show basic sections of a bubble-memory: a nucleate generator (left), a shift register (middle) and a bubble detector/expander (right).

tiple-bit-wide organizations from Burroughs (San Diego, CA) and folded-loops from Texas Instruments in Dallas.

The folded-loop design, according to TI's Magid Dimyan, is implemented at TI in a 550-kbit test chip using standard 3-μm bubbles and conventional 16-μm periods. Occupying the same area as a 254-kbit already introduced by TI, the folded loop will probably be used with a standard chevron permalloy pattern to produce a 1-Mbit, 1-cm^2 device that will fit in the same package as the 254-kbit array.

But for faster, limited-storage applications, 4-bit wide bubble chips are the route to take, says Sid Schwartz of Burroughs. Throughput is faster because four parallel arrays are designed on one chip.

4-bits in several sizes

Several 4-bit output chips are being evaluated by Burroughs, and they range from 409 kbits to 1.146 Mbits. The chips are divided into four equal blocks, each complete with its own decoder, detector, generators and gating logic.

TI may be using chevron propagation structures, but the work being done at IBM as well as Bell threatens to put a cloud in chevron propagation's future. For example, a new design structure called a "contiguous-disk" follows the same lithography rules used to make today's 256-k devices, but could permit four times the memory density. As described by Susan Kane of IBM in Yorktown Heights, NY, the structure looks like overlapping disks.

The more density available, the merrier—but it won't do much good if the bubbles aren't detected properly. Fortunately, this constant problem is being scrutinized constantly by chip designers, who are responding with detector and bubble-stretcher improvements as well as improved bubble generators (nucleators). For example, new detector geometries unveiled by D. Asama of Fujitsu Laboratories (Kawasaki, Japan) promise to improve noise-immunity margins. Another solution is to use rf signals to sense the bubble's presence.

High-accuracy control

Another problem is to produce enough bubble memories to make

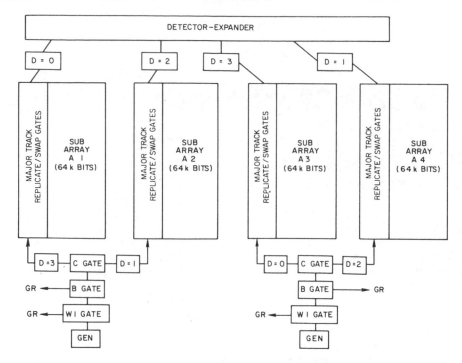

By organizing a megabit chip as a 256-k × 4 array, Burroughs effectively quadruples memory throughput. Each of the four main arrays is further subdivided into the four 64-kbit subarrays shown here. The "D" blocks are delay stages that prevent simultaneous data readouts.

them commercially practical—that means a lot of them. This problem is being solved too, thanks to advances in material processing and the ability to analyze the material to a finer degree. Bubble manufacturers are using many of the techniques developed by the semiconductor industry for high-accuracy impurity control and mask generation.

Both Bell and IBM are at the forefront again, using ion implantation to help fabricate device elements with 8-μm periods and 1-μm bubbles. The implants are typically used to define the propagation paths within the epitaxial magnetic material by distorting the material's magnetic properties. All the basic functions necessary for a major-minor-loop chip organization can be realized.

Meanwhile, the nonplanar deposition used by most bubble memories—several layers of metal separated by oxide insulating layers—is headed for competition. Research by several companies demonstrates that fully planar structures are possible—as a result, so are improved reliability and higher efficiency.

One outgrowth of such effort comes from Rockwell International (Anaheim, CA), which is experimenting with permalloy devices using 2-μm bubbles and planar topology. So far,

both a 256-kbit device have been prototyped and are being evaluated, reports Rockwell's Leonard Tocci.

Planar work is also going on at Hitachi (Tokyo), which has realized 2-μm bubble devices. According to H. Yamada, a proprietary polyimide resin called PIQ is used to fabricate permalloy circuits on the surface of the cured resin. Hitachi claims good reproducibility and reliability for the PIQ bubble devices. Moreover, 256-kbit memories are now being fabricated with 8-μm periods.

Different applications

And there's more good news, this time on the application front. Beyond the minicomputer bulk-memory applications that bubbles were intended for, new, nonstandard applications are springing up. One of them is an optical use developed by Plessey Research (Northants, United Kingdom).

Using a 3 × 3-mm array of bubbles, a magneto-optic page composer has been developed to permit the high-speed visual recording of data, reports Plessey's Joe McCarthy. Organized into 4096 elements (64 × 64), the array of 8-μm bubbles is imaged with a laser and the data are recorded on film in just 4.1-ms for every 4-k block.

The bubble group works as an array of electrically controlled light valves—after imaging onto the film, the bubbles are erased and a new "page" of data is fed in.

A page composer based on bubble technology is particularly attractive for data-acquisition applications since the array can act as the information-storage medium during acquisition. Acting as a serial-in (electrical) to parallel-out (optical) shift register, it permits any number of input bits to be fed-in on just two input lines, and yet transfers a complete page of data.

Once all the manufacturing problems are licked, the next problem the bubble manufacturers and users have to contend with is testing the complex devices.

Basically, however, testing considerations bog down over one big question: How much testing should be done on the manufacturing level and how much on the user level?

Even the tester manufacturers can't agree on the important aspects. At any rate, a tester from Fairchild's Xincom Division will be a general-pur-

pose system that's supposed to handle many different chips. And a tester under development by Watkins-Johnson (Palo Alto, CA) for Intel Magnetics' (Santa Clara, CA) as yet unannounced bubble-memory products is supposed to be general enough for bubble products from several companies. And it's hoped a system being designed by Megatest (Sunnyvale, CA) will fit the same bill as the other two. Most bubble vendors, however, are designing their own testers to keep most design details close to home. ∎∎

Bubble Chips with 256 kbits Are Here

DAVE BURSKY
Senior Editor, Semiconductors,
Electronic Design

The 256-kbit bubble-memory devices from Rockwell and Texas Instruments have the commercial marketplace all to themselves for now, but they should have plenty of company before the year ends. What's more, the companies joining the bubble fray will not start with low-density devices as Rockwell and TI did: National Semiconductor (Santa Clara, CA) will announce a 256-kbit chip—and Intel (Santa Clara) will actually go beyond that with a 1-Mbit device.

Both newcomers, National's NBM2256 and Intel's 7110, will use the block-replicate architecture instituted by TI and Rockwell. Both will have families of support circuits introduced with them. But additional details of the NBM2256 are sketchy at best.

What is known is that, housed in a 16-pin package, the device will have the lowest pin count of any 256-kbit unit, even though it uses a redundancy loop on-chip to store its band-loop map. In addition, the NBM2256 will tolerate external magnetic fields up to 40 Oe without any data degradation, and will offer an isolated detector output to minimize false sensing due to noise.

National does have plans for a 1-Mbit device, and further generations of National bubble devices are expected to use a 1.25-μm bubble diameter so that units with 1-Mbit capacities and more can be fabricated. However, Intel is already there.

Slated for sampling late in the third quarter, the 1-Mbit 7110 will offer 1,048,576 bits of storage and come in a special leadless package. Organized as a serial-parallel, loop-serial shift register, the Intel chip will contain 512 minor loops holding 2048 bits each. As a result, the structure will appear as 2048 pages of 512 bits (1 block) and each page is processed as 64 8-bit bytes. Internally, the loops will be grouped as two banks (odd and even) of 256 loops each, with a serial output channel from each bank.

1-Mbit bubble memory chip from Intel is organized as 512 loops of 2048 bits each. Basic shift rate is 50 kHz and worst-case access is 40 ms.

Operated at a basic shift rate of 50 kHz, the 7110 has a worst-case RAM-mode access time of 40 ms. However, when both banks are combined, the effective data rate becomes twice the shift rate, or 100 kHz. A page read or write requires 327 shift cycles, which translates to a 6.5-ms period and an average data rate of 78 kHz.

Not only does the 7110 offer 1 Mbit of storage, it also provides features for keeping costs down and reliability high. First off, 48 additional "spare" minor loops on the chip offer redundancy for any marginal or defective loops. Also on the chip is a loop that stores the redundancy-map data. Another part of the chip contains an error-correction code that can be used to detect and correct up to five bits long in each channel. This feature, though, can be bypassed and the user can use the 32 bits allocated to implement other error-correction codes.

Circuits to be introduced with the 7110 bubble chip will give all the support it needs. They include a bubble-memory controller (7220), a format-ter/sense amplifier (7242), a current pulse generator (7230), and a coil pre-driver (7250).

Plenty of support

The 7220 controller, an HMOS LSI device in a 40-pin package, will provide the bus interface, generate all memory-system timing and control, maintain memory-address information, and interpret and execute user requests for data transfers.

The 7242 amplifier will perform the output sensing of the two detector outputs from the bubble-memory chip, handle the redundant loops, and buffer the data. It will also provide the burst-error detection and correction circuits for each channel. Fabricated with NMOS technology, the 7242 will come in a 20-pin DIP.

The 7230 current-pulse generator will provide the relatively high peak currents required by the bubble chip. Built from Schottky-TTL technology and housed in a 22-pin DIP, the 7230

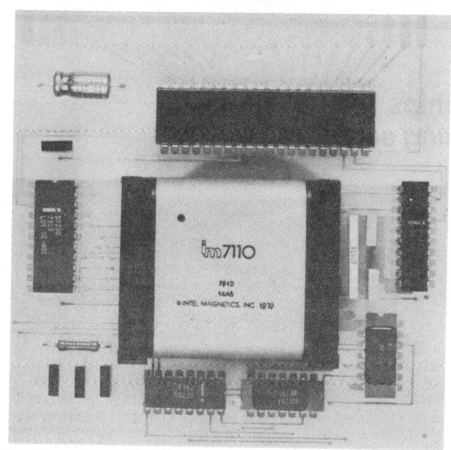

Megabit prototyping kit from Intel, to be available by fall, provides bubble chip and necessary drive circuits for $2000.

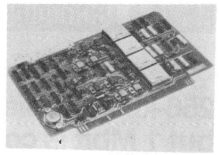

Megabit-memory module from Rockwell uses four 256-kbit bubble chips. It is used in the company's R6500 Microcomputer Development System.

will contain a power-down circuit to shut off the current sources whenever the chip is deselected, and a power-fail detection circuit to power-down the memory chips in an orderly fashion.

Currents beyond the capacity of ICs will be needed to drive the coils, so the coil predriver is designed to prepare the outputs of the controller to drive discrete transistor drivers such as quad bipolar transistor packs or quad VMOS FET transistor packs. Built from CMOS technology, the 7250 will come in a 16-pin package.

All the components will be put together in a prototyping kit, which will be offered in the fall. For $2000, it will contain a bubble chip, a circuit board and the necessary drive circuits for $2000. While not the lowest-cost memory available, it will be nonvolatile, have no moving parts, and be well-suited for harsh environments.

The bubble memory systems, though, could be assembled in several ways. For example, one 7220 controller could handle up to eight 7110 bubble devices in parallel, or eight multiplexed devices one, two, three, or four at a time. Parallel operation helps increase speed while multiplexed operation conserves power. Controllers could also be operated in parallel to provide 16-bit parallel bus widths and even larger systems, if necessary.

Companies coming

Although no manufacturer other than Intel has divulged any details about a 1-Mbit device, it's a sure bet that at least four manufacturers will be in the market in 1980. In fact, both TI and Rockwell—approaching high-volume production of their 256-kbit devices—have been showing 1-Mbit feasibility prototypes at various magnetics conferences. While production details are not yet available from either company, it has been ascertained that their devices will be binary and will offer a full 2^{20} bits of storage. In addition, TI will keep the redundancy loop on-chip while Rockwell will have to decide between that and providing it separately.

At this point, however, 1 Mbit for the most part is still a peak to be assaulted and several techniques are being examined to do just that. TI, for example,

has developed a folded-loop design that uses a 12-μm period in the input and output areas and an 8-μm period in the storage areas along with a 2.5-μm bubble diameter. While this alternative enhances density enough to reach 1 Mbit and beyond, it also increases loop length and with it the access time.

Rockwell, on the other hand, has been looking at more of a "brute force" approach—shrinking both the pattern and the bubble size. Bubble diameters of approximately 2 μm with 1-μm gaps will probably appear in the next generation of Rockwell bubble devices.

Other techniques could provide the added density and then some. Bell Labs has come up with a contiguous-disk design that replaces magnetic coils with two levels of metallization (ELECTRONIC DESIGN, Mar. 29, 1979, p. 19). This technique promises not only to improve the density fourfold but also to eliminate the bulky coils needed to move the bubbles. However, experts at Bell Labs don't expect the technique to be production-feasible for another year or two.

IBM, meanwhile, uses 1-μm bubbles and a "wall" effect to boost data storage to 25-million bits per square inch. Bubbles move around the edge of a pattern instead of directly underneath the pattern.

This technique permits minimum track dimensions to be much wider than the bubble, thus easing the photolithographic requirements. What's more, the structure adds a third layer to the commonly used two-layer garnet. The new layer consists of a 0.4-μm-thick deposition of gadolinium with ion-implanted helium atoms. The implanted atoms cause the axis of magnetization to change, which in turn causes a charged wall to be formed and thus a path for the bubbles. ∎∎

Bubble Memories Are Bursting Out

DAVE BURSKY
Senior Editor, Semiconductors,
Electronic Design

Bubble memories—they're here and promising to deliver densities unimaginable just a decade ago. Both Texas Instruments and Rockwell International have products on the market. Other manufacturers, though, aren't far away. Intel is now sampling a 1-Mbit chip, and National Semiconductor is expected to announce products this year. And though Western Electric, Bell Telephone Laboratories and IBM have been in the forefront of bubble research, they aren't likely to offer commercial products.

The recent conference on magnetic bubbles held in Indian Wells, CA (see ELECTRONIC DESIGN, April 12, 1979, p. 25) unveiled a wide array of improved architectures and chip designs, all promising to deliver densities of a megabit and higher, operating frequencies of up to 1 MHz, and reduced magnetic structures with simplified drive requirements.

Why bubbles? For starters, they offer a combination of high-demand features: nonvolatility of stored data, reasonably fast access time compared to mechanical storage systems, and relatively low-power drive requirements. And just as attractive is the very high density of a quarter of a megabit and more in a package just slightly larger than a large DIP.

Large memory systems, such as multiple-disk drives, derive their low cost per bit by spreading the high fixed costs of electromechanical components over a very large number of bits. If the actual data capacity needed in a system is less than a few megabits, disk cost per bit rises dramatically. The minifloppy-disk drive is a partial answer to the reduced storage requirements, but actually the cost per bit goes up even as the hardware cost goes down.

Smaller to larger

Bubble-memory components, however, permit the memory system to be expanded in smaller increments —92-k, 254 or 256-k, and eventually 1-Mbit steps. As

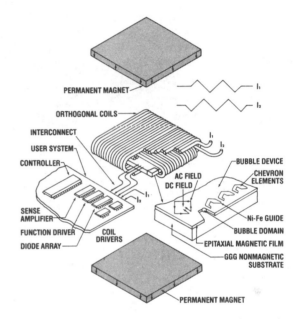

The basic bubble-memory package: The rotating field created by the orthogonal coils moves the bubbles serially through the magnetic film.

a result, the optimum memory size for a system can be designed-in immediately. The system can then be expanded in inexpensive blocks—and at all times the cost per bit stays low.

For now, the traditional full floppy-disk memory system offers a larger storage capacity than the available bubble chips. However, technological developments will bring bubble-chip cost down to that of a disk system, and soon. Right now, the two technologies can be melded together to provide fast access to often-used data, yet minimize mechanical wear and access delays.

As a matter of fact, bubble-memory technology in harsh environments is already cost-competitive and there are some applications where no other product

Where they come from

Magnetic bubbles are small, cylindrical domains formed either in single-crystal thin-films of synthetic ferrites or garnets, or in thin, amorphous magnetic-metal films when a stationary, external, magnetic bias field is applied perpendicularly to the plane of the films. These domains are mobile in the presence of a magnetic field gradient, and their direction of movement can be controlled by special structures deposited on top of the film and by a moving magnetic field.

As the bias field increases in strength toward its optimum value, randomly distributed serpentine domains in the film layer shrink until they form the cylindrical domains, or bubbles.

(What's more, the materials used in bubble devices must form uniaxial domains perpendicular to the plane of the film.)

Once the bubbles are formed, they can be moved along a path defined by a deposited layer of metal on the surface of the magnetic film. The presence of a bubble corresponds to a ONE and the absence to a ZERO.

However, bubbles aren't the only things that must be created on the chip to make a functioning memory component. Also needed are special control functions for generating, destroying transferring, and sensing (writing, swapping, detecting bubbles). All these functions are performed in aluminum-copper patterns deposited over the magnetic film. Also deposited on the chip are permalloy (80% Ni, 20% Fe) metal patterns—these patterns form an easily magnetized layer on the chip above the Al-Cu metal and are separated from it by an oxide deposition.

The permalloy pattern defines the path along which the bubbles will travel in the magnetic film. One commonly used pattern is called a chevron structure. When each succeeding chevron is magnetized by the rotating magnetic field, the patterns create magnetic polarities that pull the bubbles along.

The center-to-center spacing between adjacent chevrons (the cell period) is currently about 16 μm for today's quarter-megabit devices. However, the chevron structure is not the only one used. Earlier designs such as the T-bar and H-bar are still being used, and newer designs, half-disk and contiguous-disk patterns, are being incorporated.

Forming closed tracks, or loops, the permalloy paths contain a fixed number of bit positions. Two types of loops are formed on the chip: A major loop that holds one bit from each of the large minor loops, which actually store the data. The contents of the same relative bit positions of each minor loop in the chip represent a block of binary data.

Data are typically entered at the generators through transfer-in switches to a major loop. The desired data block is then lined up on the major loop with the desired minor loops that will actually store the block. The entire data block is then sent, all at once, into the minor loops.

Other circuitry on the chip performs the read operation. Replicate transfer gates reproduce a data block from the minor loops to the read major loop. This nondestructive readout technique prevents accidental data loss if the wrong signals are fed to the memory.

With all this happening, a bubble-memory package basically consists of a bubble-memory chip surrounded by the two orthogonal coils, which are then sandwiched between two permanent bias magnets, which provide nonvolatility and stable domains (see figure). This entire grouping is then enclosed in a magnetic shield to prevent external magnetic fields up to about 20 oersteds from affecting the data.

The bubbles, being magnetic dipoles, interact strongly and must be separated from each other by several diameters. In practice, a spacing of four bubble diameters (center to center) minimizes the interaction. The bubble diameter, however, is a function of material composition and applied bias field strength at a given temperature.

---

can do the job. Severe vibration, contaminated-atmosphere and continual-access situations are just a few where costs of 50 to 100 millicents per bit are competitive.

How rapidly bubble memories get on a par with semiconductor and disk memories depends on the ability of the semiconductor industry to solve the various technology problems that still exist. Until these problems are solved, bubble chips having 1-Mbit and larger densities will not be in high-volume production as soon as many people think.

Nevertheless, bubble-memory technology has become a design force to be reckoned with and the three articles to follow take on the various aspects of this force. Both Texas Instruments and Rockwell International have introduced commercial devices—quarter-megabit bubble-memory chips using block-replicate architecture—and so their articles explain how their devices work, and what's needed to make a complete memory system. Next, the Xincom Division of Fairchild delineates the test problems both manufacturers and users will face and some possible solutions for both. Finally, in the next issue National Semiconductor points to technological and manufacturing problems to be mastered before megabit bubble-memory chips become a high-volume production item.

All About the TIB0303 Bubble Memories

GERALD COX
Product Manager,
Texas Instruments, Dallas, Texas

WILLIAM MANCZUK
Texas Instruments, Dallas, Texas

Before you can make the TIB0303 bubble-memory chip—and its 254,688 bits of storage—part of your design, you need to know the basics: device specifications, timing requirements and pinout. Then get acquainted with basic system-design support details (drivers, controllers and interface circuits).

To start with, the TIB0303's 20-pin DIP-like package has pins on 70-mil centers and dimensions of 1.2 × 1.2 × 0.4 in. Coming soon, though, will be a package with 18 pins that are on standard 100-mil centers. Either package includes the chip, two orthogonal field coils, two bias magnets and a magnetic shield. The shield protects data in the chip from external magnetic fields of up to 20 Oe (without any noticeable degradation in data integrity).

To move the data around, the rotating magnetic fields are currently cycled at a maximum frequency of 100 kHz. Although the actual waveforms in the coils are triangular, the fields can be run at lower or higher frequencies.

The bubble chip's total storage capacity is actually 286,525 bits, stemming from 252 minor loops with 1137 bubble positions on each. However, a redundancy provision allows 28 loops to be defective—so perfect chips aren't needed. This improves yield and lowers cost. At most, then, 224 minor loops are actually used.

To keep track of the defective loops and permit the system controller to map them out of the actual memory space, a special minor loop called a redundancy loop is factory-programmed with a map of the unused loops. During system initialization, this map is read into the TMS9922 or 9923 bubble-memory controller. For a read or write operation, each bit position in a page of data is then compared with the stored map.

When an unused loop position is encountered during a write operation, a bit space is inserted into the data stream entering the write track. For a read operation, a clock-inhibit signal inside the controller causes the unused bit position to be ignored.

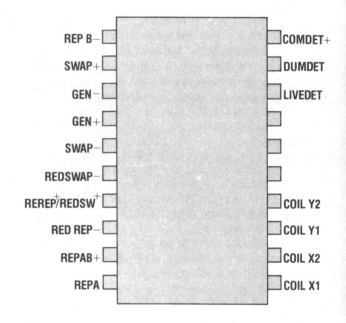

1. **A special feature of the 20-pin interface** for the TIB0303 bubble-memory chip provides separate control lines for the redundancy loop. Actually, the basic interface to the chip requires just 14 pins.

Addresses must be synchronized

The redundancy loop also stores an address-synchronization pattern that enables the controller to locate the zero-page position in the bubble chip. After a power-down cycle or after the system is turned on, this pattern is used by the controller circuits to initialize the page counter. This feature also permits data in the minor loops to be stopped in any bit position in no more than 22.5 μs. Consequently, the power-down cycle time is essentially negligible.

Moving data into or out of the bubble-memory chip is fairly simple. The storage area of the TIB0303 is divided into two banks of minor loops (even and odd banks).

With the even/odd structure, two serially connected

Two chips, different loops

A major step forward in nonvolatile memory technology introduced in August, 1978, the TIB0303-254-k bubble-memory chip has several special features, including on-chip loops that store information about address synchronization and the redundancy of the data loops. In addition, a block-replicate architecture provides a data-transfer technique that's more efficient than the simple major/minor loop structures of the 92-kbit TIB0203.

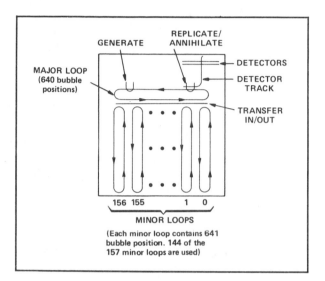

This smaller chip has a completely different loop architecture than the TIB0303, and while it is not directly interchangeable with the 254-k chip, it shares all the advantages including nonvolatility, small size for portable applications, high reliability and higher system performance for secondary storage. In addition, the 92 k oftentimes allows the designer to more closely match the desired memory size.

The architecture used for the 92-k bubble chip consists of a simple major/minor loop structure (top). Only one bubble replicator is used—before data can be read, then, the contents of the minor loops must be transferred to the major loop. Although this procedure is simple, the operation of the 92-kbit chip is slower than the 254-kbit unit, since data can only be generated in every other position. This is due to physical space limitations of the minor loops.

To increase the bubble memory's speed—it was in fact doubled by dividing the data storage area into two blocks for each page of data—Texas Instruments adopted the block-replicate architecture for its 254-k bubble memory (bottom). In this architecture, each minor loop has a bubble replicator so that instead of being transferred out of the loops, the bubbles are duplicated into the output track (for a read operation). To store bubbles, they are first generated, then shifted along the input track and finally swapped into the minor loops.

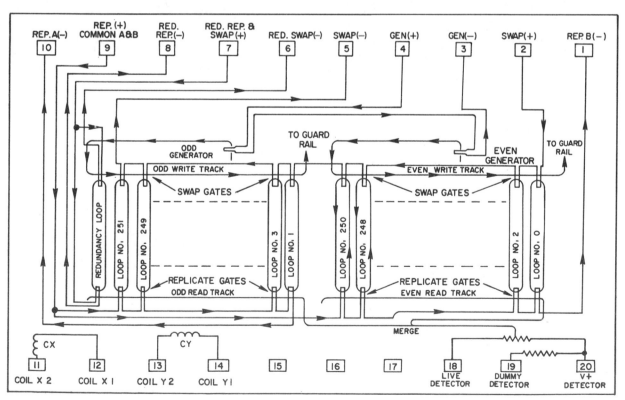

Available in both 92-kbit (top) and 254-kbit (bottom) capacities, bubble-memory chips from Texas Instruments can provide the optimum in minimizing incremental memory system costs while providing nonvolatile storage without any mechanical failure problems.

generators create identical data in both write tracks. The bubble generator for the first bank of minor loops is located one bubble position closer to the first minor loop in its storage area than the second generator is to its storage area. So when the data in the two write tracks are in position to be placed in the minor loops, the odd bits are aligned with the odd bank and the even bits with the even bank.

Once the bits are properly aligned, a current pulse to the swap gates removes any old data bits from the minor loops and replaces the bits with the new data. Since the data stored in the minor loops are split into odd and even bits, write-track data are generated in every bit position; consequently, the write-data rate is equal to the field frequency.

Data left in the write track will be shifted to a guardrail position and destroyed when the rotating

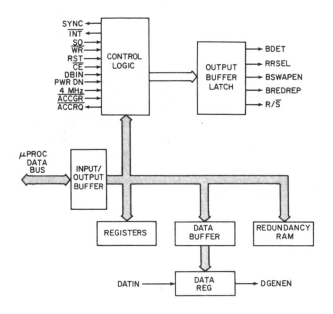

2. **Providing the interface between the bubble memory and the host CPU,** the TMS9922/23 controller does the serial-to-parallel (or vice-versa) conversion as well as keeps track of the data location in the chip.

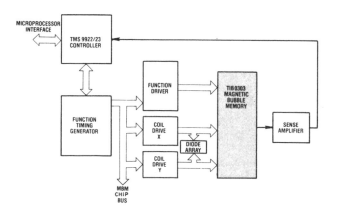

3. **The basic interface to a CPU system** consists of the controller supervising the operation of the function-timing generator and the function driver, coil driver and sense amplifier.

field is turned on for the next read or write operation. The swap function makes the cycle time for a single-page write sequence very short, since it permits data to be transferred in while existing data are transferred out. Thus, the memory looks a lot more like a RAM.

Reading data are even simpler

At one end of the minor loops, data bits are written in; at the opposite end, they are read. Once they receive a current pulse from the controller, replicate gates at the junction of the minor loops and the read track replicate data from the minor loops. Thus, it takes just one operation to duplicate an entire page of data (252 bits) in the read track. And with data in the minor loops remaining intact, data integrity is preserved.

Since the crests of the minor loops are spaced two periods apart, data replicated in the read tracks are separated by one empty bit position until the two tracks reach a common point called the merge gate. The extra bit position between bits allows the even and odd data bits to be interleaved to form the original 252-bit page of data. The bubbles are propagated along this major loop by the rotating magnetic field and directed to a magnetoresistive permalloy detector positioned perpendicularly to the loop. Here, the bubbles passing through the detector produce an analog signal output.

The chevron detector pattern causes the bubbles in the loop to stretch to several hundred times their original diameter. They then pass under the permalloy detector, which changes resistance. This changes the balance of a bridge circuit that contains two detector elements and causes a 5 to 10-mV change in the bridge output.

After passing through the first detector, the bubbles then proceed to the guardrail (located between the two detectors), and are destroyed. If bubbles are allowed to pass both detectors, the net output will indicate that no bubbles were present, since the bridge will remain balanced.

The operations inside the bubble package are controlled by signals applied to the device pins (Fig. 1). Of the 20 pins, four are used for the X and Y coil-drive power and three are used by the detector circuitry. Two others control the odd and even bubble generators, another two control the odd and even swap gates on the write tracks, and three more control the replicate gates for the read function (odd bank, even bank and common). Three other pins control the redundancy loop, providing separate replicate and swap functions just for that loop. And three unused pins separate the detector leads from the coil leads. (For the 18-pin package, there's only one unused pin, which is between the coil and detector pins.)

Where's the data?

Various control circuits are required to keep track of the data bits within the bubble memory. Developed

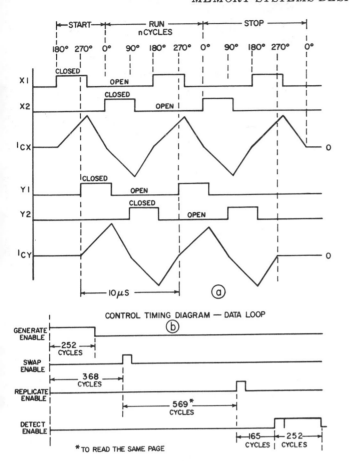

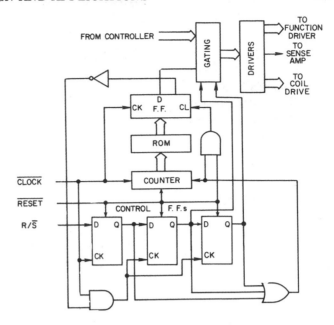

4. **For smooth bubble operation,** timing waveforms for the field coils (a) as well as the necessary pulses for the swap, generate and replicate functions (b) must be delivered in the proper sequence.

5. **Most of the memory-timing signals** come from this function-timing generator, which supplies TTL-level pulses to the coil drivers and the function drivers. The drivers, in turn, boost the voltage and current to the levels necessary for operating the chip.

with that in mind, the TMS9922/23 controller also provides the high-level interface between a microprocessor or other CPU and the bubble-memory chip (Fig. 2).

Designed to operate with the TMS9900 μP family, the TMS9922 controller has a communications-register unit-control interface to the processor. Another version of the controller, the 9923, provides a more general parallel interface for connection to almost any processor.

Basically, the entire interface for a bubble-memory system should look like the block diagram shown in Fig. 3. The controller provides the parallel-to-serial and serial-to-parallel conversion between the processor and memory. It also contains a 28-byte buffer and provides addressing and control outputs to the function timing generator. Also included in the controller are internal status registers, I/O buffer latches, and a redundancy-loop memory-map RAM.

Able to operate in either a single-page or multipage (1 to 1137) mode, the TMS9923 controller is compatible with the TMS9911 DMA controller. This cuts the CPU overhead for large data transfers.

The controller's primary functions are to start and stop bubble movement, maintain page position, and

raise and lower flags for the bubble-memory functions such as generate, swap, block replicate and redundancy replicate. Control signals are sent to the function-timing generator, which controls the coil drivers and other timing circuits. A set of the basic timing waveforms is shown in Fig. 4.

The function timing generator, a monolithic IC with low-power Schottky TTL inputs and outputs, provides the precise timing signals necessary to operate the function driver, coil drivers, and sense amplifier. The function timing generator consists of control flip-flops, a counter, a decode matrix, output latches and some gating (Fig. 5). The control flip-flops synchronize the run/stop signal from the controller with the starting, shifting and stopping sequence of the rotating magnetic field.

Each field rotation is divided into 40 intervals by the counter. The decode matrix is accessed on the rising edge of the clock pulse during each interval, and its output is latched in a D-type flip-flop. These outputs are then gated with signals from the controller to enable the timing pulses to the coil drivers, sense amplifier and function driver.

Boost the drive levels

The function-driver section of the interface converts the TTL-level signals from the function timing circuit into current pulses required by the bubble-memory chips. Inside the driver, constant-current sources are switched on and off from the external inputs. The function driver also performs temperature compensation for the generate element in the bubble chip.

Two external resistors and a thermistor set the magnitude of the generate current and determine the slope of the temperature compensation.

All output drivers are disabled when the disable input control line is held at a logic ZERO—this safeguards the data in the bubble chip during power-on or power cycling. The function-driver circuit also has a chip-select line so that multiple drivers can be used in a system.

The coil-drive circuit generates the triangular currents that create the rotating magnetic fields in the orthogonal coils. These drivers receive TTL inputs and produce a high-level driving voltage. The currents themselves are generated by applying the voltage pulses to the coils, which then integrate the voltage into a current ramp. When the pulse is switched off, the current is commutated by two diodes and allowed to ramp down to zero. At that time, the opposite polarity pulse is applied and the current ramps in the opposite direction. The result is the desired triangular waveform.

Schottky diodes reduce the voltage across the coils when the voltage drive is turned off. This helps make the triangular current waveform more symmetrical.

Sensing the output from the bubble-memory detector, the sense amplifier must be able to detect millivolt-level signals. Since the output of the detector is a differential voltage, it permits high degree of common-mode noise rejection. Amplified and then internally ac-coupled to eliminate offsets and provide noise discrimination, such a signal is then level-detected and latched by control signals provided by the function-timing circuit. The sense-amplifier output is then connected to the controller for serial-to-parallel conversion. ■■

To aid in evaluating bubble-memory systems, TI offers two interim boards: the BKA0303-4 memory board, which holds up to four bubbles, and the BCA0300 controller board. Both boards fit the same card chassis as TI's TM990/100M microcomputer. Up to eight memory boards, for a total of 8 Mbits, can be supported. By dropping in an EPROM containing demonstration software, and adding an ASCII terminal, you end up with an inexpensive development system. A redesigned one-board system holding the controller and up to eight bubbles is in the offing.

The RBM256:
A Block-Replicate Bubble Chip

WILLIAM C. MAVITY
Product Marketing Director,
Rockwell International, Electronic Devices
Division, Anaheim, California

The RBM256 bubble chip is composed of three distinct functional parts—the input port, the storage loops and the output port (Fig. 1). Bubbles are generated at the input port, stored in the loops, replicated and read out or erased at the output port. With block-replicate architecture, Rockwell's unit operates at data rates up to 150 kHz (the field coil frequency).

Power consumption for the RBM256 is about 1 W, and with a field frequency of 150 kHz, the unit accesses the first bit of a block in less than 4 ms (average). For that field frequency, the unit operates within a −10 and +65-C temperature range. If the field frequency is reduced to 100 kHz, operation goes up to 70 C. When the unit is not operating, data storage nonvolatility spans −50 to +100 C.

A considerably diverse amount of support circuitry is required to make the bubble chips operational in a system. To meet this need, Rockwell developed a controller board that uses a 6502 microprocessor as the main control element, and a 1-Mbit evaluation board that has all the basic drive, timing and sensing circuitry.

The loops on the chip are organized as two blocks of 128 data loops—an odd bank and an even bank. Actually, including the spares there are 141 loops in each. Even though each bank has its own output detector circuit and bubble generator, the chip shares the same rotating field.

The input port consists of the twin generators and transfer-in switches at one end of each data loop. In essence, the loops are long, two-bit-wide recirculating registers into which data bits are transferred on an alternate basis when write operations are performed. The output ports, located on the opposite side of the chip, consist of the dual detectors made from magneto-resistive elements. The detectors are fed by replicate/transfer switches located at the ends of the data loops opposite the input ports.

The guardrail surrounds the bubble chip's active area. A series of permalloy elements laid out as outward-bound paths, the guardrail permits bubble movement in only one direction—from the active area out to the inactive area at the chip's edge. This pulls any stray bubbles away from the active area, preventing the appearance of false data.

There are four types of pins that makeup the bubble chip interface to the control and drive circuitry—detector outputs (six pins), coil drive (four pins), operator or system control (six pins) and a shield ground pin. The one remaining pin has no connection to it, it's a spare.

The coil drive pins accept the X and Y drive signals that create the rotating magnetic field (Fig. 2). The voltages going across the coils, which are designed to handle high currents, are dependent on the desired operating frequency. At 100 kHz, the voltage required is 11 V; at 150 kHz, it increases to 16 V.

The two identical output ports each consist of three pins a common line and two detector outputs. The common pin is connected to a power supply as a return for the bridge current. The detector outputs are connected to external bridge completion resistors or current sources. A differential signal appears across the completed circuit. When a bubble passes under the detector, it provides a "sensed" signal and then a complementary—but opposite polarity—dummy signal when the bubble passes under the second resistor. The differential output from the bridge is an 8 to 15-mV signal that must be fed directly to a sense amplifier (Fig. 3). Since the signals are in the millivolt range, proper shielding and grounding methods are an absolute must to preserve signal integrity.

The operator pins are input control functions that can be driven by simple open-collector TTL gates. Conventional R, L, and C support circuits form the collector load current source, which determines the current level required during the desired pulses. The pulses are ac coupled, to eliminate "fusing" problems, if a timing signal is misapplied.

The six operator pins are grouped in pairs—one pair forms the transfer/replicate switches' terminals, another pair are the terminals for the transfer-in pulses and the last pair connect to the bubble generators. The transfer/replicate pins control two functions. During a read cycle, for replication, the bubbles are

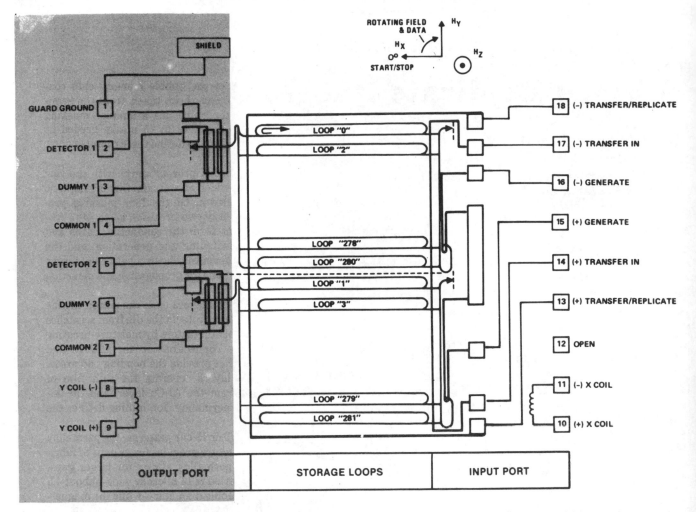

1. The RBM256 bubble memory chip's functional areas include an input section, storage section and an output section. Of the chip's 282 loops, 260 are used for data storage and each holds 1025 bits.

stretched across the switches and cut. This creates new bubbles in the output track, while the original bubbles remain in the data loop.

In a transfer, the bubbles are physically moved across the output track. After the transfer operation, the block tangent to the read track is left with all zeros. So, the transfer function during a write cycle is essentially a clear, or erase, function.

The replicate and transfer functions require different pulses, waveforms and timing requirements. The transfer-out is a simple square pulse, while the replicate pulse has a peak and a plateau (Fig. 4). Each transfer-in pulse occurring on the transfer-in terminal lines transfers a complete block of bubbles from the input track into the proper storage loops.

When the generator circuit—two generators connected in series—is pulsed, it creates two identical streams of bubbles. These bubbles form the block to be input. There is a difference of one step between the number of steps from the generator to loop 1 and from the number to loop 0. Once the transfer-in pulse is applied, all the bits line up properly. The odd bits go to the odd-numbered loops on the chip's lower half and the even numbered to the loops on its upper half.

The bubble memory's block-replicate structure has

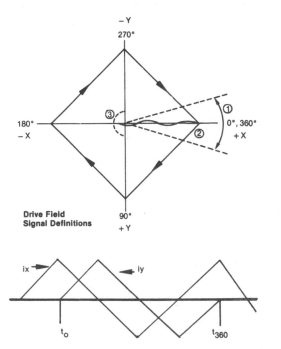

2. The two rotating magnetic fields move the magnetic bubbles around the chip, and remain out of phase by 90°. For ease of generation, Rockwell recommends triangular current waveforms.

Details of bubble-chip construction

The RBM256 packs a lot in an 18-pin DIP-like package: full binary 2^{18} bits of data storage—the largest capacity of any commercially-available bubble-memory chip. The chip's construction and packaging is similar to other commercial bubble chips. But as far as similarity to the other quarter mega-bit chip from TI goes, it ends with their block replicate architecture. First of all, Rockwell's RBM256 has a data storage capacity of 266,500 bits, while Texas Instruments' TIB0303 stores 254,688 bits. Although the bit storage difference is negligible, the TI chip's controller has to work harder if binary-sized storage areas are used.

Since the bit counts are different, it follows that the loop sizes within the chips are different. The RBM256 has 260 guaranteed minor loops of 1025 bits each and an additional 22 loops that may be defective. In many applications, four of the 260 minor loops are for "housekeeping" purposes (possibly for block address storage), bringing the actual data storage to 256 loops of 1025 bits each. In most addressing schemes the 1025 block is not used.

Unlike TI's chip, Rockwell's does not internally store the redundancy information that maps out the defective loops from the chip. Instead, the map data are externally supplied in a listing from which the user can burn his own PROM. This eliminates the need to reprogram the bubble chips in the event of a map data loss if the bubble-chip memory gets scrambled due to a fault elsewhere in the system.

A data block on the chip consists of one data bit from each of the 260 minor loops. That bit holds the same relative position in each loop. Thus, the RBM256 contains 1025 data blocks of 260 bits each. The 1025th block, however, will rarely be used in most binary applications. When eight devices are set up in a parallel system, the data field becomes 256 bytes. The extra four bits (260 to 256) in each of the eight devices provides storage for a 16-bit block address header and a 16-bit cyclic redundancy check character suffix.

Although many of the bubble memory chip construction processes have been taken from the semiconductor world, the chips use a simpler masking sequence—cutting the nine to 15 masks needed by semiconductor products to define the structures down to just four.

Rockwell's four-mask process starts with the raw garnet wafer upon which an epitaxial film of magnetic garnet has been grown. Of the four masking procedures, there are only two precision steps—the AL-Cu layer mask that form the conducting paths and loops for bubble switching and generation, and the permalloy layer to form the chevron pattern of tracks that define the locations for propagation and detection of the bubbles.

The other two mask layers open the silicon-nitride passivation layer that protects the die from scratches and from environmental factors by moisture-proofing the chip, to make connections to the CR/Au and permalloy layers that provide the bonding pad areas. Nonmasked SiO_2 layers separate the thin film of magnetic garnet from the Al-Cu layer, and the Al-Cu layer from the permalloy. Ion milling defines the permalloy pattern.

As compared to T or H-bar patterns, the permalloy pattern's basic structure provides fewer gaps to fabricate. In addition, permalloy allows for larger gaps. The chevron cell period is 14 microns wide—about 4.5 times the 3.2 μm bubble diameter—while the magnetic garnet layer has about a 3-μm thickness.

Although the Rockwell chip's fabrication process is much simpler than a semiconductor chip's, assembly is much more complex. Unique to the Rockwell package are copper-laminated covers and copper plates within the coil assemblies. The copper laminations act as both an electrostatic shield for the sense line and as an equipotential surface that forces the electromagnetic vectors to remain parallel to the chip. The net effect of such construction is a uniform field over the chip's surface.

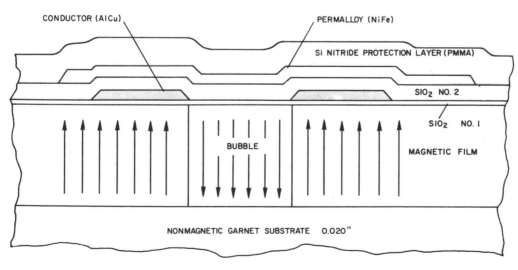

CONDUCTOR (AlCu) PERMALLOY (NiFe)

Si NITRIDE PROTECTION LAYER (PMMA)

SiO_2 NO. 2

SiO_2 NO. 1

MAGNETIC FILM

BUBBLE

NONMAGNETIC GARNET SUBSTRATE 0.020"

the same effect as moving magnetic media, providing block access to data. Individual loops are not addressed but the same relative bit in each loop is addressed.

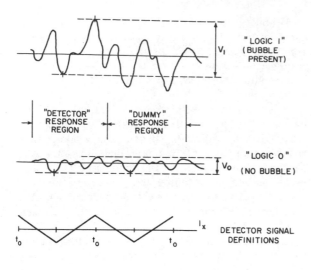

NOTE: SIGNAL POLARITY SHOWN FOR DETECTOR COMMON AT LOWER POTENTIAL.

3. **The differential output from the detector elements,** down in the 10 millivolt range, is sensed and subsequently converted to logic level signals that the digital control circuits can handle.

The read operation is then performed on a complete block at a time (the same holds true for a write).

Loops rotate to the particular bit position that corresponds to the desired data blocks. The data held in that block are then replicated onto the read track through the replicate/transfer switches. The appropriate pulse causes the blocks' odd and even halves to be either replicated from or transferred out of the loops into the read tracks. Next, the bubbles are propagated along the read tracks to the detectors, where they may be read. Their last movement is through the guardrail and out of the active die area, where they are destroyed at the die edge.

All 282 loops are now read (260 guaranteed good loops and 22 possible defective ones). After the read operation, the control circuitry, operating in conjunction with the mapping information stored in a PROM or other memory, eliminates the invalid data bits bringing the data stream back down to a 260-bit block.

To provide the logic one and zero outputs, each read track detector structure uses the magnetoresistive elements in a bridge arrangement with an external sense amplifier. The bridge configuration gives the best noise cancellation and a high signal-to-noise ratio.

Physically, the detector is a rank of chevrons interconnected by a conducting path. When a bubble

OPERATOR INFORMATION

Operator	Resistance (Ω)	Delay[1] (Deg.)*	Width (Deg.)*	Amplitude (mA)	Amplitude Deviation (mA)	Maximum Undershoot[11] (mA)
Generator	10 ± 1	120 ± 30	10 ± 5[2]	200 ± 25[5]	± 28[8]	10
Transfer In	315 ± 30	280 ± 30	220 ± 20[2]	25 ± 5[5]	± 2[8]	2
Transfer Out		280 ± 30	220 ± 20[2]	25 ± 5[5]	± 2[8]	2
Cut	330 ± 30	12.5 ± 7.5	15 ± 5[3]	100 ± 20[6]	± 5[9]	3
Replicate — Xfer			100 ± 20[4]	35 ± 7[7]	± 2[10]	

Note:
$t_{rise} \leq 100$ nS; $t_{fall} \leq 200$ nS

*360 degrees per period.
At 100 KHz, one period = 10 μS
At 150 KHz, one period = 6.66 μS

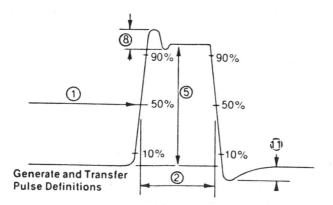

Generate and Transfer Pulse Definitions

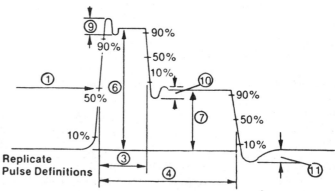

Replicate Pulse Definitions

4. **The waveforms necessary to perform the generate and transfer operations** (left) and the replicate function (right) differ considerably. The generate and transfer pulses are typical rectangular pulses, while the replicate signal has an initial pulse peak that subsequently decreases to a plateau (shown as No. 7 above).

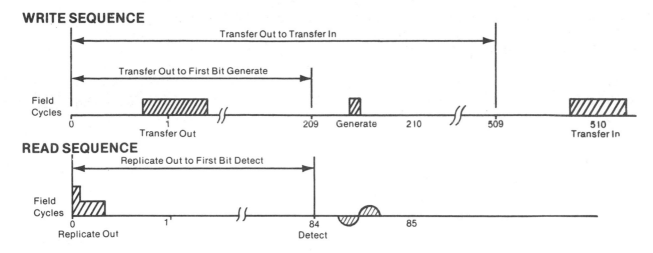

WRITE SEQUENCE

Transfer Out to Transfer In

Transfer Out to First Bit Generate

Field Cycles

0   1   209   Generate   210   509   510

Transfer Out   Transfer In

READ SEQUENCE

Replicate Out to First Bit Detect

Field Cycles

0   1   84   85

Replicate Out   Detect

5. **Timing requirements for a write or read sequence** are simple once the desired data block has been correctly positioned (accessed) at the replicate/transfer point. The sequences assume the next block is ready.

comes under the detector, the bridge resistance changes, creating an imbalance and a differential output voltage. Using two detectors maximizes the integrity of the signal and ensures the transference of the data from the chip at the rotating field rate.

The bubbles come from the chip in two steams—odd and even. The streams, each of which contains alternate data and spacer locations (spacer locations never contain bubbles), are offset by one bit position and each detector alternates in reading them. For the odd-numbered bits, 84 steps (field rotations) are traversed from the loop to the detector. The even numbered bits require 85 steps. The result is the emergence of continuous, interlaced data that are read at the rotating field frequency.

Writing is just as simple

For each generate pulse received by the chip, a bubble is generated in the device's input port. The external controller circuitry uses the data mask to direct the bit stream and insert the space "zeros" that prevent data from going into nonfunctional data loops.

The generator pair, with a single-conductor path, serially generates two identical streams of bubbles—representing two identical input blocks. The bubbles propagate along a pair of input tracks until the block's first bit lines up opposite loop 0 on the chip's even side, and the second bit is opposite loop 1 on the odd side. As before, the number of steps from the generator to the even loops differs from the number to the odd loops by one step.

Once the bubbles are lined up, a single current pulse activates the transfer-in switches and all the bubbles are simultaneously transferred to the data loops. Every other bubble generated enters a loop. The remaining bubbles—odd numbered bits from the even half and even numbered bits from the odd half—are shifted out through the guardrail later.

The timing relationships between the different functions during the reading or writing of a data block are relatively simple (Fig. 5). Some delays represent the number of drive field cycles measured from the 0° drive field reference point preceding the first function, to the 0° drive field reference point prior to the second function. The minimum delay between successive replicate-out and transfer-out operations clears the major track of any bubbles prior to the transfer or replicate function.

The timing sequences shown work under the assumption that the next block is already in position —tangent to the input or output port. If tangency has not been achieved, the data are circulated around the loops until the required block is accessed. This eliminates the additional 1 to 1024 steps that the sequences might otherwise need to reach the desired block. At 100 kHz, the time required per step is 10 μs; at 150 kHz, it drops to 6.66 μs.

Within the package, the two orthogonal coils generate the magnetic flux that forces the bubbles to advance one position for each 360° rotation. (The bubbles move only in one direction.) The coil timing is set to drive the X and Y fields 90° out of phase with the X leading the Y. The coils can be driven either continuously or in a start-stop mode without loss of data.

As far as power goes, both coils can take a common voltage supply with either sine, trapezoid or triangle current waveforms. The triangle drive is recommended as the easiest to work with.

In the RBM256, nonvolatility is guaranteed for data stored in the loops and input port. However, to ensure data integrity, operation at the output port should not be interrupted. System timing is best set to allow the completion of one rotational cycle before a replication function is attempted.

Part 2 of this article will appear in the May 24, 1979 issue of ELECTRONIC DESIGN, and will examine the various interface and control circuits needed to build a bubble-memory system.■■

Bubble Memories Are High Technology

PHILLIP D. BURLISON
Manager, Marketing,
Fairchild Test Systems, Xincom Division,
Chatsworth, California

Magnetic bubble memories are a special, complex blend of semiconductor processing and magnetic technology. It's this very combination, along with the increased memory density they will permit, that will make testing the bare chips as well as packaged devices a designer's nightmare.

The test philosophy of any manufacturing process is to detect and discard defective devices at the earliest point in the production cycle, before any added value work is done. To do this, functional testing should be performed at the earliest possible steps in the production cycle. For bubble memories, this can be done at the wafer level, although with some difficulty.

Using external electromagnets, each wafer die is probed and submitted to as rigorous an exercise as possible. After the tested dies are scribed and bonded onto a carrier, field coils can be installed and further tests can be run not only to make sure there are no failures caused by the assembly process but also to derive the optimum field-strength value for the yet-to-be installed permanent magnets. After final assembly, the package is subjected to a full battery of electrical and environmental tests.

A test system, then, must be able to fill various requirements. Before examining them, however, take a close look at the various peculiarities of bubble-memory devices, whose technology differs considerably from semiconductor technology.

Problems start with the wafer

For basic operation, the magnetic bubble memory requires several magnetic fields—and to test the bubble operation at the wafer level, these fields must be supplied. Standard IC testing, on the other hand, simply needs probes to supply the signals and power, not the special magnetic fields that must be generated to surround the entire wafer instead of just a single chip. These fields are much more powerful than the fields used for individual chip packages and are much harder to generate.

Another field problem is that the various manufacturers of bubble memories may require different

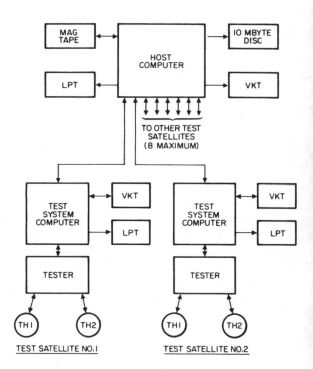

1. **A typical distributed test system** can use a host computer to down-load programs to independently controllable satellite-test-station computers.

things of the waveform used to produce the rotating magnetic fields. Thus, any test system developed should be able to handle several types of waveforms —triangular, square (trapezoidal) and sine are most common.

Because of their size, bubble-memory chips are designed with "spare" storage loops so that if only a few minor defects knock out several loops, the chip can still be used. This redundancy capability is just now being considered for semiconductor as density increases. Typically, most bubble chips developed have about 10% of their loops allocated to act as spares.

However, not all the loops allocated or mapped-out as defective are necessarily bad or nonfunctional. Testing that checks device sensitivity to variations in the magnetic field may show some of the loops to be marginal. Generally, then, the loops that are mapped out of the chip are those that exhibit the lowest bias margin, that is, the smallest range of operational magnetic fields.

Check those bias margins

Specifications for magnetic bubble memories normally guarantee bias margin—range of magnetic field strength—over which the bubble devices will operate. The optimized field bias for each chip must be specially determined and may require permanent magnet val-

as several minutes, and complex tests can take hours. A typical 256-kbit chip requires about 1 ms of dynamic testing, including a minimal nonvolatility test.

On a quarter-megabit chip, with a field frequency of 100 kHz, for example, it would take about 2.5 seconds to read out the entire chip. Cycling every loop several times with a few different test patterns, or even with the same pattern, could stretch test time very rapidly.

Sometimes, failures are caused by one bubble interreacting with a nearby one; these pattern sensitivity

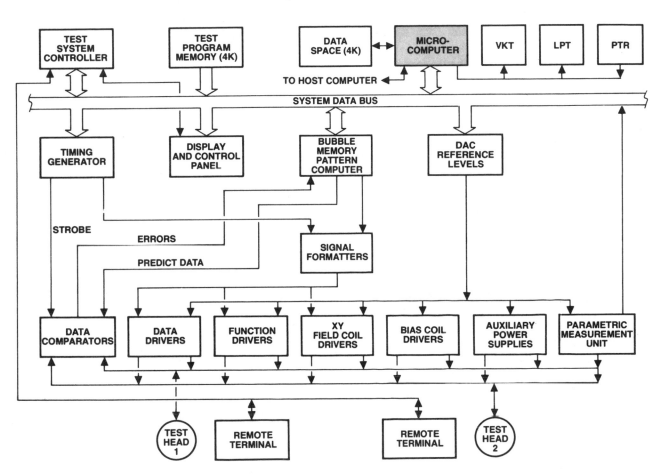

2. **Inside the 5585 bubble-memory test system,** computers control the programmable functions of the tester —a microcomputer handles the I/O interfaces, and a dedicated processor generates the memory test patterns.

ues for each chip.

The bias-margin spec is supplied to ensure the chip will perform properly over the specified temperature range. The requirements for both the permanent magnet's bias field and the ac drive's field have negative temperature coefficients, and the bias margin allows for differences.

Once the magnetic field testing is over, the next major hurdle to overcome is selecting the right test patterns for checking the bit positions in the loop, the read and write functions of the bubble device, and the pattern sensitivity of the storage areas. But with storage capacities of a quarter-megabit and more, this is now a simple task: Simple testing can take as long

failures often are hard to find. Interreaction occurs between bubbles on sequential locations of a track, between bubbles on adjacent loops, and between bubbles at the transfer gates. It's difficult to determine the most economical test or tests for the particular chip being characterized or evaluated.

Pick the tests and configure the system

Once the final layer is deposited on the bubble wafer, the devices on it are ready to be tested by a system like the one in Fig. 1. First a battery of dc and ac tests determine basic functionality of each chip on the wafer. Then they go on to determine if func-

3. Testing up to 65-Mbit bubble memories, the 5585 test system is part of the Xincom III distributed system that consists of a host computer, a tester satellite with test heads, a medium-speed printer and a CRT terminal.

tional chips meet the full specification. Testing might then follow a procedure like this:

1. Measure and verify that the resistance of the current loop function is within specification limits.

2. Measure and verify that the signal detector and dummy-element resistances are within spec limits.

3. Test the critical loops (major and bootstrap or housekeeping loops) for functionality and at the same time perform a bias search to define the bias margins for these loops. (Margins too small are rejected.)

4. Derive an optimum bias level and bias margin for which the maximum number of bad loops is maintained. Again, if the margin is too small, reject the device. In addition, prepare the loop error map for masking marginal or defective loops.

5. Test the device for extreme min/max parameter variations according to spec. Include changes in function-current levels, function-pulse delays and widths, frequency, and field-coil drive levels.

At some point in the testing cycle, the manufacturer should cut up the wafer and start working with individual chips to ease the sorting process. For the user, the test system should be able to perform many of the parametric tests on the packaged devices.

What, then, is needed to test the bubble memories? Conventional automatic test equipment for semiconductor memories can't be used for two reasons:

■ The device interface requires substantial drive capability to generate the magnetic fields. The function loop drivers, since they convert current pulses directly to magnetic fields, have some stringent performance requirements, and the signal generated by the memory requires specially designed detectors.

■ Data generation, data verification, and error processing also require techniques not provided by conventional memory testers. Bubble chips are in effect "characterized" instead of tested. The resultant characterized data are then reduced to determine whether the bias-margin distribution of a minimum number

of minor loops is adequate to qualify the device.

Besides drive requirements, the various input and output functions of the memory chip must be defined. I/O requirements differ for the commercially available bubble devices from Texas Instruments and Rockwell.

To meet both current and yet-to-be announced requirements, a test system (Fig. 2) should include the following items:

■ From eight to 16 current-loop function drivers—programmable current-source pulsers that can be independently specified for amplitude and delay/width. Currents up to 300 mA are required with voltages of up to 30 V.

■ X-Y field-coil drive for packaged devices with voltage drivers of up to 30 V, providing peak currents in excess of 1 A. Because field coils cannot be arranged properly around an uncut wafer at the wafer-sort level, substantial field-coil drive requirements are required at this stage. These may include up to +100-V swings and peak currents exceeding 5 A.

■ A programmable current source, capable of delivering up to 10 A, for an electromagnet that provides a bias field during wafer sorting and testing.

■ Signal detectors capable of monitoring the small differential signals imposed on a higher common-mode signal. The desired signal measurement examines the peak-to-peak variation of the differential signal during the cycle. Each device requires one to four detectors.

■ A precision dc measurement system capable of measuring resistances very accurately as well as detecting opens and shorts.

Function-driver control, data generation, and error detection and processing are managed by an intelligent processor. One possible approach could interface these functions to some general-purpose minicomputer via a direct-memory-access port. Strings of data would then be generated by the available lan-

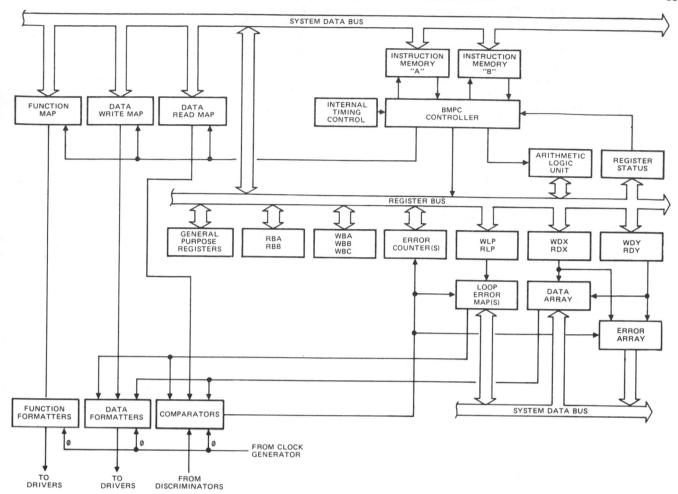

4. Generating the bubble-memory test patterns, the BMPC is actually a full computer in itself. Internal registers store error counts, while various pointers help with reading and writing data to the bubble chip.

guages, stored in a buffer, and transmitted to the device at the proper data rate.

A more efficient design takes advantage of μP computational power and uses special high-speed dedicated processors that can generate data and process errors in real time. Analog parameters can be controlled via a test program that can be used independently of the main control program for the test system. The test program operates in the foreground while the main program operates in the background.

One other factor to consider is to have a parallel testing capability in the tester, since the bubble chips have a fairly long test time and are slow enough to permit some concurrent monitoring. This type of capability can readily be added to a test system by designing the system in modules—this permits more interface "heads" with separate drivers and detectors to be added. Each of these heads, by having its own dedicated data processor, can thus preprocess data for the main system controller.

Combining all this knowledge of bubble requirements with experience in semiconductor testing, a bubble-memory test system from Fairchild's Xincom Division—the Xincom III with the Model 5585 satellite stations and the Model 7710 host computer—can test almost any type of bubble-memory device that can be built (Fig. 3).

This means handling various device architectures —single-loop, major/minor-loop, block-replicate and multiple-bit output—as well as providing both diagnostics and evaluation testing. And it means being able to test any of the currently available devices and future devices with capacities of up to 65 Mbits. Built into the system's core is a bubble-memory pattern computer (BMPC)—a high-speed custom-designed processor that provides the speed and versatility required to generate the complex test patterns for the varied chip architectures (Fig. 4).

The processor operates in a multiplex mode at an uninterrupted cycle rate of 6 MHz. It generates continuous, exhaustive test-pattern streams and monitors and tabulates the results without any noticeable system overhead. The over-all system operating speed can reach a maximum frequency of 500 kHz.

Two separate read and write programs can be held in the BMPC instruction memory and executed concurrently. The control memory holds up to 128 instructions, each 32 bits wide. The BMPC can vary parameters on the fly, perform arithmetic or logic operations.

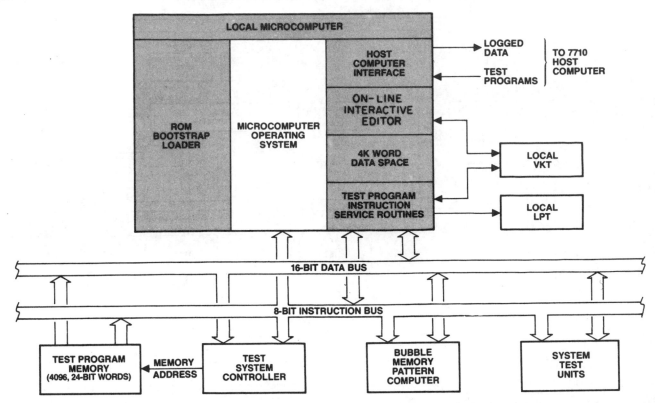

5. Controlling the operation of the bubble-memory test system, the software operating system of the 5585 satellite coordinates the activity of all the peripherals and the memory pattern computer.

change conditions and many other tasks, as the operation system of Fig. 5 shows.

Test-data patterns are defined in a 64-word-×-16-bit data array in which data are specified as they would reside in memory. These patterns can then be automatically replicated throughout the device. Each current-loop driver provides up to 0.5 A with a programmable resolution of 0.25 mA. The drivers also have a programmable edge with a resolution down to 10 ns.

Programmable drivers are provided for both the ac field coils and for the dc bias magnet. These magnets are used for wafer sort and package testing. Signal testing is done by remote, high-accuracy signal discriminators. There are at most 16 independent loop-error maps, each with a capacity of up to 1024 loops. These maps may be generated, read, or written from the device. They can also be read back by the BMPC for data logging into the host computer—a Nova 3 or Eclipse system.

Sixteen independent error counters (one per output) record the number of errors detected per device. Up to 65,000 errors may be accumulated per counter. And once an instruction is selected, the loop error may be used to mask data generation and/or subsequent data-out response for determined faulty loops.

The BMPC has no pattern discontinuities—for any programmed data pattern and sequence, testing is not interrupted even for one memory cycle for algorithmic or data masking calculations. The test-system controller may run concurrently with the pattern-controller program. At predetermined points in the test pattern, the test-system controller may vary test-condition parameters—without incurring discontinuities in test-pattern generation.

Built with ECL technology, the test system avoids the switching noise that TTL designs could create. That means there isn't as much of the noise that could interfere with the system's low-level analog measurements.

The basic test system also comes with two device data I/O channels. To test four devices simultaneously, the tester may be expanded to two test heads with four device I/O channels per head. Up to eight test satellites can operate in the system.

Dc tests are performed with a Xincom enhanced 3981 parametric measurement unit, which is interfaced to the system by a programmable relay matrix. The main-system computer provides the ability to perform high-level, on-line editing of the test program and conditions. Immediate data feedback such as plots of various device functions, bias margins and interactive data analysis are supported at local levels. The data can be output to the local video terminal or line printer, or transmitted to the host computer for extensive accumulated data analysis.

Test-system users will have the extensive Xincom III software library at their disposal. The data base includes generalized data-reduction programs and sophisticated test-management reports. The programming language is an extended version of Xintol, a high-level test language. ∎∎

Bubble-Memory Systems Go Together

TAL KLAUS
System Designer,
Rockwell International,
Anaheim, California

PAUL SWANSON
Systems Circuit Designer,
Rockwell International,
Anaheim, California

BRUCE KINNEY
Senior Design Engineer,
Rockwell International,
Anaheim, California

Magnetic bubble memories demand special design treatment all around. Having a unique structure and technology, they require a completely new set of interface and drive circuits. Moreover, since they function as large serial-storage devices, bubble memories also require special control circuits to convert from parallel to serial and serial to parallel, as well as to keep track of the data-loop positions within the bubble chips.

The RLM650 memory module holds four RBM256 chips set up to operate in parallel and provide a total storage capacity of 256 k, 4-bit words (Fig. 1). The board also contains the coil drivers and some logic control circuits.

The memory module also has a PROM that stores the redundancy data for all four of its bubble devices. This information gets transferred to the controller when the system is initialized.

Designed to interface to the bus structure used by both the System 65 development system built by Rockwell and the EXORciser development system designed by Motorola, the controller board can handle up to 16 memory cards. This provides a total system storage capacity of 16 Mbits, or 2 Mbytes, depending upon how the controller configures data outputs from the bubble devices. A microprocessor performs all the timing coordination and interface control between the bubble storage boards and the interface to the host computer system (Fig. 2).

At the system level, the controller provides three buses to the computer system: an address bus, a data bus and a control bus. Between the controller and the memory cards sit control lines, address lines, and the data lines.

Although the main interface bus supplies a clock signal for command timing control, a separate clock on the controller provides synchronization for the bubble-memory card timing.

Handling the data I/O

The memory module is set up so that the four serial inputs and outputs from the bubble devices are routed to four of the eight data bus lines allocated for bidirectional data handling. Two memory boards can be set up to operate in parallel, with their data I/O lines cascaded to form a byte-wide data word.

Basically, five sets of control and signal lines control the operation of the memory boards, including:

1. Board-select (or enable) inputs (signal names BRDENF, BRD0F to BRD2F).

2. Coil Enable, which when brought low permits

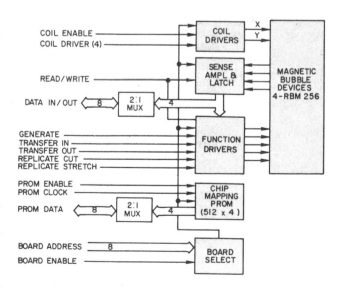

1. This detailed look at the memory module shows the various I/O lines and functions needed to make the memory chips operate.

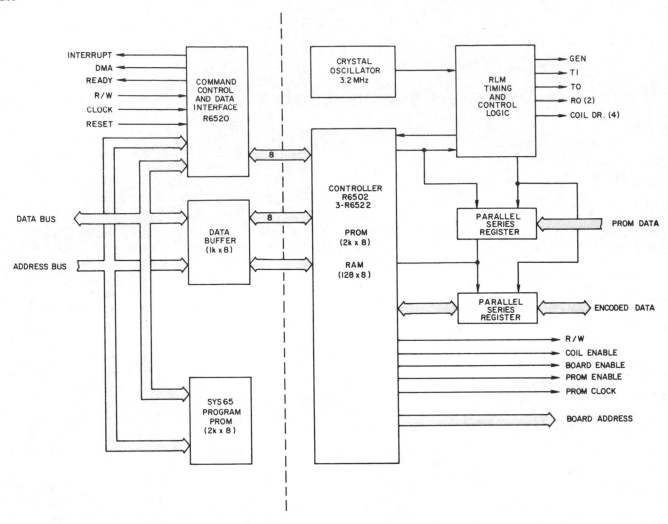

2. Using a microprocessor to provide most of the control, the controller card performs the interface job between the memory and the host computer system under software control from an on-board PROM.

bubble movement to begin (C0ILNF).

3. Read/write data control (R/WF).

4. Function commands: Transfer In, Transfer Out, Generate, Replicate-out Cut, and Replicate-out Stretch (TIF, T0F, GENF, R0CF and R0SF, respectively).

5. Reading defective loop information from PROM (P00F to P07F).

The storage modules have been designed to use TTL signal levels, with the low level serving as the active level for operational signals. (All signal names ending in F are active-low.)

When dc power is applied, the timing signal that controls the coil drivers, 0AF, must be applied at least 25 ms before any control signals are activated to maintain an internally generated voltage in the bubble devices' replicate/transfer circuitry. Leaving the timing-signal line continuously active satisfies this requirement.

The memory is now ready to accept commands. All functional elements are interlocked—no command is recognized without the presence of the module-select terms and the board enable. The four bubble chips on the board are driven in parallel by coil-driver circuitry controlled by four timing signals, 0AF, 0BF, 0CF, 0DF (Fig. 3).

The coil-enable signal, C0ILNF, activates both the X and Y coils, and with subtiming, turns the X coil on 90° before the Y coil. Each subtiming signal is 90° wide and generates the proper triangular waveforms in the coils. Phase zero is defined at the peak of the X current, and each succeeding phase is 90° further along. The fourth quadrant signal, 0DF, then, is actually the first to be applied, and establishes the X current. If the coils are turned off, a delay of 30 μs must be included before they are reactivated.

Simple control functions

The bubble-device output is sensed by millivolt-level preamplifiers, sense amplifiers, bridge-completion resistors, and data latches. Data on the output lines are valid until the next cycle, provided the module remains enabled and the system remains in the read mode.

Each bubble device has two detector/dummy output

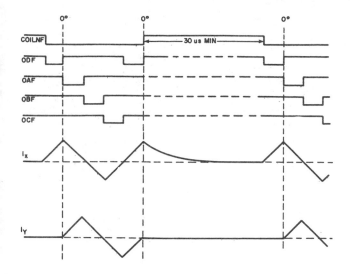

3. **Requiring triangular ac current drive,** the bubble field coils provide the rotating field necessary to move the bubbles within the chip.

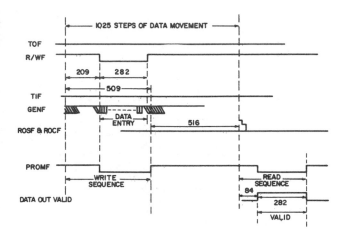

4. **The timing sequences for read and write operations** are relatively simple. The hard part is getting the correct data block lined up.

lines called odd and even, which are active during alternate cycles. The bubble signal (approx. 5 mV) is preamplified and then sensed by a level detector. A threshold voltage is determined by several resistors. And if the signal level exceeds the threshold value, the sense-amplifier (level detector) output goes high. The two digital outputs of the level detectors are gated with strobe pulses and are merged into a single data stream by a latch. The strobe pulses are derived from a flip-flop that is preset by the replicate-out pulse and then clocked every cycle.

The transfer-in, transfer-out and replicate-out circuits all operate in parallel for the four devices, while each generating circuit is driven independently. All these functions ultimately happen when a current pulse passes through the respective loop on the bubble-chip surface. Since the loop is designed to accommodate a low-duty-cycle pulse, all these functions are

ac-coupled to prevent incorrect input logic states from burning them out.

The generators may be activated every bit time; however, the other function signals may not be activated more often than every 282 bit times (the length of a data block).

Even before data can be written into or read out of the memory, the addressed block location must be placed at the proper set of transfer gates. For a write operation, actuating the transfer-out line empties the desired block of data onto the bubble-chip read track and clears the memory location. After a delay of 209 run cycles (Fig. 4), data entry begins by bringing the read/write line low, which activates the generator function (write) for all four channels and duplicates the data pattern from the four data-input lines.

The data entered must be organized so that 260 valid bits are spaced into the 282 operating loops, interspersed with 22 zero-data bits at the defective-loop locations. After 18 more run cycles, the transfer-in line is activated, and a block of data is transferred to the loop-storage area of each of the four devices. As a result, it takes 509 cycles to write an entire block. At a 150-kHz clock rate (6.66 μs/cycle), one block will require 3.39 ms, and all 1024 will require about 3.5 s.

Data are nondestructively read out of the bubble devices by first activating the replicate-out signals when the block location corresponding to the desired address is positioned at the switches. After all that, the read/write line should be set high for a read. Each bubble in the addressed block is then stretched and cut, with one bubble remaining in the loop, and its identical twin placed in the major read track.

After 84 field cycles are used to move the data to the detector, the data outputs are considered valid. The process continues for 282 bits, yielding a 282-$\times$-4 data block for the four parallel chips. The 260 valid bits in each loop of the block are identified via the loop map held in the PROM on the memory board. A minimum delay of 282 cycles is required between successive replicate-out and/or transfer-out commands. This delay ensures that the read track is entirely clear of bubbles before the next transfer or replication.

Put the memory modules into a system

The bus structure on the RLM658 modules is split into two sections: One section, on the bottom of the board, carries the power and ground, and the other section, on the top of the card, carries the bubble control signals and the data bus. The controller card also has two bus sections: The mating bus to the memory cards is on top of the card, the bus that mates to the System 65 or EXORciser bus is on the bottom.

All control and timing signals generated by the controller are transmitted over the upper bus, and the waveforms shown in Fig. 5 define most of the critical timing relationships. When the system is powered-up

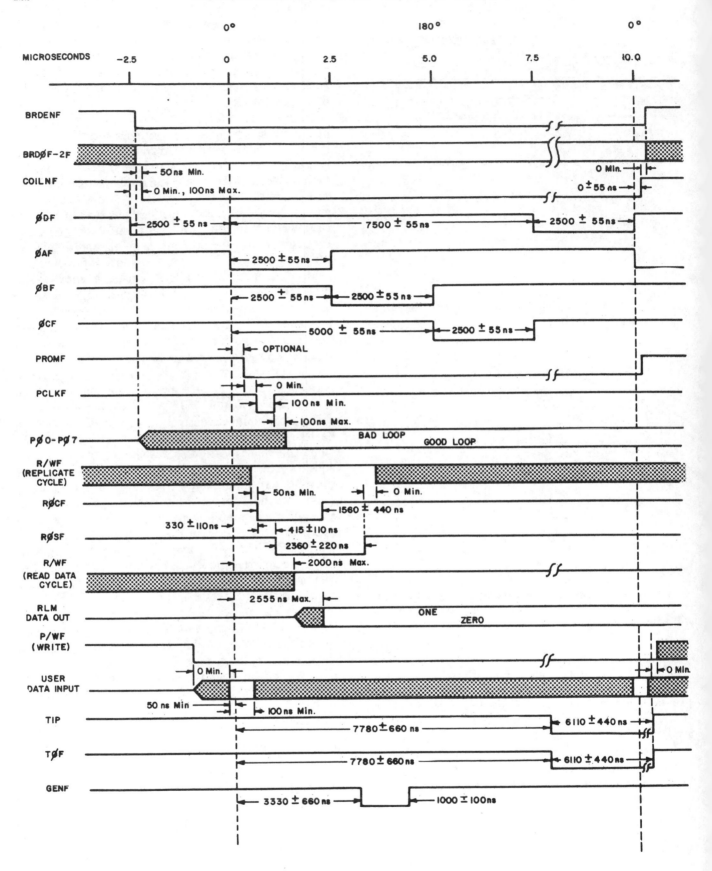

5. Interface timing requirements for the controller and the memory cards provide a considerable margin for most timing skews, as shown by the dotted areas. However, there are a few critical periods.

or reset, the controller polls each memory section (individual memory cards for 4-bit operation and card pairs for byte operation) for its current address, which is held in the controller's 128-byte RAM. With the current address of the memory modules known, the number of cycles to the next desired address can be calculated; and then the bubbles are moved the required number of steps to access the desired data block.

The control module centers on the 6502 CPU and three 6522 versatile interface adapters (VIAs) to do the control and signal interface. All the operations of the processor and the VIAs are controlled by the program stored in a 2-kbyte PROM and by the contents of the 128-byte RAM that stores the current system configuration. The 2-k program sets up automatic handshaking in one of the VIAs to communicate commands and control data to a 6520 parallel interface adapter (PIA), which provides the interface to the host system (System 65 or EXORciser)—under host-system control.

Another RAM on the controller, a 1-kbyte unit, functions as a data buffer. It is user-dedicated with one exception: Programs may not be executed from this RAM while the controller is executing a command.

Data to be stored in and read out from the bubble-storage cards are transferred to the host system by an "invisible" direct-memory access scheme (the DMA does not interfere with the host system operation) to the on-board 1-k RAM. During DMA, the controller forces access to a PIA port, which enables the port to act as a bus buffer/latch between the controller and the module's internal data bus (which is buffered from the host system data bus).

While data flow between host system and memory, the controller uses the DMA to access the data buffer. The starting buffer address and the block address in the storage module are supplied by the host system under software control. Before a read or write operation, the controller must align the requested block in the minor loops with the input or output track.

When data transfer begins, a 2-byte software-controlled shift register/latch is set up by the controller to buffer the two data rates at the input and output, and to provide serial-to-parallel and parallel-to-serial conversion. One result is that the data stream can be either expanded or contracted between the 256-byte user data block and the 282-byte data block size of a module pair (two bytes for address, 256 for data, two for spares, and 22 for defective loops).

In a typical write sequence, the first two bytes put into the data stream by the controller contain the block address. The data block is then fetched by DMA from the buffer RAM at approximately 100 kbytes/s. The controller serializes the data stream in the VIAs so that it can be combined with the PROM-mask data, and the extra zeros may be inserted at bit positions corresponding to the defective loops.

The zero insertions are performed by having the defective loop data serve as an external shift clock for the VIAs while the system clock serves to load data into a serial-to-parallel shift register. So while bits are always shifted into this register, the actual data are input only at "good" loop locations. The composite data are output to the storage modules in parallel, one byte at a time.

The opposite way

A read sequence is the exact opposite of the write sequence. First, the data from the storage modules are loaded into a parallel-to-serial shift register clocked by the system clock while the VIA serial input is clocked by the defective loop data from the map PROM. In this way, the extra bits at the defective loop positions are removed from the data stream. The controller reads the first two bytes as the block address, and then loads the rest of the data into the buffer RAM using DMA.

Although interface timing is handled by a clock signal from the host-system interface, an on-board crystal oscillator operating at 3.2 MHz provides the master timing between the controller and the memory

Compare modulo operations

Modulos	Effective sustained data rates (kbits/s) (2-RLM)	Avg random read access times (ms)	Search cycles to read next block	Read-access times to next block (ms)	Comments
282	726.2	5.96	941	10.25	Optimum for multiblock read
366	559.6	5.96	0	0.84	Fast read access
509	402.4	5.96	143	2.27	Fast write access
512	400	5.96	146	2.30	Simple half-loop
1024	200	5.96	658	7.42	Successive full loop

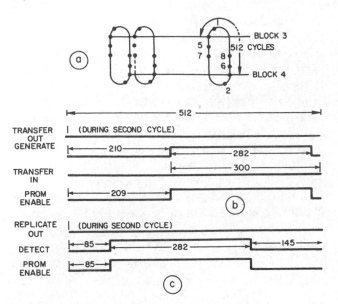

6. By using a modulo-512 count, the controller places even address blocks on half the loop and odd address blocks on the other half.

modules. The frequency of the controller clock is counted down to a 1.6-MHz rate. The clock decoder also provides the internal clocks for gating, for redundancy and data-shift registers, for generating the four-phase coil drive, and for generating the intracycle timing of the memory-card operations. The controller's CPU provides windows to gate the operator signals during read and write operations.

The controller organizes the data in memory in a modulo-512 count, which means that each subsequent block of data is separated by 512 cycles (or bubble locations). Fig. 6 shows how the modulo-512 operation places even address blocks on half the loop and odd ones on the other half. This scheme allows simple control, address searching and time for housekeeping functions, and requires no overlapping storage-module operator functions. Typical read and write sequences are also shown in Fig. 6.

The controller also permits five types of errors to be detected: invalid command code, block-address error, incorrect number of bits per block, block-size discrepancy between blocks, and read/write to a nonexistent board.

Pinning down data rate

It's important to note that system-performance limits set forth for the controller do not come directly from the bubble-memory specifications. The effective data rate, for instance, is determined by more than just the rotating field frequency—the rate of usable data bits to the total bits available must be included. In the RCM650, the data block has 256 bits, two address bits, two spare bits and 22 redundant bits. This provides an effective data rate of approximately 0.908 of the field frequency.

The modulo of operation is the spacing of successive data blocks in the minor loops of the bubble chips. The closest possible spacing, dictated by the number

of minor loops, is 282, which would be the fastest modulo of operation and the most efficient for multiple block transfers. However, it is slow for single-block transfers.

The RCM650 uses a modulo 512 because it places successive data blocks at half the loop length and allows simple algorithms for control-timing. It's a fair compromise between optimum multiblock and fast single-block read and write access times. The burst data rate of the over-all 2RLM module system for a 100-kHz field frequency is 400 kbits/s. The effective sustained data rate at modulo 512 then becomes

$$800 \text{ kbits/s} \times 256/512 = 400 \text{ kbits/s}.$$

Some comparative data rates and read-access times are given in the table so you can compare various modulos of operation.

Scrambled bits help

Spreading data from a serial input to a parallel output with the redundant loop data inserted scrambles the data to the memory module. In other words, bit 1 of a data byte does not always go to cell 1 on the memory card. The first redundant loop mask shifts this bit to cell 2 and all successive bits are shifted by one cell position.

Since the bits are scrambled, future bubble-memory cards may not require that 260 loops per chip be functional, but only 1040 of the 1128 loops on a 4-device RLM. This method, however, adds some overhead to stocking, sorting and replacing.

Connecting to the host system

To the host system, both the read and write commands to the bubble memory are identical in set-up and operation—they differ only in the direction of data flow. The user specifies the starting buffer RAM address, block address, and number of blocks to be accessed. A set of subroutines written for the System 65 and housed on the on-board PROM of the system controller, organizes these blocks into files with names that are stored in a directory along with the associated block addresses. The directory is stored in a designated location in the bubble memory. These file subroutines can be used by both the system programs (assembler, editor, loader, etc.) and the user's programs.

In the file-structure format, the directory takes the first ten blocks of memory. Each directory entry uses 13 bytes—six for file name, two for starting block address, two for block length, two for ending address and one for a code number that indicates an active or deleted file—and leaves three unused. A total of 159 files are allowed for.

More complex file routines can be derived from the four basic functions of Open File, Read Byte, Write Byte and Closed File. These include initializing directory, compressing data, deleting files, renaming files, listing files, among others. And, the 65 assembler, editor and loader can use these subroutines to manipulate the source program and object code.■■

As Bubble Density Approaches One Megabit, Problems Mount

PETER K. GEORGE
Design Manager,
National Semiconductor Corp.,
Santa Clara, California

With quarter-megabit capacity chips now available and the 1-megabit heading for prototype production, magnetic bubble memories seem destined to become a major factor in the memory market. There are, however, several production and technology problems that need to be addressed before megabit chips can be produced in high volume.

At the root of many of these difficulties is the device scaling needed to achieve high densities. Device scaling, for example, leads to high gate voltages and narrow conductor lines, which in turn cause electromigration problems. And then there are many complex interactions between the drive field, chip temperature and material requirements.

Fortunately, such problems can be solved. Using the well developed permalloy field-access technology and the popular YSmLuCaGeFeO as the base material, 2-μm bubble devices capable of 0-to-70-C operation can provide 1-Mbit densities—and be volume-produced. The next step—the 4-Mbit chip—requires smaller bubbles (1-μm diameters), but at this size, lithography and anisotrophy requirements for conventional technology can no longer be met. It is likely that the reduced lithography and drive field requirements for contiguous-disk technology will make it a candidate for these larger capacity chips.

Go back to the rules

To gain a better understanding of some of the megabit design problems, consider the device-scaling rules. Since the packing density of bubble devices increases approximately as the square of the bubble size, the smaller the bubble, the better.

Recent design innovations, such as going from the T-bar to the half disk or asymmetric chevron propagation elements, have relaxed both drive field and lithographic requirements, thus making fabrication of very large chips possible. At the same time, however, this shift to smaller bubble sizes has led to inherent —and apparently insurmountable—limits for conventional permalloy technology.

As the table shows, there are standard geometrical relationships among bubble size, gap and pattern period to be maintained as the memories are scaled down. The asymmetric chevron's larger nominal gap makes it more desirable than half-disk since lithographic requirements are relaxed. It is unlikely, however, that the period-to-gap ratio of 5:1 for 3.3-μm bubbles will actually be used in a production design. This gap size doesn't allow for variations that occur in a manufacturing environment. Furthermore, the gap is larger than the minimum chip feature of the detector, which corresponds more closely to an 8:1 period-to-gap ratio. Since the limiting detector features must be resolved and since the storage-area margin (asymmetric chevron) improves with decreasing gap, an 8:1 ratio more likely will be used in the future—particularly when the drive field begins to rise with smaller bubble size.

The curves in Fig. 1 illustrate the relationships between bubble size, gap, and period established in the table, and also give the gap tolerance corresponding to a 15% margin loss. The period here is the nominal value based on a 5:1 period-to-bubble-diameter ratio. Experimental measurements indicate that the ratio can be reduced to nearly 3.5:1 without serious margin consequences.

The bottom line is encouraging: 256-k, 512-k and 1-Mbit chips can be achieved with 3.3, 2.5 and 1.5-μm bubbles, respectively, assuming the chip size is about 400 $\times$ 400 mils and the chip-storage area occupies 80% of the total area. As a matter of fact, 1-Mbit capacity can be achieved with 1.8-μm bubbles because as capacity increases, the relative size of the peripheral area decreases. If a 10% shorter period were used, 2-μm bubbles could be fabricated in a 1-Mbit chip. This requires a minimum feature size of about 1.25 μm (8-μm period), which is pushing current manufacturing and photolithographic capabilities. Fortunately, recently developed projection aligners appear capable of achieving these requirements in production.

The field is wide open

Another important aspect of device scaling is the drive-field requirement. Since the bubble field and rotating drive field compete with each other to magnetize the permalloy-propagation pattern, minimum drive field increases as the bubble size decreases.

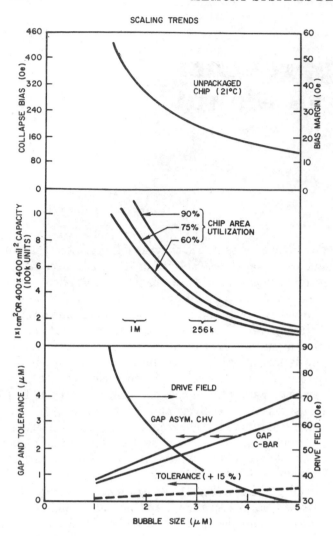

1. **The various scaling trends in bubble-memory chips** are broken down by showing how bubble size depends on bias field, bias margin, drive field, permalloy-gap dimension and chip capacity.

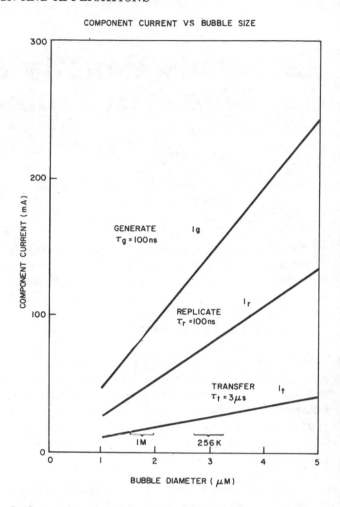

2. **Generate, replicate and transfer**—the three main functions externally controllable—have special current requirements, which are a function of bubble diameter.

Generally, about 10 Oe of overdrive are required to open up the rotating field margin and this factor has been added to the minimum-drive value to obtain the result in the table.

Fortunately, it's possible to reduce the required magnetization and with it the drive field. Up to now, it has been assumed that the diameter and height of the bubbles are about the same. Reducing bubble height will reduce the required magnetization and drive field. However, this will also slightly narrow the free-bubble stability range and thus decrease the net operating margin. In view of the larger intrinsic margin associated with smaller bubble size, this tradeoff appears favorable.

Taking stability into account, the free-bubble bias margin works out to about 10% of $4\pi M_s$ and the nominal bias field to about 45% of $4\pi M_s$. For a fully functional device, it is more common to express the bias margin as a percentage of the nominal bias. A 12.5% figure is sustained in the reduction from 6 to

3.3-μm bubbles. Preliminary results on smaller bubbles indicate that the same margin should apply right down to the lithographic limit.

Another implicit assumption so far is that vertical distances are scaled like the bubble diameter to maintain an equivalent magnetic environment. Unfortunately, as bubbles get smaller, it becomes less desirable to reduce the control-conductor thicknesses because of potential problems with drive voltage and electromigration.

Furthermore, standard device processing makes step coverage a problem as the conductor thickness increases relative to the permalloy to garnet spacing. The solution is to shift from conventional to planar processing. Several approaches using either lift-off or spun-on spacer layers are now available.

Good chip designs are configured so that bubbles start and stop only on permalloy sites having no conductor underneath them. This means that the reduction in magnetic pole strength due to the step in the permalloy height plays the important role in device operation. Because the conductor is about as thick as the permalloy, the steps at the conductor edges produce unwanted competing poles. Thus the

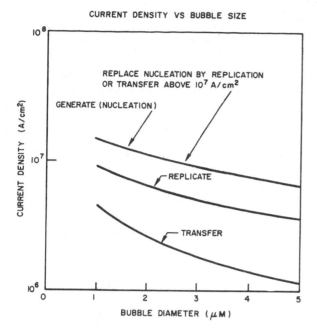

CURRENT DENSITY VS BUBBLE SIZE

3. **As bubbles approach 2 μm,** the current densities for the same functions shown in Fig. 2 are high, but do not increase to unmanageable levels.

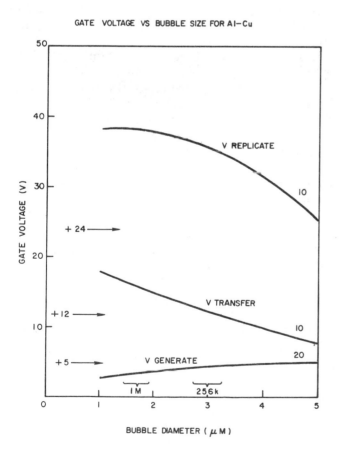

GATE VOLTAGE VS BUBBLE SIZE FOR Al–Cu

4. **Except for the generate voltage,** the gate voltages needed to perform the replicate and transfer functions go up as bubble sizes go down. The generate voltage remains essentially constant.

effect of the desired pole is reduced, and the drive field becomes too high.

Apparently, even at 3.3 μm bubble size, nonplanarity increases the drive field unnecessarily. Consequently, a planar approach appears necessary to obtain the full potential of 2 μm bubble technology. The crossover point from conventional to planar processing should occur at about 2.4-μm diameters.

Scale the conductors, too

The lateral conductor geometries must also go down much like the permalloy pattern period. This stems largely from routing characteristics and constraints related to transfer, replicate and exchange switches. Still, the generator conductor design is flexible to some extent if the permalloy-pattern period in this region is elongated.

Because the conductor line widths get very small for 2-μm bubbles, electromigration can become a serious problem as bubble sizes are scaled down. Thus it is necessary to know how the current requirements vary with bubble size for each of the components. Fig. 2 shows that in practice the required component currents decrease almost proportionally with bubble diameter. As a result, the corresponding current densities (Fig. 3) don't increase as rapidly as expected —this makes possible operation down to a 2-μm bubble size.

Because bubble generation requires the largest current, it could be a major candidate for electromigration. Flexibility in conductor design and the short generator pulse width can be used to prevent electromigration failures—especially when a planar process is used.

After all the physical parameters have been scaled, it is necessary to consider the voltage levels. Fig. 4 graphically presents the required component voltages for generating, transferring, and replicating bubbles. The curves are based on a dual-block-replicate chip in which the number of minor loops equals N/2, where N is the chip capacity. The conductor thickness is also scaled, and the component currents follow the curves of Fig. 2.

The two generators on the chip are assumed to be connected in series. Since the required generator current drops with decreasing bubble size, a +5-V supply is adequate for this component with bubbles as small as 2 μm. For the other components, the number of required switches is increasing, so the voltage goes up even though the current decreases.

This potential problem has several solutions, which involve either the processing or the design. For example, thickening the conductor by a factor of 1.5 to 2 (probably feasible with planar construction) would bring down the required voltage dramatically. Changing the metalization to lower the resistance would also help. The resistivity would very likely benefit and electromigration would decrease by using gold instead

PACKAGED CHIP TRENDS

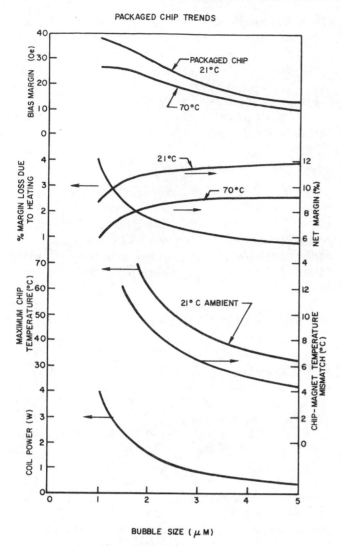

5. **Coil power, chip temperature and margins** all increase with chip density since smaller bubbles require higher drive fields.

of Al-Cu. However, gold systems have been criticized for the additional adhesion layers they require—these complicate the processing.

Even without processing modifications, the necessary chip voltages can be developed by stepping up the commonly used ±12-V supplies directly on the PC board with inexpensive circuits. For a megabit chip, however, the replicate function becomes particularly difficult to implement. Subdividing and paralleling the replicate conductor to reduce the required voltage becomes unattractive due to routing difficulties and resistance mismatches.

As a result, if the replicate function is to be retained on a megabit chip, it's likely that either the pinout or the minor-loop structure will have to be changed, the latter in order to reduce the number of switch components. Unfortunately, if the loops are folded and made longer, this increases access time, reduces data rate and—thanks to the additional corners—probably creates margin losses.

Density affects packaging, too

There are packaging problems to solve. For low-frequency operation, the material requirements for a packaged bubble memory chip are determined primarily by the problems of spontaneous nucleation at higher temperatures. To prevent spontaneous nucleation at high temperature, it is necessary to determine both the chip temperature rise above ambient due to coil heating and chip power dissipation; this way, the minimum H_k, or Q, can be found. (Q is the ratio of induced uniaxial anisotropy field, H_k, to the demagnetizing field that attempts to rotate the magnetization into the plane of the film.)

This problem is extremely complicated and depends on package geometry, thermal conductivity of the package components and coil design. The graph of Fig. 5 illustrates the power and packaged chip parameters vs bubble diameter for a 400 × 400-mil chip and a coil height of 80 mils. The on-chip power dissipation is assumed to be 150 mW.

Also plotted is the steady-state temperature difference between the chip and bias magnet, which can be used to calculate the percent margin loss due to start-stop operation, assuming that the bias margin decreases according to −0.19%/°C. The percent margin loss due to this effect, as well as the net packaged chip bias margin are also included to show that in practice the over-all bias margin does not increase as rapidly as 1/d.

When a material composition of YSmLuCaGeFeO is tested, a temperature rise causes the existing Q to decrease as bubble size decreases. Because Q is lower for smaller bubble materials and the drive field is higher, the problem is accentuated for larger capacity chip designs. If the temperature rise isn't reduced, the lower limit on bubble size for this material composition is limited to about 1.75 μm. Of course, if the operating temperature range were reduced to a range narrower than 0 to 70 C, the material could handle still smaller bubble sizes.

When evaluating thermal factors, it is necessary to consider the drive field, H, the coil design, and the thermal conductivity of the packing materials. Unfortunately, coil design is limited by inductance considerations if low-voltage supplies are to be used.

Alternatives to reducing coil power such as using silver wire to reduce the electrical conductivity—are expensive. Since the coil power varies with H^2, this is where emphasis should be placed to extend the technology to smaller bubble sizes. Contiguous-disk bubble technology is particularly attractive from both the drive field standpoint and minimum Q requirements since propagation is achieved by an in-plane garnet layer vs permalloy elements. This relaxes the nucleation criterion, and thus allows lower Q materials to be used at high temperature. And, with lithographic requirements also relaxed, the useful lower limit on garnet material is extended. In any case, however, high-frequency operation for both conventional and contiguous-disk technologies remains a major stumbling block due to the voltage requirements. The newly introduced current-access technologies, however, promise to overcome this problem.

In summary, then, bubble memories are now a commercial reality.■■

Bubbles: More Capacity and Components

DAVE BURSKY
Senior Editor, Semiconductors,
Electronic Design

From a laboratory curiosity, the magnetic bubble memory has evolved rapidly into a viable commercial device. Likewise, the range of available components has grown faster than anyone expected.

The first bubble-memory devices were 64-kbit serial shift-register architectures; this year, 1-Mbit major/minor-loop block-replicate architectures were introduced. New techniques—such as planar structures and electron-beam lithography—and improved resolution will produce devices with capacities of 4 Mbits in the early 1980s.

Modified loop architectures and various other organizations are also being examined. The TIB1000, introduced by Texas Instruments, has two complete 512 k × 1 arrays on a single chip, giving a storage capacity of 512 k × 2.

Before long, ×4 and ×8 outputs will be available. Access times have dropped from hundreds of milliseconds and will go to less than 6 ms when manufacturers realize field-coil frequencies of 200 kHz in 1980.

As the chart shows, at least seven vendors are vying for a share of the bubble-memory business and each is developing its own support components.

Bubble-memory devices

Manufacturer	Model No.	Net capacity	Organization	Package	Sample availability	Sample cost	Special support ICs
Fujitsu	FBM0102	64 kbits	Major/minor	18-pin	Stock	$100[3]	In development
	FBM0201	64 kbits	Serial/parallel single-loop	18-pin	Stock	$100[3]	In development
	FBM0301	256 kbits	Major/minor block-replicate	16-pin	Stock	$500	In development
Hitachi	HBM	64 kbits	No information available				
	HBM	256 kbits					
	HBM	1 Mbit					
Intel	7110	1 Mbit	Major/minor block-replicate	Leadless	30 days	$2000	Yes
Motorola[1]	RBM256	256 kbits	Major/minor block-replicate	18-pin	Late 1980	—	In development
National Semiconductor	NBM2256	256 kbits	Major/min block-replicate	16-pin	Early 1980	—	In development Early 1980
Plessey	PB064/S1	64 kbits	Serial shift register (no loop)	12-pin	Stock	—[4]	In development
	PB256	256 kbits	Major/minor block-replicate	18-pin	Mid-1980	—	In development
Rockwell	RBM256	256 kbits	Major/minor block-replicate	18-pin	Stock	$500	In development
		1 Mbit	Major/minor block-replicate	18-pin	Late 1979	—	In development
Siemens	RBM256	256 kbits	Major/minor block-replicate	18-pin	Late 1980	—	In development
Texas Instruments	TIB0203	92 kbits	Major/minor	14-pin	Stock	$100	Yes
	TIB0303	254 kbits	Major/minor block-replicate	18-pin[2]	Stock	$500	Yes
	TIB0250	256 kbits	Major/minor block-replicate	24-pin	2nd qtr 1980	—	2nd qtr 1980
	TIB0500	512 kbits	Major/minor block-replicate	24-pin	4th qtr 1979	$2100[5]	2nd qtr 1980
	TIB1000	1 Mbit (512 k × 2)	Major/minor block-replicate	24-pin	4th qtr 1979	$3100[5]	2nd qtr 1980

1. Alternate source for Rockwell RBM256.
2. 70-mil centers (an 18-pin, 100-mil version is also available).
3. 100-unit quantities.
4. Only board-level products will be available ($2997, 64 kbytes, SBC-80 compatible).
5. Board-level-evaluation subsystems with support ICs.

Building Bubble Memory Systems Becomes a "Family" Affair

GERALD COX
Engineering Manager,
Magnetic Bubble Memory Systems,
Texas Instruments, Dallas, Texas

Magnetic bubble memories can provide efficient and reliable performance in many applications like terminals or stand-alone computer systems. Subsystem flexibility allows the designer to trade off between system characteristics like transfer rate, access time, cost per bit, system cost, system size, system weight, power consumption, and storage capacity.

Intended to provide the designer with the flexibility and components needed to put together optimum bubble-memory storage systems, Texas Instruments has developed the TIB1000 family of bubble memory devices and support circuits. Included in the family are three new bubble memory devices (see Table 1) and associated support circuits. These devices are in addition to the already available 92-kbit and 254-kbit devices.

The largest circuit, organized internally as two separate 512 k × 1 arrays on a common substrate, but sharing the same magnetic fields, provides a total data capacity of 1,124,901 bits. All three devices will be electrically and physically interchangeable with each other, thus permitting the system designer to select the capacity necessary for his current design, and to increase it later, just by substituting a larger capacity device.

Operating at field rates of 100 kHz, the bubble memory devices (BMDs) provide an average access time of just 11.25 ms. All the BMDs retain the features of previous bubble memory chips—swap and replicate gates, a block-replicate architecture, and an on-chip map loop for the transparent handling of defective loops by the system controller.

Support chips simplify system design

New support circuits for the BMD family include a controller (BMC), a function timing generator (FTG), a data corrector/formatter (DCF), coil drivers (CD), read and write function drivers (RFD and WFD) and the sense amplifier (SA). Initially, there will be one set of circuits introduced for the design of small-to-medium size systems. In the near future, though, a more powerful set of support circuits based on a modular array concept will permit extremely large systems, such as disk replacements, as well as small systems to be structured very economically.

The current family of support and the future devices are listed in Table 2. The bubble modular array with correction (BMAC) system will permit up to 32, individually corrected, parallel channels of data to be transmitted to a host system at burst rates of up to 16 Mbytes/s. Included in the DCF circuit are data buffers that permit total isolation of the data rates on the input side from the host system, to the output side of the bubble-memory array, and vice-versa. A specially-developed error-correction code, designed specifically for the most probable error distribution in bubble-memory systems, provides unequalled levels of error-rate performance (see Table 3).

Shown in Fig. 1a is a 1-Mbit bubble-memory system in a minimal configuration. The use of the TIB0903 controller does not permit software programming of the device parameters for the bubble memories, and restricts system use to the 512 k × 1 and 512 k × 2 devices. The TIB0902 controller mask option handles the 256-kbit devices. For software programmability, the TIB0904 controller, when available, will permit the use of any of the bubble memory devices.

The TIB0902 and 0903 controller interface to the host system is compatible not only with TI's TMS9900 microprocessor family, but with the 8080A, 8085A and Z80 microprocessors as well. Other microprocessors, such as the 6800 and 6502, can mate to the controllers with some additional logic. The next generation controller, the TIB0904, will permit simple interfaces to all these microprocessors without additional logic. And, the new controller will also support the use of the DCP, thus permitting error correction and data formatting capability to be added to the system (Fig. 1b).

The TIB1000 has a gross storage capacity of 1,122,852 bits on a chip in an area of less than 1 cm². However, some of this storage capacity is used for the redundancy map and error correction, so that the available data storage capacity with error correction capability drops to a still impressive 1,049,088 bits. This translates to a full 128 kbytes of nonvolatile storage. The small area of the chip permits more

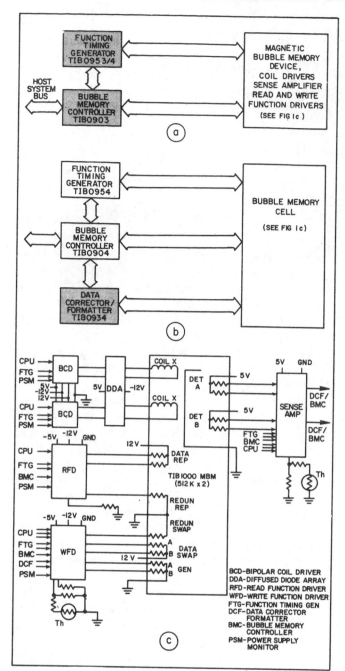

1. **A minimal bubble-memory system can be built with a single bubble-memory device and one of each of the various support circuits (a). For more complete system capability, including error correction, the data corrector/formatter circuit can be added (b). The basic bubble-memory cell shown in detail in (c) must be repeated for each bubble device used.**

devices to be processed on a given wafer, which will further reduce cost per bit, while the redundant data loops increase yields by preventing a few defective loops from ruining an otherwise functional chip.

Compact packages boost density, too

The external packaging has also been rearranged and the small size of the new package (1.3 × 1.4 ×

0.37 in.) allows two bubble memory devices and the associated system circuitry to be mounted on a 25 in.² card with a storage capacity of 256 kbytes. For increased-capacity systems, the controller has an internal data accumulator that provides a parallel interface for one to four DCFs operating either one at a time or in parallel. By simply changing the memory devices, the same board can change capacity; ranging from 64 kbytes to 256 kbytes.

For maximum channel width, though, the controller can accommodate bus widths from 5 to 32 bits by using the same number of DCF integrated circuits. In this mode, the BMC merely supervises the DCF circuit transactions rather than acting as a bus-width conversion device. Other features include detailed status of bubble-error correction; data transfers selectable via polled I/O, interrupts, or DMA; single-page or multipage data transfers; and operation with up to a 200-kHz bubble-memory field frequency. The DMA mode allows programmable burst length as well as a programmable interval between bursts.

Examine the timing considerations

The speed that data in the loops can be accessed and transferred out of the bubble memory depends on several factors. Additionally, there are different ways to specify the performance of the memory. Access time, for instance, can be described in several ways: One of these, which might be called loop access time, is the average time required for a desired page of data to circulate through the minor loops to replicate or swap gates, which is equal to half the length of the minor loop divided by the bubble field frequency. In the TIB1000, there are 2049 bits per loop, and an initial field frequency specification of 100 kHz, which yields a loop access time of 10.2 ms. In the near future, the design goal of 200 kHz will be achieved, and the loop-access-delay time will drop to 5.1 ms.

Another way to specify access time is by the delay associated with propagation of the bubble along the read or write tracks. This write/read track delay equals 100 field cycles, so that the average access time is half the minor loop length plus 100 divided by the bubble field frequency. This can be computed to be:

$$t_{av} = [(2049 \times 0.5) + 100] \div 200 \text{ kHz} = 5.6 \text{ ms.}$$

In many applications, however, you must know the worst-case access time. To compute this, you must assume that the desired page of data is at the furthest possible point from the replicate gate and must circulate through all 2049 bit positions before being transferred to the read track. The worst-case access time then equals 2049 plus 100 field cycles, for the read track delay divided by the frequency; the resulting time is 10.7 ms at 200 kHz.

Another important measure of bubble-memory performance is the average data rate. Once the starting point for a block of data has been reached, the average data rate in the multi-page read or write mode equals

Table 1. Comparison of bubble-memory devices

Model number Array organization	TIB1000 512 k x 2	TIB0500 512 k x 1	TIB0250 256 k x 1
Available capacity (bits)	1,122,852	561,426	280,850
Architecture			
- Page swap/replicate			
- Total loops	300 x 2	300	300
- Good loops	274 x 2	274	274
- Data loops with ECC	256 x 2	256	256
- Data loops w/o ECC	272 x 2	272	272
- Bits per loop	2049	2049	1025
Access time (ms)	11.2	11.2	5.6
Data throughput			
- Field rate (kHz)	100	100	100
- Burst data rate (kb/s)	200	100	100
- Average data rate (kb/s)	170	85	85
Power dissipation (watts)	1.2	1.2	1.2
Packaging			
- Size (inches)	1.3 x 1.4 x 0.37	1.3 x 1.4 x 0.37	1.3 x 1.4 x 0.37
- Number of pins	24	24	24
- Pin spacing (inches)	0.1	0.1	0.1
- Row spacing (inches)	1.3	1.3	1.3
- Interchangeable	Yes	Yes	Yes
Temperature range			
- Operating (ambient)	0 to 50 C	0 to 50 C	0 to 50 C
- Data storage (ambient)	−40 to 85 C	−40 to 85 C	−40 to 85 C

Table 2. Summary of support components

Initially introduced devices		Future support	
TIB1000	1-Mbit BMD		
TIB0500	512-kbit BMD		
TIB0250	256-kbit BMD		
TIB0903	Bubble-memory controller (TIB1000 and 0500)	TIB0904	Bubble-memory controller
TIB0902	Bubble-memory controller (TIB0250)	TIB0954	Function-timing generator
TIB0953	Function-timing generator	TIB0934	Data-corrector/formatter
TIB0863	Read-function driver	TIB0864	Read-function driver
TIB0883	Write-function driver	TIB0884	Write-function driver
TIB0804	Coil driver	TIB0804	Same as initial unit
TIB0833	Sense amplifier (single-channel)	TIB0834	Dual-channel sense amp

the number of bits per page times the field frequency divided by the number of field cycles required to read or write a page of data. Thus, for a page of 256 bits the calculation would be:

$$\frac{256 \times 200 \text{ kHz}}{(300 + 20^*) \text{ field cycles}} = 160 \text{ kbits/s per channel.}$$

* Interpage gap.

This is the maximum average data rate that includes error correction. If the error-correction option is not used, there are an additional 18 bits of data available for each 256-bit page, which in turn yields an average data rate of 170 kbits/s. Each bubble-memory device uses a dedicated redundancy-map loop to store a map of the defective loops. During system initialization, this map is read into a RAM in the DCF

Table 3. Error-correction ability			
Definition of error within a 256-bit page in order of occurrence	**Probability of page in error***	**TI bubble code**	
		correction	**detection**
Single soft error	3×10^{-4}	100%	—
Single hard error	3×10^{-6}	100%	—
Randomly spaced double soft error	3×10^{-8}	50%	100%
Soft-error burst length 2	3×10^{-9}	100%	—
Hard-error burst length 2	3×10^{-11}	100%	—
Soft-error burst length 3 or 4	2×10^{-11}	—	100%
Randomly spaced double hard error	3×10^{-12}	50%	100%
Soft-error burst length 5	3×10^{-12}	—	100%
Randomly spaced triple soft error	3×10^{-12}	—	87%
Single soft and soft burst length 2	8×10^{-13}	—	100%
Undetected and uncorrected system-error escape rate per 256 bit/page	4×10^{-13}	—	—

* To convert to errors per bit, divide error rate by 300.

circuit. During a read or write operation, each bit position in a page of data is compared with the map stored in the DCF. During a write operation, when an unused loop position is encountered, a bit space is inserted in the data stream entering the write track. For a read operation, an inhibit signal causes the unused bit position to be ignored by preventing that bit from entering the DCF's data buffer.

Reading or writing data can be done in the single or multi-page mode. During a multi-page data transfer, the write command causes the bubble memory controller to wait for a page of data to be received from the CPU. The controller then writes that page to the bubble memory and continues writing pages of data until the number of pages indicated by the page-count register have been transferred. An interrupt signal is generated each time the data buffer is emptied so the CPU can start writing the next page to the DCF buffer. Multi-page transfers can be stopped and started, if desired. Depending on the command used to stop the data transfer, the multi-page operation can resume with the next consecutive page or at a new page location, as determined by the contents of the page-select register.

Data transfers from the DCF to the CPU occur up to a maximum of 4 MHz. Of course, at that rate, the data buffers are emptied very rapidly, and for small systems, the CPU must wait for the buffers to be refilled. In an expanded system, though, many bubble memory devices can operate in parallel and it is possible to read the data at a continuous 4-MHz rate per channel.

LSI provides system support

Bubble memory components, as dense as they are, require a considerable amount of external support,

since circuits (aside from the memory array) cannot be fabricated on the same chip. In fact, in any system consisting of multiple bubble memory devices, each bubble memory must have its own coil drivers, function drivers and sense amplifier. This bubble memory cell, or modular memory unit (MMU), shown in Fig. 1c, then interfaces to the controller, function timing generator, and data corrector/formatter.

To provide the interface between the microprocessor or computer and the memory subsystem itself, the TIB0904 controller does the basic manipulation, such as starting and stopping the bubble movement, maintaining the page position, and raising and lowering flags for bubble memory functions, such as generate, swap, block replicate, and redundancy replicate.

The controller also maintains detailed status in-

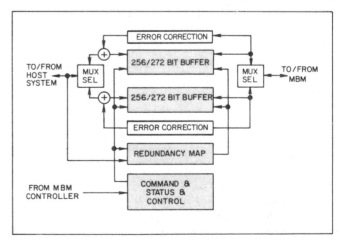

2. Providing error correction using a proprietary algorithm, the data corrector/formatter circuit also buffers the incoming and outgoing data so that the host system's data-transfer rate is independent of the bubble-memory speed.

Take a look inside the TIB1000

The TIB1000 offers the highest data capacity of the three bubble-memory devices just introduced by Texas Instruments—1,122,825 bits. Organized as two side-by-side 512-k x 1 arrays on the same garnet chip, the TIB1000 comes in a package that also includes two permanent magnets, two mutually perpendicular coils, and a magnetic shield.

The magnets provide a magnetic field that stabilizes the magnetic-bubble domains even when power is off. Both of the coils provide a rotating magnetic field that propagates the bubbles in shift-register fashion through the magnetic layer. An external shield protects the data from magnetic fields of up to 20 oersteds that the device may be forced to operate within.

Control functions of the memory include generation, replication, and swapping of data, and the replication and swapping of redundancy information. A new, advanced planar structure is used along with bubble diameters of $2 \mu m$ to provide the high density. The bubble control functions are accomplished by accurate current pulses flowing through the planar aluminum-copper patterns that have been deposited on the surface of the chip above the magnetic film.

The memory array itself on the TIB1000 has the two separate 512-kbit blocks set up to operate in parallel. The BMD pinout of Fig. A shows the two totally separate sets of control and output lines. Each array on the chip has its own mapping loop; however, only one of the map loops is actually connected to the external pins of the package.

Each subarray has 300 minor loops of 2049 bits each. A page of data consists of bubbles from 256 of those loops. Of the 44 remaining loops, 18 can be used for error correction and as many as 26 are allowed to be defective. As shown in Fig. B, each section has its own independent read track and detector.

Each of the arrays within the chip uses a new double-period gate that effectively closes the distance between minor loops, and eliminates the need for odd and even storage banks within an array. The number of generators per bank is reduced from two to one and the merge gate in the output track is eliminated while preserving data-shift rates equal to the field rate.

For write operations, data are generated on every field cycle and shifted two normal periods on each field cycle until aligned with the minor loops. Then a swap pulse exchanges data in the top bit position of each minor loop with data in the input write track. The old data are shifted to a guard rail on subsequent operations and destroyed.

A read operation begins at the opposite end of the minor loops where block replication of the bubbles duplicates an entire page of data and transfers it to the read tracks in one operation. Again, data bits travel two normal periods per cycle and close normally present data gaps to allow data to be read on every field cycle.

The bubbles are then propagated to the detector, where the magnetoresistors sense the presence or absence of the bubble and feed their output to an external dual-channel sense amplifier set up in a balanced bridge configuration. This bridge operates similarly to the bridge in the older TI bubble-memory devices (see "All about the TIB0303," ELECTRONIC DESIGN, May 10, 1979, p. 56).

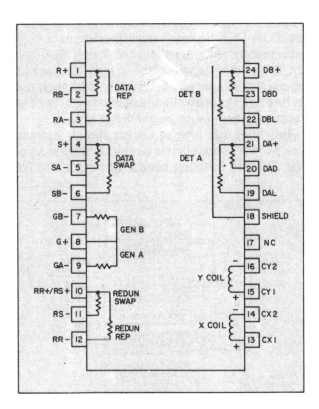

(cont'd on next page)

formation regarding bubble error correction and controls the DCF devices which provide data buffering and error correction. Fabricated with NMOS technology, the controller will come in a 40-pin package and operate from a single, 5-V supply. Although not used at its limit, the controller has a maximum bubble field-frequency rate of more than 200 kHz.

Providing the precise timing signals necessary to operate the various driver circuits and sense amplifier, the TIB0954 function timing generator receives the control signals from the controller and carries out each instruction. this circuit has standard low-power Schottky TTL inputs and outputs for simplified interfacing to the other support circuits.

In the earlier, 92-kbit, and the TIB0903 megabit bubble memory systems, the controller section performed the functions of data buffering and redundancy handling in addition to the main control of the bubble memories. In the new BMACS family of memory components, these functions and error correction are performed by the TIB0934 DCF (Fig. 2). Data buffering of 274 bits can be performed for one 512-bit section of the TIB1000 at a time. Although a single DCF circuit can be shared by both sections of the 1-Mbit bubble memory via multiplexing, higher operating throughput rates can be obtained by using one DCF for each 512-kbit section.

The error-correction circuitry takes care of any single-bit random error or 2-bit burst error and detects any randomly spaced double-bit error in a page of data. In fact, 50% of the randomly spaced double-errors are corrected. The significance of this correction capability lies in the fact that most burst-error correction codes do very poorly for the same problem. Thus, to see any significant improvement in error-correction capability, this area must be addressed well before burst-error correction can be attempted.

The DCF circuitry has the capability to correct both redundancy loop data and regular data. Internal error correction can be disabled, thus increasing the maximum page size to 274 bits of pure data. The DCF is fabricated with NMOS processing, is housed in a 16-pin package, and operates from a 5-V supply.

Individuality for coil drivers

In any bubble memory system, individual bubble memory devices require support circuits that provide coil drive for just that device. To directly support each bubble memory device, several circuits are needed. Included would be the field coil drivers; in this case, the TIB0804 which uses the +5 and ±12-V supplies. Each supply can vary, independently, by ±5%.

These circuits receive TTL inputs from the function timing generator and produce a high-level driving voltage that is integrated into a current ramp by the field coils, thus producing a triangular waveform. The diode arrays minimize the voltage loss across the coils

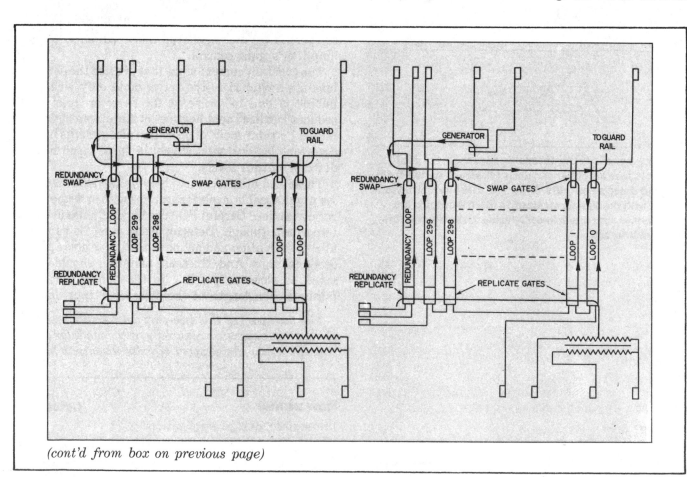

(cont'd from box on previous page)

when the driving voltage is turned off, thus making the triangular current waveforms more symmetrical. For bubble devices operating one at a time, the TIB0804 drivers offer the best solution. However, for parallel bubble device operation, discrete VMOS power transistors offer the best solution.

Converting the TTL signals from the controller into current pulses required by the bubble memory, the TIB0863 and 0883 function drivers provide the current pulses needed by the bubble memory for the actual operations of bubble generation, swapping, and replication. The drivers have an internal time-out circuit to prevent burn out of the bubble memory elements if a timing fault should occur in the memory system. A chip-select input on the function driver permits drivers to be multiplexed, and a disable input lets all the outputs of the circuit be disabled to inhibit transients during power cycling.

The disable signal comes from a centralized power-supply monitor circuit that makes sure that all function drivers and coil drivers are enabled or disabled at the same time. The monitor also detects when the supply levels have dropped to below 95% of their nominal value, to warn the bubble system that something is amiss in the system.

The bubble memory architecture directly influences the design of the function driver, and vice versa. The block-replicate section of the memory consists of a bubble-stretch-and-cut gate structure at every junction of the minor loops and the output track. At 2 μ design rules, the electrical resistance of each gate is about 0.5 Ω; and when 300 are connected in series, the resistance is such that about 20 V, max, must be used to drive the control element. This requires that linear process technology be used in the fabrication of the support circuit. Since linear processes have only about 1/3 the packing density of digital processes, two separate chips must be used, ergo the separate function drivers for the read and write operations. However, this is a small price to pay compared to the alternative—half the number of loops but double the access time.

Sense the bubble's presence

Receiving the millivolt signals from the dual bubble-detector elements, the TIB0834 sense amplifier provides amplification for the weak signals. The dual sense amplifier contains phase-tolerent clamp circuitry that enables amplification of the optimum input amplitude for a maximum output signal.

Shown in Fig. 3a is an ideal case when negative and positive peaks occur at the clamp and strobe times, respectively. However, in the real world (Fig. 3b), the signals are often delayed and the effective amplitude

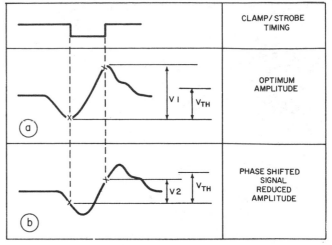

3. Using a phase-tolerant sensing approach, the dual-channel sense amplifier can detect the weak signals from the BMD detector outputs. Shown in (a) is an ideal detector output with the signals in phase. In (b), the outputs are out of phase, and much lower in value in the window time frame of interest.

is diminished, such that detection may not occur. The TIB0834 uses a window-sensing technique that searches for the negative-most peak and uses it as its reference. The amplifier then searches for the most positive peak in the timing window and stores the peak value. The resulting signal is presented to the input of the threshold circuit and later strobed into a latch.

Additionally, the sense amplifier is temperature compensated to maintain constant-signal amplitude to the threshold circuit. At low temperatures, the amplitude is at its maximum, and at high temps, at its lowest. The entire amplitude span is so large, that the amplifier has a special temperature sensing provision to change the gain as a function of temperature. A special clip mounts a thermistor in contact with the case of the bubble memory device to sense the temperature; the signal is then fed back to the amplifier's gain control.

The constant current sinks that provide the detector bias are switched to the active state only when the bubble is due to arrive at the detector area. This reduces localized spot heating by more than 90%. The pulsed detector mode of operation also permits higher detector bias currents, which, in turn, mean higher detector output levels.

These and other features help reduce soft errors to very manageable levels for systems with or without error correction. Careful PC-board layout rules are still important, though. Detector leads must be run parallel to each other and not be located near noisy power or signal runs. And, the sense amplifier should be located as close as possible to the bubble device to minimize the length of the detector output lines.■■

Build Compact Bubble Memory Systems

GEORGE F. REYLING, JR.
Subsystems Manager,
National Semiconductor Corp.,
Santa Clara, California

PETER K. GEORGE
Design Manager,
National Semiconductor Corp.,
Santa Clara, California

With bubble-memory devices and LSI support components becoming available from several major manufacturers, system designs are emphasizing lower costs at the subsystem level. For small-capacity applications (such as portable terminals, instruments and programmable calculators), costs can be reduced only by combining a complete family of support circuits with a bubble memory device that has a small die size. This combination is currently practical at the 256-kbit level. The graphs in Fig. 1 illustrate some of the cost trade-offs per bit and per system.

Five custom LSI circuits support the NBM2256 bubble memory device from National Semiconductor in a complete, yet economical subsystem. The NBM2256 stores 256 kbits on the smallest die currently used for a commercial 256-k bubble product in the United States. Because of the small die and because just five support circuits are needed, the complete bubble memory system fits on a printed-circuit board area of just 9 sq in. (Fig. 2). At a thickness of 0.36 in., the NBM2256 package allows tight board-to-board spacing, unlike some other bubble memory devices.

The combined NBM2256 and support circuits also promote modular, cost-effective expansion of systems that range in capacity from 32 to 256 kbytes. In even larger systems, they provide parallel control or bank-select operation.

The general operating characteristics of the NBM2256 are summarized in the table, and the package is described in "Just What Is an NBM2256?" It has a total data storage capacity of 262,144 bits (32 kbytes). Six additional loops detect and correct data errors. The nominal field frequency of the NBM2256 is 100 kHz, which provides a data throughput of 100 kbits/s. The first bit of a random data block is accessed with an average latency time of 7 ms.

External circuits control input/output

Since any bubble memory device contains no built-in control circuitry (aside from the swap and replicate

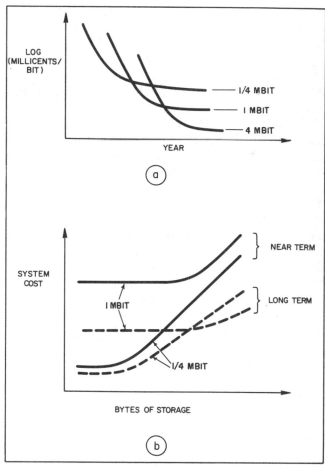

1. As bubble memories become denser, the cost per bit decreases dramatically (a). The expected entry cost for entire bubble memory systems will be lower for those incorporating smaller-capacity memory devices (b).

gate functions), external circuitry must take care of the addressing, the mapping of data into good loops and the counting of the data block positions for input and output. The control requirements are roughly equivalent to those of a small disk, which is implemented with as many as 40 to 100 standard MSI circuits.

The five specially developed circuits that support the NBM2256 are:

- The controller
- Two coil drivers
- The function driver
- The sense amplifier.

All but the controller are bipolar; the controller is an NMOS device. The bipolar process is well suited to the high currents and voltages required to manipulate the bubble memory. The bipolar circuits must be duplicated for each bubble memory device used, but their simplicity makes them inexpensive.

The more costly INS82851 controller, housed in a 40-pin DIP, can be shared by up to eight memory devices. It handles all the basic system timing and control functions for each bubble memory device. (Fig. 3).

At system initialization, the controller resets all control and status registers and transfers the bubble-memory redundancy map from the map loop to an on-chip buffer in the controller. Because a read error at this time would appear in all future data input and output operations, an error-detection capability is included in the bubble memory device and in the controller to ensure that the map data have been read correctly. Once initialized, the controller is ready to accept commands and data over National Semiconductor's well-defined Microbus interface. This bus is easy to use with most available microprocessors.

Read and write commands handle single or multiple blocks of data using program controlled, interrupt driven or DMA transfers. An internal 16-byte FIFO buffer facilitates responses, and the six error-correction loops of the bubble memory device verify data integrity.

The error most likely to occur during data transfer is a transient or soft-read error in the sense circuitry. The nondestructive read of the block replicate architecture prevents this error from affecting the data stored in the bubble memory. The most reliable error-correction strategy is to reread the block when an error is detected. If the error is redetected, the error can be assumed to be in the stored data, which can be corrected and rewritten.

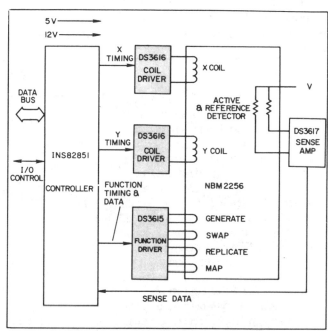

2. **The basic bubble memory subsystem consists of the bubble memory device, two coil-drive circuits, a function drive, the sense amplifier and the bubble memory system controller. The entire system only occupies a printed-circuit board area of 9 sq in.**

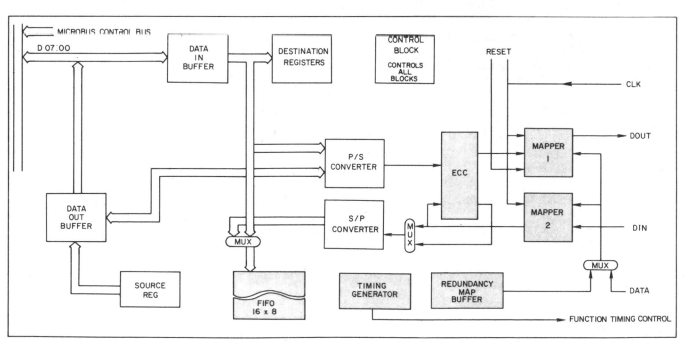

3. **A complex NMOS circuit, the system controller includes a FIFO register, error correction circuitry,** mapping registers, all timing control and redundancy map information, for controlling each bubble memory device.

The controller can operate with as few as one bubble memory device, or with two, four or eight devices in parallel, given the addition of a few low-cost TTL support circuits. Thus, the cost of the controller can be amortized over many bubble packages. For systems requiring higher data rates than the 100-bytes/s provided by one controller and eight bubble devices, multiple controllers can be operated in parallel.

Providing all the required system timing pulses, the controller interfaces directly to the coil drivers, the function driver and the sense amplifier. These other support circuits come in dual-in-line packages of 14 to 2 pins, depending upon the options provided.

The coil driver is perhaps the simplest of the support circuits (Fig. 4a). The DS3616 accepts the low-current logic inputs from the NMOS controller and translates them into the high-current triangular waveforms used by the field drive coils and the bubble memory device. The inductive load of the coils requires high-current clamp diodes in the driver. Power supplies for the driver can be limited to 5 and 12 V because the driver has a built-in voltage booster for upper-drive transistor biasing. An internal supply-voltage sensor guarantees glitch-free outputs during power up/down.

The generate, swap, replicate and map inputs to the bubble memory all require pulsed constant-current

Just what is an NBM2256?

The NBM2256 bubble memory device uses a dual block-replicate architecture and has several features not available in other bubble memory devices. The memory array on the chip is organized into even and odd loops of 1024 bits each, which are loaded through swap gates and read via replicate gates at opposite ends of the storage loops (see Fig.). The use of swap gates gives a considerably better performance than the use of transfer-in functions for write operations.

The total array stores data in 256 loops and an error correcting code in six loops. The remainder of the 282 potentially good loops provide redundancy to minimize problems from production defects. Thus, the usable data storage capacity is 262,144 bits (32 kbytes). Two additional loops are provided for storing a redundancy map; however, only one loop is actually used. The other loop is transparent to the user and provides additional redundancy for the map loop.

The minimum device geometry of 1.5 μm gives a storage cell of 12 $\times$ 12.5 μm for a bit density of 6.7 $\times$ 10^5 bits/cm^2 and an overall die size of 300 $\times$ 320 mils. Fabricated using projection lithography with a direct wafer stepper, the chip is expected to have high yields.

Housed in a 1.2 $\times$ 1.1 $\times$ 0.36 in. DIP and using only 16 pins, the NBM2256 can operate over a temperature range of 0 to 70 C (case). It can be stored between -40 and 100 C. With its support circuits, the NBM2256 requires 5 and 12-V power supplies; the bubble memory device itself dissipates just 0.75 W typical.

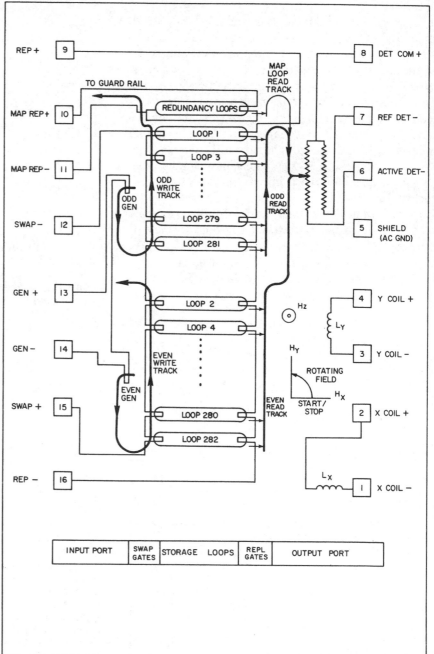

drivers. But the resistance on the replicate and swap inputs is so high that the IR product exceeds the voltage of the 12 V supply. Thus, a high-voltage source is required. Some vendors divide the replicate and swap lines into sections and run them in parallel to reduce the voltage, but this procedure also reduces the current margin (as a result of resistance mismatch) and complicates package interconnections.

Instead, National Semiconductor's DS3615 function driver (Fig. 4b) changes the logic-level outputs of the controller into higher voltage and currents by means of the inductive voltage-boost circuit that runs off the 12-V system supply. The driver is designed to limit the boost voltage to avoid possible burn-out of the replicator if a short occurs. An external capacitor and resistor are used to protect the generator. The function driver also features low-current np inputs, protection to ensure glitch-free power up/down and external control of current scaling.

To sense the millivolt outputs from the detector on the bubble memory device, the DS3617 sense amplifier (Fig. 4c) uses peak sensing with a considerable tolerance of phase shift in the signal. Bubbles are detected by the change in differential resistance between a reference cell and an active detector. A resistance change occurs when the bubble passes under a magnetoresistor element, and this change is transformed into a voltage change.

One commonly used approach senses the peak-to-peak signal excursion using a clamp and strobe technique. However, this approach tends to be sensitive to signal timing, which is affected by coil driver supply voltage, driver saturation voltage and manufacturing tolerances.

With its peak sensing approach, the DS3617 avoids this problem. If the threshold is crossed anywhere within a gating window, a data latch in the amplifier

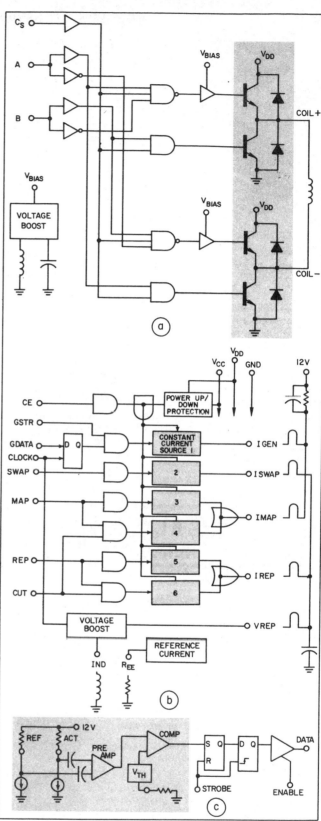

4. The DS3616 coil driver boosts the logic-level outputs of the system controller to the necessary current and voltage levels needed for coil driving (a). The DS3615 function driver (b) provides the current pulses for the bubble memory control functions (such as generate, swap replicate and map loops), and changes the controller's logic-level signals into the higher voltages needed, by means of a built-in voltage booster (b). Sensing the detector's millivolt-level outputs, the DS3617 sense amplifier has a phase-tolerant circuit designed to minimize errors (c).

Characteristics of the NBM2256

NBM2256	Characteristics
Capacity (net)	262,144 bits
Organization	Block-replicate
Minor loops (total)	282
Useful minor loops	256 data plus 6 ECC
Minor loop capacity	1024
Bubble size	2.7 μm
Storage area period	12 $\times$ 12.5 μm^2
Minimum geometry	1.5 μm
Chip size	300 $\times$ 320 mil^2
Operating frequency	100 kHz
Data rate	100 kHz
Average access time (first bit)	7 ms
Operating temperature (case)	0 to 70 C
Nonvolatile storage range (nonoperating)	−40 to 100 C
Package size	1.2 $\times$ 1.1 $\times$ 0.36 in.
Pins (dual-in-line package)	16 (100 mil centers)
Weight	28 g
Shielding capacity	20 Oe
Power requirements	+5, +12 V
Power consumption	0.75 W, typical

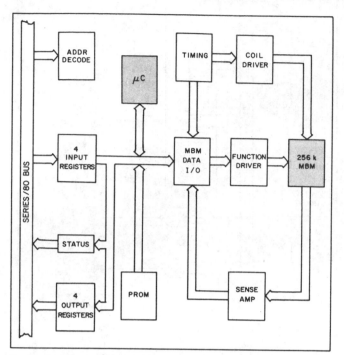

5. Until the custom LSI support is available, the NBS100 bubble memory board will provide equivalent functions by using a microprocessor and standard, off-the-shelf, MSI circuits. A 128-kbyte expansion board is also available.

is set. Constant current sources are used on the input to maximize input impedance and to reduce signal loading. The sense threshold can be externally adjusted, and the output can provide three-state levels to multiplex many devices.

Device evaluation starts here

Samples of the NBM2256 bubble memory device will soon be available; however, the support circuits will be in development a little longer. Until the support circuits are available, a basic evaluation board containing the subsystem functions is available. It uses standard ICs compatible with the company's Series/80 microcomputer boards and systems. The NBS100 evaluation board will contain one bubble memory device and all necessary drive and support circuits, as well as a microprocessor-based controller (Fig. 5). An expansion board, capable of providing an additional 128 kbytes, can be added.

These fully functional, bubble memory subsystems are suitable for applications where reduced component count is not critical. The System/80 bus is also fully compatible with the popular Intel interface. Thus, the NBS100 evaluation board will operate in any SBC-80 microcomputer system.■■

Serial or Major/Minor Loop?

GEORGE NEENO
Marketing Service Manager,
Component Sales Division, Fujitsu America,
Lake Bluff, Illinois

Magnetic bubble memories are organized in long serial loops or broken up into several minor loops that interface a so-called major loop. Each configuration has advantages, suiting it to specific classes of applications.

The serial bubble memory is much simpler than the major/minor version, but the serial unit has a much longer average access time. For example, Fujitsu Ltd.'s FBM31DB serial loop accesses in about 370 ms; its FBM32DA major/minor loop memory takes only 4.5 ms. Those applications that do not need the faster access time—like memories for storing program steps sequentially or for logging large amounts of data—can take advantage of the much simpler interfacing requirements of a serial loop.

Bubble memories have the speed and soon should have the price to compete with disk, cartridge and cassette units. They combine the advantages of volatile semiconductor memories with the advantages of nonvolatile magnetic-based memories. Bubble memories have no moving parts and low power consumption like semiconductor units, and they are smaller, lighter and nonvolatile like the conventional magnetically based units. Moreover, just two film masks are needed in the photo-etching process to make a bubble memory. Most semiconductor memories need many more.

In Fig. 1a, various conventional memories are compared by prices and access time; Fig. 1b compares applications with storage capacities. Existing technology for bubble memories can provide the 2-μm precision required for a chip as large as 256 kbits, and soon 1-μm precision will provide 1-Mbit chips.

Both loop configurations available

For the present, Fujitsu supplies two, nominally 64-kbit, bubble-memory packages—a serial loop (Fig. 2a) and a major/minor loop (Fig. 2b). Even though the major/minor loop configuration is considerably more complex than the serial, both types are housed in 18-pin DIP-like packages (Fig. 3).

Although the housings include magnetic shielding, any external magnetic field should not exceed 50 Oe, when the units are operating, and 100 Oe for preserving stored data.

Bubbles form in a thin, single-crystal film of garnet that is deposited, on a gadolinium-galium-garnet (GGG) substrate. A permanent magnet biases the film, and orthogonally mounted coils provide a rotating field to "step" the bubbles when writing or reading (Fig. 4).

The orthogonal coils (X and Y) are each driven with a 100-kHz triangular wave for a data transfer rate of 100 kbits/s. Synchronously operating switching

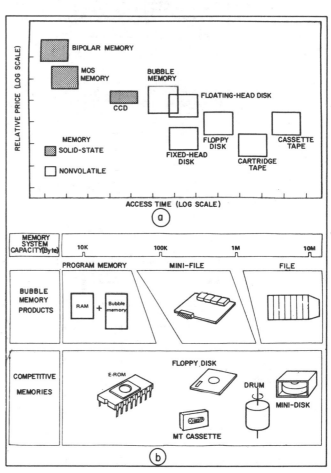

1. **Faster than most nonvolatile magnetomechanical memories, the bubble memory also costs more (a). But bubble prices should come down as production volume expands. When individual bubble-memory units are combined, they can handle as many bytes as much larger disk, cassette and cartridge units (b).**

circuits, represented by switches S_{X1}, S_{X2} and S_{y1}, S_{y2}, pulse currents through the X and Y coils in the sequence shown in Fig. 5. Coil inductances shape the current flow into the triangular waves. The two waves are 90° out of phase with each other.

Pulses in time sequence

Generating, replicating and annihilating bubbles requires current pulses—peak values of 260, 140 and 55 mA, repectively—from a constant-current source. The pulses must be delivered in a proper time sequence with the rotating field and with the proper polarity.

The current pulses pass through a conductor loop to generate a magnetic field that aids or opposes the biased field. The loop is a thin-film pattern of conducting nonmagnetic material that acts as a single-winding coil.

A bubble is generated whenever the current pulse passes through the loop, in the direction of the arrows in Fig. 6a (to oppose the bias), when the unit's rotating

field is oriented as shown. Orthogonally mounted coils provide the rotating field. Information is written bit by bit as each bubble is stepped to the left by the rotating field as soon as it is generated.

A conductor-loop, similar to the generator, copies magnetic bubbles. A bubble aproaching from the right is replicated when a current pulse passes in the direction of the arrow in Fig. 6c, as long as the direction of the rotating magnetic field is within the cross-hatched area shown. One bubble transfers upward, and the other transfers leftward. This action results in nondestructive reads, because one bubble is read and the other is recirculated in the loop.

Magnetic bubbles are detected by exploiting the magnetoresistive properties of some magnetic materials: The electrical resistances of these materials increase under the influence of a magnetic field. Since the increase in resistance is greater with larger bubbles, the bubbles are enlarged, or stretched, several hundred times in the direction of their motion as they pass under chevron-shaped elements (Fig. 7) before passing under the detectors. They are then detected more easily.

The detecting elements are electrically arranged in a differential-bridge pattern to eliminate the effects of the rotating field. Bubbles unbalance the bridge to supply an output of 5 to 10 mV. This output must then be amplified to required logic levels.

Card circuits interface TTL

To interface the bubble-memory packages with TTL, Fujitsu mounts them on circuit cards. Its FBC304D2A memory card is a high-speed unit containing four major/minor loop packages to provide 32 kbytes of memory. It can be connected to an 8-bit μP bus via a separate FBC304C2A control card, which can handle up to 256 kbytes, or eight memory cards,

SERIAL LOOP

A: ANNIHILATOR   G: GENERATOR   D: DETECTOR   R: REPLICATOR   T: TRANSFER GATE

(a)

MAJOR LOOP

— CONDUCTOR PATTERNS

— PATHS OF BUBBLE TRANSFER

MINOR LOOPS

(b)

2. Serial-loop configurations are simpler to make and interface (a). However, major/minor-loop arrangements (b) have much shorter access times.

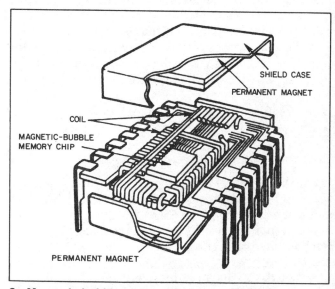

3. Magnetic-bubble memory devices are housed in shielded DIP-like packages. Several such packages on a plug-in card with appropriate driver circuits can be used as a minifile, and several cards can make up a file with megabyte capacities.

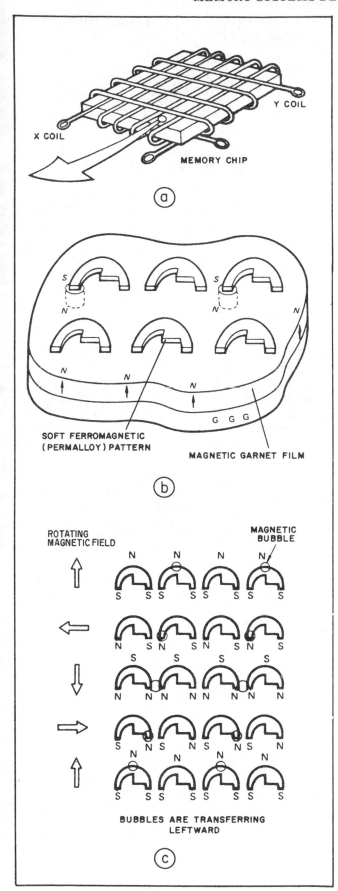

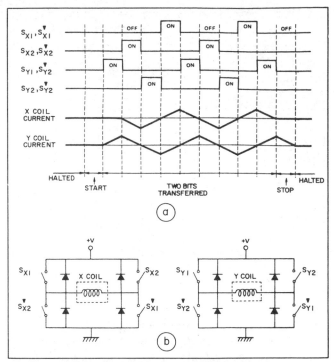

5. The triangular waves for the orthogonal coils, X and Y (a), are generated by synchronously driven switch pairs, S_{X1}/S_{X2} and S_{y1}/S_{y2}, which are 90° out of phase (b).

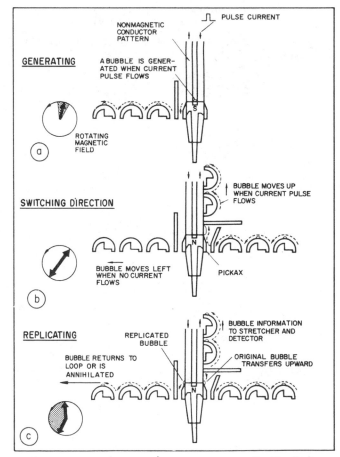

4. Orthogonally mounted coils (a) are driven with triangular waves that are 90° out of phase with each other. The coils produce a rotating field parallel to the garnet-film surface. A specially patterned overlay of soft ferromagnetic material (b) guides the bubbles to the left (c) as the field rotates counterclockwise.

6. Bubbles are generated by current pulses flowing in a nonmagnetic conductor loop, with the rotating-field and current-pulse directions as shown (a). Changes in bubble direction (b) and the replication of bubbles (c) occur when the current pulse flows in the opposite direction but with different rotating-field positions.

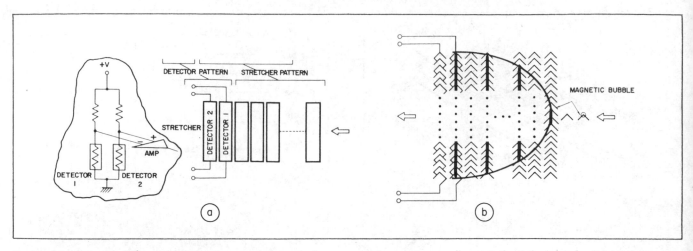

7. Bubble detection is accomplished by magnetoresistive material arranged in a bridge circuit (a). The bubbles pass under a chevron-shaped stretcher pattern (b), which enlarges the bubbles to facilitate their detection.

in a high-speed random-access file.

Where speed is not important, the FBC304M1A card (which also supplies 32 kbytes of memory) contains four serial loop packages instead of the much faster major/minor units. The one card contains all the control circuits—coil drivers, constant-current sources, sensing amplifiers, timing generators and others—to interface directly with an 8-bit μP, possibly as a program memory or even as a low-speed data file.

Bubble memories can be used in the following applications:

- Program memory
  Loaders for terminal equipment
  Program loaders for testing machines
  Program loaders for NC machines
  Memories for microprocessor systems
- Minifile memory
  Auxiliary memories for small-scale computers
  Air-borne memories
  Pattern memories for generating kanji characters
- File memory
  Files for electronic switching systems
  Voice recorders for audio service systems.

LSI Support Circuits Take Trouble Out

DON BRYSON
*Formerly Marketing Manager, Intel Magnetics,
Santa Clara, California*

DAVE LEE
*System Design Manager,
Intel Magnetics, Santa Clara, California*

Designing bubble memory systems is no more difficult than designing semiconductor memory systems. For several reasons, it may even be easier. Bubble "chips" offer high density. They are non-volatile. Perhaps best of all, support circuits for bubbles have just been integrated on a few specialized LSI chips. Six support packages are all it takes to stuff a 1-Mbit bubble system onto a single circuit card.

Bubble-systems offer several other advantages, including improved power dissipation and reliability. Compared to moving media memories (such as disks and tape), bubble memories operate over a much wider environmental range, without the periodic maintenance required by moving parts. The system can be easily expanded—memory is added in 1-Mbit blocks —by slipping another package onto the circuit board.

The bubble-memory chip—whether a circuit or an array—depends upon external circuits to provide timing and control pulses. Fig. 1 shows a minimal bubble-memory system organized as 128 kbytes. Supported by four LSI control circuits and two coil drivers, Intel's 1-Mbit 7110 exemplifies the internal capabilities of a bubble-memory chip.

256 loops and 48 spares

The 7110 has a serial-in, parallel-loop, serial-out array structure, and a gross-storage capacity of 1,310,720 bits. Each of the 256 data-storage loops contains 4096 bits, for a total useful storage capacity of 1,048,576 bits. In addition, 48 spare loops (also 4096 bits each) provide redundancy, so that fewer bubble chips must be discarded because of slight imperfections.

The spare loops on the chip can be mapped into the array via a boot loop, which contains a "map" of the known good loops on the chip. When the boot loop is read out during system initialization, the controller can avoid the bad loops. For even greater reliability, another 16 loops on the chip store an error correction code.

To get a reasonable data rate, the usable memory array on the chip is divided into two smaller arrays of 128 loops each. Each array bank feeds its own detector, which senses the absence or presence of a bubble and supplies the result to the external sense amplifiers.

The Intel bubble-memory chip comes in a dual-in-line leadless package; most of the other manufacturers of bubble memories use leaded packages. (See "The Whys and Wherefores of DIPs and Leadless Packages," p. 151.) The leadless package contains permanent magnets to maintain the bubbles in the magnetic material and contains orthogonal-field coils to create the rotating magnetic fields that move the bubbles within the material.

The outer case of the package serves as a magnetic shield for the internal return path of the magnetic flux. It also protects the stored data for external magnetic fields of up to 40 Oe. Weighing approximately 0.16 lb (74 g), the package mounts in a socket that occupies a total board area of 3.5 sq in. (Fig. 1b). The socket and package are keyed to guarantee correct insertion of the memory array.

The magnetic fields that move the bubbles are presently specified to operate at a rate of 50 kHz. With the dual-detector structure of the internal memory array, the effective maximum data rate is actually double the field rate or 100 kHz.

Bubble memories are well suited to standard printed-circuit boards since no special environmental conditions have to be met. Power to the bubble memory chip comes from a single 12-V supply. Because the memories require only ordinary supply voltage (5 and 12 V), the extra capacity of most power systems can probably support a reasonably sized subsystem.

Interface the array to a system

Like all bubble devices, the 7110 needs several kinds of support circuits. Typically, jobs can be divided into major subsystems and then developed into dedicated circuits as follows:

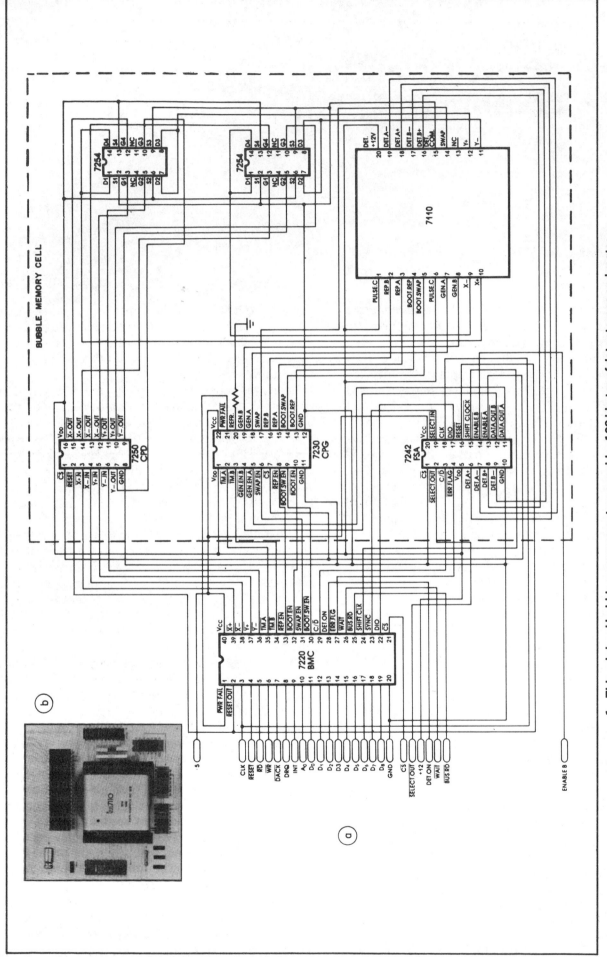

1. This minimal bubble memory system provides 128 kbytes of data storage and mates to an 8080/8085-compatible bus. Just six support packages are needed to make the subsystem operational (a). On a 4.5-sq-in. board, the entire 128-kbyte memory system can be transported and plugged into another system without any data loss (b).

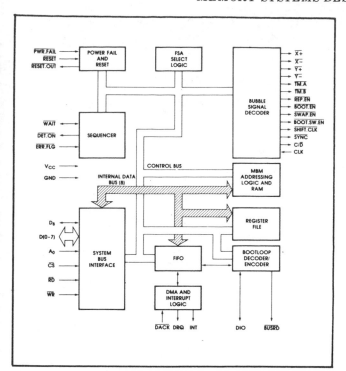

2. Providing the system bus interface and controlling up to eight 1-Mbit bubble memory devices, the 7220 BMC also permits DMA operations for high data throughput when large amounts of data must be transmitted.

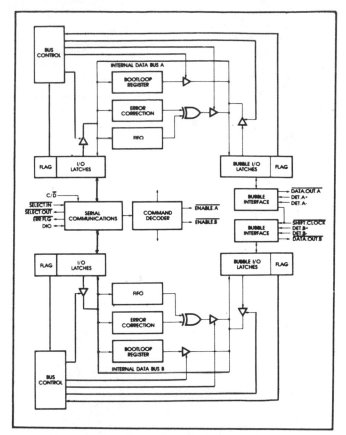

3. In addition to sensing the bubble detector outputs and converting the analog levels into digital form, the 7242 FSA contains the error-correction logic needed to eliminate all single-bit errors and burst errors up to 5 bits.

Table 1. Power dissipation of components

Component	Standby power (W)	Active power (W)
Bubble memory	0.29	1.9
Controller	0.5	0.5
Formatter/sense amp	0.6	0.6
Current pulse generator	0.23	0.64
Coil predriver	0.05	0.7
Drive transistors	0.0	0.7

- Bubble-memory controller (BMC)
- Current pulse generator (CPG)
- Formatter/sense amplifier (FSA)
- Coil predriver (CPD)
- Two coil drive transistors (CDT).

The controller is the interface for any bubble-memory system. In Intel's system, the controller is the 7220 BMC, an LSI device that provides the system timing, addressing, control and bus interface (Fig. 2). Housed in a 40-pin DIP, the circuit is TTL compatible and operates from a 5-V supply. One 7220 can control up to eight 1-Mbit devices (i.e., 1 Mbyte of storage).

The bus interface of the 7220 is 8080/8085 compatible. The 7220 has DMA handshake capability and can transfer both single and multiple-page blocks. Interfacing as many as eight 7242 FSAs, the controller reformats the serial data coming from the bubble memory into a 9-bit parallel data bus (the ninth bit can be used as a parity bit or can be eliminated). In the reverse mode, the circuit accepts an 8 or 9-bit word from the data bus and serializes it for the bubble-memory serial inputs.

The 7242 FSA provides most of the data handling and sensing for a bubble memory system (Fig. 3). Millivolt-level amplifiers on the FSA boost the weak signals from the bubble-memory detector outputs and then determine whether each signal represents a ONE or a ZERO. Each bubble-memory device is a system needs one 7242 to provide two channels of signal conditioning.

The FSA handles the redundant loops built into the chip and corrects errors. It generates and checks a 14-bit code for correcting burst errors (Fire code) of up to five bits. This code is attached to each 256-bit data block, and resides in the 16 storage loops which are reserved for this purpose on the bubble-memory chip.

Housed in a 20-pin DIP, the 7242 requires 5-V and 12-V power supplies. The circuit includes an FIFO data block buffer that holds 272 data bits when the FSA operates in the no-error-correction mode and 270 bits in the error-correction mode.

Convert TTL levels to current pulses

The TTL levels of system signals that are used by the interface circuits must eventually be converted

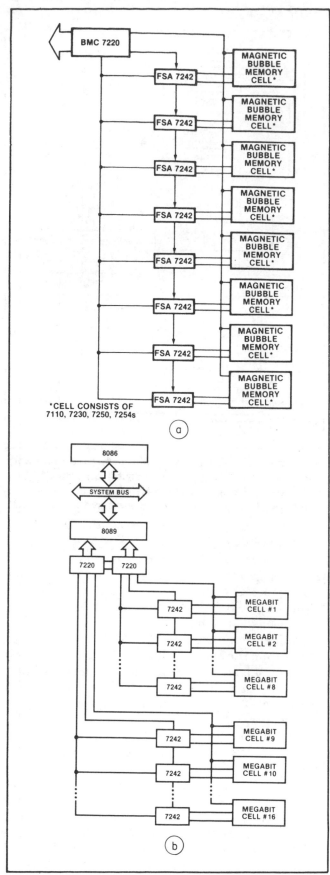

*CELL CONSISTS OF
7110, 7230, 7250, 7254s

(a)

(b)

4. To expand the bubble memory system beyond the 1-Mbit level, eight bubble-memory cells can be paralleled with one controller to make a 1-Mbyte system (a). Two controller chips can be paralleled under the control of an 8089 I/O processor to make a 1-M word system (1024 k × 16) that is compatible with the 8086 bus structure of the (b).

Table 2. Performance comparison for 1-Mbyte system (100% duty cycle)		
No. of active devices	Power (W)	Data rate (kbits/s)
0	10	0
1	12.6	68
2	15.5	136
4	20.9	272
8	32	544

Table 3. Comparison of error rates		
Probability of error	Mean time between errors (raw)	Mean time between errors (corrected)
10^{-8}	33.5 min	49.5 yr
10^{-9}	5.5 h	5000 yr
10^{-10}	5 5 h	>500k yr

into current-pulse control signals for the use of the memory device. Housed in a 22-pin DIP, the 7230 CPG takes advantage of the drive capability of bipolar, Schottky, TTL circuits to convert the TTL-compatible input signals into current pulses.

Drawing its power from 5-V and 12-V supplies, the CPG provides a power-fail signal to the system when the voltage levels of the supplies drop 15% below nominal. It interfaces directly with the controller and the memory chip and delivers the current pulses needed for replicate, swap, generate and boot replicate operations.

Finally, the basic coil-drive components are split into two sections: The predrivers take the TTL levels and reshape the signals into the 12-V levels needed for driving power devices; and the high-power transistor arrays deliver the current drive to the magnetic field coils. The 7250 predrivers are built from CMOS since they are used to drive VMOS power devices. The VMOS devices require only a voltage swing on the gate and little gate current. The predrivers operate from a +12-V supply and are housed in a 16-pin DIP.

The 7254 is a quad-transistor package that contains two n-channel and two p-channel VMOS transistors. They connect directly to the predrivers and to the bubble-memory package and require neither biasing resistors nor capacitors. Each bubble-memory device needs two 7254s.

With these components, a complete bubble memory subsystem can be designed with a minimum of parts. When configured on a printed circuit board, the entire 128 kbytes of the system fit in 16 sq in.

Expanding the system

The system block diagram in Fig. 4a contains a complete, 1-Mbyte (8,388,608-bit) bubble memory sys-

The whys and wherefores of DIPs and leadless packages

The leadless package selected by Intel was picked primarily to minimize damage to the bubble-memory device during handling or installation. If a standard dual-in-line package weighed as much as the 7110 (3 oz, or 74 g), its leads could easily be bent or damaged during normal handling.

Also, when soldered into a printed-circuit board, the leads may not be strong enough to hold the device on the board if it receives a shock or is vibrated. Thus, a leadless package was deemed necessary to simplify removal and installation, and a socket with clamping arms was developed to hold the device more firmly (see Fig.).

The socket also compensates for the tilted bubble-memory ceramic substrate and lifts the device 30 mils off the board. Traces can then be run under-neath the memory device.

To make installation almost fool-proof, the device can be inserted only one way: The bubble memory package has a polarization tab on one side and the socket has a slot that matches.

In the short term, the leadless ceramic package will be more expensive than the dual-in-line, but many production efficiencies can be gained by using a drop-in package. Since the redundancy map of the bubble memory is stored on the chip itself, the 7110 memory devices can be swapped from board to board or replaced when necessary without any loss of efficiency or need for system reprogramming to compensate for the change in good loop addresses.

Testing is another area where a drop-in package is advantageous. Intel has a dummy package available

that provides an equivalent to the 7110 device, in terms of the coil load, resistances and other electrical characteristics that the support circuits would have to match. Thus, before the bubble memory devices are plugged in, the entire board can be checked for all electrical parameters. This eliminates the possibility of accidentally "blowing up" a good bubble memory device because of an electrical problem on the board.

---

tem, in which one controller manipulates eight memory cells. Each cell contains one 1-Mbit bubble memory chip (the 7110), a current pulse generator (the 7230), a coil predriver (the 7250) and two drive transistors (7254s). The 7242 FSA for each cell is connected to a 7220 BMC via a high-speed serial bus.

Within 86 sq in. of board area, the nonvolatile system uses 6 sq in. for the 7220 BMC and 10 sq in. apiece for each 7242 FSA and 7110 cell. Mounted in its socket, the bubble memory device stands about 0.46 in. above the surface of the board. The center-to-center board spacing (0.625 or 0.75 in.) must allow for board thickness, warpage and lead protrusion. All together, 54 to 65 cu in. are required for 1 Mbyte of memory.

Most of the weight of the system is contributed by the bubble memory devices. Eight 7110s weigh about 1.28 lb or 590 g. The PC-board, peripheral circuits, sockets and miscellaneous components weigh an additional 1.23 lb, so the entire subsystem will weigh approximately 2.5 lb or 1150 g.

The system shown in Fig. 4a, can be operated in several user-programmable modes. Even though the

system contains eight bubble-device packages, all eight do not have to be accessed simultaneously. The various software-programmable modes can access devices in groups of one, two, four or eight. The user may, therefore, trade off data rate for power dissipation, since the standby power for a bubble device and drivers is significantly less than the active power.

In fact, the standby power of the bubble device is zero, if the user elects to switch the detector off. This choice is provided by the controller, which has a "detect enable" signal output. Table 1 summarizes the power dissipation of each of the components in a system, and Table 2 summarizes the power dissipation and data rate of the various system modes. Additionally, since bubbles are nonvolatile, the entire system could be switched off for those applications in which power is critical.

In Table 2, the data rate (which is an average) is less than the maximum, because of the redundant loops, error-correction bits and overhead functions. Very few systems will maintain a 100% duty cycle, so the average power will usually be somewhat less than that shown. Because bubbles can be started and stopped on a page basis, no additional access time is incurred for consecutive pages (sectors) when data are processed between I/O accesses.

Parallel controllers for larger systems

Memory systems even larger than 1 Mbyte can be built very easily with the bubble devices. For example, Fig. 4b shows a 1-Mword system, which consists of 16 bubble memory devices that can be configured for use with an 8086 16-bit microprocessor and associated support circuitry. The system uses two 7220 BMCs that are synchronized to provide a 16-bit data bus.

Each 7220 handles eight bubble memory devices.

The system can be expanded to 10 Mbytes by synchronizing additional controller systems. This system will be relatively error free, since each of the bubble-memory devices provides its own error correction. Typically, errors will be caused by detection failures, rather than by bubble loss, and will be single-bit errors. However, error correction can control even relatively high error rates.

Table 3 compares the effect of the correction on device error rate, assuming single-bit errors. The Fire code can detect and correct 1-bit or 2-bit errors in a burst of 5 bits or less, using 14 check bits. ▪▪

Off-the-Shelf Discrete Components Give Custom Performance

PAUL SWANSON
Strategic Applications Manager,
Bubble Memory Products,
Rockwell International,
Anaheim, California

Avoid waiting six months or more for specialized IC devices for bubble memories. Conventional ICs and discrete components can generate and sense bubbles and drive the coils. When they become available, custom circuits will require fewer parts and less board space and, in sufficient quantities, will cost less. However, off-the-shelf ICs and discrete components work just as efficiently and are available now.

For example, the Rockwell RBM256, 256-kbit, bubble memory device requires a sense amplifier circuit, a coil-drive circuit, a generate circuit, a replicate/transfer circuit and a transfer-in circuit. All these can use commercial, discrete components.

Common components sense bubbles

On a bubble memory device, a bubble is "sensed" when the resistance of one magnetoresistive element (the detector) changes in reference to another (the dummy) in a common bridge circuit. Detecting the presence of magnetic bubbles requires the following elements (Fig. 1):

- A completion bridge, consisting of simple resistors or current sources
- Ac coupling, if the bridge is highly unbalanced
- A preamplifier (UA733) to boost the millivolt-range signal to detectable levels
- Additional ac coupling after the preamplifier to eliminate circuit imbalances in the preamplifer
- A sense amplifier (HAI4905) and data latch (74LS74)
- Control for edge gate or clamp and strobe detection.

All the components are ordinary stock items, chosen according to the frequency of operation, the power levels available and bubble signal characteristics.

In designs for bubble memory sense amplifiers, the bridge completion resistors and the preamplifier must be placed close to the bubble memory device. Parallel lines are needed to the preamplifier inputs, and no signals which switch during the sensing times may cross the input detector lines. To avoid noise problems, the power supplies must also be filtered adequately

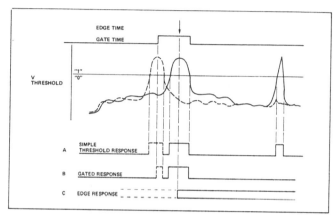

1. Three methods of bubble detection—simple threshold, gated and edge response, in order of increasing complexity—show the various methods of separating data bits from surrounding noise.

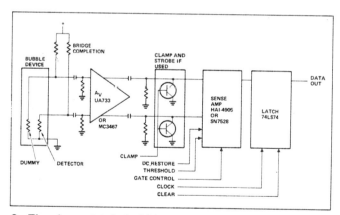

2. The elements of a bubble-memory detector circuit are generally-available stock items, chosen to accommodate the desired frequency, power and signal characteristics for the memory system that is being designed.

and a ground plane used, if possible.

A typical bubble signal is shown in Fig. 2. The dotted lines indicate some of the noise that may result from power variations, temperature changes, component aging and other factors. Unwanted signals include random output signals that result when the rotation of the magnetizing field causes nonlinear switching transients in the detector. Noise also occurs from the cross-coupling of large current/voltage switching in the coil drivers. Finally, a data pattern several bits away or in adjacent loops may cause bubble-to-bubble interaction.

Bubble detection methods that ignore the noise while sensing the difference signal are obviously essential. The most common detection approaches are simple threshold, threshold plus edge strobe, threshold plus gate strobe, and clamp and strobe.

The most common of these, the simple threshold method, is the easiest to mechanize but has the greatest disadvantage: It is highly prone to errors caused by random noise spikes that exceed the threshold voltage (V_{th}). As indicated in Fig. 2a, whenever the signal rises above the threshold line, it is defined as a ONE; any noise pulse of sufficient amplitude can produce a ONE output and thus an error.

An improvement on the simple threshold is the threshold plus edge strobe. In this method, a signal is defined as a ONE only when it occurs on the edge strobe (arrow in Fig. 2c). However, if the bubble signal shifts with drive field variations, like those shown by the dotted line in the figure, the edge trigger point does not shift correspondingly. This results in a lost signal and no bubble is detected.

In the threshold-plus-gate-strobe method, the bubble signal is allowed to drift within a certain "window" (top of Fig. 2) or period of time, and is still detected as a ONE. Thus, the signal is captured even if it shifts; but unwanted signals, falling outside the "windows," are ignored. Rockwell uses this method on its RLM658, a megabit bubble-system linear-storage module.

A more sophisticated approach than the previous three is the clamp-and-strobe method. It is used either in extremely noisy systems, where dc restore of the signal occurs prior to threshold sensing; or when the detector signal is both plus and minus with respect to a baseline and is too small for simple amplitude detection. This method is expensive because it requires additional components. It has been used on a 100-Mbit bubble memory system in a space flight recorder which Rockwell developed for NASA, to make the flight recorder totally reliable despite an unusually harsh environment.

Several other bubble manufacturers are currently designing bubble memory sense amplifiers for use with specific memories. Standard devices, such as the Motorola MC1444 plated-wire sense amplifier, will work as well, although the relatively low threshold voltage makes the layout critical. Because the threshold is set at 1 mV, detection is susceptible to low-level noise. In general, however, the circuit layout requires no more extra care than would be required for any other low-level circuit.

Three types of waveforms drive coils

Most often coils are driven with a sine, a triangle or a trapezoid waveform. The sinusoidal system may be driven directly from a linear amplifier. This arrangement is most useful in a test station but impractical elsewhere, because of the amplifier's large size and power consumption.

An alternative is to use a tuned circuit and recharge it once every cycle to replace its losses (see Fig. 3). The tuned circuit consumes less power than the linear

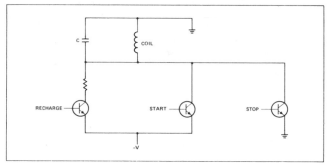

3. A tuned tank circuit, composed of a capacitor and an inductor paralleled in the collector circuit of three transistors, forms a sine-wave coil driver for which power requirements are very low.

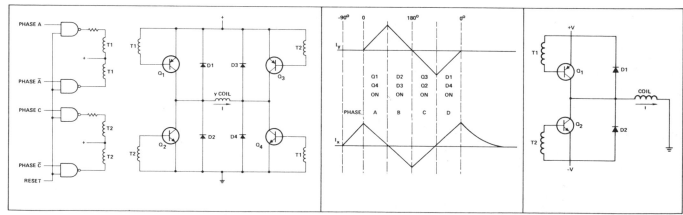

4. Triangular-waveshape coil drivers can be implemented with a circuit that operates from a single power supply, but at the cost of more circuit components (left). An alternative circuit design uses two supply voltages but fewer components (right). Both produce a triangular waveshape (center).

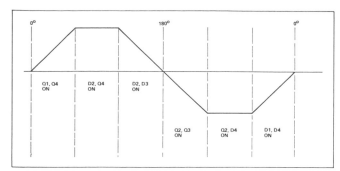

5. Trapezoidal-waveshape coil drivers produce a waveshape containing six equal phases. The drawback: more noise than from the other coil drivers.

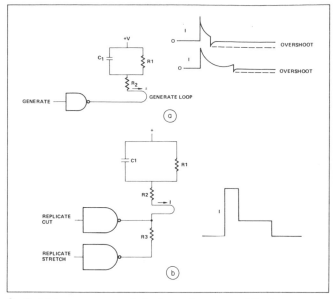

6. Bubbles are generated when a large-amplitude, narrow, current pulse passes through a conductor (a). In bubble replication, large, short pulses stretch and divide the bubble; longer, smaller-amplitude pulses complete the bubble transfer (b).

amplifier but cannot start and stop as quickly and is prone to overshoot on turnoff. Because a capacitor cannot be instantly charged from zero to full voltage (nor instantly discharged back down to zero), the choice of start/stop transistors involves trade-offs of size, speed and cost.

Triangle and trapezoid circuits are identical except for timing. The triangle drive is more common—Texas Instruments and Intel use it, as does Rockwell on its RLM658.

As shown in Fig. 4a, operation of the triangle drive begins at phase A by turning on transistors Q1 and Q4. Current builds up in the coils, as shown in Fig. 4b. When phase A is turned off, the current decays through diodes D2 andD3 in an almost linear fashion (since L/R is large compared to frequency). During phase C, transistors Q2 and Q3 are turned on. Coil current flows in the opposite direction and is discharged during phase D, through diodes D1 and D4. The second coil drive operates similarly, beginning at phase B.

The system shown in Fig. 4c operates like a triangle drive but with only half as many components. It does require an additional power supply, and two supply variations cause a change in peak-to-peak currents that increases distortion in the drive field.

Fig. 5 shows the timing for the trapezoid drive, which operates in six equal phases. The trapezoid waveform, including the X and Y portion, is more circular than the triangle waveform. Because the current is switched more often than triangular drivers, trapezoid drivers create more noise in the detector signal.

Two circuits are required per system, one for the X coil and one for the Y coil, with X leading Y by 90°. Bubble devices may be operated in parallel, if the coil parameters are matched sufficiently to make drive levels uniform.

Each of the bubble drives has a built-in holding field (tilt) to keep the bubble in proper position; excessive overshoot when the X coil is tuned off negates the tilt and causes a loss of data. One method to minimize overshoot is to allow the X current to decay exponen-

tially through the circuit impedances when the coils are turned off.

The following equation defines the pertinent relationship between the parameters for assessing a driving system:

$$I = \frac{V}{R} \left(1 - e^{\frac{-TR}{L}}\right),$$

where V is the power supply in volts
L is coil inductance in microhenrys
R is coil ac resistance in ohms
I is current in amperes
T is the phase time period in microseconds.
If the frequency (reciprocal of T) for a given current were to be increased (say, from 100 kHz to 150 kHz), then more voltage would also be required. Coil inductance would remain constant but the ac resistance would, of course, change with frequency.

Generation/replication/transfer

A bubble is generated by passing a high, narrow pulse of current through the conductor loop, resulting in a highly localized field. Bubbles are replicated in a similar fashion (replication is the transferring of a bubble from the storage area to the read track in a nondestructive manner). Bubble transfer other than replication requires less current over a longer period of time. Each process can be driven directly from an open collector driver IC; for example, one of the 75450 series.

Each function loop of a bubble memory is designed to operate in a low-duty cycle mode. Improper input signals can destroy devices. The most common method to prevent device destruction is to ac couple the current into the device (in Fig. 6a), thus restricting the maximum current to $V/(R_1 + R_2)$. The time constants must be chosen to obtain adequate peak power while limiting the dc power to specified limits, as defined in the device specifications.

Overshoot may also be limited by using a current source to control the turnoff current or by extending the on-time. In the latter case, the current reaches the dc level; it is turned off when overshoot would not cause a problem (Fig. 6a).

The typical replicate current in Fig. 6b needs large short pulses to cut the bubble and a longer, lower pulse to complete the transfer. Bubble devices may be operated in parallel merely by connecting the replicate pins in parallel at the driver, assuming the resistances match.

During power on and off the driver IC is controlled by interlocking the interface signals with a reset control. This interlock avoids accidental transfers of data in or out or starting the coils out of sequence.

In designing a system, an early decision is necessary on how many devices will operate in parallel. Replicate/transfer and coil driver circuits lend themselves to parallel operation, but obviously generation and sensing circuits do not. ■■

SECTION VI

Charge-Coupled Devices: Are They or Aren't They?

Although a promising technology, the charge-coupled device has run into a sort of technology roadblock—the development of the 64-kbit RAM and the large bubble-memory devices have almost eliminated the need for this memory element. It can still be used in many application areas; however, the technology used to make it has lost some of its supporters and most of the companies that were trying to produce the devices have stopped trying. So, at least for the present, there is only one company actively trying to get the CCD memory components designed into new applications—Fairchild Camera and Instrument Corp., Semiconductor Division.

The articles in this section serve as a guideline to those who are considering using CCDs in future systems. They outline the basic system considerations that must be examined before a design is committed to, as well as the basics of operation for the CCDs themselves. If future devices are introduced, expect them to contain much of the system support that was external to the older devices. And you can probably expect the next step in density—from the current 64-kbit level up to 256 kbits on a single chip. Educated guesses put the introduction date for such a device into late 1980 if at all. In the meantime, let's look at some hard design information.

Charge-Coupled Devices for Bulk Storage

CHARLES B. MITCHELL
Manager, Central Applications,
National Semiconductor Corp.,
Santa Clara, California

Charge-coupled devices provide the highest capacity for memory applications of any semiconductors. CCD capacity generally has been about four times that of a dynamic random-access memory, which has long held sway as the most widely used semiconductor memory device.

Since existing CCD memories, particularly 64-kilobit and greater density devices, exhibit large capacitances between clock lines, as well as between clock pins and ground, they generally require multiple high-level clocks—usually three or more. Such high capacitance has often meant one clock driver for every three CCD packages.

Even more important than the effect these drivers have on package count is their impact on system power levels. Although CCD memories consume little power at low clock rates, numerous clock drivers mean a significant increase in system power requirements.

However, a new 64-k CCD memory, the MM2464, incorporates buffers that permit a single 5-volt clock driver to service a megabyte or more of memory. Even a pair of TTL or CMOS logic gates are enough to provide the appropriate clock signals for a system with low distributed capacitance.

Besides offering this ease of interface, the MM2464 is configured as a short-loop device, so it can operate at high data rates yet keep power dissipation to a minimum, as well as offering short latency time. (See "CCDs: the semiconductor answer to bulk storage.") Thus, the chip is a viable memory component for a wide range of applications.

Clocking the memory

The MM2464 (Fig. 1) requires only two TTL-level clock signals, sense enable (SE) and synchronize (SYNC), with the latter occurring once for every four SE cycles. The SE signal appears to clock the 256-bit shift registers, but actually each shift register contains four 63-bit CCDs (plus a one-bit delay to form the 64th bit), as well as a decoding/sense-amplifier/multiplexing circuit, with SYNC providing the stimulus for clocking the array. This multiplexed parallel arrangement makes the MM2464's 256-bit registers faster than continuous 256-bit registers while maintaining a single sense amplifier.

The power a CCD dissipates depends directly on the clock rate. Since SYNC occurs at one-fourth the rate of SE, increased speeds are possible for a given power dissipation. SE provides the clocking signal for multiplexing and selects each of the four register outputs for amplification, at the same time refreshing the four bits in the holding register. The SYNC signal then clocks four new data bits into the register, and the sequence is repeated.

Refreshing the data

A refresh cycle is a single regenerative passage of all data bits through the sense amplifier. Thus, refresh takes place every 256 SE cycles. CCDs require refresh because of charge degradation due to thermally-generated "dark current" and transfer inefficiency between cells. Therefore, in systems with controlled environments, the refresh operation, or maximum page time requirements, may be adapted to temperature conditions. (The refresh interval can be halved for every 10 C decrease in temperature.)

All told, the MM2464 has 257 registers with the 257th providing a reference level for the sense amplifiers. Through comparison and feedback techniques using the reference loop, noise immunity is significantly enhanced. The remaining 256 registers are available for storage.

(Providing power-supply and temperature-stable reference voltages this way reveals another advantage of the short-loop configuration. The addition of a 256-bit reference loop requires only 1/256 of a 64-k device's die area. In a 4096-bit, 64-k oriented device, 1/16 of the die area would be necessary to construct a similar loop.)

Each register I/O in the memory array is accessible through a data-steering multiplexer, which is controlled by an 8-bit address port. The three-state data-output and data-input ports may be tied together in common-bus systems if, when writing data into the part, the write enable (WE) signal is lowered before or simultaneously with chip enable (CE). The 256-bit page may be used as read-write memory.

Power-supply voltage requirements of the MM2464 are 12 V, -5 V and ground. Power-supply current, I_{DD}, may vary widely according to system design, mode of operation, and clock speed (Fig. 2). Clock frequencies should not exceed those needed for required system performance. Adaptive clocking (i.e., minimum clock rate during periods when the system is not in use) may also be advantageous. Even the page mode of operation can be extremely attractive, since I_{DD} is generally low even for high frequencies.

The reduced number of clock cycles permits far lower power-supply drain in page mode than that in serial mode though data rates are higher. In Fig. 2,

the page-mode current characteristics reflect the use of a burst-refresh scheme, where the burst frequency is either the CCD's maximum clock frequency or a frequency given by

$$f = \frac{256}{t_{REF} - Nt_{CYC}}$$

where t_{CYC} is the read or write cycle time in the page mode, and N is the number of memory-access cycles required during the refresh period (t_{REF}) to achieve a given data rate.

During page-mode operation, there will be current variations on system power-supply lines. So the designer must provide bypass capacitors to ground, located near the V_{DD} pin, for each device in the system.

CCDs: the semiconductor answer to bulk storage

Charge-coupled devices are prime candidates for bulk-storage memories and other applications usually handled by read/write or rotating magnetic memories. Access time, probably the key parameter for any memory device, is on the order of hundreds of microseconds. CCDs, then, fall between high-speed medium-density devices like semiconductor RAMs and magnetic cores (which have access times of 1 or 2 microseconds) and high-density low-speed devices such as tapes and discs (which offer tens-of-milliseconds access times).

In general, there are three things you should know about designing with CCD memories:
■ They store information as charge on a capacitor, so like MOS dynamic RAMs they must be refreshed.
■ Since they are serial devices, their memory-system architecture will reflect their sequential nature.
■ Because they are constructed with MOS processes much like those used for dynamic RAMs, they have similar interface and power-supply requirements.

For digital storage, CCD memories come in either long-loop or short-loop configurations, which reflect the size of the internal shift registers. In both cases, the devices resemble a number of recirculating shift registers arranged in parallel (see figure), with each register input and output addressed through a data multiplexer to provide a path to the package I/O pins.

Long-loop CCDs seem to have reached a *de facto* standard of 4096 bits, while short-loops are generally 256 bits. Since short-loop devices generally operate with higher signal levels than long-loops, their refresh requirements tend to be less demanding. Also, short-loop designs usually have a simpler manufacturing sequence, as well as more efficient sense-amplifier circuits.

On the other hand, long-loop CCDs may be clocked faster than short-loop components, although clock rate is not the only speed parameter. Latency time —how long it takes to get to any given word—may be more critical, depending on the application. Due

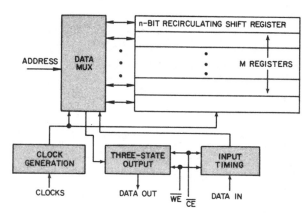

to the relatively few clock cycles required in a short loop, both the average and maximum latency times of a short-loop CCD are much less than those of a long-loop device.

Long-loop CCDs normally work in a serial mode— a 64-k bit part, for example, would be treated as, say, 16 dynamic shift registers. However, with a short-loop CCD, a page (a position within the shift registers) can be 256-bits wide, a practical size for treatment as read/write memory. With such treatment comes high data rate and greatly reduced power dissipation.

Besides bulk storage, CCDs can be useful for:
■ Serial formats—when sequential ordering of information is inherent is the system philosophy.
■ Low latency—when rotating memories must be replaced or augmented to achieve greater bandwidth.
■ Human interface—when dense random-access storage is required and a speed slower than conventional RAM is not detrimental.

Finally, because CCDs store charges in closely packed MOS capacitors, their memory-cell circuitry is not as detailed as that of dynamic RAMs. Moreover, since they are fabricated with MOS processes, CCD products should mature in much the same way as MOS dynamic RAMs and microprocessors—with costs and sizes decreasing and speeds rising.

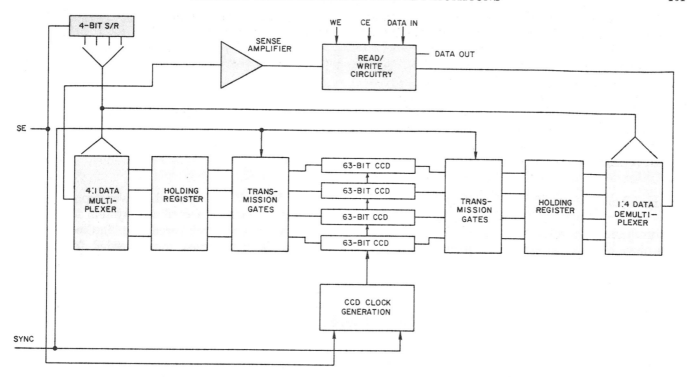

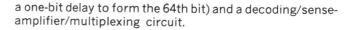

1. **Each of the 256-bit shift registers** in the 64-kilobit MM2464 memory is composed of four 63-bit CCDs (plus a one-bit delay to form the 64th bit) and a decoding/sense-amplifier/multiplexing circuit.

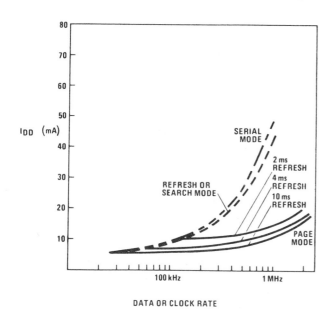

2. **The smaller number of clock cycles** in page mode, compared to serial mode, reduces power-supply current drain, even though data rates are higher.

These capacitors should be relatively large (0.1 μF) in the early development stages and then adjusted for acceptable noise levels after the PC board has been laid out.

Similar precautions should be made with respect to V_{BB} transient currents. Power-supply layout and distribution should follow the same rules as those used in dynamic-RAM design. Although clock and data distribution will be far less critical than in CCD or RAM designs with high-voltage and/or high-capacitance clocks, good practices will always provide more margin for noise immunity and device variation.

Clock, refresh and search

The design of the clock circuit will, of course, depend on the specific system. Figure 3 depicts several clock-generation circuits for SE and SYNC: one logic realization for a 1-MHz clock rate (a), another 1-MHz generator but altered to allow maximum clock rates (b), and a less complex circuit that you can put together with CMOS logic (c). Each of these designs includes a clock-enable input to allow page or search-mode operation. If clock rates exceeding 770 kHz are not required, you may use a simple 50% duty-cycle SE clock (Fig. 3d).

Several refresh techniques are available, including:

■ Burst refresh, with a burst consisting of 256/b clock cycles at maximum clock frequency, where b is the number of bursts during the refresh period, t_{REF}.

■ Distributed refresh, with one clock cycle each $t_{REF}/256$ microseconds.

■ Adaptive refresh, with a circuit to monitor how the CCDs are used within a system. The adaptive-refresh circuit also keeps tabs on timing restrictions placed upon the memory and takes command of the system to provide clocking when those restrictions are exceeded.

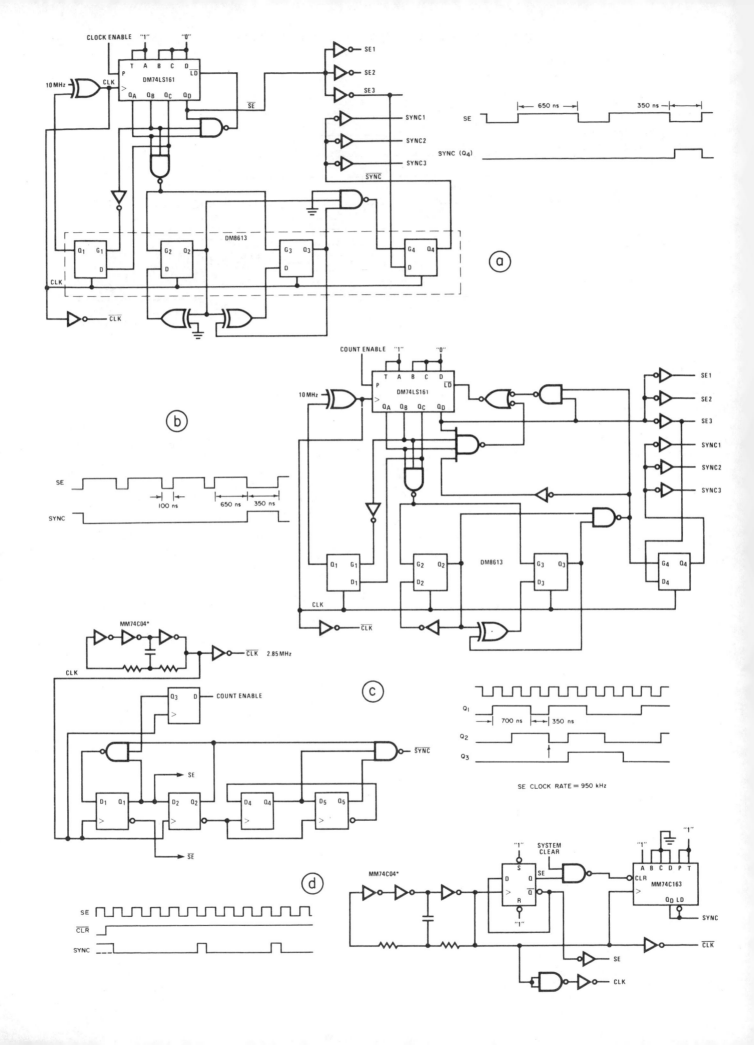

3. **The choice of logic realizations** for obtaining the two clock signals (SE and SYNC) required by the MM2464 includes: a 1-MHz generator (a), a modified version for a 1.23-MHz clock rate (b), a less complex CMOS circuit for a 950-kHz generator (c), and a simple 50% duty-cycle SE clock for 750-kHz operation.

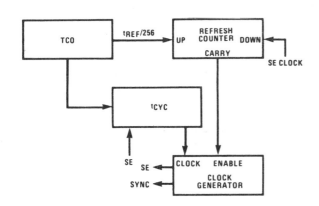

4. **An adaptive-refresh circuit** monitors system use of CCDs and the various timing restrictions placed upon the memory. Temperature may be added as a parameter to determine refresh and maximum page times.

For the adaptive-refresh subsystem of Fig. 4, temperature has been added as a parameter to determine the maximum page times and t_{REF}. The refresh counter is counted up by the temperature-controlled oscillator and down by the SE clock.

A carry enables a CCD clock cycle. A counter determines page time and is reset each time SE occurs; whenever a carry is generated, a clock cycle is enabled. Although this type of refresh control is the most flexible method, many serial-data applications, such as a CRT display, either won't need refresh control or will use much simpler techniques involving fewer components.

Search mode for fast register advance

Search mode differs from refresh mode only in speed. While refresh mode implies clocking at very low rates to maintain data integrity, search mode is intended to advance the shift registers to a desired page as quickly as possible. To achieve this, a counter must keep track of the present page location. To access a particular page, the controlling system loads the corresponding address into a register whose output is compared to the count state. When the proper page is reached, the clock is stopped, and the system is alerted that it may access the requested page. Fig. 5 shows a block diagram of a typical search-mode circuit.

As mentioned earlier, the MM2464 may be treated as read/write memory, permitting the use of the same design techniques for this CCD as for a static RAM. An address latch or register may be needed at the card edge for buffering and for satisfying address hold-

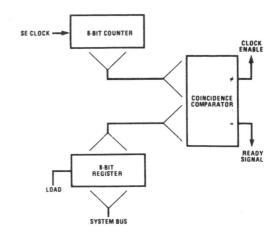

5. **To advance shift registers quickly** to a desired page the controlling system loads the address of the page into a register whose output is compared to the count stage.

time requirements. Check the data sheet for the Chip-Enable and read/write input specifications.

A ready or busy signal should be sent to the main system to prevent short cycling of the system or the MM2464. This signal may be the "page change required" signal of an adaptive-refresh circuit in faster systems or a decoded output of the page time counter in slower systems.

In the serial mode, you treat the MM2464 as a series of addressable parallel shift registers—a good configuration for display and scanner applications. However, because of the power and speed considerations and because there is no penalty in support parts count, you should, in most cases, use the CCD in page mode with a counter doing the addressing.

There is an important exception: systems in which data may be accepted with a random starting location. There is no latency time; the shift register desired is immediately selected, and data manipulation starts at once. When using the MM2464 this way, be careful with clocking schemes like the one shown in Fig. 3b. Here the SE off time with no SYNC pulse has been reduced to data sheet minimum, which is less than the minimum Chip Enable time. Regardless of the mode—pay attention to the parameters describing the relationship of SE and SYNC to CE. One way is to ensure that Chip Enable is active (low) only when both SE and SYNC are in the low state.

Although the MM2464 may be used in a page mode, you may find the limited maximum page time imposing restrictions that are unacceptable. A read/write memory buffer may help. Fig. 6 shows a memory configuration consisting of a page-mode-driven array of MM2464s that supplies data to, and accepts data from, a buffer 4-k static RAM. A 0.5-Mbit memory consisting of 16 memory devices and associated logic will fit on a reasonably small PC board and consume far less power than a system consisting entirely of RAM.

You can expand this array system several ways. For

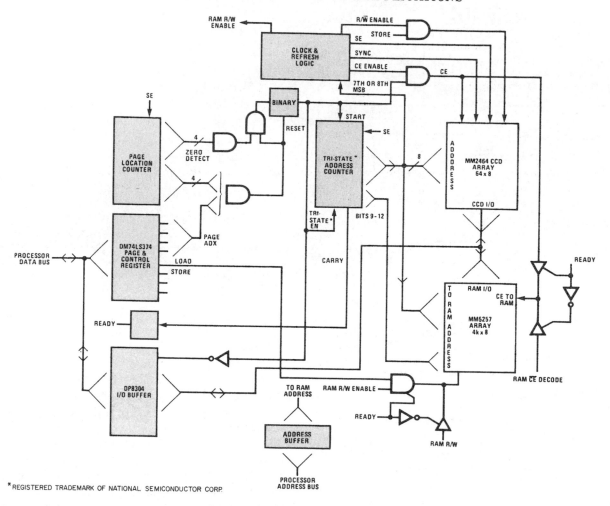

*REGISTERED TRADEMARK OF NATIONAL SEMICONDUCTOR CORP.

6. So as to ease timing restrictions, a page-mode-driven array of MM2464s supplies data to, and accepts data from, a buffer array of 4-k static RAMs. Moreover, there are several simple ways of expanding this array system.

example, you can easily add CCD storage to form multiple-megabyte capability. For more throughput, you can add a RAM page. Loading or storing one page while using the other may, in effect, reduce latency time to zero.

Another way to expand is to switch from the absolute addressing of Fig. 6 to a scheme in which the processor assigns a label to each 4-k page by writing the label in the first location in the page. To find that page, the control system compares the input label to shift-register data in location zero while operating in a serial mode. When the label is found, a switch is made to page mode; data is transferred to or from the buffer.

In large systems, this content-addressable expansion may be put to work by implementing wide word lengths and searching with masked "don't care" states using either page/serial or serial/page techniques. As a result, information retrieval may be of the type used in large data-processing systems, resulting in minimal CPU time. Bulk-memory formats may consist of these techniques or others, but in any case, recognition of both the strengths and weaknesses of CCDs can result in high-performance architectures.

Sequentially formatted data obviously fits CCD applications and especially the "square" arrangement of the MM2464. The block diagram of Fig. 7a depicts a possible configuration for a CRT graphics system; four MM2464s arranged in parallel. The resulting 1024-bit word contains the video data for two 512-bit horizontal scan lines of the CRT. The scan lines are arranged one above the other on the screen in an interlaced display; consequently, one of the 512-bit words is accessed during each vertical scan.

The CCDs are read via page mode (during the horizontal sweep) at a rate of 2.4 MHz, allowing for 10 μs of horizontal retrace time. However, clocking the CCD once during horizontal retrace will not maintain data at extended temperature ranges. You can use the clocking scheme shown in Fig. 7b. Here the MM2464 is clocked eight times during the first 31 horizontal retrace periods; on the 32nd retrace the device is clocked nine times. In this way, the CCD page sequence is 0, 7, 15, ..., 223, 231, 239, 248, 1, ...

As a buffer or swapping memory

Multitask or multple-user processing systems are often limited in their performance by the latency time

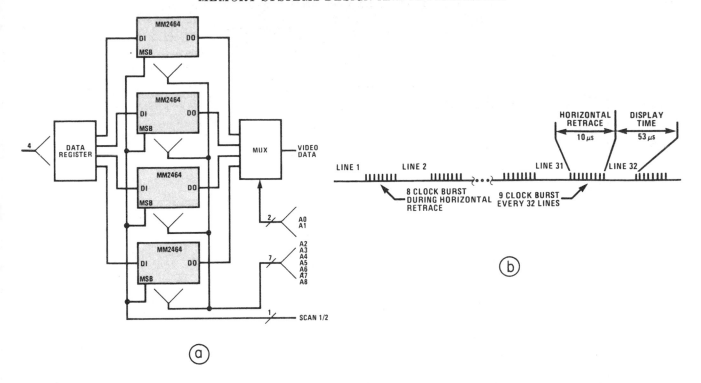

7. Parallel arrangement of four MM2464s (a) provide a 1024-bit word containing the video data for two 512-bit horizontal scan lines of a CRT graphics system. Each CCD receives multiple clock burst (b) during retrace periods.

of disc and tape memories. You can improve performance by adding a buffer or swapping memory to take contents of the rotating memory. The MM2464's lower latency time (orders of magnitude) and density make it a good swapping memory. Moreover, you can greatly increase computer bandwidth for a fraction of the cost of other techniques. The configuration of the MM2464 allows you to construct a disc-like, sector-oriented architecture that permits you to use the same software drivers used for the rotating device. So not only do you increase user capacity, but you also avoid the costly penalties of having to do software revision.

Another possible application is calculators. Couple a single MM2464 to a single-chip microprocessor or calculator-oriented device such as the COP420. The MM2464's low-power operation and easy interfacing, plus the processing device's programmability, results in a programmable calculator with 8192 possible (8-bit) program steps or memory locations. The processor can easily drive the two CCD clocks, data input and Chip Enable with flag and data lines, as well as the address port with its own address lines or latched data port.

CCDs may also be used in distributed systems such as point-of-sale terminals that reload data each day from a central processing or storage unit and require only human interface speed for random access.

In short, CCD memory technology has progressed to the point where a practical device for bulk memory storage has evolved. This device, the MM2464, is a TTL-compatible 65,536-bit CCD organized as 256 pages of 256-bit memory. The CCD fulfills a requirement for a dense memory with access times far less than those of rotating magnetic media, permitting its use in a wide variety of applications in many different types of systems.■■

Bibliography:

Melen, R., and Buss, D., editors, *Charge Coupled Devices: Technology and Applications*, IEEE Press, NY, 1977.

Sequin and Thompson, *Charge Transfer Devices*, Academic Press, NY, 1975.

Single-Chip CCD Memory Really Delivers

DAVID SITRICK

Applications Engineer, MOS Memory Division, Texas Instruments, Houston, Texas

With 64-kbit units now available and 256-kbit complexities already on the drawing board, charge-coupled devices are a full generation ahead of dynamic random-access memories, which now offer 16-k sizes with 64-k units yet to come. And one of the most cost-effective memories today is the TMS3064, a 64-k CCD.

Besides low cost and high-speed, this CCD offers the highest density of any available semiconductor read/write memory—and the lowest power consumption per bit. Yet in terms of systems use, the 3064 is quite similar to today's dynamic RAMs. It requires the same power-supply voltages (−12 V and ±5 V), fits in the same 16-pin sockets, and is fully TTL-compatible, except for its two clocks and chip enable, which must be 12-V, MOS-level signals. Furthermore, it is fabricated with the same n-channel silicon-gate process that has become the standard for the manufacture of MOS LSI memories.

CCD needs less power

At its maximum clock frequency of 5 MHz and in its worst-case write mode, the 3064 at most consumes just 320 mW—a far cry from the 462-mW power drain of a typical 16-k dynamic RAM for its minimum cycle time. That means the RAM uses 50% more power for one-fourth the 3064's memory capacity, or practically six times more power per bit. Moreover, the CCD can retain data in its recirculate mode while consuming no more than 50 mW.

In terms of speed, that 5-MHz clock frequency translates into a CCD cycle time of 200 ns, as opposed to the 375-ns cycle time of a typical 16-k dynamic RAM. However, not every bit is accessible during that cycle time because of the serial nature of a CCD.

Perhaps a better way to compare speed performance is to look at data-transfer cycle times in the page mode, which is ideal for a CCD since it normally holds data formatted into blocks or pages. The fastest 16-k dynamic RAM, with a maximum access time of 150 ns, takes a minimum 170 ns in page mode—which is really just about the same 200-ns speed that the 3064 offers.

Its long-loop organization (see "The advantages of long-loop CCDs," p. 167) and its single-chip design make the 3064 truly cost effective. Furthermore, CCD technology permits cell size to be approximately one-third that of a dynamic RAM's, so this 64-k CCD takes up about as much silicon real estate, yet provides four times more memory capacity.

The 3064 CCD—a powerful chip

The TMS3064 (Fig. 1a) is organized externally as a 65,536-by-1-bit serial memory, addressable as 16 loops of 4096 bits each. These loops are arranged in

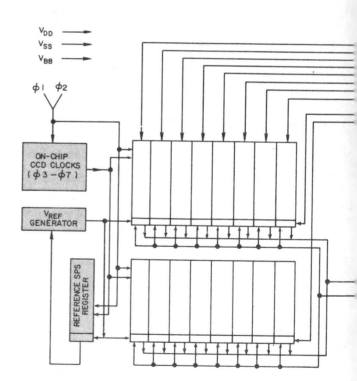

(a)

166

parallel and individually addressable. Each loop consists of a 4096-bit serial-parallel-serial (SPS) CCD shift register for data storage, a regenerator for refreshing the data, and an I/O interface circuit for data transfer to and from the loop.

A 17th SPS register, which is not addressable, operates in conjunction with a reference circuit to generate a voltage that is compensated for leakage current. This reference voltage is used by the regenerators at each loop.

Data are shifted into the SPS register (Fig. 1b) along a 32-bit input serial shift register, then demultiplexed

---

The advantages of long-loop CCDs

Charge-coupled devices intended for memory applications come in either long-loop or short-loop configurations, which determine how large a block of data may be serially accessed at one time. But there are some advantages to long-loop.

For one thing, long-loop 64-k CCDs, like the TMS3064, are usually organized as sixteen 4096-bit loops, so a 4-bit address is sufficient to provide random access to any one of the 16 loops. But same-size short-loop CCDs typically consist of 256 loops, each containing 256 bits. Thus selecting the proper loop requires an 8-bit address.

In general, long-loop minimizes system complexity because it requires only four address lines on board layouts, as opposed to the eight needed by short-loop. What's more, the long-loop 3064 in particular requires just two clock lines, which not only simplifies board layout further but also reduces clock-driver requirements and clock-timing/generation circuitry.

Long-loop organization also minimizes on-chip peripheral circuitry, which holds down chip size and cost. Since each CCD loop must contain a sense amplifier and regenerator to detect and refresh data circulating in the loop, short-loop CCDs require 256 amplifiers/regenerators, while long-loop devices need just 16.

Short-loop organization does allow shorter latency time—after all, each loop is 16 times shorter than a 4096-bit long-loop organization. But the time savings isn't as great as all that. A long-loop like the 3064 transfers or shifts data at a rate of 5 MHz, compared to 1 MHz for short-loop CCDs. Since latency time is actually the product of loop length times shift rate, the short-loop latency advantage is actually reduced to a factor of three, or about 130 μs vs the average long-loop latency of 410 μs.

John Hewkin, Strategic Marketing Manager, MOS Memory Div., Texas Instruments Inc., Houston, TX.

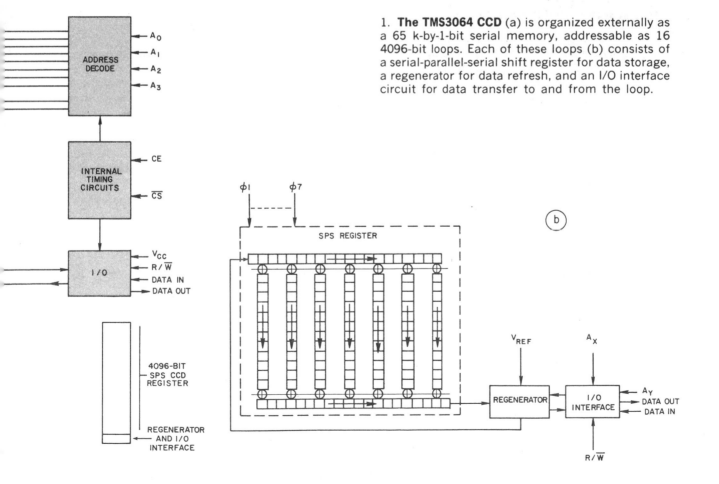

1. **The TMS3064 CCD** (a) is organized externally as a 65 k-by-1-bit serial memory, addressable as 16 4096-bit loops. Each of these loops (b) consists of a serial-parallel-serial shift register for data storage, a regenerator for data refresh, and an I/O interface circuit for data transfer to and from the loop.

Looking inside the registers

Basically, the TMS3064 CCD transfers data with a two-phase shift register. Although the device requires seven clocks internally, the user has to provide only two of these, $\phi1$ and $\phi2$, and the CCD generates the other five on-chip.

In effect, $\phi1$ and $\phi2$ advance the charge in the input and output serial shift registers, although actually $\phi1$ and $\phi7$ are applied to the input serial shift register. The $\phi7$ clock is derived directly from $\phi2$, except $\phi7$ "misses" every 32nd pulse due to an idiosyncracy of the transfer-gate timing from the input serial shift register to the parallel-storage serial shift register.

Clocks $\phi3$ and $\phi4$, which simultaneously advance the parallel main-storage serial shift registers, are modulo-32 (occurring only once every 32nd main clock cycle), and are derived from and in sync with $\phi1$ and $\phi2$. The $\phi4$ clock is delayed from $\phi3$ because of the design and timing of the transfer gates of the input and output serial shift registers.

Clocks $\phi3$, $\phi4$, $\phi5$, and $\phi6$ all run at the same frequency and in sync with each other, but provide staggered pulses of varying widths. Since the bulk of the stored charge is advanced only once for every 32 $\phi1$-$\phi2$ clock pairs, the CCD dissipates much less power than other possible internal storage architectures. What's more, speed is not compromised to get this lower power—data rates up to 5 Mbits/s are obtainable.

Regenerator provides data refresh

Data are stored mainly in the serial-parallel-serial register, but input and output, as well as refresh, operations require that the SPS register interact with its regenerator. Assuming that the charge is in a fully-loaded serial output shift register of the SPS, the charge then shifts from the SPS output register into the regenerator, which senses the logic level and regenerates (refreshes) it to a MOS level. This signal is now available for transfer to the output buffer (for a read cycle) and to the SPS input register (for read and recirculate).

During a write cycle, the SPS output register transfers the charge into the regenerator, which again senses and refreshes the logic level to a MOS level. The read/write signal controls the I/O buffer. Active low enables the input buffer circuitry, which in turn transfers the appropriate charge into the regenerator, overriding existing contents. The charge is then transferred into the SPS input register. This process repeats for 32 cycles until the SPS output registers are empty and the input registers are full.

When the output registers are empty, internal clock $\phi6$ enables the parallel-to-serial transfer gates to allow new data to be loaded into the SPS output register from the parallel storage registers. Meanwhile, internal clock $\phi5$ enables the serial-to-parallel transfer gates, permitting new data to be loaded from the SPS input register into the parallel storage registers. This process repeats 127 times until all data have been refreshed (recirculated). At that point, the initial data (location) is again at the regenerator, and one refresh cycle has been completed.

Examining cell structure

Each shift-register (cell) location in the 3064 has a two-part storage structure. As the figure shows, an electrical charge packet is shifted from cell to cell and within the cell from storage well to storage well, on respective phases of the nonoverlapping clocks.

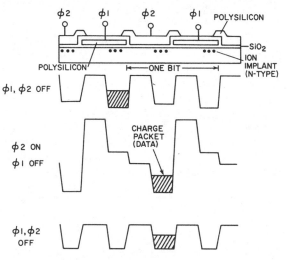

Charge must be restored (refreshed) to offset the degradation that occurs during the dynamic shifting and quiescent storage of data. In other words, in the transfer of charge packets, some charge is lost (escapes) due to a nonperfect medium. During quiescent storage, normal (inherent) capacitive cell leakage occurs.

This charge degradation can result in loss of data unless the charge is periodically regenerated before reaching nonrecoverable levels. The refresh period is the maximum time, 4 ms in this case, the data will be guaranteed to be valid without regeneration. The minimum clock frequency, 1 MHz for the 3064, is a function of the refresh period (at 70 C) and the size of the SPS loop.

The worst-case refresh conditions occur at high temperature, which accelerates charge leakage. Both ambient temperature and chip temperature (due to device power dissipation) contribute to the temperature the device encounters. In addition, high-frequency operation increases chip temperature because it increases power dissipation. However, this effect may be offset by more frequent refresh—for example, a clock frequency of 5 MHz yields a refresh period of 0.82 ms.

(every 32nd clock) into 32 parallel 127-bit shift registers (these form the bulk memory array), and finally multiplexed (every 32nd clock) into a 32-bit output serial shift register.

The regenerator detects the small charge quantities being transferred and converts these charge levels to voltage levels for comparison with the reference voltage (V_{REF}). The output of the regenerator is a 0-to-12-V digital signal that, during a read or recirculate cycle, drives the input gate of the CCD so as to refresh the stored data.

The I/O interface circuit controls data transfer to and from the loop. During a write cycle, transfer of data to the loop occurs via the I/O interface, then via the regenerator and into the input serial register.

All the user need supply are two simple nonoverlapping clocks, although internally a total of seven different clocks are required to operate the SPS registers (see "Looking inside the registers," p. 168). The five additional clocks are generated on-chip, decoded from and synchronized to the user-supplied $\phi 1$ and $\phi 2$ input clocks.

Clocking the device

These internal clocks perform various functions that are transparent to the user. Essentially, the clocks recirculate and refresh the data storage in the loops. Within each loop, clock pulses $\phi 1$ and $\phi 2$ access the data serially until the desired bit (location) shifts to the output of the selected SPS register. (Each $\phi 1$-$\phi 2$ clock pair advances the bit forward one step.) At the register output, the regenerator refreshes the data, which, in a read cycle or recirculate cycle, is returned to the input of the register again.

Data at the output of any regenerator are read by: setting the appropriate address (which selects 1 of the 16 SPS registers), setting $\overline{CS}$ low and R/$\overline{W}$ high, and then pulsing CE high. Data output will be valid one data delay time following the rise of CE (access time from CE). For writing data into a particular loop: the address and data inputs are set, $\overline{CS}$ and R/$\overline{W}$ are set low, then CE is pulsed high.

A given bit may be read and then modified in the same clock cycle by performing a read-modify-write (RMW) operation. This consists of first performing a read cycle (as just described), then while CE is still high, setting data input and pulsing R/$\overline{W}$ low. The RMW cycle may be used to interchange the contents of two 3064s by connecting the data output of one to the data input of the other and vice-versa.

For support

Common to all applications for the 3064 memory is a basic group of CCD support circuitry, the most obvious being clock and timing generation. In addition, the device requires such other commonly used functions as: loop (bit) address location tracking, address matching between the CCD and its support circuitry,

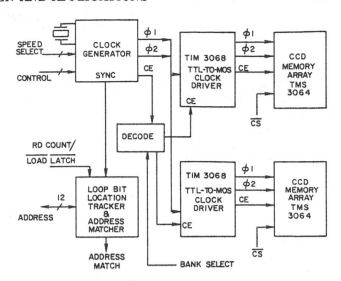

2. **Support circuitry** for the 3064 includes just a single clock generator and combination location-tracker/address-matcher, in addition to appropriate decode circuitry and clock drivers proportional to the size of the array.

TTL-to-MOS clock drivers, serial-to-parallel and parallel-to-serial bus transceivers, cueing-sorting control, and system master control.

Several of these support functions are universally needed in all CCD systems. As Fig. 2 shows, a typical CCD memory system requires only one clock generator and one location tracker and address matcher, with the number of clock drivers proportional to the size of the CCD memory array. Specialized applications, like a multiple-board system where every board except the selected one is in low-power-recirculate mode, may need additional clock generators and location trackers.

The 3064 requires a nonoverlapping two-phase clock plus a synchronized chip enable (CE), all at MOS levels (12-V swing). A fourth signal, called SYNC, is useful to indicate that data read from the CCD are valid and that a new memory cycle has just begun.

Figure 3a shows one implementation for a 1-to-3-MHz CCD clock generator. Here, the 4-bit counter and the NAND gate perform as a modulo-8 counter whose outputs drive the three-to-eight decoder. Positive transitions of the clock input increment the modulo-8 counter, while on negative clock transitions, the decoder's outputs go active to preset and clear the appropriate flip-flops, thereby creating the desired clock signals.

With an alternate clock generator (Fig. 3b), you can cut package count to two and three-quarter ICs, compared to the four and one-third devices required for the circuit of Fig. 3a. This package reduction, though, comes at the minor expense of some increase in wiring complexity.

From TTL to MOS

As already indicated, the 3064 requires MOS-level signals for the two-phase clocks and the chip enable.

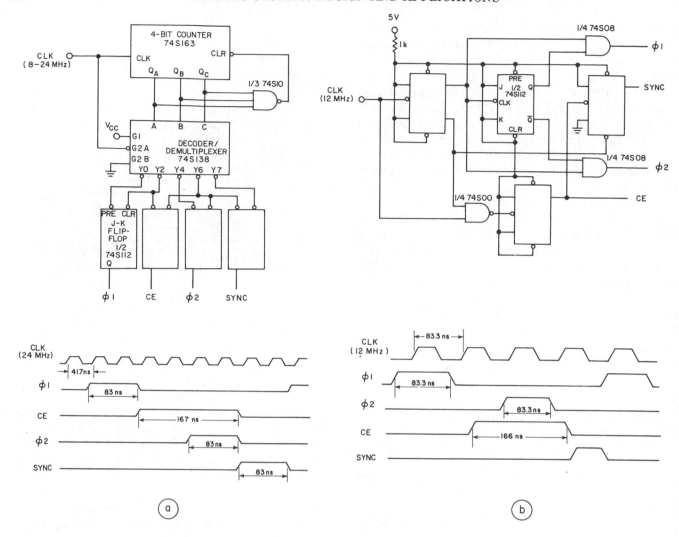

a

b

3. **Clocking the 3064 is easy.** From two user-supplied nonoverlapping clocks, the device generates the other five clocks it needs on-chip. A simple circuit (a) for 1-to-3-MHz operation provides both these clocks, as well as chip enable (CE) and SYNC. An even simpler circuit (b) cuts package count to 2-3/4 ICs for the same clock function.

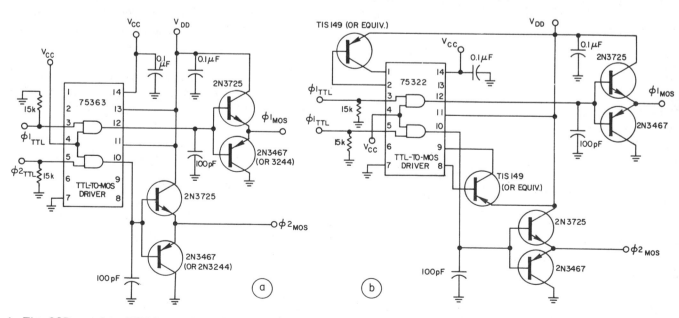

a

b

4. **The CCD requires MOS-level signals** for the two-phase clocks and chip enable. Either of these circuits will buffer the TTL-level signals from the clock-generator circuits of Fig. 3. Circuit (b) offers lower standby power.

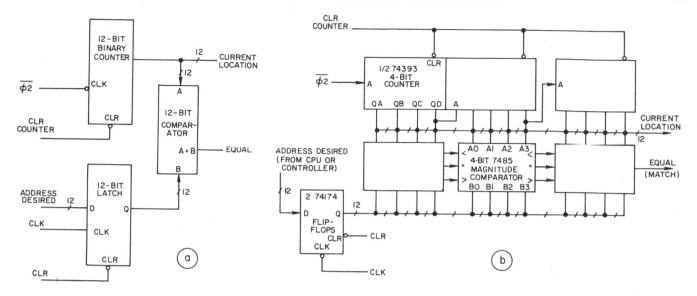

5. **A tracker/matcher** (a) keeps tabs on which bit position within a loop is accessible. The binary counter maintains the current loop location, while the 12-bit latch holds the desired address. The comparator produces an output when the two addresses match. Circuit (b) shows one possible implementation requiring only 6½ ICs.

Fig. 4 shows two circuit configurations for buffering the TTL-level signals from the clock-generator circuits. One (a) is the better choice for smaller systems, while the other (b) is more appropriate for larger systems because of its lower standby power. However, this latter circuit does require two extra transistors for the TTL-to-MOS driver.

Within each of the 16 addressable loops (registers) of the 3064, data are accessed serially by pulsing clocks $\phi1$ and $\phi2$, until the desired bit is shifted to the output of the selected register. To keep track of which position, of the possible 4096, within a loop is accessible at any given time, an external address assignment must be made when the 3064 is first powered up, and that address assignment must by synchronously updated each memory cycle. (This initial address assignment is usually zero.) In addition to knowing the current data location, it is often necessary to know when a specific address is accessible.

The circuit that does both of these jobs is called a location tracker and address matcher (Fig. 5). As its functional block diagram (a) shows, a 12-bit binary counter, which is clocked at the beginning of $\phi2$, maintains the current loop location. Optionally, at power-up, this counter may be cleared.

To access a specific memory loop position, the 12-bit address for that loop position is loaded into the 12-bit latch, and then this desired address is compared to the address of the current location in the counter. When the address desired matches the current location, the EQUAL output becomes active, signalling that a read, write, or read-modify-write cycle may begin. (This circuit includes an optional clear input to the 12-bit latch holding the address desired.) One possible implementation (b) for the tracker/matcher requires only six and one-half ICs.

Adding address and data latches to the clock generator and tracker/matcher circuits produces a basic CCD controller (Fig. 6). The latches simplify interfacing to the CCD array by synchronizing the address and data information to the clock signals and by assuring that the set-up and hold-time constraints of the CCD array are met by the system.

Building a basic controller

This controller uses still another technique to generate the $\phi1$, $\phi2$, CE, and SYNC signals, employing the 74LS321, a 16-pin device containing an oscillator plus a modulo-8 counter. The f/2 and f/4 outputs from this counter are decoded into four timing pulses that are used to strobe the 74S112 latches, thus creating $\phi1$, $\phi2$, CE, and SYNC signals that the 3064 needs.

During a read cycle, the data outputs of the selected CCDs go to the high-impedance state with the rising edge of CE. The one data delay time later (150 ns max), these outputs go to a low-impedance (logic 1 or logic 0) state, where they remain latched until the beginning of the next CE pulse.

The prerequisites for a read operation are that the loop address and encoded chip select inputs be stable and that the CCD write (CCDWRT) input be logic 1 before the end of the SYNC pulse. Because of the timing requirements of the 74S373 flip-flops, these same signals must also remain stable for 25 ns afterward.

In applying the controller, a valid chip select will not be encoded until the proper loop address is reached, producing the EQUAL (match) signal from the address matcher. Since the current location information in the address matcher is updated at the beginning of $\phi2$, this gives the length of $\phi2$ (83 ns) to set up a

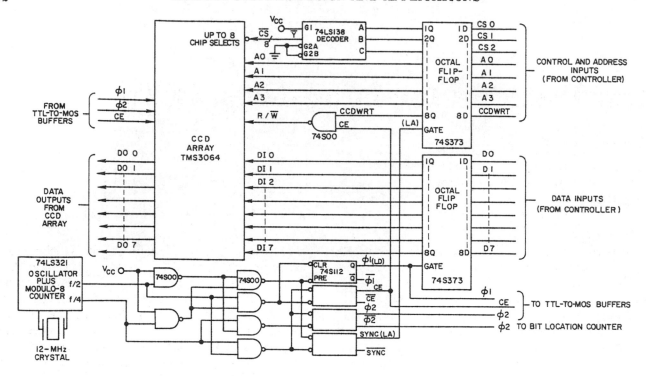

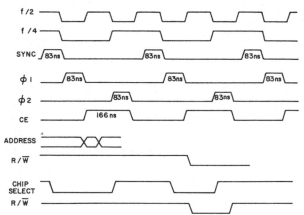

proper loop address and encoded chip select to the 74S373 address latch.

During a write cycle, the same addressing constraints apply as for a read cycle, except that the CCDWRT input must be logic 0. In addition, the data inputs must be stable before the end of $\phi1$ and remain stable for 25 ns afterward (again for the 74S373). Thus, once the address matcher indicates a match, the time before the data must be stable is $\phi2$ plus SYNC, or approximately 166 ns. (Note that the CCDWRT signal is gated with a CE pulse, so write setup and hold times are easily met.)

The 74S138 three-to-eight decoder is optional, depending entirely upon the complexity of the application and, hence, the size and organization of the CCD array. In many applications, it may be omitted.

More to come

One of the most frequently asked questions about CCDs is where are they used. The answer is not simple, for because CCDs are a serial storage medium capable of high-speed and low-power operation, their applications are numerous. For example, with only some slight modifications to the basic controller of Fig. 6,

6. **In this basic CCD controller,** the latches (both octal flip-flops) not only synchronize the address and data information to the clock signals but also assure that set-up and hold-time constraints are met.

the 3064 CCD memory may be used for bulk storage, fast disc replacement, or as a file manager, a buffer/cache, or a data compressor. The next article on this device will show you how to do these applications and more.■■

Applications for Long-Loop CCDs

DAVID SITRICK
Applications Engineer, MOS Memory Division,
Texas Instruments, Houston, Texas

Charge-coupled devices have become a logical choice for many mass-storage solid-state memory applications. Moreover, their speed, high-density, and low power consumption make them ideal not only for bulk storage but also for disc and cassette interface, file swapping and management, video-terminal refresh, and even front-end data compression and processing.

In fact, for applications that limit power consumption or space, CCDs may very well be the one choice that makes sense. And most medium to high-speed applications involving bit-serial data manipulation can use them to advantage.

Versatility and more

One new CCD memory that is a natural for all these applications is the TMS3064, a 64-k long-loop device. Its single-chip construction and high storage density make it one of the most cost-effective semiconductor read/write memories available. What's more, the device offers extremely low power consumption per bit and high-speed operation, rivaling the cycle time of the fastest 16-k dynamic RAMs operating in page mode.

Furthermore, the 3064 is easy to apply. All the user has to provide is the appropriate power-supply voltages and the usual support circuitry, which includes a clock generator, clock drivers, a combination location-tracker/address-matcher, and address and data latches to simplify interfacing. The clock generator need only produce two nonoverlapping clocks, in addition to chip-enable and sync signals. The two clocks and chip enable are all that have to be buffered to a MOS level.

Fig. 1 shows how to wire the 3064 with two location trackers to build a storage memory. The size of the CCD array and its organization depend on the particular application, as does the number of serial-to-parallel (SP) and parallel-to-serial (PS) registers. Generally, both types of registers are needed because of the speed difference between the CCD memory and the device (or memory space) to and from which data transfers are made, and the need for random access —not purely serial access—to the CCD array.

To access the CCD memory, the block-transfer controller (BTC), not shown in Fig. 1, loads the block-transfer size (number of bits) into the righthand location tracker and the transfer-start address into the lefthand location tracker. The controller then sets a ready signal and waits for an address match. Once the loop address equals the transfer-start address, a match signal releases the clear-counter input to the righthand location tracker.

As data bytes are written to or read from the PS registers, the counter in the righthand location tracker counts from zero until it reaches the proper value (between 1 and 4096 bits) of the block-transfer size. Once the entire block has been transferred, the done signal becomes active, alerting the controller to set up for the next data transfer.

Bridging the access gap

Until now, there's been no cost-effective way to bridge the access gap between fast semiconductor memories (less than 1-μs access time) and slower magnetic serial-access memories (greater than 5-ms access time). CCDs have become that cost-effective bridge.

Currently, large computer systems rely on fixed or moving-head discs for storing bulk data and program segments. Typically, the difference in access time between the main semiconductor memory and the disc bulk storage is on the order of 10^5. Such a mismatch, with a single program executing, can easily hike a CPU's idle time to 75% or more.

Obviously, as the size of main memory increases, requests to the disc decrease—but a smaller memory would hold down system cost. One lower-cost alternative to adding main memory is to use a CCD as a cache—a small high-speed memory residing between the disc and main memory—to decrease access-time mismatch.

In Fig. 2a, the CCD functions as buffer/cache between main memory and disc and acts as an intermediate storage device for all data transfers between them. It could also be used as a temporary-save space for swapping program segments between the main memory and itself.

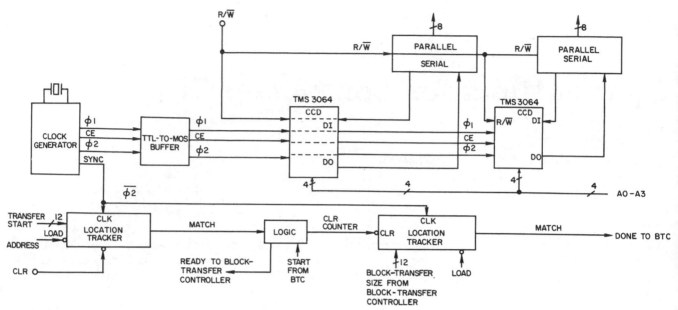

1. Building a storage memory with the TMS3064 CCD requires only minimal support circuitry. The lefthand location tracker matches addresses, while the righthand tracker matches the block-transfer size.

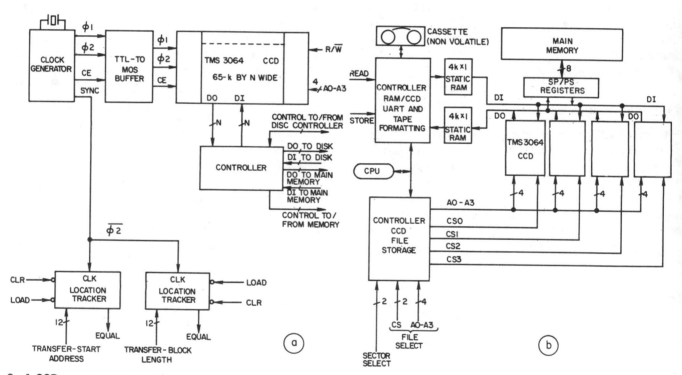

2. A CCD memory array reduces the mismatch in access time between main semiconductor memory and a disc (a) or a tape cassette (b). The smaller the mismatch is, the shorter the idle time of the mainframe CPU.

With the CCD cache, the mismatch ratio plummets to around 2000. In many cases, you can even reduce processor idle time to the point where you won't need any additional main memory and/or multiprogramming techniques.

In small computer systems, the access mismatch can be just as severe between the main program memory and the cassette tape typically used for storing bulk data or nonvolatile programs. Moreover, because of memory-addressing limitations, it is seldom possible to increase program memory size or employ multiprogram techniques.

CCD interfaces tape cassettes

To decrease CPU idle time in a small computer system, you can turn to a CCD cassette interface like the one in Fig. 2b. The four 3064s provide 262 kbits (32 kbytes) of buffering between main memory and tape cassette. The SP and PS devices allow data to

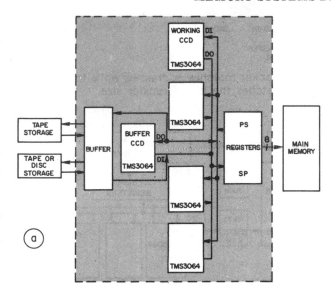

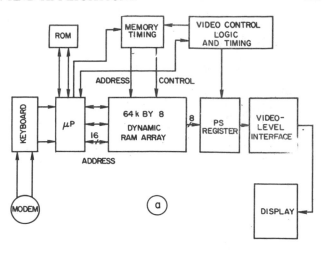

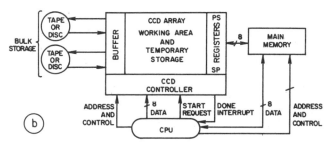

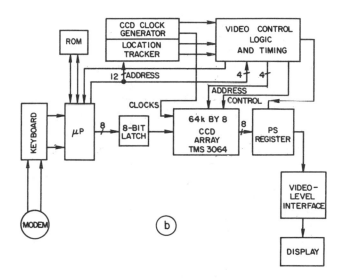

3. **The 3064's read-modify-write cycle** permits a given bit to be read and modified in the same clock cycle. This capability makes it easy to build a high-speed file swapping memory (a) or even manage files (b).

be transferred between main memory and CCD memory at 3 Mbits/s, while 4-k static RAMs (shift registers) allow for the typical tape speed of 1800 bits/s.

Besides compressing data between main memory and cassette, this CCD interface can also serve as a temporary storage area, or as a final linking area for working files in the main memory. Since the 3064 is arranged as 16 loops of 4096 bits each, you could let one tape sector be 128 bytes or 1024 bits, so that each CCD loop contains 64 files, or a total of 256 sectors from tape.

Another attractive feature of the 3064 is that it can make high-speed serial data exchanges and modifications—since a given bit may be read and modified in the same clock cycle. This read-modify-write (RMW) operation means that the contents of two CCDs can be exchanged in less than 20 ms simply by connecting the data output of one to the data input of the other and vice-versa. Even if you want to fill one memory from another, rather than swap data, the RMW cycle permits an 8-bit byte transfer at a rate of 2.4 μs/byte, or over 416,600 bytes/s.

Fig. 3a depicts an array of 3064s organized as a high-speed file swapping memory that takes advantage of the RMW cycle. Four CCDs make up the working-file area, while one CCD serves as a buffer memory to

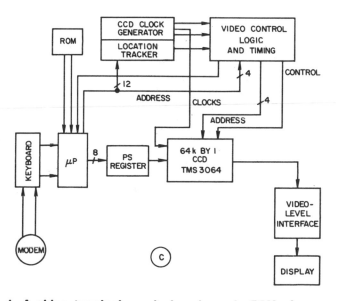

4. **A video terminal employing dynamic RAMs for refresh** (a) needs a lot of space and has a limited addressing scheme. Using CCDs for the refresh memory instead (b) not only saves space and power but also speeds up the rate at which data may be changed in the array. And CCDs remain a good choice for a simpler dot raster (c).

and from disc or tape storage. As a result, the working-area CCDs can swap files at full speed. The working file goes to the buffer file while the buffer file, which contains the next file from storage, goes to the working file. Similarly, as the buffer CCD is dumping to one of the storage devices, it is refilling from one of the other storage devices.

High-speed file management

High-speed file-swapping is just part of the story. Combine CCDs with a sophisticated controller, as in Fig. 3b, and you can do high-speed file management, performing operations like file exchanges, extractions, deletions, insertions, and modifications. The CCD controller performs the actual data exchange, while the CPU is relegated to file-table management and system control.

In this system, the processor directs the controller by giving it a function code, source and destination addressing information (when appropriate), a transfer count (from 1 to 4096) to indicate the size of the file to be moved, and a start signal. The controller then performs the function transparently to the processor and, when finished, interrupts with a done signal.

Meanwhile, the processor updates its file table with any new file locations, modifies files in main memory if needed, and prepares the next request to the controller. The file table must include information about each file, such as file-code identification, a complete file address, file length, a memory-start address, and tape identification. With this information, the processor can spend more time directing how the files are to be fetched, modified, and stored—and less time doing the actual modifications.

Frequently, a high-resolution television image requires 1 or 2 Mbits of stored information. Even a rather standard 256 × 256 video display, with 8 bits/pixel (256 bits for colors or grey-scale levels), will require 524,288 bits of memory.

Fig. 4a shows how a video terminal of comparable size might be configured to refresh a large amount of memory while maintaining fast access. Besides an 8-bit microprocessor and its support ROM, the terminal consists of 512 kbits (64 kbytes) of dynamic RAM for video refresh, video control logic and timing, memory-timing circuitry, a PS shift register, and a video-level interface.

The microprocessor fills the video refresh RAM a byte at a time on a cycle-steal basis. (Data are written to the video memory while data shifting is inhibited.) The processor must share the address lines with the memory-timing circuitry, and it can write data to the video refresh memory only when data aren't being written to the PS shift register, or in this case only during retrace periods.

In addition, consider the sheer space consumed by the 64-k-by-8 video refresh memory. To build it with 4-k dynamic RAMs would require 128 16-pin locations, and even the denser 16-k dynamic RAMs would take up 32.

A refreshing alternative

With long-loop CCDs (Fig. 4b), a video terminal may be designed more simply, yet provide several advantages over a dynamic-RAM approach, notably in the addressing scheme, memory timing, system size, power consumption, reliability, and processor support. At present, the memory cost will probably

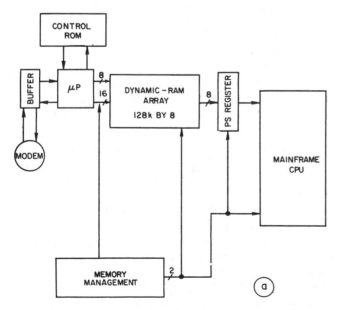

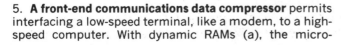

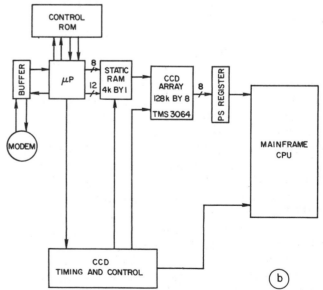

5. **A front-end communications data compressor** permits interfacing a low-speed terminal, like a modem, to a high-speed computer. With dynamic RAMs (a), the micro-processor must keep track of received data while filling the memory array. But the microprocessor's data-saving task is lightened considerably with CCDs (b).

increase slightly, depending on the value of circuit real estate. By late 1979, however, you might break even or even save a little.

As before, the processor produces a 16-bit address and an 8-bit data word. But the location tracker holds the upper 12 address bits while the video control-logic-and-timing circuitry holds the lower four address bits. The 8-bit latch holds the data byte. Now when the correct memory location comes along, the timing circuitry, not the processor, writes data to the video refresh memory, a CCD array in this case.

Because of its read-modify-write cycle, the long-loop 3064 allows data to be written during both retrace and display scanning. So not only is timing removed from the processor routine, but the rate at which data may be changed in the array is increased. What's more, the CCD video memory takes up four to 16 times less space than the dynamic-RAM one, while consuming five to 20 times less power.

For a less complex dot raster, say, 256 × 256 with a dot frequency in the 5-MHz region, the size and power savings of the CCD approach, though significant, take a back seat to the simplicity of designing the timing and interfacing. In such a simple terminal (Fig. 4c), the PS shift register replaces the 8-bit latch, and the CCD produces a single serial output that drives the video-level interface directly.

Within the single 16-pin CCD, each bit of memory corresponds to one particular dot location on the TV raster. Again, the processor can write to the video memory without timing constraints, while the video control logic and timing circuitry place the data in the correct location of the ever-cycling CCD.

Besides serving as video memory, CCDs are well-suited for interfacing a low-speed, data-originating device, like a data terminal or modem, to a high-speed data acceptor, like a mainframe computer. Such a front-end data compressor accepts data in the range of, say, 300 to 4800 bits/s and stores the data for bursting into the high-speed communications channel of a mainframe CPU. The burst rate is typically very high, around 20 Mbits/s.

In a data compressor built with dynamic RAMs, as in Fig. 5a, the microprocessor stores information as it is received. If the 1-Mbit dynamic-RAM array is not full, the received data are simply written directly to the array. If the RAM array becomes full, however, the memory management circuitry starts bursting the memory contents to the CPU, and a small RAM storage area saves the received data until the burst is over. Then the μP must begin filling the memory array with that saved information without missing or misplacing the data it is receiving.

A CCD alternative, as shown in Fig. 5b, simplifies the microprocessor's data-saving task considerably. The CCD timing and control circuitry, and not the μP, transfers received data into the storage area—in this case, a 1-Mbit CCD. As a result, received data may be written to the 4-k static RAM with at most 1 byte

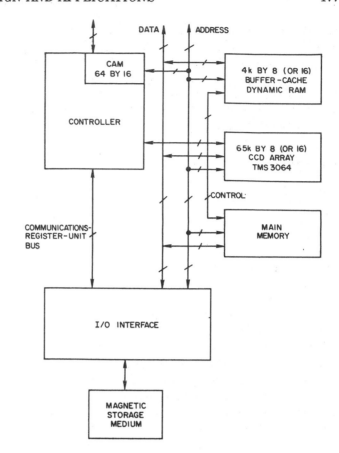

6. **CCD latency can be reduced by a factor of 64** with a system whose buffer-cache RAM holds sixty-four 64-word files and their starting addresses, while the content-addressable memory (CAM), holding the current file addresses, compares the 64 addresses simultaneously. If the addresses match, the desired file is in the cache.

of buffering, whether or not the high-speed burst is in progress.

With data storage on a first-in, first-out basis, the CCD timing-and-control circuitry needs only a single indication of when the static RAM is full. Then this circuitry cues received data into the CCD array, while remaining completely transparent to the μP.

The static RAM, organized as 4-k × 1 bits, does slightly increase the complexity of the CCD timing-and-control circuitry, but it does save the μP some data shifting, especially at slower data rates. This RAM could just as easily be organized 8-bits wide, which would simplify the control and timing; but then the microprocessor's task would grow more complex as would memory size.

In general, however, the long-loop CCD implementation simplifies memory addressing and control while reducing space, power, and cost. And, eventually should save a lot of money. There's another, not so obvious advantage. The dynamic-RAM configuration operates very near its read-cycle time limit, with 20 Mbits coming from the PS shift register every second. But since the 3064's read cycle can be as fast as 200 ns, the CCD configuration can transfer data at up to 40 Mbits/s.

Sometimes you won't require as large a memory as you do for video-terminal refresh or front-end data compression. But you may still need fast data throughput—for example, with a synchronous commutator/decommutator for a time-division multiplexing system. In such an application, data may have to be stored, read or manipulated in a way that will make PS shift registers awkward or even impossible for interfacing memory or increasing data throughput.

That's the time to consider data interleaving, which simply involves skewing the chip-enable inputs to the CCDs in time to stagger memory access. With timing like that, data can be obtained from an array of N CCDs at a rate equal to N times the 5-Mbits/s limit of one CCD. However, you won't get this faster throughput without more complicated memory-timing circuits.

Reducing CCD latency time

Another way to speed up data transfers is to shorten CCD latency time. Fig. 6 shows you how to cut CCD latency by a factor of 64 on the average. The 4-k × 8 buffer-cache dynamic RAM holds 64 data blocks each made up of 64 words. The content-addressable memory (CAM), shown as part of the controller, is arranged as 64 words of 16 bits each.

Each word is loaded in the cache with the starting address of a file, making that data available for

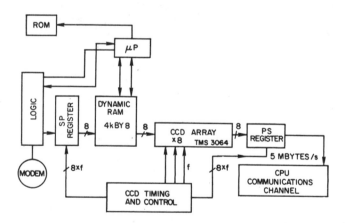

7. **This intelligent front-end processor** transfers data from the RAM working area to the CCD array very quickly. As a result, the microprocessor has enough time to manipulate data before writing to the CCD array.

retrieval. After receiving the current address, the CAM makes 64 simultaneous comparisons for an address match. If the addresses match, the file you want is in the buffer cache. No match means the desired file isn't there, and a seek-and-load cache cycle begins.

An access from CCD bulk memory causes the controller to write that location to the buffer cache. Then the next CCD location is written and so on until the file has been completely transferred to the cache. Depending on the time between CPU accesses, there may be as many as four transfers between each CPU memory cycle. It is also advantageous to allow continuous transfers at certain times, for instance, when an arithmetic-logic-unit cycle is in progress.

An intelligent front-end processor

Another applications area to which CCDs are well-suited is communications. In conjunction with the microprocessor, many schemes are being used to minimize message errors, boost throughput, and increase the accuracy of translating messages from one format to another. In any case, the data received must be "preprocessed." One good way to do it is with a long-loop CCD array, like the one in the intelligent front-end processor of Fig. 7.

This front-end processor operates very much like the front-end data compressor of Fig. 5b. However, with the compressor, writing speed is not critical provided that the information is written to the CCD array as fast as it's received from the modem. The front-end processor, on the other hand, requires a good deal of microprocessor time to manipulate the data before writing to the CCD array for high-speed bursting.

Therefore to let the μP spend more time processing data, the CCD array is arranged as a wide word and preceded by a SP register as well as an 8-bit-wide RAM working area. As a result, data transfer to the CCD array from the RAM working area is eight times faster than in the data compressor.

On the other hand, CCD timing in the front-end processor is the same as in the data compressor, and the shift clocks for the SP and PS registers may usually be derived from the main CCD clock generator. And as for the data compressor, the processor's CCD timing-and-control circuitry needs just one alert to move RAM data into the CCD array. ∎∎

SECTION VII
System Application Examples Using RAMs

System design with RAMs offers designers many challenges: packing the most memory into the least area, minimizing errors due to noise on the signal lines, and preventing problems or data losses due to power-supply failures, to name a few. Some of the articles in this section are basic design guidelines, such as how to build a refresh controller for dynamic RAM systems. However, other articles show how to develop large memory systems that can provide megabytes of memory for large computer systems.

Additional articles show how to take advantage of high-speed RAMs and use them in some unusual applications, such as data multiplexing or telecommunications. However, no matter what your application, many of the design hints shown in these articles can probably be applied to it and provide a beneficial result.

Take the "Dynamics" Out of Dynamic RAMs

BRUCE McCORMICK
Product Marketing,
Intel Corp., Santa Clara, California

CRAIG PETERSON
Design Engineer,
Intel Corp., Santa Clara, California

You no longer have to give up the good points of dynamic RAM because of its bad points. With an IC controller taking care of the refresh and address clocking, you won't have to resort to static RAMs as the best way out. That's fortunate, because dynamic RAM offers more than static: It's four times denser—only one or two transistors are required per cell vs four or more per static cell. Smaller die size means more memory in one DIP—which generally brings down cost. With care, 64 kbytes of fully-interfaced dynamic RAM can fit into 16 in².

Another dynamic attribute is lower power consumption (Table 1). Storing information on a capacitor-type cell consumes much less power than a continuously-on flip-flop. As a result, dynamic RAM is less expensive to operate.

But up to now, there was a big catch: the problems of refresh and address clocking. And up to now, the approaches developed to eliminate those problems didn't provide a total solution (Table 2). For example, the popular Intel 3242 and Zilog Z80 microprocessors help simplify the dynamic-RAM interface, but that's about all they do.

Now, however, the whole problem is being attacked by three different solutions, each of which makes dynamic RAM appear static to the processor. The TIM 9915, MOT 3480 (chip sets) and Intel 8202 (one IC) apply to any microprocessor environment and can handle at least 64 kbytes of memory. All three provide some means of refreshing and, with some external circuitry, hidden refresh.

Taking the pain out of refresh

The beauty of the 8202 is that it handles the problems of refresh and clocking regardless of reset, DMA transfers or the CPU relinquishing the bus. For normal refreshing, the 8202 controller requires very little overhead since it doesn't need an acknowledge from the processor to perform a refresh. Instead, it

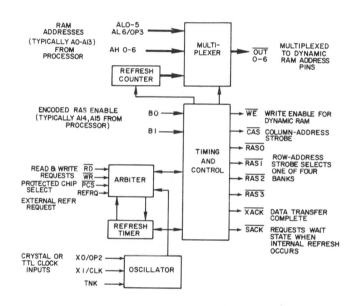

1. **A new dynamic-RAM controller** takes the pain out of refreshing and clocking. The chip not only provides address multiplexing and fail-safe refresh without wait states, but also allows DMA operation.

takes advantage of wait states whenever a memory cycle is requested during refresh: Refresh/memory arbitration takes place inside the 8202; the processor doesn't do it.

TI's component set also allows for an optional fail-safe refresh. Motorola's 3480 component, which complements the company's 3242A, 3222A (similar to Intel's 3242, 3222), uses a request/request-granted structure.

But where both TI and Motorola lean on analog techniques for timing control, the 8202 goes with a simpler, more accurate digital approach. And with one crystal (up to 25 MHz) controlling all timing, multiplexing and refresh generation, 8202 component count is minimized.

Not only that, the timing is flexible, because the 8202 operates over a large band of frequencies and,

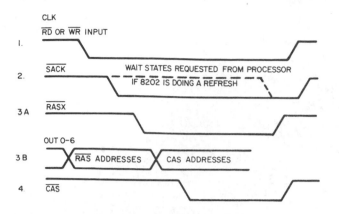

2. When a memory cycle is requested, $\overline{\text{SACK}}$ returns to tell the processor that memory is ready (for refresh, $\overline{\text{SACK}}$ stays high until completion). Addresses are then set up for RAS, and RAS goes low. Next, column addresses are set up, while CAS goes low to strobe into dynamic RAM.

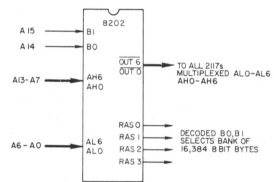

AO–A6 ARE THE RAS ADDRESSES AND A7–A13 ARE THE CAS

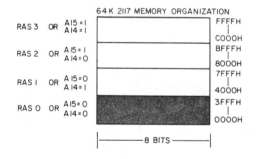

3. How the 8202 addresses dynamic RAM: With A_0 through A_6 as the RAS addresses, and A_7 through A_{13} as the CAS, all 16 address bits are used.

through spec definition, is compatible with industry-standard 4 and 16-k dynamic RAMs (16-pin).

Basically, the 8202—bipolar and packaged in a 40-pin DIP—does all the system support to operate and refresh up to 16 kbytes of 2104A or 64 kbytes of 2117/2118 in 8080A, 8085A, 8086 systems, or 128 kbytes of 2117/2118 in an 8086. The 2104A and 2117 are 4096 × 1 and 16,384 × 1 industry-standard dynamic RAMs, whereas the 2118 is a new, 5-V only, 16-k × 1 RAM offering a choice of speeds higher than the ones available with 2117 and 2117-compatible components.

To interface with the dynamic RAMs, the 8202

■ *Provides address multiplexing:* The multiplexed bus can drive up to four banks of eight RAMs each (with additional buffering, four banks of 16 each for a 16-bit system). The chip generates all the necessary RAS (Row Address Strobe), CAS (Column Address Strobe), WE (Write Enable) and CS (Chip Select) signals.

■ *Provides fail-safe refresh:* Memory gets refreshed in a distributed manner without having to ask the processor to hold the bus. The processor waits only if it requests a memory cycle during a refresh cycle.

■ *Provides an externally controlled refresh option* for those who want sync or hidden refresh.

■ *Allows direct interface* with the 8080A bus, the 8085A demultiplexed bus, the 8086 demultiplexed bus and DMA controllers.

■ *Allows convenient and compatible debugging* with Intel ICE modules, μscope and SDK kits.

■ *Allows memory and refresh requests to be asynchronously requested*—a very flexible system solution.

All these capabilities add up to a simple solution to dynamic RAM interface (see Fig. 1). The 64-kbyte card interfaces with a microprocessor bus as easily as any static RAM.

Arbitration is the key

The crystal-controlled internal shift register in the 8202 gives the fine timing resolution needed for dynamic RAMs. All the RAM-controlling signals are generated by tapping an internal traveling-ONEs shift register. The taps provide integral increments of the clock period for generating RAS, CAS, WE and CS signals (see Fig. 2). The crystal inputs (which also can be driven by external TTL) provide for up to 25-MHz operation.

Externally, a memory cycle can start from one of three inputs: memory-read, memory-write or an external-refresh request. Internally, memory cycles are initiated from an internal refresh-timer request. Arbitration between memory or refresh requests occurs within the 8202.

To perform arbitration, a refresh request (internal or external) clocks-in on the falling edge of the internal clock. If no memory cycle is in progress, the refresh logic activates on the subsequent falling edge of the internal clock. At this time, the refresh address (taken from an internal counter) is multiplexed out to the memory, and a refresh cycle occurs. However, if a memory cycle is in progress, the refresh request is latched until serviced (at the end of the current memory cycle).

Conversely, if no refresh cycle is in progress, a read or write can occur with the 8202 performing the synchronization. Because of arbitration within the chip, the 8202 clock, system clock, refresh requests

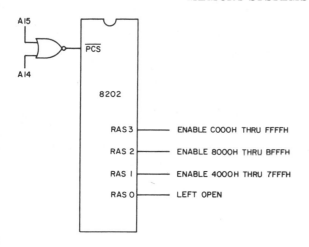

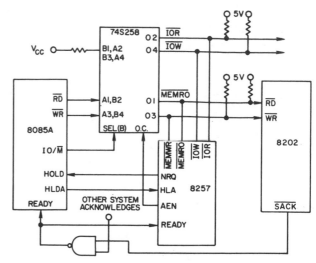

4. **Arrange address space any way you want** by NORing A_{14} and A_{15} together to keep the 8202 off the bus for the first 16 kbytes.

5. **To perform a direct memory access with the controller,** interconnect the processor and memory-control lines as shown. A DMA-controller is also used.

and memory read or write requests can all be totally asynchronous. Because the 8202 controls all timings, you don't have to worry about system timing being compatible with the complex clocks of dynamic RAM. All that is necessary is that the memory provide the data in time for the processor and vice versa for a write.

Refreshing takes place in a distributed manner as a RAS-only cycle, an approach using less power than other methods. Through a user-selectable option, the 8202 configures itself to be compatible with the 64-cycle/2-ms refresh rate required for the 2104A, or the 128-cycle/2-ms for the 2117. When a memory cycle is requested while the 8202 performs a refresh cycle, wait states are injected until the refresh is complete (Fig. 3). This is accomplished through an output called SACK (System Acknowledge), which is gated with other similar system-acknowledge signals and applied to the ready input of the processor.

Full address space is used

To see how the 8202 addresses the dynamic RAM, check Fig. 4. With 2117s, and using the full address space of the 8-bit processor, all 16 bits of address are given to the 8202. The B_1, B_0 inputs are decoded to select one of four RAS lines. Using the processor's address lines, A_{15} and A_{14}, for B_1 and B_0 gives the address map shown in Fig. 3. The remaining 14 address lines are multiplexed to the dynamic RAM on the OUT $_{0-6}$ output pins. The sequence of addressing, with the RAS and CAS clocks as shown in Fig. 2, is compatible with 2117s and 2104As.

To inhibit one of the RAS lines, all you have to do is deselect the 8202 while the prohibited address space is being accessed. This is accomplished through a PCS pin (Protected Chip Select) on the 8202. Using this input to disable the 8202 won't disturb a cycle already in progress. In Fig. 4, A_{15} and A_{14} are NORed together to prevent the 8202 from using the bus in the first

16 kbytes of address space. Extending this technique allows you to break up your address space any way you desire.

DMA interfacing with the 8202 is just as easy. Fig. 5 illustrates the control-line interconnect of the 8085A processor, 8257 DMA controller and the 8202. The memory read and write lines of the 8257 DMA controller are wire-ORed with the demultiplexed read and write control signals from the processor. The system-acknowledge signal, which notifies the processor when a wait state is required, also notifies the DMA controller when a refresh cycle is being performed.

'Hidden' refresh obviates waits

To avoid using wait states during normal processing, you can opt for an external refresh-request input. A pulse on this input causes the 8202 to perform a "hidden" refresh cycle (with the same arbitration as noted before), if the pulse appears in conjunction with an instruction fetch or decoded CS for other address spaces.

If external refresh fails to occur—as may happen during reset, single-stepping, or relinquishing of the bus by the CPU—the 8202 will take over and perform the refresh. With a proper external refresh, you can ignore the SACK line and so eliminate wait states.

In a typical 8085A configuration (Fig. 6), the system interfaces with a 64 kbyte 2117 array. The 8202 also provides an XACK (Transfer-Acknowledge) signal, which can latch output data into a data buffer—very useful with nonlatching memories in which data may have to remain valid for long periods. This configuration takes advantage of the full address space of the 8085A processor. Note that you might want to have PCS disabled initially to allow a bootstrap ROM to "bring up" the system.

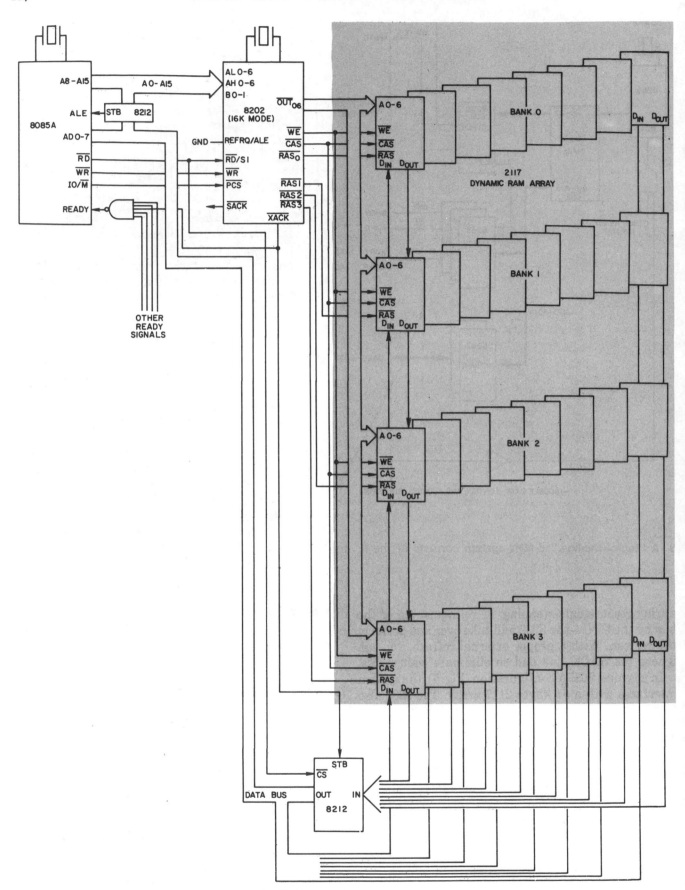

6. **Configuring an 8085/8202 system** with 64 kbytes of
2117 memory will make use of the full address space of
the processor.

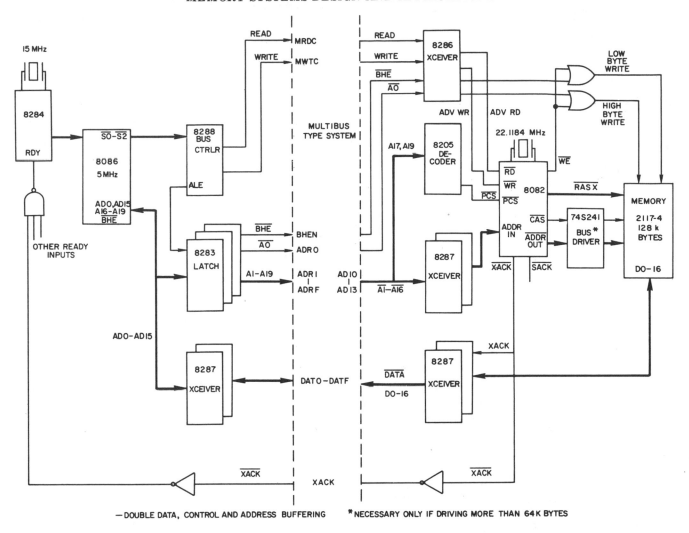

7. A "top-of-the-line," 5-MHz system consists of the IC controller, the 8086 16-bit μP and 128 kbytes of memory.

The dynamic-RAM memory array in Fig. 6 could just as easily have been made up of 16 kbytes of 2104A. The 8202 has an option that allows you to configure the device into a 2104A mode (AL6 is tied to 12 V). The highest address of the higher seven CAS addresses, AH_6, now becomes a CS input to the 2104A via OUT_6. The 8202 knows to treat it as such because of the selected option, which also configures the 8202 to perform a 64-cycle refresh, as compared to 128 cycles required for 2117s.

Perhaps even more dramatic are the possibilities the 8202 allows with the Intel 8086, a 16-bit, 5-MHz processor that can address directly up to 1 Mbyte of memory, and can work with both 8 and 16-bit data

words. To change word size, either A_0 or BHE (Byte High Enable) qualify WE from the 8202 so that an 8-bit byte or 16-bit word is written to as desired. The 8202 can control up to a full 128 kbytes of memory space via address lines A_1 through A_{16} from the demultiplexed 8086 bus (Fig. 7).

Eight 8202s can function with the maximum-mode 8086 system to provide control and addressing for 1 Mbyte of memory (except for chip select). Just nine cards are needed—one processor and eight memory cards. Each memory card, acting as a subsystem, can provide its own decoding, refresh and address control. And all cards can work totally asynchronously with the processor board. ∎∎

Keep the Memory Interface Simple

GARY FIELLAND
Microcomputer Applications Engineer,
Intel Corp., Santa Clara, California

KEN OISHI
Dynamic RAM Applications Engineer,
Intel Corp., Santa Clara, California

Dynamic random-access memories, which offer about four times the density of static memories, are prime candidates for many microprocessor-system designs. With the increased use of programmed logic, the pervasiveness of high-level languages, the rising power of the microprocessors themselves, and the dropping costs of RAMs, system memories are increasing in size at an almost unbelievable pace.

But a dynamic RAM isn't as easy to design into a microprocessor system as a static unit. Not only do you have to worry about special access timing requirements, but you also have to decide which form of memory-refresh system will work best with your application. And, depending on the size of your memory system, it may be more economical to use static devices. For systems requiring less than 8 kbytes of memory, static devices are probably the better alternative. For systems above 16 kbytes, dynamic RAMs are more economical, even with the cost of the refresh circuitry. In between the two ranges, the choice depends on many factors—cost, ease of design, parts count, familiarity, etc.

There is no RAM component easier to use than the static device. Still, you can design a dynamic-memory system that is every bit as reliable and perhaps, more cost-effective. One of the biggest challenges you'll encounter, though, is to determine the minimum access time needed by the RAMs.

Understand memory speed requirements

Memory speed, or access time, for either static or dynamic RAMs is a fairly complex characteristic. Considering a typical microprocessor memory read cycle (Fig. 1a) will help bring the term "access time" into focus. A typical microprocessor presents its memory address to the memory address bus, followed some time later (typically 100 ns to allow for stabilization) by its memory-read (MEMR) strobe. This strobe asks that the selected memory device provide the addressed data on the microprocessor's bidirectional data bus.

Providing the address early in the cycle allows address decoding and module selection to be performed before the MEMR strobe occurs, and heads off any bus conflicts. Some time (typically 350 ns) after the MEMR strobe is issued, the processor expects valid data at its input port. If the data are not available in the allotted time, the processor can be forced to wait by having its Ready input (assuming an 8080A processor) pulled to the inactive state. As long as the Ready is false, the processor will wait an integral number of processor clock periods (wait states).

To meet the "no-wait-state" timing for the processor, the memory system must be no slower than the processor's required read access time. One of them, t_{ACA}, is the time between a stable processor-supplied memory address and the arrival of valid data at the processor's input port—typically 450 ns. Another read access time is t_{ACR}, the period, after a processor-supplied read strobe, during which the processor can expect valid data at its input port—typically 350 ns.

Read access time, t_{ACS}, for a static memory component (Fig. 1b) is the delay between a stable address input and valid data at the RAM output. A static memory will begin accessing the addressed bit cell(s) the moment the address becomes available. If there are multiple banks of static memory, each bank will access the addressed bit cell(s), though only one bank will be selected by the high-order address-bits decoder. So by ignoring bus and bus-buffer delays, a static memory with $t_{ACS} \leq t_{ACA}$ will satisfy the no-wait-state criterion.

On the other hand, the read access time t_{ACD} (Fig. 1c) for a dynamic-memory component is the time from its clock input until the data at the RAM output are valid. Assume that the address is set up at the address inputs of the dynamic RAM some time, t_{ASU}, before the clock input is activated—typically 0 to 10 ns. For a simple system design, the clock input can be activated by the MEMR strobe. This means that the dynamic memory doesn't have as much time as a static memory to access its data.

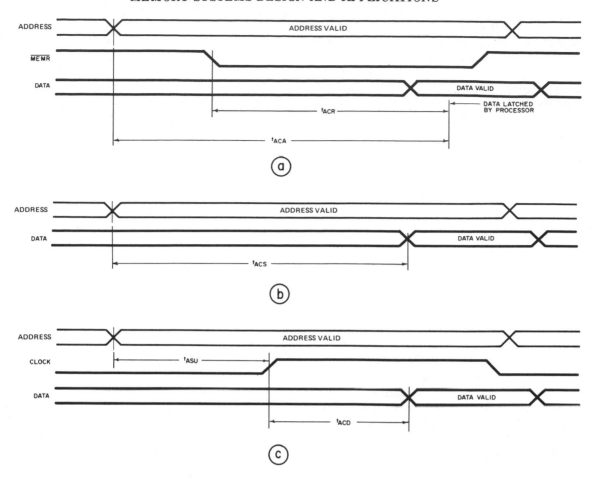

1. **A typical microprocessor no-wait-state memory Read cycle** (a) shows the memory-system access time required from address (t_{ACA}) and Read strobes (t_{ACR}). For a static memory system, access time (t_{ACS}) is measured from address valid to data valid (b). Access time in a dynamic memory system (t_{ACD}) is measured from the start of the clock to the beginning of the data valid, with an implied address set-up time, t_{ASU} (c).

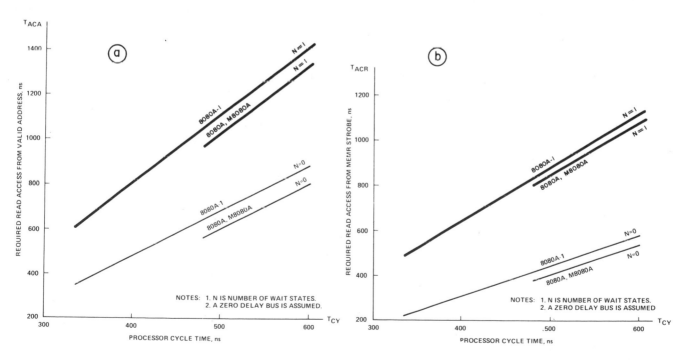

2. **Able to operate with a wide range of memory-access times,** the 8080A processor family can perform with or without wait states. The minimum read access time from a valid address (a) and from the MEMR strobe (b), shows a difference of about 100 ns for the same speed/processor cycle time and 0 or 1 wait states.

Not only that, but 50 to 100 ns are typically lost in the dynamic-memory controller itself. To satisfy the no-wait-state criterion, a dynamic memory must provide a $t_{ACD} \leq t_{ACR}$ (typically 50 to 100 ns less). Thus, a dynamic memory must have an access time some 150 to 200 ns faster than a static memory to satisfy a microprocessor's no-wait-state access requirement. Fig. 2 graphically depicts the memory access time requirements for an 8080A microprocessor.

Memory refresh: crucial for data retention

Another crucial requirement is that the dynamic RAM be refreshed so that none of the data held inside will be lost. Most of the 4 and 16 k dynamic RAMs available today specify that each bit cell within the array be refreshed every 2 ms.

A dynamic RAM has its cells organized in arrays —4096-bit memories have a cell array of 64 rows and 64 columns. All columns in a single row are refreshed simultaneously so that you need only provide 64 refresh cycles (each with a different row address), each 2 ms. The 16,394-bit memories have two identical cell arrays each with 64 rows and 128 columns. Again, all columns in a single row in an array are refreshed simultaneously. This means that you must supply 128 refresh cycles (each with a different row address) during each 2-ms period.

A 6 or 7-bit counter supplies the refresh row addresses (for 4 k and 16 k memories, respectively). It must be incremented after each refresh cycle (Fig. 3). A two-input row-address multiplexer is also used to multiplex either the processor-supplied memory address or the counter-supplied refresh address onto the dynamic memory row address inputs.

Refresh cycles may be a set of contiguous cycles known as burst-mode refresh, or they may be discrete nonadjacent cycles known as distributed or single-cycle refresh. You choose one method over the other based on memory-availability requirements and ease of over-all system design. In either case some means must be provided to arbitrate between processor memory cycles and refresh cycles. The design of this refresh arbiter can be simpler or complex, depending on the method chosen.

More than one way to refresh

There are three ways to refresh dynamic RAMs. Each differs slightly in complexity, generality, and memory availability (Table 1).

The *asynchronous* method assumes that refresh is inherently a real-time event—one refresh cycle every 31 μs (64 cycles every 2 ms)—and is independent of the state of the processor. This popular approach yields the most flexible system since it is very loosely coupled. The asynchronous memory system normally has its own dedicated control logic and may run independently of the microprocessor. The local control

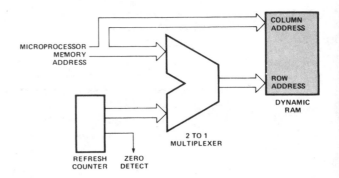

3. **The basic circuit for a dynamic RAM refresh system** includes a refresh counter and row-address multiplexer. If burst-mode refreshing is done, zero detection in the refresh counter is very helpful.

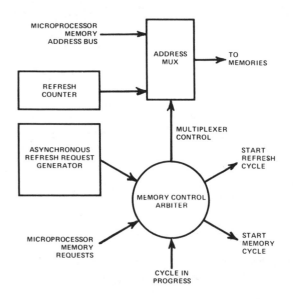

4. **An asynchronous memory system** requires that you design a very complex controller that must be able to resolve contention problems.

logic supplies refresh as needed and couples with the processor only to provide Read or Write cycles.

In most implementations, the memory system is unaware of the processor state or any other processor particulars. Indeed, an asynchronous-refresh memory system may be designed to operate with just about every microprocessor. At the other end, the asynchronous-refresh memory appears no different than static memory to the microprocessor, except that the processor may occasionally have to wait for service if the memory is busy performing refresh.

While an asynchronous-refresh memory system offers the most modular approach to design, it frequently suffers from a high degree of complexity, which degrades performance. One big reason is that you have to design a reliable, high-speed memory controller that arbitrates between asynchronous-refresh requests and microprocessor memory requests —a demanding job (Fig. 4). This problem is further complicated since the beginning of the memory cycle must now be delayed until the requests have been

Three ways to refresh

Asynchronous	—	Refresh is performed asynchronously with respect to the microprocessor.
Synchronous	—	Refresh is performed in synchronism with microprocessor events.
Semisynchronous	—	Refresh is performed in synchronism with the microprocessor clock, but asynchronously with respect to microprocessor events.

definitively resolved and appropriate address, data, and control set-up times have been supplied. So this request resolution adds time directly to the system access time for each cycle.

Synchronize the μP and the refresh

The *synchronous* method of refresh, on the other hand, can improve the performance and apparent availability of a memory system. Refresh cycles are forced to occur synchronously with microprocessor events, and the event usually chosen is a cycle in which the microprocessor won't be using the memory. Hence, there is no contention for the memory and the refresh cycles do not detract from apparent memory availability. This hiding of the refresh cycles when the memory would otherwise be idle is often called Invisible Refresh since the processor sees no delay due to refresh.

As a result, the memory is available to the processor without conflict every time the memory is requested. This absence of contention leads to a not-so-obvious but significant performance improvement. The memory address and data multiplexers may select the microprocessor bus before the cycle begins. Then, once the microprocessor issues a request, the cycle begins. The processor can provide sufficient address and data lead time to satisfy all address decoding, propagation delay, and memory device set-up times.

Synchronous system-access time is determined only by the memory and timing-generation circuitry, with no time added for arbitration or multiplexer settling. Thus, with today's dynamic memories, you can guarantee memory cycles that require no microprocessor wait states. Dispensing with wait states yields a significant performance improvement—about 500 nanoseconds' worth for each state.

The heart of an efficient synchronous refresh microprocessor memory system is the refresh scheduler accepts status inputs from the refresh timer and the microprocessor, and based on its knowledge of that processor, schedules the refresh cycles into idle portions of the processor cycle.

Obviously, construction of the scheduler is dependent on the particular microprocessor used and its application.

An override must be provided to guarantee refresh, should the microprocessor be detained from reaching the normal refresh event—such as when the microprocessor enters the Halt, Reset, Wait, or Hold states. But this override will introduce some asynchronism back into the system, for the processor may begin again at any time.

Semisynchronous refresh is a combination of asynchronous and synchronous refresh. For one thing, it simplifies an asynchronous system's request arbiter. Moreover, the memory requests initiated are synchronous with a clock edge. Thus, if the refresh request is synchronous with the opposite clock edge, the two request transitions will never occur simultaneously.

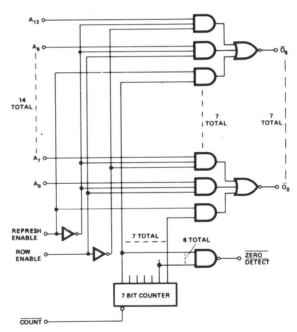

NOTE: A_0 THROUGH A_6 ARE ROW ADDRESSES.
A_7 THROUGH A_{13} ARE COLUMN ADDRESSES.

TRUTH TABLE AND DEFINITIONS

REFRESH ENABLE	ROW ENABLE	OUTPUT
H	X	REFRESH ADDRESS (FROM INTERNAL COUNTER)
L	H	ROW ADDRESS (A_0 THROUGH A_6)
L	L	COLUMN ADDRESS (A_7 THROUGH A_{13})

COUNT – ADVANCES INTERNAL REFRESH COUNTER.
ZERO DETECT – INDICATES ZERO IN THE FIRST 6 SIGNIFICANT REFRESH COUNTER BITS (USED IN BURST REFRESH MODE)

5. **Containing both the refresh counter and the address-row multiplexer,** the Intel 3242 helps simplify the circuitry needed to build a refresh controller for a dynamic memory system. It comes in a 28-pin DIP.

Except for the synchronization of refresh requests to the microprocessor clock, semisynchronous refresh is very similar to asynchronous refresh. There must still be memory-cycle-vs-refresh-cycle arbitration since one cycle may already be in progress when the other is requested. However, this arbitration can be made much simpler.

Using a microprocessor other than an 8080A might require a slight modification to ensure the mutual exclusion of refresh and processor request transitions. The memory controller must still arbitrate between requests and lock out the tardy one. Hence, refresh is still visible, and the processor may have to wait for the refresh cycle to be completed before gaining access to the memory.

Which refresh method do you choose? If you select the synchronous refresh methodology, your next question might be whether or not to perform invisible refresh. First, consider the loss due to visible refresh. Assuming a nominal memory cycle time of 500 ns, 4000 memory cycles will be available in each 2-ms refresh interval. During an interval, 64 refresh cycles must be provided, which causes a loss of almost 2% in memory availability.

Looking at the same numbers from the processor's point of view, the situation is similar. A typical processor machine cycle takes 2 μs, so assuming instant memory availability and no loss due to refresh, 1000 machine cycles can be performed each refresh interval. Now if 64 of those machine cycles were delayed one memory cycle (500 ns) for visible refresh, only 984 machine cycles could be executed each refresh interval, for a processing loss of about 2%.

To maximize performance, you can *improve* performance about 2% by using invisible refresh. But then you get penalized by the added cost and complexity of the refresh-scheduler design. In some implementations this cost may not be much. There are some LSI devices that can reduce system package count in a dynamic memory controller by providing a major portion of the necessary control logic.

The 3242 refresh controller from Intel, for example, contains an address multiplexer and refresh counter (Fig. 5), and is designed for use with 16-k dynamic RAMs. It multiplexes 14 bits of system-supplied address onto 7 output pins. The 7-bit refresh-counter outputs can be multiplexed onto the refresh controller's output. Since they are externally controlled, either distributed or burst-mode refresh may be used.

Now that you're ready to design a microprocessor/dynamic-RAM interface, be prepared to make tradeoffs. The first involves system requirements. Do you want, for example, a dedicated memory system where low cost is more important than generality, or do you want a system where generality is critical? But if cost and performance are your key objectives, choose the synchronous method of refresh, and don't even try to make the refresh invisible.

Design a dedicated system

When trying to decide how to design the synchronous refresh scheduler, consider this: Clearly, the scheduler must have intimate knowledge of the processor state and be able to predict the appropriate moment to perform refresh. Conveniently, an 8080A already has an inherent scheduling function under another name; and what has better knowledge of the processor state than the processor itself?

Two pins in the 8080A, HOLD and HLDA (Hold Acknowledge), indicate internal processor states. HOLD is an input used by the memory to request that the 8080A suspend its use of the bus as soon as possible, and HLDA is an output that the 8080A uses to signal that it is about to yield the bus.

In an 8080A system, HLDA is commonly delayed until the trailing edge of the $\phi2$ clock, which yields HLDAD (Hold Acknowledge Delayed), which in turn is used to gate off the 8080A bus drivers.

So actually you've got a scheduler without any design work. All you have to do is rename the signals generated by the basic processor configuration shown in Fig. 6: HOLD becomes RFRQ (Refresh Request); HLDA becomes RFAK (Refresh Acknowledge); and HLDAD becomes RFAKD (Refresh Acknowledge Delayed).

Before going any further, however, examine the system limitations stemming from your choice of scheduler. First, there are several conditions under which refresh will not be provided due to the use of the 8080A HOLD feature. Refresh will not be provided while the 8080A RESET pin is active, so don't maintain RESET for too long if you want to preserve your dynamic memory's integrity. Similarly, refresh will not be provided while the 8080A is in the Wait state; that is, READY is false. This should be no problem unless READY is being used to single-step the processor.

Finally, refresh will not be provided while in the interrogation mode if you're using the Intel 8080A in-circuit emulator on a system under development. While in that mode, the user system is virtually without a processor, so it obviously will not respond to requests.

With the scheduler design completed all that remains is to provide a source of refresh requests and an interface to the dynamic RAM or RAMs.

Take advantage of 16-k dynamics

With the 16-kbit dynamic RAMs in 16-pin packages, you can build a 64-kbyte memory array on a printed-circuit board area of 16 square inches.

The use of the 16-pin package is made possible by multiplexing the 14 address bits onto seven address input pins. The two 7-bit address words are latched into the RAM by two TTL clocks—Row-Address Strobe (RAS) and Column-Address Strobe (CAS). No chip select is included on the 16-k RAMs; however,

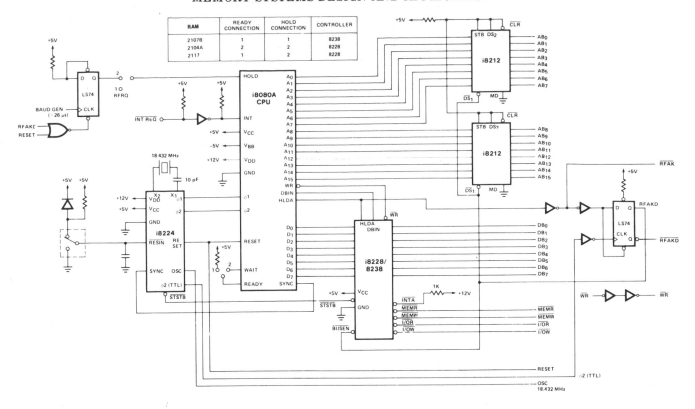

RAM	READY CONNECTION	HOLD CONNECTION	CONTROLLER
2107B	1	2	8238
2104A	2	2	8228
2117	1	2	8228

6. **To design a dedicated memory controller**, you must assume a certain processor configuration. This 8080A-based CPU structure provides all the signals needed by a dynamic-RAM system.

the output is brought to a high-impedance state by the positive transition of CAS.

Refreshing can be accomplished every 2 ms by either of the following methods:

1. RAS-only cycles on 128 addresses A_0 to A_6.
2. Normal read or write cycles on 128 addresses, A_0 to A_6. Remember, when using a write cycle for refresh, 127 cells are refreshed, but the selected cell will contain the data written based on the state of the data input pin.

A 64-kbyte RAM's synchronous-controller-refresh memory system can be built using 2117s, a 3242 controller (Fig. 7), and the 8080A processor group (using the 8228 bus controller). An output ($\leq 15\ \mu s$ period) from a baud-rate generation chain is used to set the refresh request (RFRQ) flip-flop. This RFRQ is applied to the 8080A's HOLD input, while HLDA is used as refresh acknowledge (RFAK).

This design emphasizes maximum performance, in spite of the consequent cost increase. All 64 kbytes are available to an 8080A system (488-ns clock) without any wait states. The primary cost penalty is the need for high-speed RAMs.

System interface is simple

In the system, accurate timing is generated via a shift-register technique. The register is built from 74LS174 D flip-flops. Since the 2117 dynamic RAM doesn't have a chip-select pin, the devices are selected by decoding some of the addresses to generate separate RAS inputs for each row of the memory array, while all devices receive common CAS. A device receiving CAS but no RAS performs no memory operations. Its output remains in the high-impedance state. Only the group of devices receiving both RAS and CAS are enabled to perform memory operations.

Data from the 8080A are transmitted along its bidirectional data bus and buffered by 8216 buffers to the data input pins of the RAMs during a write cycle. During a read cycle, data out of the selected RAMs are buffered by the 8216s and sent to the 8080A. The three-state 8216 outputs are enabled and drive the 8080A data bus during all memory-read cycles, as long as the inhibit is inactive.

The 14 low-order address bits are fed directly into the 3242 multiplexer, whose seven outputs are connected to the 2117's memory-address inputs. Address bits A_{13} to A_7, A_6 to A_0, or the internal 7-bit counter may be presented on these seven outputs, depending on the state of the Row Enable input and the overriding Refresh Enable input. The Refresh Enable input is activated at the start of a refresh cycle (REF), whose trailing edge can be used to advance the internal refresh counter. The two high-order addresses (A_{14} and A_{15}) are decoded and used to select one of four banks of 16-kbyte memories.

Any memory-cycle request (including refresh) will set the Cycle Request (CYRQ) flip-flop and start the timing chain. Note that for a refresh cycle RFAKD,

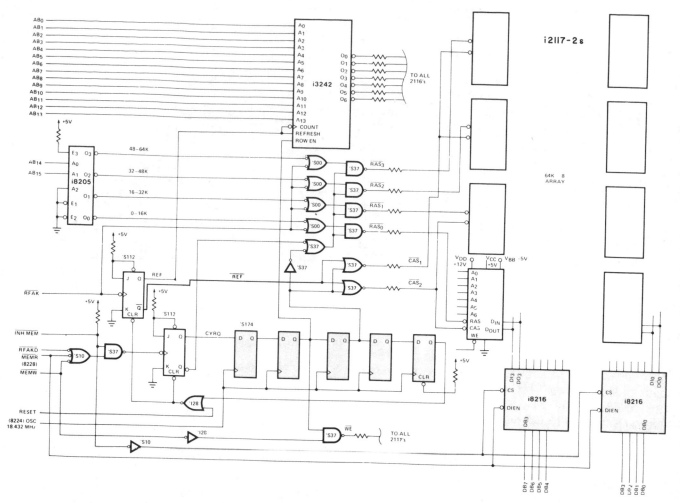

7. A 64-kbyte dynamic memory system, built using 16-k RAMs, requires less than a dozen ICs in addition to the memory chips and the 8080A-based processor array described in Fig. 6.

the REF flip-flop will have already been set by RFAK. Setting the refresh flip-flop early gives the multiplexer outputs time to settle on the refresh addresses from the internal counter. It also enables all four RAS drivers, and inhibits CAS for RAS-only refresh operation.

Once set, the cycle request is immediately applied as RAS and also synchronized with the 18.432-MHz oscillator (from the 8224) and propagated down the shift register (74S174) in 54-ns steps. This is the earliest that RAS can be applied and it must be done this early for the memory to meet the 8080A no-wait-state access requirement. When a ONE reaches the final shift-register stage, the cycle-request, and refresh (if applicable) flip-flops are cleared, which permits ZEROs to propagate down the register.

Clearing the refresh flip-flop also advances the refresh counter and returns the multiplexer to its system-address multiplexing function. All the critical timing intervals, including the generation of RAS, CAS, Row Enable, and the Write-Enable signals, are derived from two taps on the shift register.

Because of the maximum speed requirement, this interface design has the synchronizing delay inside the timing chain. The cycle-request flip-flop is set on a valid cycle request, which immediately applies the row-address strobe (RAS).

One advantage is that the memory access may start as soon as possible, rather than after a synchronizing delay. The disadvantage is that now the time ambiguity is a part of the RAS pulse. This is inconvenient but not insurmountable. Just ensure that all memory set-up and hold times will be met for either extreme of the ambiguous synchronizing interval. Keep the ambiguity in mind when you calculate the worst-case system access time.

Too much memory? Try overlapping

By now you will have realized that a processor system with 64 k of dynamic RAM as its only memory is virtually useless. Two techniques will help circumvent this problem. Both involve overlapping a ROM or PROM into the memory-address space and require an inhibit feature on the dynamic RAM system.

Because semiconductor memories are available in discrete sizes, you may have to have two memories

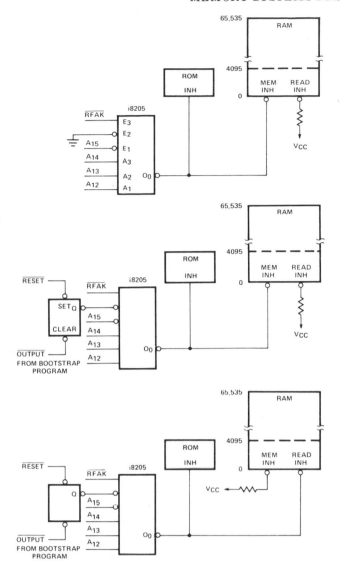

8. Memory can be overlapped by any of three methods: permanently disabling specific RAM locations (a); inhibiting the RAM only during start-up (b); or inhibiting only RAM read operations during start-up (c).

overlap in address space. For instance, if you have a system with 4 kbytes of ROM in addresses 0 to 4095 and 60 kbytes of RAM in addresses 4096 to 65,353, you can implement the system very economically with 16-k RAMs. But then this 64-kbyte RAM would also occupy the first 4 kbytes where you would like to place the ROM.

Mapping the ROM into the first 4 kbytes would essentially discard the first 4 k of RAM by preventing the RAM from ever functioning while in that address range. You can do that with an address-decoding network and memory-inhibit (INH MEM) line as shown in Fig. 8a.

Another thing you might want to do is put the ROM in the address space and inhibit the overlapped RAM only at system start-up. Then, once the system reaches steady state, the bootstrap program can perform an output, which inhibits the bootstrap ROM and enables the overlapped RAM. Thus, the overlapped RAM is

Asynchronism and bistable hang-up

Though most activities of a computing system are synchronous, occasionally asynchronous events must be introduced. Handle this introduction with great care. Bistable devices are normally designed with an input set-up and hold-time requirement with respect to the "clock" input (see Fig. A). This timing requirement ensures that the bistable won't be forced into its astable state. Thus, knowing the normal delay paths, you may specify the delay time required to change state. This delay time, however, is only valid so long as the required set-up and hold times are honored.

Whenever the data input occurs asynchronously to the clock input, it's possible the set-up time will be violated. If this happens, the bistable may "hang" in its astable state for an indeterminate amount of time and extend the specified delay. This hang-up, under forced conditions, has been observed to last as long as 20 ns with a 74S74 flip-flop (Fig. B). Furthermore, during this hang-up time, the outputs are undefined. Depending on the circuit design, they may do nothing, exhibit a slow transition, or even oscillate (Fig. C).

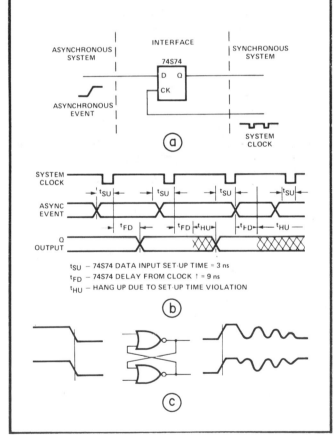

t_{SU} — 74S74 DATA INPUT SET-UP TIME = 3 ns
t_{FD} — 74S74 DELAY FROM CLOCK ↑ = 9 ns
t_{HU} — HANG UP DUE TO SET-UP TIME VIOLATION

not discarded forever; it is simply switched out while the ROM is being used to bootstrap the system and possibly load new programs into the remaining RAM. This allows an easy start-up while retaining the flexibility to later exchange the ROM for RAM. Such a system could be implemented with an address-decoding network, an output port and RAM memory-inhibit line (Fig. 8b).

A slight modification of such a bootstrap technique inhibits the RAM only during start-up for Read cycles. The read inhibit (INH RD) in the RAM module simply keeps the data-bus drivers in their high-impedance state (Fig. 8c). Then, all Reads in that address range will be from ROM, but all Writes will be to both. In effect, the Writes are directed only to RAM since a Write to a ROM is a no-op. As a result, a bootstrap ROM can load a program into RAM—even in locations currently occupied by the bootstrap ROM itself.

In fact, a bootstrap ROM can even copy itself into corresponding RAM locations. Of course, after steady state has been achieved, the ROM may be completely disabled, which would allow both Reads and Writes from the RAM.

Watch out for circuit bugs

A dynamic RAM is a highly complex analog and digital system. It contains differential sensing amplifiers that must detect decivolt signals buried in noise and must operate in tens of nanoseconds. When the device is deselected (RAS and CAS High), the power dissipation is minimal. However, when the memory receives a RAS signal a high current transient is generated on the supply lines.

Proper printed-circuit layout can contribute much towards achieving a reliable dynamic memory system design, which should have an effective gridded power-supply-distribution network to supply current adequately and minimize inductive effects. How the circuit ground is distributed makes a big difference when you're trying to reduce ground noise and inductive offsets, and provide a ground plane for the signal lines.

Another concern during layout is to find a geometry that minimizes the length of the signal and clock lines. Drivers and receivers should be placed as close as possible to the array to minimize the line lengths.

The importance of bypassing the power supplies cannot be overstressed. Large current transients are inevitable, and capacitors must be provided to handle these transients. The capacitors fall into two categories. One covers capacitors that are physically small, with low inherent inductance—such as monolithic and other ceramic capacitors. These should be used quite liberally throughout the array.

The other type includes large-bulk capacitors used to prevent supply droop. This type should also be included within the array for good distribution.

Vendors' literature will normally make specific recommendations for capacitive bypass. For instance, Intel recommends a 0.1 μF ceramic capacitor be connected between V_{DD} and V_{SS} at every other device in the memory array. A similar arrangement between V_{BB} and V_{SS} is also recommended (preferably the alternate devices to the V_{DD} decouplings). For every 16 devices a 25 μF tantalum or equivalent electrolytic capacitor should be connected between V_{DD} and V_{SS} near the array. An equal or slightly smaller bulk capacitor is also recommended between V_{BB} and V_{SS} for every 32 devices. A 0.01 μF ceramic capacitor should be used between V_{CC} and V_{SS} for every eight memory chips.

By carefully laying out the circuit to minimize the length of the signal path, you can reduce the detrimental effects due to the transmission-line properties of a printed-circuit line. Most clock drivers, for instance, include clamps that help minimize over and undershoot. Another frequently used and recommended technique is to put a series resistor in the line to help match impedances and damp out reflections.

The optimum value of the series resistor depends very much on layout and driver and receiver characteristics, and is normally determined empirically. A value of 20 to 30 Ω is a fairly good starting value. When using a series resistor, you must also ensure that the voltage drop across it does not severely degrade the logic level noise margins.

Crosstalk is usually not a severe problem, but you must allow for it during layout. Avoid the temptation of running two or more signals very close together for long distances.

If your system design uses asynchronous refresh, be very careful with the refresh arbiter. It's quite tricky to design, and can arbitrate between asynchronous requests very rapidly. Most circuit-design problems in asynchronous-refresh memory systems are found to be linked with refresh interference—an extremely annoying problem because it occurs infrequently and unexpectedly.■■

RAM-Based Multiplexer Systems

ZAHEER M. ALI
Member, Technical Staff,
COMSAT Laboratories,
Clarksburg, Maryland

Usually, the number of logic devices needed to build a multiplexer for a digital data transmission system having N channels increases at a rate 2N (twice the number of channels). But in a multiplexer using a random-access memory (RAM), hardware increases at one eighth the number of channels (N/8).

Multiplexer circuits in digital-data transmission systems select one of N input data sources and transmit the selected data to a single information channel. For long-distance communications, data must be transmitted serially, because a serial channel is the only type available from common carriers. An example of serial data transmission is a pulse code modulation system for voice channels. Each channel is sampled at an 8-kHz rate, and is then digitized into 8 bits of companded data. The overall transmission rate is 64 kbits/s, and to multiplex N channels a transmission rate of 64 × N kbits/s is required.

But at data-processing sites, parallel data may be transmitted when computer channels are directly coupled to each other or to terminal equipment. In either case, there are two different ways to multiplex —bit interleaving and word interleaving. So to appreciate how much hardware you'll save with a RAM multiplexer, examine both conventional types of multiplexers.

A bit-interleaved multiplexer requires demultiplexing at the receiver end of the line to convert serial data to parallel for presentation to a processor. On the other hand, serial data in a word-interleaved multiplexer must be stored at the transmission end.

Bit or word interleaving?

A bit-interleaved multiplexer like the one shown in Fig. 1 is a parallel-to-serial converter at the transmission station. Each of the N channels has M-bit data words. And bits from all N channels are clocked in parallel to a shift register and readout serially.

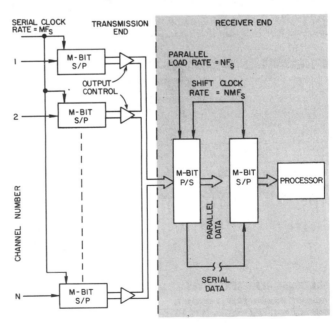

1. **Bit-interleaved multiplexing** requires a parallel-to-serial conversion at the transmitting station. And demultiplexing is used at the receiver end to present data in a parallel format to a processor.

2. **In this word-interleaved multiplexing scheme,** parallel data are formed at the source or transmitter. If a processor is at the source, parallel data can be fed-in directly; but long-distance transmission requires the multiplexer to generate serial data.

If you designate the sampling frequency by F_s, then bits are clocked into the register at a rate of MF_s and read out serially at NMF_s. At the receiver, demultiplexing is performed by an N M-bit serial-to-parallel converter. Data signals from the output of the N and M sections are multiplexed and sent to the processor as parallel data (double lines). A bit-interleaved multiplexer can be built from AND-OR select gates, and controlled by the address provided for each data channel.

If you choose TTL logic for system hardware, a three-state bus can replace the multiplexer. But you must provide the proper output enable signals for the M-bit registers, and this requires that address lines be decoded for serial selection.

Word-interleaved multiplexing is similar to bit-interleaved except that parallel data are formed at the source, not at the destination. In the word-interleaved multiplexer of Fig. 2, you can use parallel data at the sending end for transmission to local processors, while serial data must be used if you transmit information to remote sites.

For TTL, selecting 8-bit registers and 8-to-1 multiplexers is a low-cost approach, but three-state bus logic will give you a lower device count. And three-state makes your system faster, since all channels will be only one level deep in delay.

To start building the multiplexers in Figs. 1 and 2, examine how the total device count is determined by referring to Fig. 3. Here, three-state logic is assumed for each multiplexer. An N-bit shift register is needed to provide output-enable-select control for three-state registers, and a ONE is circulated in all stages of the register.

When you add the first column in Fig. 3, you'll find the number of logic devices required for a bit-interleaved multiplexer is proportional to $NM/4 + 3N/8$.

Type of device	Bit-interleaved multiplexer	Word-interleaved multiplexer
Parallel-to-serial shift registers	$\dfrac{2N}{8}$	$\dfrac{2M}{8}$
Serial-to-parallel shift registers	$\dfrac{MN}{8}$	$\dfrac{MN}{8}$
Buffers	$\dfrac{MN}{8}$	$\dfrac{MN}{8}$
Decoders (4:16)	$\dfrac{N}{8}$	$\dfrac{N}{8}$
Total	$\dfrac{NM}{4}+\dfrac{3N}{8}$	$\dfrac{MN}{4}+\dfrac{M}{4}+\dfrac{N}{8}$

3. **No matter which system you build,** bit-interleaved or word-interleaved, the hardware tally will be the same for systems with many data channels. You find the hardware count by adding component entries in each column; total chip count is shown at the bottom of each column.

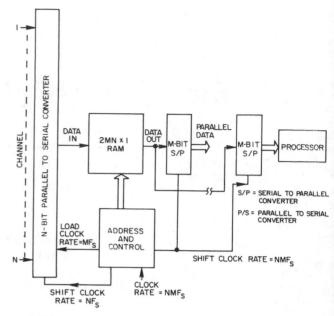

4. **Build your multiplexing system with RAMs** and you'll save a tremendous amount of hardware. For conventional multiplexers, the number of devices increases at twice the number of data channels. But hardware in this RAM-based scheme increases at a rate of only one eighth the number of data channels.

And for a word-interleaved multiplexer the device count is proportional to $NM/4 + N/8 + M/4$.

As it turns out, the expressions are equal, so you don't save any hardware by selecting one multiplexer system over another.

Either system can be applied in pulse-code-modulated (PCM) voice channels where each voice channel is sampled at an 8-kHz rate and digitized into eight bits of companded data ($M = 8$). If there are many channels, the hardware-count expressions in Fig. 3 for both bit-interleaved and word-interleaved multiplexers approaches 2N.

So that's why if you double the data channels in a large, conventional multiplexer system, you'll end up having to double the hardware to build it. On the other hand, a RAM-based multiplexer's hardware grows larger at a rate that is 16 times less than that of conventional multiplexers.

RAMs shrink multiplexers

The RAM multiplexer in Fig. 4 is an N-channel system with M word bits per channel. Parallel data are latched into the parallel-to-serial converter, and transmitted out serially to a RAM. Data are stored in the RAM, which is divided into two equal parts.

Since the RAM must be able to read and write, a so-called "ping-pong" operation is required between the read and write functions. Say that part A of the memory supplies output data while part B stores input data. This action continues until NM bit locations are filled; then parts A and B exchange roles or ping-pong.

Word interleaved data leaving the RAM in serial form are loaded into an M-bit serial-in parallel-out

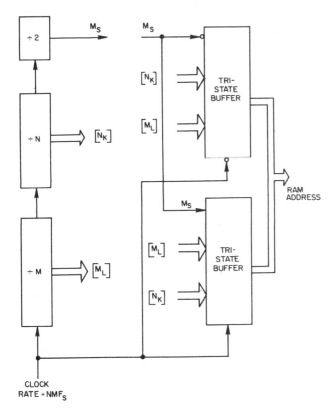

5. Three free-running binary counters form the addressing section of a RAM-based multiplexer. Counter inputs are fed to two buffers, which then generate the read and write addresses for the RAM.

shift register, which can be located at either the source or destination end of the line.

RAM operation is controlled with two special addresses, one for writing information in, the other for reading out. Anytime you change the address from read to write or vice-versa, the memory is remapped. If memory is divided into N words of M bits each, writing is done along the columns, and reading along the rows. If a frame is defined as MN, then the memory size must be 2MN to store all the data. The RAM can also be used for demultiplexing, with writing done along rows and read-along columns.

To control and address the memory, you need a clock rate of NMF_s, where F_s is again the sampling frequency, and M and N are binary integers. Since memories are only available in multiples of binary integers, you may have to add a few dummy channels for N or some dummy bits for M, if the data don't fill the memory capacity. When memory-cycle time is less than clock period NMF_s, read operations are performed during CLOCK time and write operations during $\overline{CLOCK}$.

Addressing the RAM requires three binary counters connected in a free-running configuration as shown in Fig. 5. The divide-by-N, or channel counter has a vector output of N_K. And the divide-by-M counter is the bits-per-channel counter with vector output M_L. Together, the outputs form the composite vector $N_K M_L$, which approximates the write address W_A. But to form the complete write address and establish ping-

pong operation, you must include the output of the divide-by-2 counter, M_s. Now the write address can be written as

$$W_A = N_K \ M_L \ M_s \tag{1}$$

where $K = 0, 1, \ldots , \log_2 N$ and
$L = 0, 1, \ldots , \log_2 M$.

Note that M_s can only assume two values, 0 and 1. Since N bits belonging to N channels occur serially, they must be stored in one of M columns, and M_s determines which half of the memory is to be used.

The read-address composite vector, R_A, has the same factors as the write address. In a read operation, M bits belonging to the same channel must be retrieved, and the read address is defined as

$$R_A = N_K M_L \overline{M}_s \tag{2}$$

where K and L are defined as in Eq. 1.

The difference in the two equations is that the complement of M_s is used in the read address, and the true output is used in the write address. In Fig. 5, W_A and R_A are multiplexed through three-state buffers, with R_A controlled by $\overline{CLOCK}$ and W_A by CLOCK. For demultiplexing, R_A and W_A are reversed since memory contents are rearranged as M channels of N bits each. This enables you to change from bit-interleaving to word-interleaving and vice-versa.

Now you're ready to calculate the amount of hardware you'll need to build a RAM multiplexer.

Finding total chip count

To find out how many ICs will be needed by a RAM multiplexer, assume that you can get octal parallel-in, serial-out registers for sending data into the RAM. For an N-channel system, you'll need N/8 parallel-to-serial devices.

If the RAM cycle rate is F_c, the data rate is

$$F_c = MNF_s, \tag{3}$$

The total capacity of the memory is 2MN, and the length of the address vector is $\log_2(2MN)$. Assume that the RAM is a common 1-k $\times$ 1.

To find out how many devices you'll need to build a RAM multiplexer, look at the chart of Fig. 6. Putting in your values for M and N, add up the entries for each device, as you did for the one in Fig. 3. The total number of devices will be the result of,

$$\text{Total chip count} = \frac{N}{8} + 2MN \times 10^{-3} + \frac{2 \ \log_2(2MN)}{8} \tag{4}$$

$$+ \frac{M}{8} + \frac{\log_2(2MN)}{8}.$$

Type of device	RAM multiplexer component count
P/S registers	N/8 (next higher integer)
RAMs chips	2MN × 10⁻³ (next higher binary integer)
Address multiplexers	[2 log₂ (2MN)]/8 (next integer)
Output S/P register	M/8 (next integer)
Counters	[log₂ (2MN)]/8 (next integer)

6. **To get the hardware count for a RAM multiplexer,** substitute your values for M and N in this table and add up the entries. Go to the next-higher binary integer if your computation doesn't give you a binary integer.

Now that you've got an equation to determine chip count in a RAM multiplexer, you can figure how much hardware you'll save with the RAM approach.

Say you're building a PCM multiplexer with an M of 8, an $\dot{F}_s$ of 8 kHz and a memory cycle rate (F_c) of 8×10^6. Say also that the system-clock rate NMF_s is equal to F_c. From Eq. 3, figure the number of channels that can be multiplexed:

$$N = \frac{F_c}{MF_s} = \frac{8 \times 10^6}{8 \times 8 \times 10^3}$$

$$= 125 \text{ channels}$$

To multiplex 125 channels, the memory capacity must be

$$2MN = 2 \times 125 \times 8 = 2000 \text{ bits.}$$

Actually, with 2^{11} the nearest binary integer to 2000, the capacity is 2048. With a 2048-bit memory, figure the total chip count from Eq. 4:

$$\text{Chip count} = 16 + 2 + 3 + 1 + 2$$
$$= 24 \text{ devices.}$$

The same system, built with conventional multiplexers, would take over 250 devices. Doubling the number of conventional-system data channels, you'd need 500 logic elements. Doubling the number of channels in the RAM multiplexer would bring the device total all the way up to 42.

Multiplexing techniques can also be used to handle other types of signals. For example, signals from remote sensors can be fed to digitizers, whose outputs are then fed serially to a computer that uses a multiplexer. After collecting data, the computer regulates the entire process. Another application of a RAM multiplexer is to form elastic buffers with variable word-length inputs. If the buffer has a word length equivalent to the read time of the RAM, data transmissions can be made at variable speed. But this means that you must reconfigure the channel slots in a particular timing frame by changing the algorithm for the read address.■■

Fast LSI Memories Cram More Information

BRADY WARNER, JR.
Assistant Manager,
Multiple-Access Digital Techniques Department,
COMSAT Laboratories, Clarksburg, Maryland

LSI memory chips can help raise the channel capacity of communications systems in many ways. Using baseband signal-processing techniques based on IC biopolar RAMs, you can stuff more data into a transponder's limited bandwidth. Nowhere is the efficiency increase more welcome than in expensive satellite-communication systems. Satcom can benefit from several techniques that employ RAM chips:

- Time-division multiple access (TDMA).
- Digital speech interpolation (DSI).
- Frequency-division to time-division multiplex converters (FDM/TDM), often called transmultiplexers (XMUXes).
- Video processing.
- Asynchronous interfaces using elastic buffers.

One major advantage a TDMA satcom system has over a conventional frequency-division multiple-access system (FDMA) is that it needs only one carrier per transponder, which means the transponder can operate at amplitudes near saturation. An FDMA system must restrict its transponders to the linear region to prevent carriers from being intermodulated, among other problems that come up as a result of

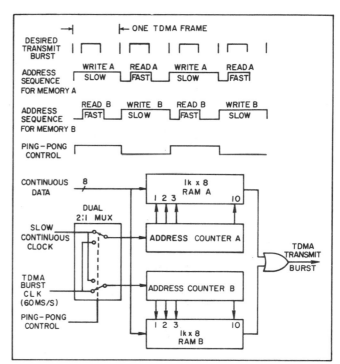

2. **Two RAMs per compression buffer operating in "ping-pong" style** at the transmitting end solve the problem of overlap between the continuous input and burst output. Similarly, two-RAM buffers are needed at the receiver.

using more than just a single carrier frequency per transponder, as in TDMA systems.

Blocking more data in

Compared to traditional methods, TDMA can improve bandwidth use tremendously.[1,2] Each earth station transmits its information via high bit-rate bursts in preassigned time blocks. These blocks are timed into repetitive frames. Time-sharing these frames among system channels requires buffer memories at both the receiving and transmitting sides of each earth station (Fig. 1).

Before transmission to the satellite, a buffer compresses the relatively slow, continuous digital information into high-speed bursts. After reception, another terrestrial buffer re-expands the data into their original format.

In TDMA, transponder bandwidth primarily de-

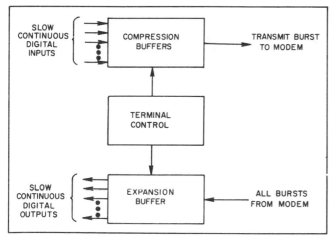

1. **TDMA earth stations require buffer memories** at both the transmitting and receiving ends. Before transmission, one buffer compresses the slow-input data into high-speed output bursts. After reception, another buffer reverses the process by scaling the data rate down.

termines the maximum data rate. For example: In Intelsat IV and IV-A, bandwidths of about 36 MHz —under four-phase, phase-shift-keying (PSK) modulation—support TDMA rates of 60 Mbits/s. The planned TDMA transmission rate for Intelsat V is 120 million bits per second.

At 120 Mbits/s, a TDMA system can handle about 900 8-bit channels. The exact capacity depends on the amount of guard time used between bursts, the burst-preamble bit length and the number of bursts in a frame. For burst formats containing no more than half the available channels, a single buffer must process a maximum 3.6 kbits—that is, 450 channels—in order to keep the frame time at 125 μs.[3] Frame times of up to 15 milliseconds have been proposed for time-division multiple-access systems, despite the high-capacity buffering that such long delays would require of the system memories.

Splitting the load

Either the output or input of these buffers is continuous. When they coincide, extra memories must store the overlap—a single RAM can't be accessed simultaneously for both reading and writing. A good solution is to use RAMs in a "ping-pong" fashion. Here each memory is split in two: For odd-numbered frames, part A is read while part B is written into. For even-numbered frames, the data are read out of Part B while data are simultaneously written into part A of the random access memory bank.

Depending, of course, on the amount of memory required, you can speed up processing by organizing the RAMs for a parallel-word format. Let's look, for example, at a standard voice PCM scheme with an 8-bit sample each 125 μs (8-kHz sampling). Such a 60-Mbit/s TDMA system, having a 750-μs frame, requires buffering of 48 bits per channel. For such a system, a 1-k × 8-bit memory—made of 1-k × 1-bit RAM chips—could handle about 170 channels at read/write speeds of 7.5 Mbits/s. Two such RAMs are needed at both the transmitter and receiver in the "ping-pong" scheme shown in Fig. 2.

Even if suitably long and fast shift registers were commercially available, LSI bipolar RAMs would still make a better choice for TDMA buffers. The random-access feature of RAMs can be used for channel routing by mapping the transmitting or receiving-side addresses during respective read and write operations. By assigning an auxiliary random-access memory, whose stored information is under microprocessor control, the channel-routing mapping can be on a dynamic basis as demand warrants. By using a read-only memory the mapping can be preassigned.

RAM compression/expansion buffers can also interleave bits to break-up paired errors, which are commonly caused when PSK-modulated data are encoded differentially to resolve bit-ambiguities. By writing data in rows and reading them in columns,

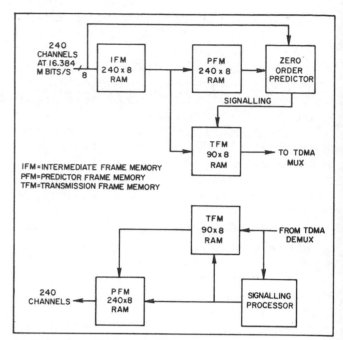

3. **Speech-predictive encoding** (SPEC) developed at Comsat Labs has been demonstrated to more than double a transponder's capacity. With the required bit rates, SPEC can service 48 to 240 voice channels.

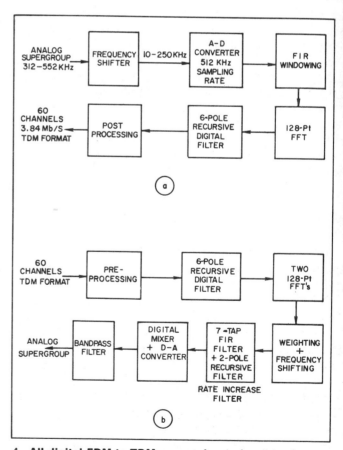

4. **All-digital FDM-to-TDM conversion** is feasible. Comsat Labs' version of a digital transmultiplexer translates a 60-channel analog supergroup, whose 4-kHz channels are stacked from 312 to 552 kHz, into 60 digital channels in a 3.84-MHz TDM format (a). The process is carried on in reverse by the TDM-to-FDM subsystem (b).

RAMs help correct errors by randomizing them.

Not only that, but with TDMA in place for voice channels, you can more than double a transponder's capacity with DSI.[4,5] That's because the average activity on a one-way voice channel is below 50%. (One party usually listens while the other speaks and the speaker pauses between phrases.) The trick is to have enough simultaneously active channels available for sampling. Under such conditions, Comsat's Speech Predictive Encoding (SPEC) DSI system has already demonstrated a two-to-one capacity increase.

Interpolating digital speech

SPEC's switching scheme sorts each digital voice channel as to the difference between the present samples and the ones just transmitted. Channels with the greatest differences are transmitted first, then, less active channels and those with smaller differences are taken—up to the system's transmission capacity. For untransmitted channels—those with the combination of lowest activities and smallest differences between samples—data are predicted at the receiving end from information contained in previously transmitted samples.

Fig. 3 shows the block diagram of an experimental SPEC system, built at Comsat Labs, incorporating several 256 × 8 RAMs. With appropriate bit rates, this system can handle anywhere from 48 to 240 voice channels. The memories used are small, byte-oriented, TTL-compatible, 256 × 8 RAMs.

Speed isn't a major factor when selecting RAMs for the essentially continuous transmission used in FDMA systems. In TDMA systems, however, the digital-speech interpolation memory doubles as the burst storage—then, of course, speed is essential.

For DSI, each voice channel must be available to the processor as a digitally coded TDM signal. But most terrestrial voice-channel interfaces are analog supergroups formatted in FDM. In order to digitally interpolate speech in the conversations carried in this frequency-division multiplexed signal—60 contiguous, 4-kHz channels from 312 to 552 kHz—must be reformatted into 60-channels of time-division multiplexed information.

Conventional FDM-to-TDM conversion equipment employs analog mixers and filters to separate the 60 baseband channels while they're still in analog form. Then a separate 60-channel a/d converter digitizes and recombines the data into one TDM stream. At the receiver, a d/a decoder reverses the process. All this analog circuitry, of course, can be sensitive to the usual error sources: aging, temperature, humidity, noise and power-supply drift.

Transmultiplexing instead

However, digital signal-processing should be relatively immune. What's more, though necessarily complex, an all-digital FDM-to-TDM transmultiplexer

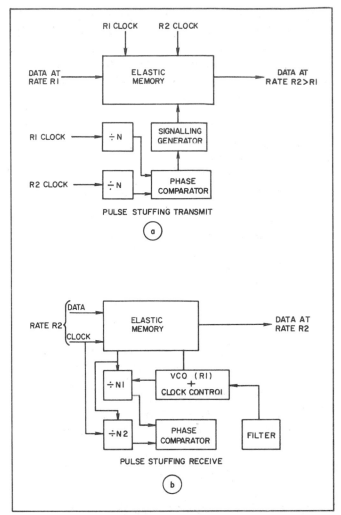

5. **Pulse stuffing makes memories "elastic."** On the receiving end (a), the read/write lines of both RAMs control stuffing. On the transmitting end (b), the incoming clock synchronizes writing, while data from the other RAM are read out at the transmission rate.

(XMUX) is feasible.[6,7] Fig. 4 shows the block diagram of Comsat's version. In the FDM-to-TDM direction (Fig. 4a), the XMUX uses supergroup a/d conversion; finite-impulse-response (FIR) windowing; a 128-point Fast-Fourier Transform (FFT); and six-pole, recursive, digital filtering. Going from TDM back to FDM (Fig. 4b) also takes six-pole recursive filtering, but this time two 128-point FFTs are needed. FIR windowing then leads to a supergroup d/a.

Comsat's XMUX design uses a TTL 256 × 4 RAM, primarily because of its configuration and speed.[8] But the RAM's speed is limited, so only half its memory can be used in the 128-point FFTs. Memories with faster access—for example, a 128 × 8-RAM with the bit speed of the 256 × 4 unit—could halve the bit width of the data bus.

Memories are now the factor limiting parallel arithmetic-processing speed. High-speed parallel multipliers on a single large-scale-integrated chip like those from TRW LSI Products, Redondo Beach, CA, and Monolithic Memories, Sunnyvale, CA, have seen to that. In communications applications, the faster the memory, the more useful and more cost-effective parallel processing becomes. Even if the amount of storage required isn't reduced by using faster random-access memory devices, the increased speed can substantially reduce the controls required.

Arithmetic and other communications processing often uses small, byte-oriented memories. A 256 × 8 chip could be tremendously useful, especially if it were fast. Denser and faster memories of course could be even more useful.

Previous XMUX designs used serial processing because dense, parallel multipliers weren't available. Serial processing requires long, high-speed, shift-register-type memories. Such shift registers, over 5 kbits long and working at 43 Mbits/s, have been made from 1024 × 1 RAMs in speedy ECL and have been used for recursive digital filters.

RAMs on television

Bipolar RAMs also play an important part in processing video for satellite transmission. They are particularly useful in techniques to reduce transmission bandwidth by storing complete lines of digitized video information. Once stored, digitized lines are available for processing—elements of one line can be correlated with elements of the previous line to help predict the present element. Within reasonable limits, such processing can reduce the required amount of information that must be transmitted.[9] Also interelement correction techniques can be adapted to reduce the effects of noise at the receiving terminal.

With a sampling rate three times the 3.58-MHz color subcarrier (or about 10.7 MHz) generally required, a RAM must perform its full-cycle (read and write) operation in about 93 ns for adequate line buffering. For 8-bit pulse-code-modulation formatted data, there are 5460 bits per line. Thus, ECL 1024 × 1 RAMs, in a 1024 × 8 configuration, work well as line buffers.

Buffers that stretch

So far, the buffers discussed have been fixed in length. But when separate digital systems with different clocks work into one another, the required interface must often be asynchronous. Common communications-systems examples include:

■ T1-carrier, T3-carrier or video to TDMA.
■ Four T1-carrier systems to T2.[10]
■ T1-carrier to CEPT's 2.048-Mbits/s, 30-channel, PCM.
■ Video to T3.

To retain all information, clock-rate differences must be taken up by pulse stuffing. One solution is to transmit at a rate slightly exceeding the incoming rate (Fig. 5). This technique forces a timing error to accumulate until a preassigned number of dummy bits are generated to take up the slack.

Manipulating the read/write control of two RAMs gives the required results. On the transmit side (Fig. 5a), incoming data are written into one of the RAMs in synchronism with the incoming clock. At the same time, stuffed data from a previous frame are read out of the other random-access memory—at the transmission rate. In this way the transmission and reception rates are made to depend on their respective independent clocks. Thus so long as the memory capacity isn't overtaxed, the transmission and reception rates need not be related.

In succeeding stuff frames, the functions of the two RAMs are reversed. Any number of bits can be deleted from the transmission by controlling the switching from write to read on the random-access memories.

On the receiving side (Fig. 5b), the action is similar, except that a voltage-controlled oscillator reproduces the originating clock. In addition, a factor that determines the data rate required to fill the buffer is translated into dc voltage. This "fill-factor" voltage then controls the oscillator frequency.

The receive-side RAMs are controlled by counting real-information bits from the transmitter. This way, the buffer memories can accommodate differences between the input and output clocks. The buffers themselves, changing their contents as necessary, are thus elastic. Their sizes depend on the maximum deviation of the periods from each other (slip rate).

Clock rates are generally tightly controlled, so the buffers are correspondingly small. The speed required of these memories, of course, depends on the data rates involved. In addition to RAMs, another possible implementation might use a high-speed first-in, first-out (FIFO) like the Monolithic Memories 67401 64 × 4 with a half-full flag. ■■

References

1. Gabbard, O. G., and Kaul, P., "Time-Division Multiple Access," EASCON, 1974.
2. Dill, G. D., "TDMA, the State of the Art," EASCON, 1977.
3. Dill, G. D., Deal, J. and Maillet, W., "INTELSAT Prototype TDMA System," IEEE Intercon Conference Record, 1975.
4. Sciulli, J., and Campanella, S. J., "A Speech Predictive Encoding Communications System for Multichannel Telephony," IEEE Transactions on Communications, COM-21, July, 1973.
5. Campanella, S. J., "Digital Speech Interpolation," Comsat Technical Review, Spring, 1976, pp. 127-158.
6. Freeny, S. L., Kieburtz, R. B., Mina, K. and Tewkesbury, S., "Systems Analysis of a TDM-FDM Translator/Digital A-Type Channel Bank," IEEE Transactions on Communications Technology, COM-19, December, 1971, pp. 1050-1059.
7. Ballanger, M.D., and Daguet, J. L., "TDM-FDM Transmultiplexer: Digital Polyphase and FET," IEEE Transactions on Communications, COM-22, September, 1974, pp. 1199-1204.
8. Ali, Z., "A High speed FFT Processor," Comsat Laboratories Technical Memorandum CL-42-77.
9. Gatfield, A. G., Suyderhoud, H., and Wolejsza, C. J., Jr., "System Design for the Digitally Implemented Communications Experiment (DICE)," ICC IEEE International Conference on Communications 1977 Conference Record, Vol. I, 1977, pp. 1.1-1 to 1.1-5.
10. Bruce, R. A., "A 1.5 to 6-Megabit Digital Multiplex Employing Pulse Stuffing," Proceedings of the 1969 IEEE International Conference on Communications, Boulder, CO, pp. 34-1 to 34-7.

Bibliography

Johannes, V.I., and McCullough, R. H., "Multiplexing of Asynchronous Digital Signal Using Pulse Stuffing with Added-bit Signaling," IEEE Transactions on Communications Technology, COM-14, October, 1966.

Get the Most Out of Top-Performing RAMs

KAZUHIRO TOYODA
Chief Engineer, Bipolar Memory Section,
Bipolar IC Engineering Department, IC Division,
Fujitsu Ltd., Kawasaki, Japan

Although tradeoffs are unavoidable, memory systems using ECL RAMs can deliver both high speed and high packing density. Within a specific system design, it is possible to calculate the system parameters that will give maximum density and minimal delays.

In CPUs built with subnanosecond logic, ECL RAMs are necessary even though less-expensive MOS memories have begun to approach their speed. Subnanosecond bipolar RAMs are too expensive to use throughout an entire memory system, unless a cache design is used. However, the slower cache can limit the CPU's overall performance. With an appropriate system design, special high-speed ECL RAMs can overcome this limitation.

For example, the MB7071 accesses in 10 ns maximum and stores 1024 bits, organized as 256 words × 4 bits. Its input/output levels are compatible with the 10-K ECL family of logic circuits offered by several manufacturers. The RAM uses a −5.2 V ±5% power supply. The circuit's typical speed-power product is 6 pJ; typical access time is 7.5 ns (10 ns max); typical power dissipation is 0.8 mW/bit (1 mW/bit max). As the graph of Fig. 1 shows, these specifications meet the highest performance levels of current products.

The internal ECL circuits of the RAM are optimized for the speed-power product. The memory cell is a nonsaturated emitter-coupled design with Schottky-barrier-diode clamped loads (Fig. 2a). An adaptation of passive isolation and fine-pattern geometries results in a 4.27-mil² cell area and top performance.

Each of the RAM's blocks can be selected by one of four block-select pins (Fig. 2b). Each of the blocks also has its own data input and data output pins, thus permitting the maximum data rate. Eight address

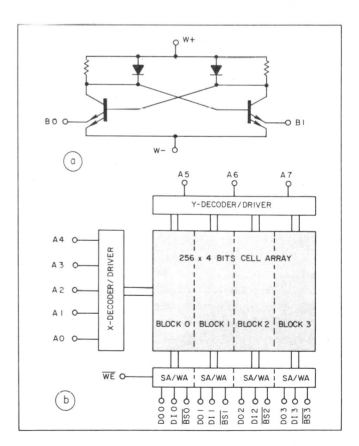

2. **Optimized for the best speed-power product,** the memory cell in the MB7071 dissipates just 1 mW (a). Organized as four "independent" 256 × 1-bit blocks, the memory chip has a select line for each block, as well as separate data in and data out lines (b).

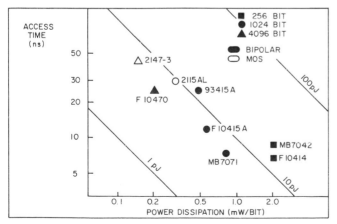

1. **For high-speed memories, access time and power dissipation per bit** are inversely related—the faster the RAM, the less dissipation per bit.

lines and a read/write line (write-enable, WE) control the entire array.

Functioning like ordinary chip-select pins, the block-select pins can be used to change the "effective" organization of the RAM. The RAM can be made to appear to have 256 × 4, 512 × 2, 1024 × 1 or any other combination of 256 × 1 blocks by simple changes in the block-select inputs and external decoding (Fig. 3). The block-select inputs are set up so that all blocks are selected (the 256 × 4 configuration) if the inputs are left open-circuited.

Compact package saves board area

Because of the high-speed capability of the circuit, the MB7071 is housed in a 24-pin package (the QIT-24), that has pins on all four sides (Fig. 4). The RAM can also be purchased in a 22-pin DIP; however, in this version (the MB7072), two of the block-select pins are connected together to make a 512 × 2 array.

The QIT-24 helps to reduce the interconnect delays introduced in memory systems when many packages are mounted on a printed-circuit board. Since the packages are mounted close to each other on 75-mil centers, the delay caused by signal transmission is shortened. Less delay between memory cards means better system performance.

As an illustration, compare a QIT-24 with a "standard" 24-pin, 400-mil-wide DIP. The area of the QIT package can be calculated as follows:
$$(0.575 + 0.075)^2 = 0.36 \text{ in.}^2,$$
where the package side is 0.525-in. long and one pin space is 0.075 in. Similarly, the area for the DIP is:
$$(0.4 + 0.1) \times (1.2 + 0.1) = 0.65 \text{ in.}^2,$$
where the package has a length of 1.2 in., a width of 0.4 in. and two extra pin spaces of 0.1-in. Thus, the QIT package requires about half the board area of the DIP, and a memory system can be built with half as many cards or with twice as much memory in the same sized box.

Fig. 4 shows a typical memory board with support circuitry; on this board even the support circuits are housed in QIT packages for maximum density and minimal delays. Measuring 18 × 18 cm (about 7.5 × 7.5 in.), the board contains 2 kbytes of RAM. A larger memory system, containing 4 kwords × 9 bits, is shown in Fig. 5. This system has two MB7071s sharing a common I/O and uses a 1-of-8 decoder to switch eight block-select inputs to make 4 kwords to a column.

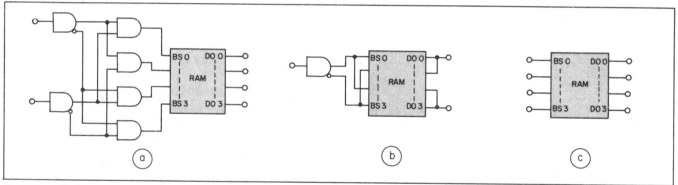

3. **When the block-select lines are externally decoded,** the RAM organization can be altered to suit the system application. The user may choose such organization schemes as 1 k × 1 (a), 512 × 2 (b) and 256 × 4 (c).

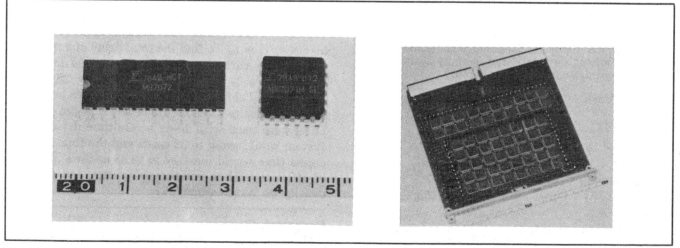

4. **Use of the unusual 24-pin square package** (center) almost doubles the packing density over 22-pin DIPs (left) and gives even greater density than 24-pin DIPs. Use of the 24-pin QIT package for support circuits maximizes board density. The board shown at right measures 18 × 18 cm but holds 2 kbytes of high-speed RAM.

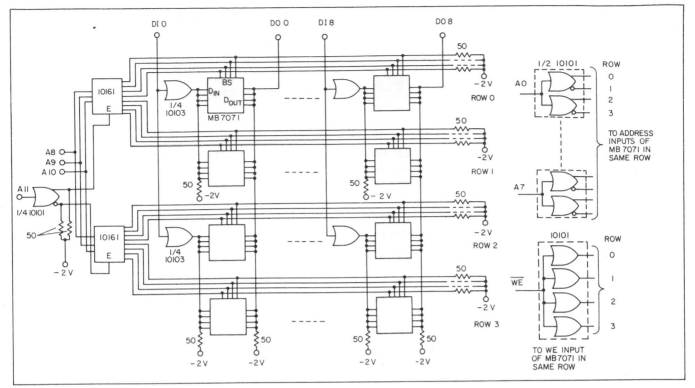

5. **In a typical 4-kword × 9-bit memory system using MB7071s,** two of the chips share a common I/O to reduce the support circuitry needed. Eight block-select inputs are switched by a 1-of-8 decoder.

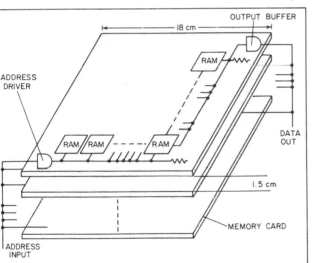

6. **All the internal propagation delays must be taken into account** in the modeling stage to ensure the proper amount of access time for large memory systems, like this 64-kbyte high-speed buffer memory.

Before building, estimate the limits

In building a 64-kbyte system with memory boards using the ECL RAMs, some general system parameters and constraints should be kept in mind:

- Capacity per card   = 4 kbytes
- Card size   = 18 × 18 cm
- Card-to-card spacing   = 1.5 cm
- Delay on cards or between   = 100 ps/cm

- RAM access time (tm)   = 10 ns
- I/O device delay (t_g)   = 2 ns
- Load delay of RAM or I/O   = 20 ps/pF
- I/O load on memory   = 4 pF
- Fanout   = 8.

To put together a 64-kbyte system, 16 cards are needed. Given these parameters, the over-all system performance can be at least partially calculated. First, the delay (t) caused by cards at the most remote part of the array can be found as follows:

$t_1 = 16 \times 1.5$ cm $\times 100$ ps/cm $\times 2 = 4.8$ ns.

The worst-case delay within a card to the furthest RAM in the array is:

$t_2 = 18$ cm $\times 2$ sides $\times 100$ ps/cm $= 3.6$ ns.

Now, the delay resulting from loading factors can be calculated:

$t_3 = 8 \times 4$ pF $\times 20$ ps/pF $= 0.64$ ns.

The delay time from wired-ORing of eight outputs is identical: $t_1 = t_3$. To find the total delay of a memory system, the various times must be added together:

$t_{Total} = t_1 + t_2 + t_3 + t_4 + 2t_g + t_m = 23.68$ ns.

If memory chips with 20-ns access times are used, t_{Total} increases to 33.68 ns. However, if 24-pin 400-mil DIPs were used with 10-ns access-time devices, the system would grow to 32 cards and the total system access time would increase to 28.48 ns for a 20% loss of efficiency. Thus, memory efficiency and packing density go hand-in-hand. ∎∎

Versatile Memory Bus Handles Mixed Memories Compatibly

ROBERT L. PAPENBERG
Manager, Memory System Operation,
Intel Corp., Sunnyvale, California

MOHAMMAD RYDHAN
Design Engineer, Memory System Operation,
Intel Corp., Sunnyvale, California

An architectural first: A memory system interconnected by a dedicated bus over which different memory types—static, dynamic or almost any other—can operate compatibly. It even lets bus cable lengths extend a relatively long 20 ft, and sometimes more. Moreover, Intel's Series 90 System with its byte-exchange path (BXP) bus (Fig. 1) is flexible enough to take advantage of memory developments as they occur. The memory modules first interface with the BXP bus, which, in turn, interfaces with the user's bus via a control module. The memory modules include control circuitry for independent operation up to the BXP bus.

Synchronous or asynchronous

The system is versatile, with a choice of synchronous or asynchronous operation.

When all memory modules are of the same speed (100-ns static modules) and are operating with peripheral devices of equivalent speed, then synchronous control is naturally the choice. Even a system with all-dynamic memory modules can operate effectively in the synchronous mode, provided dynamic-memory refresh operations are synchronized by the CPU as interrupt subroutines or as internal asynchronous refresh loops. With synchronous operations, round-trip control loops are unnecessary, so that cycle time is not affected by cable length.

Asynchronous control, however, is the user's choice when a variety of functions with variations in cycle times is anticipated. A mixed memory system of fast, static modules operating together with the slower refresh-dependent dynamic modules demands the flexibility of asynchronous control, since the cycle time can be matched to the memory system to allow each to operate at its own optimum speed.

The BXP bus, with a 100-ns data-transfer "rate," also can handshake between CPU and memory at 100-ns intervals; thus, data can be transferred at up to 10 megawords per second with word lengths to 88 bits. In this way, both 100-ns static-memory modules and slower, 400-ns dynamic, high-capacity refresh-type memory modules can be handled efficiently in the same system without impairing the performance of the fast static memory.

In addition, the system can handle the different address-boundary requirements of memories with mixed capacities and not hang up should a nonexistent block of memory be addressed. In that event, instead of waiting in vain for a cycle-acknowledge signal from the memory, the system generates a nonexistent-memory (NEM) flag that is returned to the CPU in place of the normal cycle-acknowledge signal. The flag enables the CPU either to start an interrupt routine or enter an error (or reset) state before going to another location. Also, a memory refresh cycle is initiated to protect dynamic-memory storage data.

Tight handshake reduces cable-delay effects

Providing all these bus features allows a tight handshaking loop to minimize the effect of cable delays—typically about 80 ns for a 20-ft cable between the CPU and the memory. This delay, combined with inherent logic delays, can be a serious problem in a 100-ns handshaking loop, and virtually impossible with a conventional protocol (Fig. 2a).

However, the Series 90 system overcomes cable-delay problems with a double look-ahead pipeline technique with two levels of see-through (open-window) registers: one set in the control/interface modules, and the other in the memory modules (Fig. 1b) where they store data, address and control signals. The pipeline, thus formed, is transparent to the user.

With the pipeline, the system generates two independent cycle-acknowledge signals to the CPU: a conventional signal (CYACK) from the memory module and a look-ahead acknowledge (LOKACK) from the control module. LOKACK occurs 50 ns earlier than

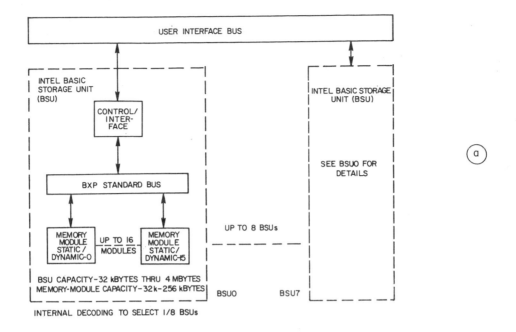

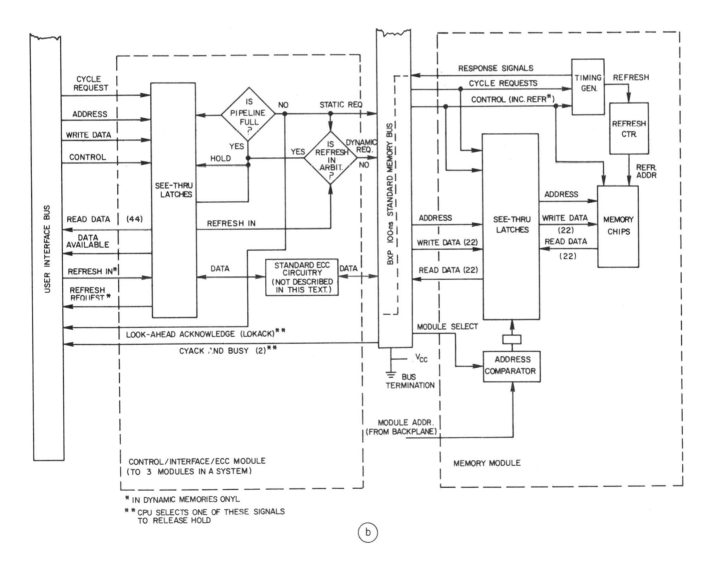

1. As many as 16 mixed-memory modules can be handled on a BXP bus with a single control/interface module (a). A "pipeline" system, employing transparent-to-program-mer latches (b), allows the use of relatively long cable lengths between the memory system and the CPU and remote control of memory operations.

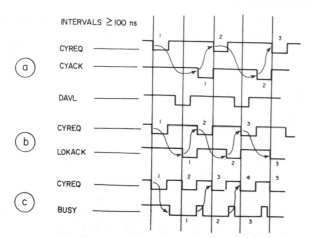

2. In a conventional handshaking protocol (a) the leading edge of a memory-acknowledgment signal (CYACK) closes the loop to the CPU, which then can send back a request (CYREQ). With this protocol, memory execution time (between CYREQ and CYACK) can be limited by the cable round-trip time. Thus cable length limits data-transfer speed. A look-ahead technique, however, can increase the over-all data rate because its acknowledge signal (LOKACK) occurs 50 ns before CYACK, thus allowing more frequent CPU CYREQ signals (b). Moreover, with the pipeline registers in the system, the CPU can issue CYREQs at 100-ns intervals—the tightest handshake loop possible—without waiting for acknowledgements between them. Instead, BUSY-signal trailing edges returned to the CPU can initiate subsequent CYREQs (after the second), provided the first BUSY is received at the CPU before the third CYREQ is needed (c).

CYACK, provided at least one set of registers is empty; otherwise, it occurs as soon as a register set becomes available.

One way the look-ahead-acknowledge signal reduces the effects of round-trip cable delay (Fig. 3b) is during a refresh-cycle operation: Although CYACK is inhibited until the refresh is complete, the earlier LOKACK is

enabled (if the registers are empty to receive data); thus helping to reduce the delay.

Without the pipeline, the CPU would hold (or freeze) until the memory provided a response signal—CYACK or DAVL (for read-only mode)—to its request for data to close the handshaking loop. With a refresh in progress, if a CPU request were issued, the memory wouldn't respond before completion of the refresh cycle, which would take two cycles.

The pipelining, however, allows the CPU to execute two cycles prior to looking for a response from memory (Fig. 2c). As a result, with a BUSY response signal in the system, round-trip cable delays can be longer, before handshaking requirements affect the cycle time. In this mode, the user must incorporate a self-clearing counter into the CPU hold circuitry.

Thus, with double look-ahead pipelining, asynchronous operation can handle many combinations of mixed memory modules and produce little or no degradation in access or cycle time.

Nevertheless, some mixed memory configurations do require extra time to set up address mapping for the module selects. A PROM in the Series 90's control/interface module maps module-address configuration for memories of different capacities with a setup time of 50 ns. To avoid adding time to every cycle, a boundary-detect circuitry restricts setup time to module-boundary crossovers, which occur typically once in 32,000 random addresses. Only when the need for such a module-address change is detected is the PROM enabled and an acknowledge signal inhibited until the setup delay is over.

Bus contention eliminated

The basic asynchronous characteristic—fitting cycle time to function—eliminates the possibility of bus contention (two or more signal sources trying to

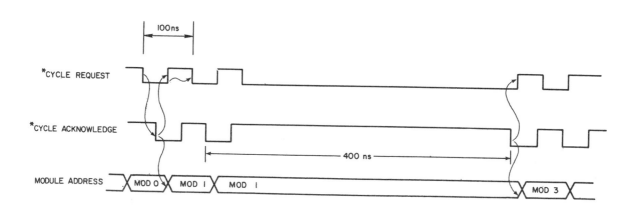

*CYCLE REQUEST AND ADDRESS ARE HELD UNTIL THE REQUESTED MODULE RESPONDS WITH A CYCLE ACKNOWLEDGE.

3. In the asynchronous mode, the memory cycles of modules with the same access speed can be interleaved to increase the data-transfer rate. Interleaving (character-

ized by partially overlapping cycle times of two or more memory modules) can be at any rate up to the maximum allowed by the bus protocol.

put data on the bus at the same time). With a long bi-directional bus, read data could be still on the bus as write data are being presented to it. However, the Series 90 asynchronous protocol takes care of this eventuality by extending the read-to-write-cycle time to clear read data from the bus, but only before transferring to write operation. This cycle extension is automatic and controlled by optional combinational circuitry at the memory, which identifies the read-to-write transition in conjunction with user logic. Because this time extension is automatic, it is transparent to the programmer.

Interleaving speeds data transfer

With bus contention taken care of, data transfer between the CPU and memory can be speeded up by interleaving—overlapping the memory cycles of several memory modules or addressable memory blocks. Although interleaving usually is associated with synchronous operation, the Series 90 makes it available for the asynchronous mode as well; thus, when the user program calls for sequential addressing, the memory modules will interleave even with the asynchronous protocol. And when the program branches to a nonsequential address, the protocol delays the cycle-acknowledge signal to the CPU until the latter can respond and put the system into random-access mode.

Fig. 3 shows the timing requirements for a high-speed asynchronously-interleaved operation. Four 400-ns dynamic-memory modules operating at a 100-ns data "rate," when interleaved, increase throughput four times.

Further, the asynchronous protocol ensures that no module is accessed faster than its minimum cycle time —the system provides a 100-ns (or more) interval between commands.

Thus, the Series-90 memory system, with its choice of synchronous or asynchronous protocols, is equally effective for relatively simple or complex computer configurations. With asynchronous operation and double look-ahead pipelining, cable-length limitations are minimized—mixed static and dynamic memories can operate at optimum cycle times without the need to place the memories near the CPUs. The system provides full remote control of all memory functions, such as read, write, read/modify/write, swap and refresh. In addition, the control/interface module (Fig. 1), which includes special features such as error check and correction (to 80 bits), refresh arbitration and nonexistent-memory flagging, helps ensure trouble-free operation.

The system's extreme flexibility allows application to a very wide range of computer configuration that can be readily updated as memory technology advances. ∎∎

SECTION VIII
System Reliability
and Testing Hints for RAMs

Facing an ever-increasing RAM size, testing the memory has become an ever more complex job. Not only does it take longer because the tests are more complex, but there's more of a chance that there will be a problem. Helping to ease the testing and evaluation problems, these articles cover some of the basic guidelines for evaluating memory reliability and developing some of the optimum test procedures to eliminate the marginal as well as the defective memory chips. Of course, the topics covered in these articles can readily be applied to other types of memory circuits, with the appropriate modifications for the new memory type.

Memory Density Quadruples Again

DAVE BARNES
Western Editor,
Electronic Design

DAVE BURSKY
Senior Editor, Semiconductors,
Electronic Design

There's more to memory design these days than increased density. There's increased reliability, too. For sure, memories keep growing, from chips to boards to systems. At the moment, chips are getting as high as 64 k in RAMs. Bubble memories reach as high as 256 k. Boards easily hold megabytes, and the sky's the limit for multicard systems.

But with system memories swelling, higher data reliability becomes more urgent—especially as mini and microcomputers move into more critical, larger-scale applications. That's why one of the more outstanding trends in memory design is error-correcting coding (ECC). Luckily, the decreasing cost of memory chips is making ECC more affordable. What's more, there's an increasing user demand for it, especially in accounting and process-control applications, where uncorrected errors can cause dollar losses or process shutdown or damage.

are also being added to the stockpile of high-density circuits. However, the list of available sources for CCDs has been dwindling instead of growing because of both unexpected production problems and the sooner-than-expected emergence of the 64-k RAM.

Using various forms of scaled NMOS technology, over a dozen companies have or are developing dynamic RAMs capable of storing 65,536 bits. However, unlike the 16-k RAM, there are at least three major differences among the various 64-k devices (see Table 1):

1. Single supply vs multiple supplies.

2. No-connect vs special function on pin 1.

3. Refresh—128 cycle, 2 ms vs 256 cycle, 4 ms.

Indeed, only TI and National Semiconductor use a 256-cycle refresh, while only Motorola and Mostek plan special functions for pin 1. Some com-

panies have already put aside pin 1 for a second power supply that could well disappear with the second-generation 64-k memories.

These super-high-density RAMs are possible thanks to combined processing and photolithography improvements as well as improved cell and sense amplifier designs. Electron-beam mask generation, combined with projection printing and plasma etching, permits the fine lines and tolerances needed to cram close to 100,000 devices on a chip.

Technology permitting, dynamic 64-k RAMs will be available in limited quantities this year from a dozen or so manufacturers. And, with the fine-line technology used, transistors on a chip will be closer and smaller, which will shorten propagation delays as well as over-all access times. That means 64-k access should range from 80 to 150 ns instead of the 120 to 250 ns typically

Memory chips: not just silicon

The memory-density breakthroughs that have spawned the need for greater data reliability stem from a variety of technologies. For one thing, combinations of NMOS and PMOS (CMOS) as well as bipolar technology have gained firm footholds in the high-performance areas, with both ECL and I²L devices.

But it isn't just silicon. Magnetic-bubble serial memories on garnet substrates have become commercial realities, and they promise to not only quadruple the capacity of MOS devices, but throw in nonvolatility, which is needed for many critical storage applications.

Other serial memories—silicon-based charge-coupled devices (CCDs)—

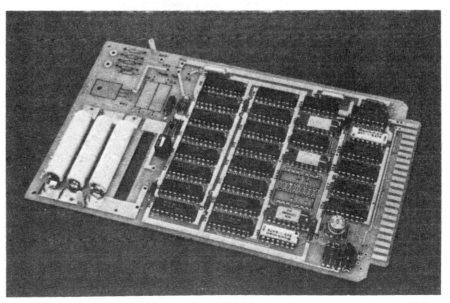

Bringing down the cost of low-power CMOS memory, RCA offers this 4-kbyte board, plus a 16-kbyte version and an 8-k board with on-board batteries to preserve data during power outages. Though its 4-kbit CMOS chips cost 40% more than NMOS, the CMOS board costs only 10% more.

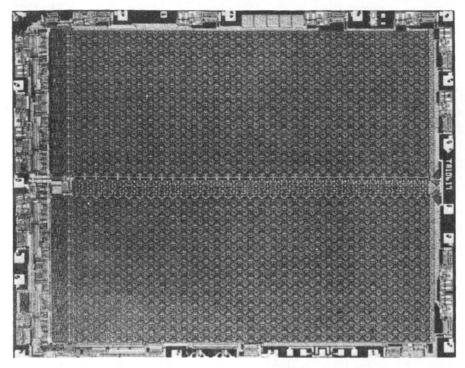

This 4-kbit static RAM, developed with SOS technology by RCA, doesn't have the biasing access time of a 2147, but dissipates just a few milliwatts.

available on today's 16-k RAMs. Not only that, but 64-kbit prices should tumble as dramatically as 16-k bit dynamic RAMs', which in two years dropped from $20 to $7.

Mature devices still maturing

Meanwhile, the 16-k RAM market has matured to the point that well over a dozen vendors offer multiple-supply devices. Interim devices such as Mostek's MK4332, which combines two 16-k chips in a dual-cavity 18-pin DIP, provide a partial solution to the density problem. Fujitsu, among other prospective vendors, will offer another solution: 32-k partials of its coming 64-k MB8164. However it won't be long before another half-dozen companies or so will be added to the list of 64-k RAM developers—Advanced Micro Devices, Fairchild, Signetics, and others are all preparing target specs for their versions.

However, one effect of the emergence of the 64-k RAM has been the development of a single-supply 16-k dynamic RAM. Here, again, there's a split as to how to make the device compatible with 16 and 64-k units. Several vendors, eying upward compatibility, are making the chip pin-compatible with the next-generation 64-k RAMs. However, several other vendors are making the chips pin-compatible with the current multiple sup-

ply 16-k's, and leaving the system modifications waiting until the 64-k's must be inserted. (To do this, the power supply pins not used are left as no-connects, and the 5 V supply has to be enhanced.)

Most of the coming crop of 5-V, 16-k × 1 RAMs will permit simple system upgrades to 64-k units. However, they will require minor redesigns of current 16-k systems—changing the bypass capacitors, strapping the supply pins, and modifying the address connections, and perhaps even altering the refresh timing.

Memory areas other than the × 1 organizations are just as active with both 4-bit and 8-bit-wide static RAMs growing in popularity for small systems, and the very-high-speed × 1 static RAMs surging tremendously. The 4 and 8-bit units are very popular in microprocessor and bit-slice systems that use wide words without parity checking. And the × 1 products are getting into microprogram writable control stores, which need very fast access times to speed instruction execution.

Speedy statics offer more

In MOS technology, the 2147 type 4-k × 1 static RAM has captured the designer's fancy—with its 55-ns maximum access time, it provides almost bipolar performance. Developed by Intel and soon to be available from almost

a dozen sources, the 2147 RAM also offers a power-down capability that permits current to be reduced from the 150-mA or so active level to about a 10-mA standby level.

For large memory systems, the power-down feature can cut power consumption and heat generation considerably. But this technique is benefiting more than high-speed devices. Some of the × 4 and × 8 RAMs are also using this technique to keep system power requirements minimal.

Speaking of × 4 and × 8, the 1-k × 4 static RAM was just about the only choice for wide-word but short depth systems. In fact, the most prevalent part, the 2114 and all its varieties, will soon be available from a dozen or so manufacturers. Some versions will offer the standard access time of 200 to 450 ns, others will offer improved access times—possibly with versions as fast as 70 ns—and others will have reduced power requirements.

However, some manufacturers now feel that the days of the 2114 are dwindling to a precious few as the byte-wide static products start to take over many of the same applications. Ever since the 8108, a 1-k × 8 static RAM, was introduced by EMM Semiconductor early last year, many more companies have announced target specifications and started sample evaluation of not only 1-k × 8 units, but 2-k × 8 static devices as well.

But now the static and dynamic markets are starting to come together with the introduction of pseudostatic products (see Table 2). These dynamic RAMs with built-in refresh circuitry can offer even higher densities—Zilog, National, Intel, Motorola, and many others have announced either 4 k × 8 and even 8 k × 8 devices. Although the pseudostatic devices won't access as fast as the fully static units, there are two distinct applications areas:

Bipolar—still the speed champ

The very-high-speed devices will go into writable control stores that need sub-100-ns access times, while the slower units (150 to 400 ns), fitting very nicely into microprocessor systems, will be used for program workspace. All versions of the byte-wide RAMs, though, will be pin-compatible with the standard UV erasable PROMs (the 2708, 2716, etc.) to facilitate program development and storage.

For speed, though, NMOS devices still give way to bipolar technology.

Emitter-coupled logic still offers the best speed, and companies such as Fairchild, Fujitsu and Motorola have pushed the technology to obtain devices like the MB7071/72 (Fujitsu). The 1-k RAM has an access time of just 10 ns and comes in either of two package configurations—a quadrilateral 24-pin version and a standard DIP. Internally, the RAM is set up so that it operates in a block-select mode that permits it to be addressed as either a 256-×-4 or a 1024-×-1 array.

Even higher memory densities are also available—4-k × 1 ECL RAMs such as the 10470 provide access to data in a mere 25 ns. And, soon to be introduced will be some 1-k × 4 ECL RAMs intended for microprogram storage applications. The first of these looks to be the MB7077 from Fujitsu, and it'll have an access time of 25 ns

and come in a 22-pin 400-mil-wide DIP.

Densities above 4 k, however, require a lower power bipolar technology like I²L. In this area, Fairchild has led the attack with its 93481, a 4-k bipolar dynamic RAM, and with its soon-to-be-introduced 93483, a 16-kbit dynamic unit. The only bipolar dynamic RAMs available, these perform about 20% better than equivalent NMOS devices. And with their bipolar background, these devices have found many homes in the military and high-reliability applications.

Also strengthening their foothold in the military and high-reliability areas are CMOS static RAMs, with their extremely low supply-current drain and wide range of performance levels. Access times below 200 ns for 4-k devices and power requirements of less than 40 mW will no longer be mutually

exclusive. Developments in silicon-on-sapphire as well as basic technology improvements will permit high-performance low-power requirements to be filled.

Moreover, as pinouts become further standardized, CMOS equivalents will appear for available NMOS devices. NEC Microcomputers, for one, will soon introduce the uPD444, a CMOS pin-equivalent to the 2114 static RAM. However, unlike the NMOS market where prices for the next larger size started out at just above four times the cost, the recently introduced 4-k CMOS devices cost less than four times that of the 1-k RAMs.

This year will also see 16-k CMOS RAM samples being introduced by at least two companies—both RCA and Harris are developing byte-wide CMOS RAMs that will be pin-compatible with

Table 1. 64-kbit dynamic-RAM developments

Manufacturer	Model	Access time	Refresh	Supplies	Active P$_D$	Pin 1 use	Availability
IBM	—	300 ns	128 cy 2 ms	8.5, 3.5, -2.2 V	360 mW	Non-std pinout	Internal use
Intel	2164	100 to 200 ns	128 cy 2 ms	+5 V	Under 200 mW	No connection	Samples 2q 1979
Mostek	MK4164	Below 100 ns	128 cy 2 ms	+5 V	300 mW	Special function	Samples 2q 1979
Motorola	MCM-6664	150 to 200 ns	128 cy 2 ms	+5 V	Under 250 mW	Refresh control	Samples 1q 1979
National Semiconductor	MM5264	150 ns max.	256 cy 4 ms	+5 V	Under 200 mW	No connection	Samples 2q 1979
Texas Instruments	TM4164	100 to 150 ns	256 cy 4 ms	+5 V	250 mW	No connection	Samples 4q 1978
Fujitsu	MB8164	120 to 200 ns	128 cy 2 ms	+7 V/ -2 V	385 mW	Power supply	Delivering prod quant
Hitachi	HM4864	120 ns max.	128 cy 2 ms	+5 V	350 mW	No connection	Samples 1q 1979
NEC	N/A	150 ns max.	128 cy 2 ms	N/A	400 mW		Samples 1q 1979
OKI	N/A	N/A	128 cy 2 ms	+7 V/ -2 V	Under 400 mW	Power supply	Delivering in Japan
Toshiba	N/A	N/A	128 cy 2 ms	+5 V	Under 400 mW	No connection	Samples latter 1979

Values are all typical unless otherwise specified.

the 2-k × 8 UV EPROM pinout. In fact, there may even be a family of 16-k devices—16-k × 1, 4-k × 4 and 2-k × 8 organizations—to satisfy a wide range of memory requirements.

Bubbles: bulky alternatives

Going past the dynamic and static RAM technology for large amounts of bulk serial storage, charge-coupled devices and bubble memories offer the possibility of four times the density of the 64-k RAMs. And with bubbles there's an added advantage not offered by statics or dynamics—nonvolatility in the event of a power loss.

This nonvolatility will make bubble memories, now available in 92-k (from TI) and 256-k (from Rockwell International and TI) arrays, an attractive alternative to mechanical storage devices. Providing an access time (for the next bit out) of 7 to 10 µs, the arrays, just in the early development stages,

operate at clock rates of 150 and 100 kHz, respectively. Latency time (to reach a desired bit) can reach 10 ms, maximum, but in most cases will average less than 5 ms.

Samples of both the TI and Rockwell 256-k chips can be purchased for $500 each, with production quantities not expected until the latter half of this year. Of course, larger arrays are also on the horizon.

But with CCDs, there are problems. They've turned out to be more complex than first realized. And now only Fairchild and Texas Instruments are left in the CCD race, so the question of product life and viability becomes more difficult to answer.

The Fairchild F464 CCD is fairly complex, but accesses faster than disc-file systems. Soon to follow will be a 256-kbit CCD brother, which will reduce clock-phase requirements from four to two, and thus simplify some of the basic system design. TI's TMS 3064

is already two-phase.

At any rate, memories are cramming in more and more, regardless of their type. But as density grows, so do electrical and radiation-caused problems. In the 16-k RAM, for example, alpha-particle scattering of electrons can cause errors. This effect is much more noticeable in the 16-k because of its much smaller cell capacitors and sensitive sense amplifiers.

Various RAM manufacturers report various levels of alpha-particle sensitivity (see Fig. 1). While larger cell capacitances would help, there are many design tradeoffs for the IC manufacturer to consider. For example, since a prime source of alpha radiation is the plastic and glass materials in the DIP packaging itself, these are being revamped.

However, improving RAM reliability at the system level is bringing one particular alternative to the fore—incorporating error-correction capability

Table 2. Who makes what in RAMs

	NMOS — Fully static				Pseudo static		NMOS — Dynamic			CMOS — Static RAMs				Bipolar (ECL) — Static RAMs				Bipolar (TTL) — Static RAMs			
	4k×1	1k×4	1k×8	2k×8	4k×8	8k×8	4k×1	16k×1	64k×1	256×4	1k×1	4k×1	1k×4	256×4	1k×1	4k×1	1k×4	256×4	1k×1	4k×1	1k×4
Advanced Micro Devices	•	•		★			•	★	★												
American Microsystems	★	★		★						•	★	★	★								
EMM Semiconductor	•	•	•	★																	
Fairchild Semiconductor	•	•					•++	•++	★					•	•	•	•	•+	•	•	•
Fujitsu	•	•					•	•						•	•	•	•				
Harris Semiconductor										•	•	•	•								
Hitachi										•	•	•	★								
Hughes Aircraft										•	★	★	★								
ITT Semiconductor							•	•													
Intel	•	•	•				•	•★	★	•											
Intersil	•	•					•	•*		•	•	•									
Matsushita	★	•		★			•	•	★	•		★									
Micropower Systems										•	★	★									
MOS Technology		•																			
Mostek	•	•	•	•	★	★	•	•★	★												
Motorola	★	•	★	★	★	★	•	•★	★	•	•	•	★	•	•	★				•	
National Semiconductor	•	•		★			•	•★	★	•	•	★		•	•	★				•	
NEC Microcomputers	•	•	•	★			•	•		•	•	★	★								
OKI Semiconductor							•	•	•												
RCA										•	•	★	•								
Rockwell	•	•																			
Siemens							•	•	★												
Signetics	•	•		★			•	•	★									•+	•	★	
Solid State Scientific										•	★		★								
Synertek	★	•		★																	
Texas Instruments	•	•	•	★	★		•	•	★												
Toshiba	•	•					•	•	★	•	•	•									
Zilog	•	★		★	★		•	•	★												

Notes: • At least one product in production. ★ Product in development or sampling
+ 256 x 8 and 256 x 9 units also available. ++ Bipolar 5-V only versions also available
* Also offers 8k x 1 dynamic RAM

within the systems. That's where ECC comes in.

Error-correcting coding, long standard in large-mainframe MOS memories and now getting into minis and micros, is related to the Hamming codes used to protect digital telemetry data from errors. In digital computing, the familiar parity check is a simple 1-bit example of redundancy checking, a primitive form of ECC.

Parity adds one redundant bit to each byte or word, to indicate whether the 1's in the word are odd or even. ECC goes further, adding several bits per byte or word. The number of added ECC bits determines how many errors, out of all the possible errors that could occur, can be detected and corrected. The more added bits, the more error-proof the system.

Memory systems: how reliable?

So how much does ECC raise reliability? An impressive factor of 60, according to one minicomputer manufacturer. That is, the MTBF of that company's memory boards is increased by about 60 times, by using 22-bit error-correcting codes to implement the 16-bit memory. The cost increment (about 30% to add ECC in 16-bit memories, and lower percentages for wide-word systems) is slowing acceptance, of course.

Today's memories with ECC usually have what's called single-bit error correction, which means that enough ECC bits are added to guarantee that appropriate logic can correct any single-bit error (where only one bit out of the eight or more bits of the word has changed value), and detect errors that change the value of two bits of the word.

Here's how the bit count stacks up for the popular level of ECC correction: For eight bits per data word, five ECC bits are added; for 16 bits, 6 ECC bits; for 32 bits, seven ECC bits; for 64 bits, eight ECC bits. These bit counts provide for correction of all single-bit errors and detection of all double-bit errors. But some memories add only five bits, not six, to protect a 16-bit word. This level of ECC protection also corrects all single-bit errors, but detects only 42% of all double-bit errors. How much does that matter in the real world?

"It's a judgment call," says Ben

System costs plummet when function duplication is designed out. While most minis duplicate read/write and control electronics for each board of memory DIPs, Interdata makes one read/write/control set serve more memory, by using eight little "daughter boards." This packaging also simplifies reconfiguration and speeds up field repair.

Auten of General Automation. "Some companies only use 21 bits total for 16-bit data, and they take the chance of missing a few double-bit errors. Our designs are more conservative, using the full 22 bits, so that all double-bit errors do get detected."

Computer Automation designers chose 21-bit ECC for their new PRO-TOS, a high-end minicomputer system. They explain that since single-bit errors occur at the rate of only one every 20 weeks in their 65-kbyte systems, double-bit errors, occurring hundreds or thousands of weeks apart, will be of no practical concern.

ECC fights brownouts

ECC memory is also effective in recovering from power outages. If power is interrupted on a RAM memory system with battery backup, error-causing glitches may occur during the loss of power or its return.

"If you have only parity in the memory, and you find some errors, you probably have to reboot the system," says Joel Korelitz, president of Mupro. "This could cost a special trip to a remote location and hours of lost time.

But with ECC, you can do a memory read, and correct the errors."

Mupro's present 16-bit boards for 8086-compatible Multibus use are available with 16, 32, 48, or 64-kword capacities (each word is 16 bits). Already alone in offering 128 kbits, the board is laid out to accept either of two 64-k RAM types in place of the 16 k's. So getting a half-megabyte SBC-80 board with ECC will be easy when the 64-k's are available. Power-supply strapping on the Mupro board permits the use of either the Fujitsu +7, −2-V 64-k RAM, or the Texas Instruments 5-V-only 64-k RAM.

It's not surprising, then, that more and more system designers are working in ECC, for applications ranging from point-of-sale to process control. Certainly, extra bits per word cost money and increase system size, and the extra steps of generating and checking ECC may add 50 ns to memory cycle time. But even so reliability is improved dramatically, and service problems are simplified. Board-edge indicators show when and where errors occur, and marginal operation of RAM chips is easily detectable. Service organizations can cut board inventories when this self-check feature keeps a good board from being marked bad.

So much for today's ECC. But what's the next trend in ECC?

13 bits in every byte?

As memory costs continue to drop, it may become standard to spend 13 bits for every 8-bit byte, even in wide-word machines. Because byte operations are so common, 32-bit machines may be built with separate error correction on each byte, instead of a single 7-bit error-correction field for the 32-bit word.

This will not only provide higher data integrity but also eliminate the additional logic operations that revise the ECC field every time a byte is written into a word. For example, envision what happens when an Intel 8086 microprocessor executes byte-write commands (sending data to a 16-bit ECC memory board, but transferring it eight bits at a time over the Intel Multibus). The Mupro memory board immediately accepts each byte from the Multibus, telling the 8086 that the transfer is complete and releasing the Multibus only 50 ns after the write command.

But actually the memory board has only latched the new byte into an input

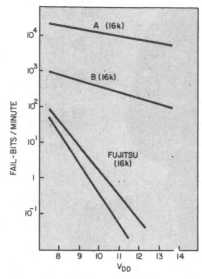

1. Comparing the soft errors of various 16-k RAMs, this graph, compiled by Fujitsu, shows the best and worst-case failure rates for the Fujitsu RAMs compared to several other manufacturers' equivalent products.

buffer. To store the byte away, the board next performs a read/correct/modify/write operation. The target word already contains two bytes, and the new byte is to be placed in half of that 16-bit word. The memory control logic reads the word, corrects it if need be, substitutes the new byte, generates a new 6-bit ECC field for the two bytes together, then stores the whole 22-bit word. In this case, the memory board is busied out for about 500 ns for each such byte transfer, but could do the job in 350 ns if the memory were organized with separate ECC for each byte.

ECC goes LSI

Whether a byte-oriented ECC trend really takes off or not, Fujitsu is ready. The first semiconductor firm with a single-chip LSI logic solution for ECC, the company has a chip, the MB1412, that can generate five ECC bits for an 8-bit byte, or form groups of two, four, or eight chips to handle ECC generation for 16, 32, or 64-bit words.

Meanwhile, Mupro is implementing the ECC function with six parity-generator chips, two Exclusive-OR chips, and three custom programmed MMI PALs (programmed array logic chips). Other semiconductor vendors are tackling the ECC problem, so more LSI ECC chips will be arriving in the next 18 months.

"If the MTBF for each RAM chip stays the same as density increases, the memory size above which we start using ECC will move up, proportional

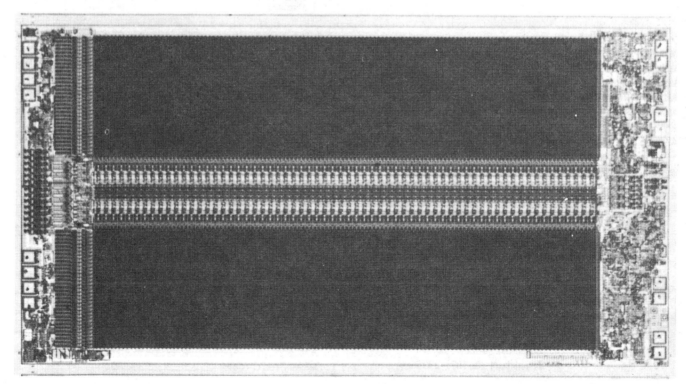

The new breed in dynamic RAMs: 64-kbits in the same space as 16-k memories. Yet this chip, from Texas Instruments, dissipates a mere 200 mW of power and provides an access time of only 100 ns.

to density," points out Mike Gutman, Digital Equipment's product manager for storage systems. Today's product offerings from DEC use ECC in systems of 64 kbytes or more based on 4-k chips, but in systems of 256 kbytes or more when 16-k chips are used. It's too soon to say, but it seems probable that the 64-k dynamic RAM will move this boundary to 1 megabyte.

At the Memory Systems Division of Intersil, 16-ks were the basis of all new design work as much as a year ago, for minicomputer add-on memories. But the story is entirely different for Intersil's plug-compatibles for IBM computers, where higher speeds count more than higher bit count per chip. While IBM is just making the transition from 1-k and 2-k statics to 4 k, Intersil's UMS-1 products for the IBM 370/158, 168, 3031, and 3032 use 8-k dynamics, and its UMS-2 product line for smaller IBM mainframes is based on 4-k statics. Since the rest of the plug-compatible industry is at 4-k, Intersil is almost alone in being able to put 16 Mbytes on a 370/168, twice IBM's capacity, with the 8-k dynamic UMS-1 product line.

With the average amount of memory per system definitely soaring, very large systems are bound to proliferate. DEC's 11/70 can address up to 4 Mbytes, which means four boxes of memory, totaling 64 boards with the 4-k dynamics. That shrinks to 16 boards in one box with the 16-k dynamics, and to only four boards with 64 k's. There is every indication that system sizes will continue to press up against the upper limit, namely the maximum address space designed into the CPU. And with big memory come some clever schemes to ease initial configuration and field reconfiguration of the memory-board complement.

Reading its own mind

For example, Computer Automation holds patents on a self-organized addressing scheme for memory. When the CPU is powered up, it checks to find out what memory it has. If a 16-k module is plugged in place of the first 8-k while the power is off, the CPU will notice and renumber the memory addresses accordingly.

Use of the standard CA Maxibus in almost all CA minicomputers makes memory interchangeable between machines. RAM, ROM, or core can be plugged in any board slot, regardless

Fast enough for the whole range of IBM mainframes, the Intel 7700 add-on memory gets 64 kbytes per board and up to 2 Mbytes per box, using the 70-ns 4-k × 1 Intel 2147 static RAM. Error-correction coding, long standard on maxicomputers, is now finding its way into some mini and micro-based systems.

High-performance memories are being built today with a variety of methods. This 16-k RAM, from Fairchild, uses an I³L arrangement.

of the capacity or speed of the board.

With a wide variety of boards offered, this means real economy in configuring CA systems, since large or small increments can be added anytime. It also means field performance can be optimized. What's more, now that 11-k dynamic RAM chips are in full production, memories may be packaged more economically. For this reason, Interdata is using ECC for the first time in its new Series Sixteen minicomputers. Models Sixteen-10 and Sixteen-20 have single-bit parity but ECC is standard in the top model, the Sixteen-30 minicomputer system.

The PC-board economy is possible through the use of "daughter boards," strips that are 8-in. long, 1-in. wide and plug into the 15 × 15-in. memory board itself. Not only does this mean that 256 kbytes can be packed on the board instead of 32 or 64 kbytes, it also means that function duplication is cut back.

As a result, the read/write control logic that would have been duplicated on a series of 64-kbyte boards appears just once on the 15 × 15-in. motherboard, serving all 256 kbytes. Larry MacPherson, Interdata product manager for the Series Sixteen, points out that this unusual modularity makes it easy to add and subtract memory in the field, and slashes the cost of incremental memory increases.

There are only 17 chips in the daughter-board strip for parity memory and 22 chips for ECC memory, yielding 32 kbytes per strip.

Although earlier Interdata models using core memory are still available, all Series Sixteen models are based on MOS memory. Why has core been left out of future planning? MacPherson points to cost. "The 16-k RAM will just cinch the cost argument for MOS versus core. But less obvious than the parts costs itself is the fact that MOS memory saves power, and so cuts system costs again. In a 256-kbyte memory, the power savings are about 4-to-1."

But Interdata used MOS memories as early as 1971, in its Models 80 and 85. Why is ECC only now being offered? MacPherson echoes the general industry opinion in pointing to three answers. First, the emphasis in the minicomputer market place in the early 1970s was on fast performance, not reliability. Second, while it was recognized that MOS memory might not come up to core levels of reliability, it wasn't until MOS memories spent time in the field that anyone saw the re-

This totally shielded motherboard prevents ringing in the bus lines by using dynamic termination that doesn't load down the signal drivers. Artec Electronics offers a 16-slot model in addition to the 10-slot S100 assembly above. Both use ⅛-in. epoxy glass boards and quality Masterite connectors.

liability problem clearly. Third, only now are ECC comparator chips appearing to make the addition of error correction easy and economic, in tightly-packed boards.

With so much attention focused on silicon memory devices, it is easy to overlook core—which is still growing in use, especially in process-control and military applications.

Speaking of core...

The core-vs-RAM picture is complex. IBM is almost 100% RAM. Three years ago, after a spurt to build inventory, one mini vendor shut down its core plant. Yet today EMM, which has built both types of memories for years, is investing in a new core plant. Why?

The explanation is that there may be a good future for core—replacing fixed-head discs. From the core-makers' point of view, CCDs may not make it: Major memory manufacturers seem to be backing off on CCD efforts, and bubbles may not make it until 1981 or later, when a 1-Mbyte chip appears.

For now, cores can use their advantages in reliability and nonvolatile data retention. Not only that, but cores are achieving their lowest cost per bit in history in such devices as the Ampex Megastore, the EMM Megabyte, and the Dataram Datastore, which are disc-replacement core boxes announced in the last year. The EMM Megabyte unit uses one board and one core stack for a full megabyte of storage. A 4-Mbyte system requires only 17.5 in. of rack space, including a custom interface. And similar core stores may be coming from Fabritek, Standard Memories, Data Products, and others.

Still, what is often called an emotional attachment to core has to break down eventually in the face of price decreases on the order of 30% a year for MOS—core prices are more or less stabilized. Digital Equipment's Gutman says the emotional problem dissolves once the customer has educated himself about his software and planned ways to make the RAM appear nonvolatile. The user looks through all the applications software and determines how each application reacts to power interruptions. If the interrupted jobs start all over again in the core version, there is no problem. Otherwise, rewrites are inserted.

Nonvolatility, Gutman points out, takes two solutions: A short-term solution is battery backup; a long-term solution is an interruptible power supply and/or added smarts in the software to back files up on disc periodically and so provide solid restart check-points. ■■

A design horror story

Here's a tale of woe from Computer Automation that should interest every memory designer who uses LSI parts. Unknown to CA, one of its memory-chip suppliers changed its production process, to shrink the RAM die size. The performance specifications of the part didn't change and the part continued to meet all specs. The part number and appearance were also unchanged. For some time, it was hard to determine why the CA memory boards, long in production, no longer worked correctly.

The problem centered around the address inputs of the RAM chips. The key difference between the original RAM chips and the shrunk version was the amount of charge returned to the address lines when CE (chip enable) was activated. The Computer Automation address drivers could no longer hold the address lines at correct voltage levels because the smaller die dumped more charge back into the address lines than the original chip.

Because system shipments were slowing down, and CA couldn't change the board design, it changed RAM vendors and substituted core memories wherever possible.

But this overloaded both the core suppliers and the new RAM vendor. Shipments went farther off-schedule, and all told, the company ended up with a multi-million dollar problem.

What is the lesson here? That every significant parameter of a part be specified tightly? Not really. According to the company, the parameter that changed, the amount of charge dumped back into the address lines, is not specified for any RAM chip. The part was second-sourced, but the second vendor couldn't gear up production fast enough.

The lesson is this: Officially, the design engineer may not be responsible for vendor evaluation. But then, leaving it to someone else could put a dent in the design engineer's paycheck.

Testing 16-k Dynamic RAMs

ROBERT W. OWEN
Product Engineer, Mostek,
Carrollton, Texas

Test a 16-k RAM inadequately, and you're on your way to a migraine headache. Two ways to get into big trouble: Forget about temperature effects, and ignore important test-pattern sequences. Analyze both, and you'll save your aspirins for later. Storage time is a case in point.

Charge storage on a 16-k MOS RAM is, of course, dynamic in nature, since the charge on the MOS capacitor eventually will leak off. Storage time is an intrinsic device parameter. Refresh time—more properly, refresh interval—specifies a maximum allowable interval. The interval separates two operations (on the same storage location) that will re-establish the full charge on a partially decayed HIGH level.

Performance varies with temperature

But remember: Storage time depends on temperature:

$$T_S = A \exp(-BT),$$

where T is the junction temperature in °C, B is a variable relating the magnitude of the generation-recombination current to the junction temperature (units of $1°C$), and A is a scaling constant reflecting such variables as junction area, bulk-defect density, and sense-amplifier design.

Note that B is not a constant. Normally, it is assumed that the storage time doubles for every 10-C decrease in junction temperature—which is equivalent to assuming that B = 0.069. Data show that 0.055 is a typical value for B—but the number varies at least ±30% from the typical (Fig. 1).

The storage time at T_J = 25 C for the hypothetical device of Fig. 1 will lie somewhere between 50 and 381 ms. If room-temperature testing is to be attempted, the refresh interval should be set at 381 ms, since any lesser value won't guarantee the assumed minimum storage time of 2 ms at 100 C. Devices failing such a test won't necessarily be failures at 2 ms and 100 C, and would therefore have to be rescreened at 100 C.

The efficiency of the procedure depends upon the number of good devices found by the first screen, but in general the number of units requiring a second test is so great, you may as well go ahead and eliminate the first screen in favor of a 100% screen at the maximum-junction temperature.

Besides storage time, access time, power dissipation, and input/output levels all need to be verified over the temperature range. Access time and power dissipation are functions of transistor gain, which is temperature-dependent (through carrier mobility) and about 25% lower at 100 C than at 0 C. Therefore, access takes longer at elevated temperatures. The memory will dissipate more power at low temperature. However, note that much of the power required is capacitive and thus related to frequency rather than temperature.

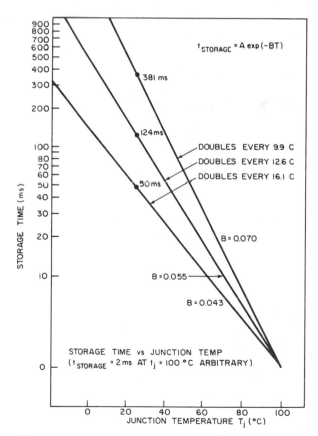

1. **Storage time doesn't necessarily double** for every 10-C decrease in junction temperature, as the "conventional wisdom" states. Setting the correct refresh intervals during testing requires an accurate knowledge of the minimum storage time for the memory.

Signal levels are functions of transistor-threshold voltage, which decreases about 2 mV for every 1-C increase in temperature. Input HIGH levels and output HIGH and LOW levels are normally the worst at low temperature and must be guardbanded if you test only at high temperature. (One 16-k RAM, the Mostek MK 4116, incorporates an integrated reference voltage for address and data inputs—which removes the threshold-voltage dependence and the temperature dependence along with it.)

A few timing parameters become worst-case as the memory becomes faster, and you must guardband these if you test only at high temperature. On balance, however—primarily because storage time varies radically with temperature—it is best to conduct tests at the maximum junction temperature only and guardband parameters that aren't worst-case.

Calculating temperature rise

The two junction temperatures singled out in Fig. 1 are not chosen at random. The equation describing temperature rise over an ambient is given by:

$$T_J - T_A = \triangle T = \theta_{JA}P_D,$$

where θ_{JA} is the junction-to-ambient thermal resistance (for a 16-pin ceramic DIP mounted in a socket on a double-sided PC board, the most widely accepted value is 70 C/W), and P_D is the power dissipation of the device under the conditions of interest.

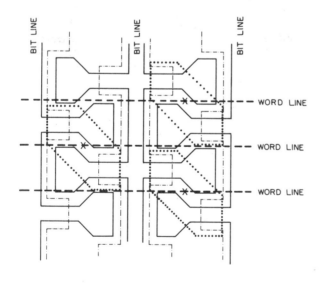

———————	ACTIVE
—·—·—·—·—	POLY I
··················	POLY II
— — — — —	METAL (NOT DRAWN AS RECTANGLE, LINE ONLY)
X	POLY II TO METAL CONTACT

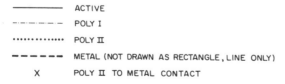

2. **Cell layout of the MK 4116 16-k RAM** locates adjacent cells on the same row or on rows separated by one word line, but always on adjacent columns. The two-polysilicon-level construction may call for further testing, for instance, of cell-to-cell interactions.

To get $\triangle T$, assume the following specified values
$$I_{DD} \text{ (active)} = 35 \text{ mA},$$
$$I_{DD} \text{ (stand-by)} = 1.5 \text{ mA},$$
$$V_{DD} \text{ (maximum)} = 13.2 \text{ V},$$
$$t_{cycle} = 375 \text{ ns}.$$

Assume that the refresh test writes 16,384 bits at the 375-ns cycle rate, pauses in the stand-by condition for the refresh interval, then reads all bits again at 375 ns. With t(refresh) = 2 ms, calculate the rise in junction temperature as follows:

$$\text{duty factor (DF)} = \frac{2 \ (16,384) \ 375 \text{ ns}}{2 \ (16,384) \ 375 \text{ ns} + 2 \text{ ms}}$$
$$= 0.86.$$

Therefore:
$$\triangle T = \theta_{JA} \ [P_D \text{ (active)} \times \text{(DF)} + P_D \text{ (stand-by)} \times (1 - \text{DF})]$$
$$= 70 \text{ C/W} \ [0.035 \times (13.2) \times 0.86 + 0.0015 \times (13.2) \times (1 - 0.86)]$$
$$= 28 \text{ C}.$$

With t(refresh) = 381 ms,
$$\text{(DF)} = \frac{2 \ (16,384) \ 375 \text{ ns}}{2 \ (16,384) \ 375 \text{ ns} + 381 \text{ ms}}$$
$$= 0.03.$$

Therefore:
$$\triangle T = 70 \text{ C/W} \ [0.035 \times (13.2) \times 0.03 + 0.0015 \times (13.2) \times (1 - 0.03)]$$
$$= 2.3 \text{ C}.$$

The junction temperature of a device undergoing a 381-ms refresh test at T_A = 25 C will rise only 2.3° to 27.3°, while the same device executing a 2-ms refresh test at T_A = 70 C will rise to a whopping 98 C.

Strictly speaking, the foregoing calculations are true only if you allow the junction temperature to stabilize by running the refresh test in a continuous mode. The thermal mass of the device is not negligible. In fact, θ_{JA} is a function of time and has a time constant of approximately 60 s in most test situations.

Is it the pattern or the temperature?

Interestingly, much of the effectiveness of the N^2 pattern test is attributed to elevated junction temperatures occurring during the test interval. An N^2 pattern, with N equal to 16,384 and a cycle time of 375 ns, requires 100 s. The value of θ_{JA} after 100 s of testing is about 80% of its final value. The junction rise for P_D = 462 mW is

$$T = \theta_{JA} \ P_D$$
$$= (0.8) \ (70 \text{ C/W}) \ (0.462)$$
$$= 26 \text{ C},$$

and this rise occurs during the test.

The storage time of the device may be reduced by as much as a factor of six, with the device speed approximately 10% less. You can attain these benefits, of course, without resorting to N^2 patterns: pre-calculate the final junction temperature and set the

Possible minimum test sequence for 16-k RAM

Test Description	Data Pattern	Function	Power Supplies V_{DD}	V_{BB}	Cycle Count
Maximum cycle	Diagonal	Functionality	13.2	−4.5	2N (t_{cyc} = 10 Ms)
	$\overline{\text{Diagonal}}$		13.2	−5.5	2N (t_{cyc} = 10 Ms)
	Diagonal		10.8	−5.5	2N (t_{cyc} = 10 Ms)
	$\overline{\text{Diagonal}}$		10.8	−4.5	2N (t_{cyc} = 10 Ms)
Load read	Parity and $\overline{\text{Parity}}$		10.8	−5.5	2N
			10.8	−4.5	2N
			13.2	−5.5	2N
			13.2	−4.5	2N
Load read	Checkerboard and $\overline{\text{Checkerboard}}$	Bit Interactions	10.8	−5.5	2N
			10.8	−4.5	2N
			13.2	−5.5	2N
			13.2	−4.5	2N
Walking diagonal	Diagonal	Functionality	10.8	−5.5	$2N^{3/2}$
			13.2	−4.5	$2N^{3/2}$
Dynamic refresh	Alternate Rows	Data retention	10.8	−5.5	1N + 2 ms
Dynamic refresh	$\overline{\text{Alternate Rows}}$	Data retention	10.8	−5.5	1N + 2 ms
Still refresh	All Highs	Data retention	10.8	−5.5	2N + 2 ms

temperature chamber accordingly—an approach not without pitfalls.

If the test chamber is so constructed that heat is maintained throughout the test, you must consider the self-heating. If you hold the device in an elevated ambient before testing, then remove it and insert it into the test socket, you must then characterize the combined effects of heat loss in the socket and self-heating during the test.

The device itself can act as a temperature reference to accurately measure junction temperature. All signal inputs connect to pn⁺ diodes, which can easily be calibrated. Notice that if diode current is held constant, diode voltage is linearly proportional to temperature. Calibrate an input on a reference device by stabilizing the device at an accurately measured reference temperature, injecting a constant current, and measuring the diode drop (from the input to the V_{BB} pin).

When you do so at several temperatures, you can construct a calibration curve of diode voltage vs temperature, then use the device to measure unknown temperatures by injecting current, measuring the diode voltage, and referring to the calibration chart.

Once calibrated, the device can profile either heat loss at the test site or junction-temperature rise during operation—and very accurately. Some tips: A good value for the current is 100 μA; the voltage meas-

urement requires millivolt accuracy; the measurement cannot be made while the device is operating because of noise in the substrate (operate the device, then switch out the functional inputs and switch in the measurement circuitry). You must calibrate each device separately, since the magnitude and slope of the relationship are variable.

Once you've sweated through the heating tests, turn your attention to other possible memory imperfections. Selection of the right test pattern can ferret out any hidden gremlins.

Tune in to sensitive patterns

Analyzing and using test sequences that exploit possible memory weaknesses is necessary to keep test times for 16-k RAMs within practical bounds. (The following information, although believed to be general, applies specifically to the Mostek design.)

The 16-k is basically a synchronous machine built around a rectangular memory array, the coordinates of which are rows and columns (Fig. 2). The synchronous machine provides the timing control for the input latches, row decoder, sense amplifier, column decoder, write circuitry, and output latch.

Unlike earlier, asynchronous, RAMs, the 16-k nearly always fails digitally. That is, if a problem exists with the input latches, the wrong output will be generated (but not a "late" output, which is correct but delayed, for example, by poor input levels). Since there is no worst-case pattern for access time, the time is controlled by internal clock generators—which greatly simplifies the testing of gross functionality. This testing ensures cell uniqueness and output validity over the specified timing and power-supply ranges.

On the other hand, you must still check the memory array and sense amplifiers for pattern sensitivities. Consider the signal-detection capabilities of the sense amplifier and its precharge requirements. A probable worst-case pattern for a sense amplifier consists of a single bit of DATA in a field of $\overline{\text{DATA}}$.

If you run such a pattern in a "row-fast" mode, each sense amplifier will be required to perform some number of $\overline{\text{DATA}}$ reads and a single detection of DATA, and complete the scan by reading $\overline{\text{DATA}}$.

If the DATA bit occupies, at some time, each of the locations along the digit line, you will have checked the ability of the sense amplifier to pick a signal out of noise and to dispel completely any influence of preceding cycles on the present cycle. Note that this pattern requires only as many scans as there are bits per sense amplifier, and that you can check all columns simultaneously.

When considering the row-select function, here, too, noise-coupling considerations indicate that a worst-case pattern might be either a single DATA bit in a field of $\overline{\text{DATA}}$ or a solid field. Here also the word "field" has restricted meaning, applying only to all cells connected to a single row-select line.

Which pattern?

Several patterns check the fore-mentioned failure modes efficiently. One pattern, the $2N^{3/2}$ "moving-diagonal," requires 128 write-read scans through the entire array.

On the first scan, all bits are written to $\overline{\text{DATA}}$, except for the 128 bits along the major diagonal, which are written to DATA. The read scan verifies the correct operation of the array under these conditions.

On each succeeding scan, the position of the diagonal of DATA is shifted until, on the 128th scan, it has occupied every possible position in the array. Thus, each cell has been the only DATA cell in a row and column of $\overline{\text{DATA}}$. This pattern proves to be quite effective in screening the 16-k.

Refresh tests can be classified as either still or dynamic. For still tests, write all locations, pause for the refresh interval with $\overline{\text{RAS}}$ and $\overline{\text{CAS}}$ inactive (HIGH), and read all cells. The pause allows the cells to leak LOW, but also allows internal nodes (which are bootstrapped above V_{dd} by the trailing edge of $\overline{\text{RAS}}$ or $\overline{\text{CAS}}$) to decay so that you end up testing both the cells and the dynamic periphery.

Unfortunately, such a test normally isn't the worst case for the cell, for noise generated during active cycles can contribute to the loss of data in the cell.

The dynamic-refresh tests write data into some subset of the cells (normally half the cells). Then, during the refresh interval, they perform either read or write cycles on the cells not being tested to couple charge-degrading noise onto the unaccessed test cells. Both tests are necessary to guarantee functionality.

Be careful: Testing at maximum cycle time gives noise an opportunity to couple onto the row-select lines (which should be off to prevent a partially selected transfer gate), allowing cell data to leak onto the digit lines.

This test might perform a write scan with minimum precharge times (t_{RP}), and maximum active time (t_{RAS}), followed by a "read-modify-write" scan under the same basic timing conditions, which is then followed by a read scan to verify the "modify write" operation. This important test is often overlooked but is, in fact, the worst case for many of the internal circuits.

The patterns discussed provide a basic but adequate test sequence, a good starting point. The table summarizes a sequence that should provide a reasonable degree of confidence in any RAM that passes. Special timing modes and certain timing parameters are left unchecked, but you can easily add if desired.

The sequence requires $28N + 4N^{3/2}$ cycles, of which all but 8N can be at the fastest allowable cycle rate. The 8N are at the slowest allowable cycle rate (maximum cycle length). If the fastest cycle is 375 ns, and the slowest is 10 μs, then the sequence executes in just over 4.5 s, excluding tester overhead and power-supply settling times. ∎

Bibliography

Ahlquist, C.N., et al, "A 16,384-bit Dynamic RAM," *IEEE Journal of Solid-State Circuits*, Vol. SC-11, No. 5, October, 1976, pp. 570-573.

Barrett, C.R., and Smith, R.C., "Failure Modes and Reliability of Dynamic RAMs," *COMPCON Spring 1977 Technical Digest*, March, 1977, pp. 179-182.

Brown, J.R., Jr., "Timing Peculiarities of the 16-pin Multiplexed Address RAM," *Burroughs Technical Memorandum*, November, 1976.

Cocking, J., "RAM Test Patterns and Test Strategy," *1975 Semiconductor Test Symposium, Digest of Papers*, October, 1975, pp. 1-8.

Feldmann, D., and Healy, J.E., "Probleme bei der Freigabe-und Wareneingangspruefung von Halbleiterspeichern", *Elektro-Anzeiger*, No. 18, Sept. 24, 1976.

Foss, R.C., and Harlan, R., "MOS Dynamic RAM—Design for Testability," *1976 Semiconductor Test Symposium, Digest of Papers*, October, 1976, pp. 9-12.

Huston, R.E., "Testing Semiconductor Memories," *1973 Symposium on Semiconductor Memory Testing, Digest of Papers*, October, 1973, pp. 27-62.

Kuo, C.K., et al, "16-k RAM Built with Proven Process May Offer High Start-up Reliability," *Electronics*, May 13, 1976, pp. 83-86.

Peck, D.S., and Zierdt, C.R., "The Reliability of Semiconductor Devices in the Bell System," *Proceedings of the IEEE*, Vol. 62, No. 2, February, 1974, pp. 185-211.

Schroeder, P.R., and Proebsting, R.J., "A 16-k × 1-Bit Dynamic RAM, *ISSCC Digest of Technical Papers*, February, 1977, pp. 12-13.

1977 Memory Products Catalog, Mostek, Carrollton, TX, pp. VII-1 through VII-15.

Speed Up 4-k or 16-k RAM Evaluation

JIM LOCKHART
Project Engineer,
Computer Systems Group,
Burroughs Corp.,
Piscataway, New Jersey

To evaluate your 16-pin 4-k or 16-k RAMs quickly before using them, go with a raster-scan tester. Almost instantaneously, the unit displays all cell errors as well as the results of varying voltages and refresh rates. What's more, it requires little or no time to set up or program.

Either 4 or 16-k RAMs can be tested at the flip of a switch, and a remote test head provides for temperature evaluation. Since an external pulse generator forms the main clock, you can adjust the frequency to test the fastest RAMs at their minimum cycle times —read-modify-writes of 500 ns or less. Of course, you'll have to adjust the RC networks to correspond to the various respective RAM minimum timing parameters. Plug-in modules make it easy.

Watch the low end

At the other frequency end, you can reduce the clock to a rate that will cause refresh failures. You'll find that some RAMs contain cells that can store information without error for many seconds at room temperature. Minimum clock frequency is limited only by the external pulse generator; the raster tester has no lower limit.

The voltage tolerances for the tester voltages are all $\pm 10\%$. The shmoo (characteristic error pattern) voltage ranges depend on the power supplies selected. Those in this tester provide the following ranges to shmoo the RAM you're testing:

Nominal Value	Range
+ 12 V	+ 2.5 V to + 16.5 V
+ 5 V	+ 2.5 V to + 11.0 V
− 5 V	0.0 V to − 7.0 V

The tester can be put in a stop-on-error mode, while V_{DD} or V_{BB} are decreased from nominal until the first RAM error occurs. The tester then stops and displays the address of the first failure. Failures are shown on LEDs in binary form and on a raster scan in matrix form (Fig. 1).

You can decrease the main clock rate until the first cell fails because of marginal refresh. Then, tests will pinpoint the most marginal cell in the array. Or, for multiple failures, you can change voltages from nominal, with the tester in the "run" mode (don't stop on error). The raster display then indicates weak areas in the array and gives the device's operating margin.

Looking at the inside

To see how the tester works, divide it into two subsystems: basic test logic and display logic (Fig. 2).

The basic test logic consists of a timing generator, an address generator, a premultiplexer, an address multiplexer, output drivers, a remote test head, a comparator, an error latch, and a pattern generator.

The timing generator, a group of monostable multivibrators, provides the proper timing for memory signals and controls events in the tester itself.

The address generator consists of a synchronous binary counter that provides not only up to 16,384 unique binary words for addressing the memory, but also the basis for generating data patterns.

The 4-bit multiplexer chips make up the premultiplexer, which arranges sequential addressing for a 4 or 16-k RAM, depending on where the selection switch is pointed. The premultiplexer permits one address generator for both RAM types.

The address multiplexer also consists of two 4-bit multiplexer chips, but here they divide the address field, whose halves are then presented to the memory in the required sequence.

Line-driver output circuits provide the signal power for the cable to the test head and its termination resistors. The test head contains a socket for the device under test and an output driver to send the data-out from the memory device back through the cable to the tester. A single Exclusive-OR gate compares the data from the memory with the expected data. When the memory data do not agree with the correct data, a cross-coupled-gate flip-flop sets to an error state.

How errors are spotted

When you set an option switch to Error Stop, and an error occurs, the error latch stops further clock

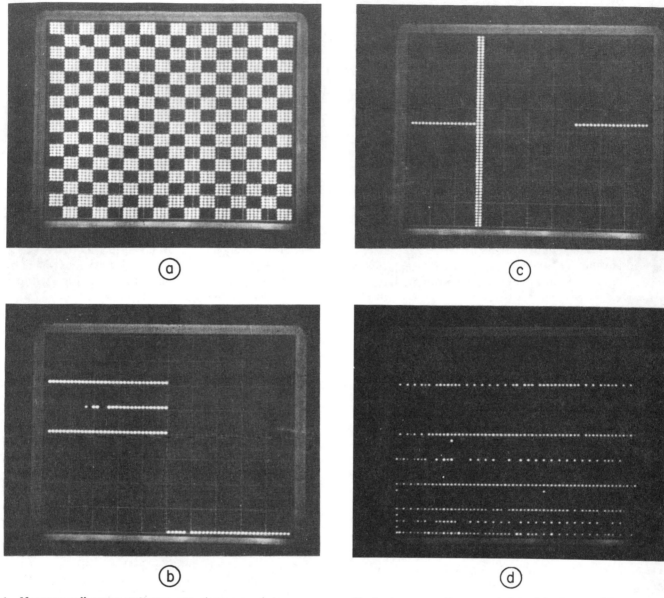

1. Memory-cell error patterns are shown as dots representing either ONE-to-ZERO or ZERO-to-ONE errors, depending on the position of a switch. A checkerboard pattern represents a typical data input to a 4-k RAM (a).

Typical error patterns consist of bad rows (b), errors in two columns and one row (c), and random errors in some rows (d). Complete row or column failures are shown, not simply "stop on first error."

pulses from advancing the address counter, so you can discern the error address.

At the same time, clock pulses are kept from the timing generator to stop all tester and memory activity. But if you want testing to continue after an error, set the option switch to Auto Reset. The error latch will set and an indicator will light. The latch will be cleared when the address counter reaches its end count.

The pattern generator uses the address generator and also contains some mechanical switches and gates. Select the appropriate switch and you'll get row bars, column bars, or checkerboard patterns that are 1, 2, 4, 8, 16, or 32-bits wide.

To best understand the tester's other major block, the display logic, divide it into two major functions.

One is translating the RAM's binary-address information into positioning information for the CRT, so that each memory address defines a corresponding location of the electron beam on the face of the tube (16,384 points for a 16-k × 1-bit memory device). This is done using two d/a converters, each translating binary-address information to dc voltage levels. Each unique binary-address combination produces a corresponding level that, in turn, provides a unique position for the electron beam.

The memory-device row addresses are presented to one converter, which controls the vertical position of the electron beam. The memory-device column addresses go to the other converter, which controls the horizontal position. Thus, one point is defined for each memory address.

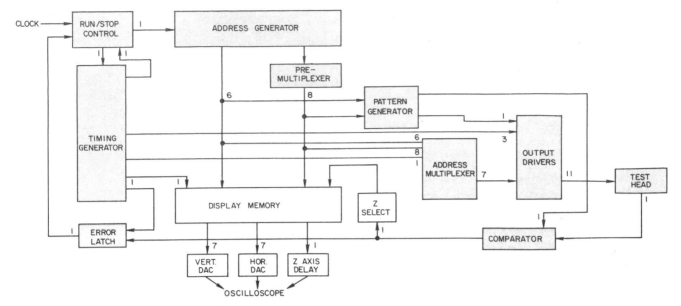

2. **Test and display logic** for a raster-scan memory tester revolve about an address generator, to produce patterns, and a display memory, to define electron-beam locations. Up to 16,000 words can be addressed.

RC timing values for memory testing

R1	R2	R3	R4	C1	C2	Sig.
5 k	5 k	5.6 k	5.6 k	220 pF	30 pF	Adv. Add. M
5 k	5 k	5.6 k	5.6 k		150 pF	$\overline{RAS}$
5 k	5 k	5.6 k	5.6 k	39 pF	150 pF	$\overline{CAS}$
5 k	5 k	5.6 k	5.6 k	175 pF	20 pF	Write $\overline{(WE)}$
5 k	5 k	5.6 k	5.6 k	100 pF	6.8 pF	Data Strobe
5 k	5 k	5.6 k	5.6 k	86 pF	8 pF	Error Strobe

Display options can be switched

The second major function of the display block is to provide specific information at a particular address by controlling the electron-beam intensity. Since the dot brightness imparts the desired information, you can select a particular kind of information by setting three toggle switches to:

■ Intensify the dot at all addresses where a data error exists, regardless of whether the error is a ONE or a ZERO.

■ Intensify the dot at all addresses where a ONE error exists.

■ Intensify the dot at all addresses where a ZERO error exists.

■ Intensify the dot at all addresses where a ONE data output is expected from the memory device.

One thing you should do is to make the display system as functionally independent of the basic test's logic timing as possible, so that clock-rate changes won't adversely affect the display. To accomplish this, row and column-address registers store the address location until a new address update occurs—no matter when. Similarly, an information-bit register stores the

intensification information (oscilloscope Z-axis information) until a new address update occurs.

The display logic needs four inputs from the basic test logic: address information, expected data, error information, and a strobe (or latch) command. The error information is the latest available information in the basic test cycle: When it becomes available, the first three inputs are then available. At that instant, the X address, the Y address, and the Z-axis information are all latched into the display system.

Since the system then stores the displays until a new cycle occurs, it is insensitive to tester repetition-rate changes, at least up to 3.33 MHz. At faster rates, the display-system response time becomes significant, and trace lines between the dots become evident.

A multitap delay line in series with the Z-axis allows a timing adjustment for the time response of the scope Z-axis input, which is shorter than those of the vertical and horizontal channels.

Standard circuits cut cost

The simplicity of the logic is immediately obvious (Fig. 3). With the exception of the two d/a-converter modules and a delay line, all circuits are standard TTL that can be placed on a standard 5-1/2 × 7-1/2-in. wrapped-wire board (Augat or equivalent). The RC timing networks associated with the 74123 circuits can be built on DIP headers and plugged into the logic board (Fig. 4). Typical values for the timing shown in Fig. 5 are given in the table. Other modules can be made to provide a quickly pluggable means to reprogram the tester for other timing.

The digital-to-analog converter are standard modules (Hybrid Systems Corporation, DAC 395-12C). The delay line is a 50-ns unit with taps every 5-ns (An-

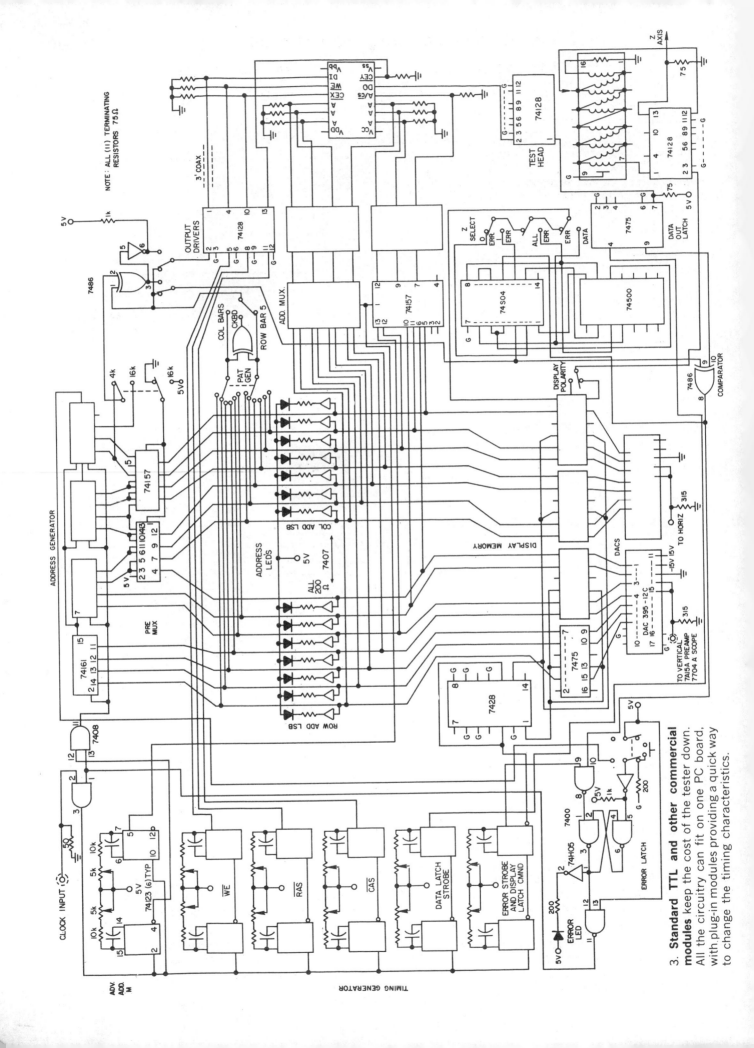

3. Standard TTL and other commercial modules keep the cost of the tester down. All the circuitry can fit on one PC board, with plug-in modules providing a quick way to change the timing characteristics.

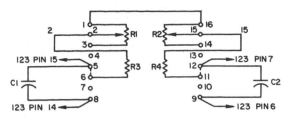

4. **Memory timing can be changed** with interchangeable RC networks, or jumper packs, which can be built on DIP headers that plug into the main board.

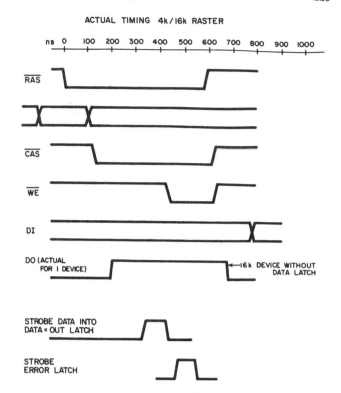

ACTUAL TIMING 4k / 16k RASTER

5. **Timing for the raster-scan tester** accommodates both 4 and 16-k RAM devices.

dersen or equivalent). It has a characteristic Z_0 of 100 Ω, with a built-in 100-Ω terminating resistor.

The Z-axis output circuitry is designed to drive the dc-coupled input of a Tektronix 7704A scope. The output of the 74128 driver provides enough contrast for that oscilloscope; other scopes may require some additional voltage amplification.

The tester is housed in a portable package, 11-in. wide, 7-in. high, and 13-in. deep. All power supplies are self-contained (Lambda Lot-W-5152-A) and include the V_{DD}, V_{BB} and V_{CC} for the device under test. Front-panel knobs adjust the voltages for shmooing.

Because 16-in, 4 and 16-k RAMs are highly standarized, you can set the timing for the slowest part; afterwards, a faster part can be tested for functionality. You can analyze failures under these conditions, since marginal timing is seldom the cause of failure. If you need to update timing for a particular part type, do it quickly with plug-in RC networks.■■

Acknowledgment

The author expresses his appreciation to Doug Haggan for his encouragement and to Peter Kerekes for an outstanding package design and construction effort.